Contemporary Management Strategies in Intellectual Property Rights (IPR) Relevant to NAM and Other Developing Countries

About The Centre

The Centre for Science and Technology of the Non-Aligned and Other Developing Countries (NAM S&T Centre) is an inter-governmental organisation with a membership of 47 countries spread over Asia, Africa, Middle East and Latin America. Besides this, 12 S&T agencies and academic/research institutions of Bolivia, Botswana, Brazil, India, Nigeria and Turkey are the members of the S&T-Industry Network of the Centre. The Centre was set up in 1989 to promote South-South cooperation through mutually beneficial partnerships among scientists and technologists and scientific organisations in developing countries. It implements a variety of programmes including international workshops, meetings, roundtables, training courses and collaborative projects and brings out scientific publications, including a quarterly Newsletter. It is also implementing 5 Fellowship schemes, namely, NAM S&T Centre Research Fellowship, Joint NAM S&T Centre – ICCBS Karachi Fellowship, Joint CSIR/CFTRI (Diamond Jubilee) - NAM S&T Centre Fellowship, Joint NAM S&T Centre – ZMT Bremen Fellowship and Research Training Fellowship for Developing Country Scientists (RTF-DCS) in Indian institutions. These activities provide, among others, the opportunity for scientist-to-scientist contact and interaction, training and expert assistance, familiarising the scientific community on the latest developments and techniques in the subject areas, and identification of technologies for transfer between member countries. The Centre has so far brought out 59 publications and has organised 91 international workshops and training programmes.

For further details, please visit www.namstct.org or write to the Director, NAM S&T Centre, Core 6A, 2nd Floor, India Habitat Centre, Lodhi Road, New Delhi-110003, India (Phone: +91-11-24645134/24644974; Fax: +91-11-24644973; E-mail: namstcentre@gmail.com; namstct@bol.net.in).

Contemporary Management Strategies in Intellectual Property Rights (IPR) Relevant to NAM and Other Developing Countries

— *Editors* —
Sarah Norkor Anku
Olufolake Sola Davies
Rungano Karimanzira

CENTRE FOR SCIENCE & TECHNOLOGY OF THE NON-ALIGNED AND OTHER DEVELOPING COUNTRIES (NAM S&T CENTRE)

2014
DAYA PUBLISHING HOUSE®
A Division of
ASTRAL INTERNATIONAL PVT. LTD.
New Delhi – 110 002

 ISBN 9789351302681

Centre for Science and Technology of the Non-Aligned and Other Developing Countries (NAM S&T Centre)
Core-6A, 2nd Floor, India Habitat Centre, Lodhi Road,
New Delhi-110 003 (India)
Phone: +91-11-24644974, 24645134, Fax: +91-11-24644973
E-mail: namstct@gmail.com
Website: www.namstct.org

Published by : **Daya Publishing House®**
A Division of
Astral International Pvt. Ltd.
– ISO 9001:2008 Certified Company –
4760-61/23, Ansari Road, Darya Ganj
New Delhi-110 002
Ph. 011-43549197, 23278134
E-mail: info@astralint.com
Website: www.astralint.com

Laser Typesetting : **Classic Computer Services**, Delhi - 110 035

Printed at : **Thomson Press India Limited**

PRINTED IN INDIA

Foreword

The 21st Century is the era of science, technology and innovation, where a nation's ability to transform knowledge into products and services and generate wealth will determine its future. Innovation holds the key to the creation as well as processing of knowledge and thereby to economic development. Consequently, issues of generation, valuation, protection and utilisation of intellectual property become critically important all over the world. A functioning Intellectual Property (IP) regime facilitates protection of IP, which encourages transfer of technology in the form of direct foreign investment, joint ventures and licensing.

Intellectual Property Rights (IPR) is the protection of research results in a knowledge-based industry prior to its public use. IPR takes a number of forms, such as copyright in case of books, paintings and films; patents for inventions; and trade marks for brand names and product logos. It is aimed at putting in place a mechanism to help the creators to safeguard the exploitation of their protected work and ensure appropriate benefit for their creation. Effective and easily enforceable IPR mechanisms help in further innovation and also provide a safe and sound system through which protected high quality work of its creator is accessible to general public.

I am delighted to learn that the Centre for Science and Technology of the Non-Aligned and Other Developing Countries (NAM S&T Centre) had organised the International Advanced Training Course on 'Contemporary Management Strategies in Intellectual Property Rights (IPR) relevant to NAM and Other Developing Countries' at Manesar (Haryana), India during 16-20 July 2012 with sponsorship from the Department of Science and Technology (DST), Government of India. The event was successful in highlighting the importance of the issues related to IPR that are of concern to developing countries including product patents and their implications on national R&D programmes. The present book titled "*Contemporary Management Strategies in Intellectual Property Rights (IPR) relevant to NAM and Other Developing Countries*" is an outcome of these deliberations and comprises 26 scientific and technical papers from the experts and professionals of 17 countries.

I am sure that this publication will serve as a useful reference material for the professionals working in the area of management of IPR and will help the developing countries in working out appropriate strategy, laws, policies and programmes for the protection and exploitation of new technologies and research results for their utilisation for the benefit of the society. I compliment the NAM S&T Centre, particularly its Director, Prof. Arun Kulshreshtha and his team, for this initiative and bringing out this very important publication for wider dissemination of IPR knowledge generated among the members of the scientific community and for enhanced south–south cooperation.

Mr. Fernando dos Santos

Director General,
African Regional Intellectual Property Organization (ARIPO),
Harare, Zimbabwe

Preface

This book is an extended and updated version of the papers presented at the International Advanced Training Course on "Contemporary management Strategies in Intellectual Property Rights (IPR) relevant to NAM and other Developing Countries", which was organised at Manesar (Haryana), India during 16-20 July 2012 by the Centre for Science and Technology of the Non-Aligned and Other Developing Countries (NAM S&T Centre) in association with the Department of Science and Technology, Government of India. The Training Programme was designed to exchange experiences, including updates on available global best practices in all aspects of IP asset development, filing and management; and to effectively leverage IPR for socioeconomic development thus encouraging members to build synergies between academia, government and industry. On the whole, the participants were expected to develop a broader appreciation of the current level of exploitation and management of IPR at the global level and the interactions of emerging IP markets within the global economic debate. In attendance were 36 senior officials from research, government and the private sector from 25 countries.

The NAM member states and others present are either members of WTO and or signatories to most WIPO treaties *e.g.*, Trade Related aspects of Intellectual Property Rights (TRIPS) Agreement and also other WIPO administered Treaties. On the whole, it was noted that developing countries have made efforts to domesticate international IPR related agreements, albeit with differing effects to national programmes, given their different levels of socio-economic development and starting points. It was noted during the training course that the low level of technological development and uptake in most of the developing countries presented a situation that could explain these countries' inability to fully exploit the benefits of the provisions enshrined in most international treaties that make certain exceptions to developing countries and right holders failure to utilize provision in their national IPR legislations.

The technical papers in this publication demonstrate the varying levels of application of IPR in the participating countries and potential and/or actual impact of the IPR regime on their respective economies, be it the state of institutional and legislative arrangements (either already functional or envisaged for the future) designed to manage the IP market locally. A number of challenges experienced in implementing a successful IP system were sighted. Resource persons served to provide insights to the current global IPR development focusing on general principles of IPR e.g protection of genetic resources and traditional knowledge, IP valuation and licensing, development of IPR policies including institutional arrangements to manage such a regime at national level, technology tracking through IP mapping, emerging dimensions in IPR such as compulsory licensing, and creation and management of IPR portfolios, among many.

Of late, Malaysia, Nigeria, South Africa, Tanzania and Turkey demonstrated advanced levels of appreciation of IPR through well coordinated, dedicated and well resourced institutional arrangements including management systems already in place and operational. The remainder of the countries presented a strong desire to embrace IP market as the future for all economies to ensure their competitiveness in a globalized village. WIPO support was therefore called upon for the development of National IP strategies to pave the way for the development of National IP Policy Frameworks. However, participants also indicated efforts by national R&D institutions (both public and private) to develop institution-specific IP policies albeit in the absence of a national IP Policy framework. An example of the success of such an approach is the outstanding achievements by Egypt where researchers managed to develop and commercialize outcomes of research results promoted by their R&D institutions for which a WIPO Award for Excellence was given.

Challenges sited by most of the country presenters included; absence of supportive institutions, lack of basic infrastructure (insecurities in power, water, general communication facilities and sometimes food and feed in times of extreme weather events); inadequate or fragmented domestic IP related legislation; absence of locally available IP capacity building and training programmes; weak enforcement procedures through insignificant penalties to discourage IPR infringement; ineffective use of intangible assets; little appreciation and awareness of the benefits and value of IP protection in all levels of production mainly through the absence of full appreciation of the commercial linkages between the processes of applied research and the needs of productive sectors in particular infrastructure. Also scarce funding in science, technology and innovation; absence of IP incentive strategies for different productive sectors designed to boost competitiveness and promotion of cultures of innovation among others. To drive the IP market, presenters highlighted the absence of supportive structures that facilitate the financial and accounting valuation of intangible assets that have been protected and where necessary, reporting on the technology balance of payments regimes as a measure for sustainable economic growth.

Generally, R&D institutions demonstrated little or no linkage between the research institutions and the industry. In addition, premature disclosure of inventions was rampant in universities and research institutions because of the 'publish or perish' syndrome. The workshop took note of the need to urgently develop technical skills and capabilities required to carry out intensive innovative and inventive activities.

While some members had long histories of IP legislation and protection (Myanmar, Nepal, Zimbabwe) the linkages of these to industry, government and academia through exploitation of Science and Technology remains a critical matter. Furthermore, the time taken from research to technology and entry onto the market of outcomes of R&D has to be fully addressed. As such developing countries either have to rely on research outputs from developed countries – thus rendering their endogenous efforts unutilized and generally deemed second rate. Nevertheless, the active participants in the IP protection systems have been mainly from the Legal divisions, attending to litigations for violations of registered IP assets from external sources. It was also noted that efforts to harmonise STI, Trade and Education Policies could be a starting point for effective management of an effective IP market in future.

An example of the Philippines four-pronged national innovation strategy called "FILIPINNOVATION" formulated jointly with the private sector was noted. Other approaches that have demonstrated positive results include Technology Transfer Institute (South Africa) or National Intellectual Property Offices (Nepal, Zimbabwe, Saudi Arabia, Uganda, Turkey) have been established to address the management, transfer and enforcement of IPRs serving as national clearing houses for entry and exit of nationally developed IP assets.

Realizing that most R&D is publicly financed, the South African Intellectual Property Rights from Publicly Financed Research and Development Act, 2008 (Act 51 of 2008) ("the IPR- PFRD- PFRD Act"), was enacted to provide a regulatory framework for the effective management of such IP. Through this legislation, Offices of Technology Transfer (OTTs) have been established within PFRDIs – R&D institutions (public and private). Through this legislation, IP from PFRDIs would be identified, protected, utilised and commercialised to benefit all - economically, socially, militarily etc. In addition a supportive regulatory authority, the National Intellectual Property Management Office (NIPMO), was also established to ensure effective implementation and adherence, by target stakeholders, to the provisions of the national IP legislation. Similar institutional arrangements designed to encourage outreach were also introduced in Philippines through IP Satellite offices and Innovation and Technology Support Offices for easy access by the general public. In Saudi Arabia King Abdulaziz City for Science and Technology (KACST) was established as an independent government scientific organization to support innovation through Technology Incubators, Science Parks Programmes, and Technology Innovation Centers (TICs). In Tanzania, the Tanzania Intellectual Property Advisory Services and Information Centre (TIPASIC) was established and to be upgraded to a full Technology and Innovations Support Centre in the near future. In Uganda, the Kampala Intellectual Property Institute (KIPI) was planned as a strategy to counter the limited facilities for specialized IPR education at national level. In addition Collective Management offices designed to manage the rights holders and acting as a single point for licencees under Copyrights supported by a specialized Policy Unit. Colleges in Uganda have been encouraged to establish incubation centres as these encourage development of various products at different stages of commercialization. In Turkey, the Scientific and Technological Research Council of Turkey (TÜBITAK), the leading agency for management, funding and conduct of research, also serves as a Patent Application Promotion and Support Programme. In Mexico, Tecnológico de Monterrey (1943) operates as a coordinated system of incubation responsible for the acceleration and landing of enterprises and creation of Technology Parks. The Mexican incubation model supports entrepreneurs to create and consolidate companies (start-up and spin off) contributing to job creation, innovation and community development. The concept of acceleration introduced by the Mexican government seeks to optimize the execution speed of different business/ companies functions, through appropriate interventions or directives - commercial, administrative, financial, and technological and/or human skills development to achieve the appropriate results. In order to realize acceptable return on invested capital levels for internally driven researches, the Mexican Government undertakes to provide financial support for the acceleration programmes. On the one hand, the landing program exclusively provides assistance to international companies that wish to establish operations and grow more rapidly in Mexico, while on the other, local companies desirous to settle in the Science Parks with a view to internationalize also benefit from this provision.

In Nigeria the National Office for Technology Acquisition and Promotion (NOTAP) plays a vital role in assisting researchers from tertiary institutions and research institutes to patent their inventions ahead of filing with the Patent Registry and pays for such services. In Indonesia, the establishment and strengthening of IPR centers/institution for IP management in University and R&D Institution have been mandated by Law No. 18 of 2002 in articles 13(3) and 21(1). However the IP management function at these institutions remains low due to inadequate institutional, budgetary and operational support. In Iran, the Parliament ratified a declaration on incentives for commercialization of IP assets including support for patent filing by inventors.

Protection of Genetic Resources (GR) and Traditional Knowledge (TK) was considered to be of great importance particularly to developing countries as it provides only checks to the exploitation of TK, particularly, regarding Licenses and Assignments but also derive maximum economic benefits to the indigenous owners of the resources. The protection of TK using the ARIPO Swakoppmund protocol was discussed from a Ghanaian point of view serving as a model law that provides that all access, authorizations, assignments or licenses granted in respect of protected traditional knowledge shall be granted in writing and be approved by a National Competent Authority, failure of which the document shall be void. It was noted that there remains a gap between the perception of policy makers and implementers of Policy on the one hand and owners/holders of IP, researchers and general users especially in relation to TK on the other. Indonesia presented a model called Indonesian Genetic Resources and Traditional Knowledge (GRTK) or I-Grest - a portal data or data base system which uses as tool for GRTKF or communality IPR management and protection system as defensive protection. The Traditional Database Digital Library of India has proven that data base system can protect Indian IP, especially for Indian GR and TK for their national prosperity and preservation programme. Both the Indonesian and Indian portals were available for application by other developing countries in pursuit of protection of Genetic Resources and Traditional Knowledge.

In relation to Copyright, enforcement in most developing countries remains ineffective. However, lessons from the Jordanian Government provided some useful insights. In particular, Jordan introduced new draft amendment to the Copyright Law - currently progressing through the constitutional stages. This new amendment would provide critical inputs to the Jordanian Customs Law review designed to strengthen *ex officio* border measures such as prosecution and administrative trademark enforcement to be administered by the Jordan Institute of Standards and Metrology (JISM) Law. *Ex officio* enforcement actions by National Library continued to effectively combat piracy in literary works while introduction of new amendments to the Public Health Law successfully imposed high fines on traders and manufacturers of counterfeit medicines.

The TRIPS agreement provides for the granting of compulsory licenses to ensure that the IP systems do not prejudice citizens of their rights to health and well being. In a recent landmark case in March 2012 India granted its first compulsory license to NATCO, a local pharmaceutical company manufacturing Bayer's patented drug Nexavar - a kidney/liver cancer drug that goes by the generic name of Sorafenib Tosylate. This generic drug was available at significantly lower price compared to the Bayer drug. In return, the local company paid 6 per cent of the net sales in royalties to Bayer. Despite the fact that the drug's landed cost to the public is significantly lower, India could face economic sanctions as a result of the European Commission directive to make it mandatory that from July 2013, all active pharmaceutical ingredients exported from India must be certified by the country's s drug controller for EU equivalence certificate. This move presents a typical non-tariff barrier under the TRIPS agreement and an unfair trade practice that is contrary to the letter and spirit of the TRIPS agreements particularly where it applies to the rights to health and wellbeing to all. Therefore by failure to meet this requirement by the EC set deadline, India could be liable to pay disproportionately large penalties on all drug exports to the EU.

Emerging Technologies offer a challenge to existing IP legislation. A huge investment is required in the research and subsequent production of goods using these emerging technologies. Highlighted in the training workshop were issues relating to Nanotechnology and Biotechnology. Most of the legal frameworks are yet to define specific protective measures for the emerging and nucleating disciplines of science and technology, the protective measures are by means of the currently available models. Thus the terrain of emerging technologies is unknown and could grow at a pace significantly faster than ICTs and therefore demanding new and innovative IPR frameworks that are yet to be developed. For developing countries, this projected rapid change of the economic development paradigm premised on future knowledge, poses a challenge that requires urgent action in all forms – skills development, curriculum, new industries including moral and ethical issues.

The concept of novelty and prior art tend to complicate matters when examining patents for disciplines like nano-biotechnology. As nano-biotechnology is a product of two pre-existing technologies - nanotechnology and biotechnology, innovations in this area are bound to find some prior art, making the inventions obvious and non-novel. However, it turned out that some of the criteria were insufficient for appropriately protecting biotechnological inventions due to the peculiarities of this discipline. The biotechnology industry and its supporters (including those in political and legal circles) are pushing for flexibilities in interpretations of novelty, industrial applicability and inventive step that give the benefit of the doubt to the applicants.

In conclusion the workshop noted efforts by regional bodies such as ARIPO that could be used as a springboard to promote and co-ordinate South-South cooperation in the development of IP. Examples of existing cooperation between India/South Africa; Turkish Patent Institute training programmes for patent and trademark attorney and Specialized Courts in the area of intellectual property rights (Turkey); IP education curriculum (Uganda); establishment of Technology Transfer Institutes, Incubation Centres, Science Parks, Acceleration and Landing Programmes (Mexico, South Africa); establishment of portal and databases for Generic Resources and Traditional Knowledge (Indonesia, India, Ghana); IP Support facilities for researchers from tertiary institutions and research institutes to patent their inventions ahead of filing (Nigeria); building synergy between Science and Technology related policies (South Africa, Zimbabwe, Egypt, Jordan, Tanzania). To counter the limited technology transfer programmes, South Africa offers short to medium term courses under (*a*) ISIS Innovation, UK: a wholly-owned subsidiary of the University of Oxford, managing technology transfer and academic consulting for Oxford, and providing consulting advice to clients around the world; and (*b*) Waikatolink, New Zealand: a commercialisation and technology transfer company of the University of Waikato.

On the whole, concerted efforts to introduce targeted interventions to redress the low-to-insignificant patent filings in developing countries against the backdrop of filings developing countries by developed country developers remaining upwards of 70-80 per cent - a situation that is untenable. It is noted that there has been marked growth in emerging developing countries. It is therefore necessary that developing country governments should introduce deliberate programmes to increase the patent filings – particularly by indigenous researchers, inventors and innovators to strengthen not only the base for sustainable economic development but also to ensure that science, technology and innovation returns its central role as the driver of national economies. In addition, as a tool to measure this progress, Gross Expenditure of Research and Development (GERD) as a ratio of GDP should also be compared against positive growth in Technology Return on Invested Capital (TRIC) that effectively indicates national contribution to internally developed and exported IP – providing an indication of increased competitiveness on the rapidly expanding global technology markets.

Sarah Norkor Anku

Olufolake Davies

Rungano Karimanzira

Contents

Introduction

The 21st Century is the era of science, technology and innovation, where a nation's ability to transform knowledge into products and services and generate wealth will determine its future. Innovation holds the key to the creation as well as processing of knowledge and thereby to economic development. Consequently, issues of generation, valuation, protection and utilisation of intellectual property become critically important all over the world. A functioning Intellectual Property (IP) regime facilitates protection of IP, which encourages transfer of technology in the form of direct foreign investment, joint ventures and licensing.

Intellectual Property Rights (IPR) is the protection of research results in a knowledge-based industry prior to its public use. IPR takes a number of forms, such as copyright in case of books, paintings and films; patents for inventions; and trade marks for brand names and product logos. It is aimed at putting in place a mechanism to help the creators to safeguard the exploitation of their protected work and ensure appropriate benefit for their creation. Effective and easily enforceable IPR mechanisms help in further innovation and also provide a safe and sound system through which protected high quality work of its creator is accessible to general public.

The WTO's Agreement on TRIPS (Trade-Related Aspects of IPR) that was negotiated in the 1986-94 Uruguay Round, introduced IP rules into the multilateral trading system for the first time. The TRIPS Agreement covers five broad issues including the application of basic principles of the trading system and other international IP agreements, adequate protection to IPR, enforcement of these rights within territories, settlement of disputes on IP between members of the WTO and the transitional arrangements during the period when the new system is being introduced. It is an attempt to narrow the gaps in the way these rights are protected around the world, and to bring them under common international rules, and establishes minimum levels of protection that each government has to give to the IP of fellow WTO members. The obligations under TRIPS apply equally to all member states, but the developing countries are allowed a longer period of time to incorporate necessary changes in their national laws. However, it is difficult to generalise the implications of the TRIPS agreement for all the developing countries, which largely vary depending on the differences existing between the IPR laws of a particular country and the standards of the Agreement, the extent of development in different sectors, and various other economic parameters Effective protection also depends on the institutions administering the system and the methods used for enforcement.

In order to discuss issues related to IPR that are of concern to developing countries including product patents and their implications on national R&D programmes especially in the area of pharmaceuticals, need for granting protection to biological products and micro-organisms and the issues relating to the protection and economics of traditional knowledge, community-based knowledge and bio-diversity, an international Advanced Training Course on 'Contemporary Management Strategies in Intellectual Property Rights (IPR) relevant to NAM and Other Developing Countries' was organised at Manesar (Haryana), India during 16-20 July 2012 by the Centre for Science and Technology of the Non-Aligned and Other Developing Countries (NAM S&T Centre) with partial financial support from the Department of Science and Technology (DST), Government of India.

The training course was attended by 36 IPR experts, professionals and policy makers from 25 countries, including Botswana, Cambodia, Egypt, Germany, Ghana, India, Indonesia, Iraq, Jordan, Kenya, Malawi, Malaysia, Mexico, Myanmar, Nepal, Nigeria, Philippines, Saudi Arabia, South Africa, Sri Lanka, Tanzania, Turkey, Uganda, Vietnam and Zimbabwe. There were nine resource persons/trainers from India to lecture on various themes related to IPR.

This publication brought out by the NAM S&T Centre is largely based on the presentations made at the training programme, that touched upon several aspects of IPR and its protection and issues related to TRIPS as well as the Status Reports submitted by various country participants in this area.

On behalf of the Centre, I would like to express our sincere gratitude to the Department of Science and Technology, Government of India for their generous support towards the organisation of the training programme which has culminated into this valuable publication. I also thank the eminent resource persons and participants of the programme as well as those who were involved directly or indirectly in making the event a grand success. Last, but not the least, I acknowledge the dynamic involvement of the entire team of the NAM S&T Centre, in particular, Mr. M. Bandyopadhyay for overall supervision, and Mr. Yasir Abbas Rizvi, Mr. Rohan Dev Talwar, Ms. Subhashree Basu and Mr. Pankaj Buttan in compiling the presented papers, getting them edited and giving a shape to the volume.

I hope that the volume would serve as a useful reference material for the professionals working in the arena of management of IPR and will help the developing countries in working out appropriate strategy, laws, policies and programmes for the protection and exploitation of new technologies and research results for their utilization for the benefit of the society.

Prof. Dr. Arun P. Kulshreshtha

Director and Executive Head,
NAM S&T Centre

Chapter 1

Analysis of Intellectual Property (IP) Rights in Costa Rica

*Cristian Miguel Orozco Vega**

Law Student/Researcher
Universidad de Costa Rica, Costa Rica

ABSTRACT

Statistics from Costa Rica have satisfactory levels of regulation of IP, although there is no actual use or knowledge of the advantages provided by the PI to the economy. The data show the need to boost investment in research and innovation, improve the competitive performance of the country, and promote the use and management of IP as a hub for the fulfillment of these purposes. In this study, we analyze the IP rights in the categories of the Costa Rican law, the indicator for assessing whether the productive sectors are making use of IP is by registering IP rights. Therefore, we analyze the data obtained from registries.

***Keywords**: Intellectual property, Copyright, Registries of intellectual property rights.*

1. Introduction: Situation of IP in Costa Rica

Costa Rica is a country with a high educational level and there is a relative knowledge of intellectual property (IP) in the economically active population. However, it is evident the lack of competitive advantages that result from obtaining formal IP titles, which is evident in the low culture of registration and protection of IP in the country.

The Competitiveness Report 2010-11 Costa Rica appears in the competitiveness index ranked among 134 nations evaluated, ranked 68 on IP protection, ranked 44 in

---

* E-mail: cristianupala@gmail.com

innovation capacity and ranked 28 in university-industry collaboration. In Latin America by the Intellectual Property Right Index 2011 Costa Rica appears in third place, behind Chile and Uruguay, in terms of IP protection. This index ranks countries in areas such as IP legal and political environment, indicators and IP rights recognized.

The statistics show that in the regulatory framework, Costa Rica have satisfactory regulation levels of IP, but not translated into effective use or knowledge of the advantages provided by the IP to the economy, record low culture and ineffective use of intangible assets. Indeed, the data show the need for action to boost investment in research and innovation, with the goal of improving the competitive performance of the country, constituting the promotion, use and management of IP a strategic axis for the fulfillment of these purposes.

The International Index of Property Rights, 2011, is an international comparative study that measures the relevant physical, intellectual and economic position of IP. The comparative study focuses on three important areas of property rights: I. Legal and Political Environment, II. Physical Property Rights, and III. IP rights. The study analyzes data from 129 countries, representing 97 per cent of gross domestic product in the world, and includes statistics derived from surveys applied by experts from different countries in 2011 on the protection of property.

In Costa Rica, the International Index of Property Rights had significant changes in the last 4 years, increasing 0.3 points due to the improvement of sub-elements evaluated, obtaining a result of 5.9 with respect to the environment legal and policy of IP. Independence of the Judiciary had the highest growth, which increased from 0.5 to 7.5, maintaining a stable 6.1. However, the physical protection of property and property registration fell 0.4 points due to limited access to credit. The IP protection increased in 0.9 points in 2011. This improvement combined with the promotion of IP crimes prosecution boosted to 5.0, the best score of IP for Costa Rica since 2007.

Regard to access to credit data, the study on Supply of Credit to PYMES, the second half of 2011report, prepared by the Ministry of Economy, Trade and Industry, were evaluated financing options for Innovation, technology transfer and IP for PYMES and the study concluded that there are in the country specific financing options of IP.

However, recently MICIT and CONICIT are promoting specific funding for PYMES through Propyme Fund, which would allow the seed capital and entrepreneurs apply for funding of IP through research and consulting units recorded in the scientific record CONICIT, being the only way currently to qualify for funds to cover costs associated with IP. These funds are to grant additional aid to promote competitiveness and development of PYMES.

It is important to note that the country has a large range of training courses on IP, from casual to programs within the formal academic university, including a master specific IP in the Universidad Estatal a Distancia. However, most courses have a strong legal approach so there is a project to formalize the IP Costa Rican academy that would have a more practical and multidisciplinary approach.

2. Materials and Methods

2.1. Research Approach

The research belongs to the quantitative approach, it uses the data collected to test hypotheses, based on numerical measurement and statistical analysis to establish patterns of behavior and test theories.

The most important quantitative characteristic present in this paper is that data collection is based on the measurement (measured variables or concepts). This collection or measurement is performed using standardized procedures and accepted by a scientific community.

2.2. Type of Study

The type of study is classified into the descriptive category descriptive studies only attempt to measure or collect information independently or together on concepts or variables to which they refer, that is, their goal is not to indicate how the measured variables are related.

This research is descriptive since its methodological purposes match with that described for this classification. Descriptive studies seek to specify properties, characteristics and profiles of individuals, groups, communities, processes, objects, or any other phenomenon to undergo a scan. That is, they measure, assess or collect data on concepts (variables), aspects, dimensions or components of the phenomenon under investigation. In a descriptive study, a set of issues is selected, then these issues are measured and information is collected about each variable in order to describe what is investigated.

In fact, this research proposes the following elements:

1. Specification of properties, features and processes profiles. The study of IP rights in Costa Rica
2. Measuring variables. With the selection of the categories of IP the subject is analyzed.
3. Selection of issues. It focused on the records of IP rights application.
4. Collection of information. By consulting the literature.

2.3. Aim of the Study

To analyze the situation of IP rights in Costa Rica in the categories of applications for the award allowed by law.

2.4. Subjects or Sources of Information

Subjects of information belong to the same unit of analysis of research project (IP rights in Costa Rica), these are the laws and rights applications.

The means of transmission are the bibliographical sources as degree theses, journal articles, reports on the topic.

The type of information sources that provide the primary sources were utilized: theses, journals, reports, among others.

2.5. Definition of Variables

A variable is a property that can vary, whose variation is likely to be measured or observed and applied to a group of people or objects, which take on different values or representations with respect to the variable. The variables selected are:

1. Patents
2. Utility models and industrial designs
3. Brands
4. Distinctive signs
5. Trade secrets
6. Copyright
7. Plant Varieties
8. Protection of test data linking drug and pharmaceutical patents
9. Protection of test data of agrochemicals
10. Analysis of registry data

2.6. Sampling

The selected sampling is described as follows.

- ✰ Applications for Registration of IP in Costa Rica: Procedures are those made by individuals or legal entities to claim IP rights in each of the categories recognized by the legislation.

2.7. Type of Sampling

For this work the type of sampling is not probabilistic. In the stratified sampling, the choice of the elements does not depend on the probability, but of causes related to the characteristics of the research or who makes the sample. The procedure depends on the type of IP right application of a person or group of people and, of course, the selected samples are due to screening criteria themselves.

2.8. Selection of Sample Elements

The non-probability samples, also called targeted samples, represent an informal selection procedure. Only typical subjects are selected with the hope that cases are representative of the population. As such, the only inclusion criterion for the selection of sample items were:

- ✰ Applications for registration of IP rights in Costa Rica.

2.9. Information Treatment

In formulating the consultation paper a literature review is carried out, which is to identify, obtain and consult the literature and other materials that are useful for research purposes and (...) extract and collect relevant information and necessary relation to the investigation.

Also, using the content analysis, this is a research technique for making inferences valid and reliable data with respect to its context. The content analysis is performed by means of coding, defining the universe, the analysis units and categories of analysis.

For the analysis of information tables are made to explain the behaviour of the variables studied. Based on inferences which are drawn up and analysis of the elements of importance for the study. Use the word processor Microsoft Office Word 2007 separately licensed.

3. Results and Discussion

3.1. Analysis of IP Rights in Costa Rica

The biennial report of National Indicators for Science, Technology and Innovation MICIT, the country provides useful information for making decisions and issuing relevant guidelines in these areas. The latest version of this document was published in May 2011 and corresponds to the results of national investment in scientific and technological and innovative capacity of firms, measured in 2009. It details: information, among others, ACT Investment, R&D, human resources devoted to ACT, and some indicators related to the internationalization of science and technology. It also includes information related to innovation in business and contains information on aspects such as innovation activities in firms, links to actors of the national system of innovation, innovation and environmental performance, and employment and organization of the work process.

It also displays information about patents. At this point, the report indicates that the number of companies that have obtained patents (8.4 per cent) reflects the kind of innovations that are being promoted, with a low number of companies making new innovations in international markets. However, a high percentage of companies report having made innovations. It is clear that the vast majority are not using patents as mechanisms of IP protection.

This agrees with the observations in the NDP to note that the democratization of scientific and technological knowledge is essential to be used by all sectors of the Costa Rican population and to increase the productivity of the Costa Rican companies. The added value of what they produce these companies could be enhanced through public policies that promote the culture and development of incubation and entrepreneurship, so as to make better use of resources and expertise in the country.

The Costa Rican companies do not lack knowledge about the scope and benefits of protecting their IP. This is seen as the 87.1 per cent of companies have obtained patents in the country or abroad despite that 90 per cent of the companies mentioned have made some kind of innovation. These reasons discourage the entrepreneurial potential of the Costa Rican and limit the development of new businesses and new jobs with advanced technology and high added value of domestic firms, which has a negative effect on the competitiveness of the productive sector in Costa Rica.

Indeed the ultimate indicator to assess whether the productive sectors are making use of IP, is by registering IP rights. It is therefore necessary to analyze the data obtained from registries

3.2. Patents

Regarding patent registration the growth of applications filed per year has sustained growth. The phenomenon of peak applications in 2008, responds to the improvement of the Costa Rican legislation on IP issues, but overall the presentation and grant applications has been increasing, but is also seen in 2009 and 2010 the volume of rejected applications is higher than requests granted.

Table 1.1: Record Patent Applications in Costa Rica

Year	*Applications*	*Granted*	*Denied*	*National*	*PCT*
2005	438	12	3	17	340
2006	593	4	0	22	546
2007	669	13	2	20	618
2008	791	45	37	21	743
2009	524	32	51	13	489
2010	614	34	53	10	578

About this data is important to consider the relationship of the Patent Office of the RPI with external examiners in charge of making the study of the substantive examination of patents. While the volume of records worldwide has exceeded the capacity of the offices in Costa Rica for the backlog of patents has produced largely by the absence of internal evaluators that in the past forced to resort to reviewers external to complete the formalities.

Until 2006, the PRI resorted to PROINNOVA office at the University of Costa Rica and the Association of Engineers and Architects to conduct assessments. From January 2007 to December 2008 managed to make formal agreements with College of Pharmacists and the Technological Institute of Costa Rica to facilitate evaluators. Since January 2010, began to give a direct relationship with each professional RPI independently, based on a contract to that effect with each evaluator. It is only since February of 2011 that finally the RPI is authorized by the budgetary authority to hire examiners plant 5.

Of the applications pending background study in Costa Rica, June 30, 2010, correspond to the following technology areas:

Table 1.2: Technology Sectors in Costa Rica by Applications

Technological Area	*Quantity*
Pharmaceutics	2000
Electromechanical Engineering	30
Chemistry	400
Building	36
Agronomy	20
Biotechnology	10
Food Technology	24

Of registration data on patents:

1. Statistics show that the bulk of applications and registrations is in the area of pharmacy and chemistry.
2. It is striking the low volume of patents in areas where the country is positioning itself at the technological, industrial and agro-biotechnology and food technology, so everything indicates that it is necessary to enhance production and registration of IP in these areas.
3. Patents required by nationals have been declining in volume while increasing the number of PCT patent. However, many national companies recognize that opt for patenting abroad and then turn to national phase applications, which led to the conclusion in the national roundtable discussion on the diagnosis of IP that there is a need to strengthen credibility in the RPI of Costa Rica to attract more records.
4. The volume of patent applications has decreased by almost 30 per cent since 2007, making it necessary to work on increasing investment in innovation and development and provide guidance to companies, universities and research institutions to develop ongoing policies of patenting.
5. The volume of records requested is vastly superior to the records completed, which is consistent with international experience and evidence of a significant gap in the volume of outstanding transactions and the volume on which they are trained to resolve the internal registration.
6. The volume of registrations granted is very similar to the volume of denied records, which merit further evaluation to analyze the reasons for such refusal.

3.3. Utility Model and Industrial Designs

In terms of utility models and industrial designs, the growth of applications has been increasing especially with a clear trend of increasing national applications, which shows that the credibility in the protection of these schemes within the population grows and industry productive.

Table 1.3: Utility and Industrial Design Applications Register

Year	*Utility Model*	*Industrial Designs*	*Nationals*
2005	11	131	21
2006	6	140	10
2007	14	146	21
2008	25	70	49
2009	14	97	48
2010	8	70	23

From the lists of applications for industrial design, industrial design and utility model above, it is not possible to determine the technical area of each application, except for site search and on each individual file. However, as reported by the Directorate of RPI, most records for parts of vehicles, furniture and electrical parts. While the number of national applications is low, it has increased in recent years, which could reflect some of the growing interest in Costa Ricans use the IP protection.

3.4. Marks

Regarding the registration of marks, Costa Rica has the same behaviour of other developing economies that have opted for the registration of trademarks and service marks as a pillar of their IP strategies. However, volume growth evidence in pending marks that have not yet consolidated their registration.

Table 1.4: Registration of Trademark Applications and Logos

Year	*Registered*	*Filed*	*Denied*	*National Registered*	*International Registered*	*Processed*
2008	12334	2723	418	5436	6829	1921
2009	12700	3443	1514	5775	5094	2905
2010	11382	1925	1148	5767	5498	7737
2011	4353	770	675	2781	3185	20700

The largest volume of trade names is presented in the following two classes:

1. **Class 5,** which covers pharmaceuticals, veterinary and sanitary preparations for medical use, food and dietetic substances adapted for medical or veterinary use, food for babies, food supplements for humans and animals, plasters, materials for dressings, material for stopping dental wax, disinfectants, preparations for destroying vermin; fungicides, herbicides.
2. **Class 29,** covering meat, fish, poultry and game, meat extracts, fruit and vegetables and canned vegetables, frozen, dried and cooked jellies, jams, compotes, eggs, milk and milk products; oils and fats.

3.5. Distinctive Signs

Statistics records for distinctive signs are detailed below:

Table 1.5: Registration of Trademark Applications

Distinctive Sign	*2008*	*2009*	*2010*	*2011*
Geographic indicator	0	0	2	0
Emblem	54	43	14	5
Collective mark	4	7	5	2
Certification mark	1	0	0	4
Trademark	932	1399	1027	533
Trademark and services	18	79	41	19

Contd...

Table 1.5–*Contd...*

Distinctive Sign	*2008*	*2009*	*2010*	*2011*
Fabric mark	5275	2576	1179	603
Fabric and trademark	717	3777	2892	1599
Trademark and services	116	145	153	60
Service mark	2374	2805	1689	926
Commercial name	1300	1537	1033	513
Advertising slogan	294	322	239	89
Sound Marks	0	1	734	0

Concerning these statistics, it can be stated:

1. Only 2 have been granted GIs. It is noteworthy that in a traditionally agricultural country, applications for OJ and IG are so rare. This is perceived as a lack of private sector, which has the advantage to have a geographical indication.
2. Most procedures are reported as OD abandoned.
3. Only 8 are reported as sound marks registered and no scent mark. Among them, the sound of Beer Imperial eagle, the whistle of the cock "solo bueno" company Gollo and related tones Kolbi Intel and ICE.
4. Only 5 certification marks are registered in the country. These are: C-Neutral and CHANGE. The latter is recorded 4 times a design, which actually means that only 2 certification marks are currently registered.
5. Only 18 Collective marks are registered in the country. Example of these are Tiara, ESPA, Montessori community, Ricalit, RIM, Seal farmer support national beans, Gusanito, Agritec, and others.
6. There are only 24 registered three-dimensional marks, the most distinguishing bottles of La Florida SA Production and other owners.
7. Despite the volume of advertising signs that circulate in the market, the number of registrations granted is low and has been declining over the past 3 years, despite being an area where greater use is made of the records of IP as a trend line with other developing countries.

3.6. Industrial Secrets

For its part, the deposit of industrial secrets increased in 2008 as an outgrowth of the approval of the amendment to the Law No. 7975 undisclosed information and the adoption of regulations for the Law of undisclosed information (Decree No. 34927-J -COMEX-S-MAG) that defined a regulatory framework for processing. The increase is also because many of the agrochemical companies waiting since 2007 for the approval of their marketing authorizations have also opted for this protective mechanism, depositing their test data and industrial secrets to the IPR, a situation which increased the volume of records up to date. Deposits recorded to date are listed below:

Table 1.6: Registration Requests for Deposits of Industrial Secrets

Year	*Granted*	*Year*	*Granted*
2001	2	2003	1
2006	1	2007	17
2008	56	2009	57
2010	54	2011	39

Since 2007, the deposit of undisclosed information has increased exponentially; with the majority of applications is the area of agrochemicals followed by the area of technology. However, the amount of secrets is little for a country supporting cutting edge technology as an export value, actually the highest percentage of deposits are foreign.

3.7. Copyright

One of the most important measurements in the country for the creative industries that are beginning to make an offer as a significant exporter is the copyright registration, which gives the following results:

Table 1.7: Register of Copyright Applications

Artwork	*Registered*	*Pending*	*Filed or Denied*
Literary Works	1989	386	297
Artistic Works	275	104	66
Artistic or literary work	220	29	11
Collective management organizations	3	0	0
Related Rights	109	41	30
Contracts	65	4	4

From the presented data it can be mentioned that:

1. Only 275 works of art are recorded, making it an extremely low amount considering the booming 2D and 3D animation industry, as well as the highest national artistic production reported by the MCJ in the field of painting, sculpture and photography, among others.
2. In 10 years, there are 1,989 records of literary works reported, equivalent to an annual average of 198.9 a year. In addition, the number of records is not consistent with the volume of publications reported by national public and independent publishers through ISBN registry reported by the National Library, which indicates that from 2004 to 2010 there are 12,601 registered literary works. This shows a low publication culture by the copyright holders.
3. Similarly, both registered only 109 works related rights balanced by the actual volume of production in the area of theater, music, dance and other arts being promoted nationally as well as rights to own the music area to

some extent themselves are being reported to the collective management organizations. From the data supplied by the ACAM, only in this entity there are dynamic repertoires registered whose volume is steadily increasing, which currently have a list of books on national average of 22,000 and works an average of 22 million of international works, which is far from the number of registered works by RDADC.

4. It is not possible to determine from the RDADC databases the specific sector of artistic area corresponding to the record because records are not kept in such detail.

3.8. Obtenciones Vegetales

In regards to plant variety registration activity which is carried in the Ministry of Agriculture, specifically the Office of seeds, from which the following data were obtained:

Table 1.8: Registration Applications for Plant Variety

Pending	*National*	*Foreign*
5	3	2

From these data it can be indicated that:

1. Of the 5 applications pending, 3 are from a national company of the same seed varieties, and 2 applications are of a foreign company.
2. It is noteworthy that there are no major local records, but there are important innovations in companies such as in the banana sector, on the rice sector and the recent range supported by the MAG hybrid known as papaya.
3. Up to date, any registration has been granted, as the authorities of the Office of seeds indicate that any licensee has failed to present all requirements in the record.

3.9. Testing Data Protection for Medicaments and Linkage of Pharmaceutics Patents

Regarding the protection of drugs testing data and pharmaceutical patents, the Ministry of Health reflects the following information:

Table 1.9: Requests for Drug Patents

Year	*Presented*	*Approved*	*Denied*	*Pending*
2009	4	4	0	0
2010	0	0	0	0
2011	0	0	0	0

The data reveal that there are only 4 steps to link approved patents. But it's only two products as the link corresponds to two patents (Patent No. 2688 and 2645) linked to 4 presentations of two products on the market under the brand Champix ® and Celsentri ® from Pfizer.

That is, up to date there are only 2 patents related to pharmaceuticals in Costa Rica, by the company Pfizer, whose patents expire in 2018 and 2020 respectively. This implies that only two drugs in the Costa Rican market are patented. It is worth indicating that none of them is included in the official list of medicines for Social Security.

To date the protected active 5 years for the non-disclosure of test data, according to the Ministry of Health, are the following eleven: Rivaroxaban, Maravoric, Varenicline, Lenalidomide, Desvenlafaxine Hydrochloride Prasugrel Hydrochloride, tenofovir disoproxil fumarate, Raltegravir, Topotecan Hydrochloride, Amlodipine Besylate And Valsartan-indacaterol maleate.

These are the 11 products that are protected with test data, according to statistics released by the Ministry of Health on its website, which regularly updated to include and exclude lists products according to their maturity.

3.10. Testing Data Protection for Agrochemicals

Regarding the protection of test data for chemicals, it is noted that since 2007 only two permits have been granted for commercialization of new products, by procedural delays, so that while there are 15 applications for protection of testing data detailed in the table below, none has been approved to date. Such applications depend on the processing of tradable permits that are overdue and the verification of compliance with defined requirements.

3.11. Analysis of Registral Data

Of the categories of IP in Costa Rica it can be mentioned that:

1. Most companies IP strategies are directed primarily to the protection of trademarks and little innovation is being protected today.
2. Companies opt to register trademarks and trade names, and designs, patents and trade secrets to a lesser extent
3. It is also clear that there is little use of copyright protection, trade secrets, collective marks and certification marks and three-dimensional, although the country is driving innovative companies that produce goods potentially subject to such legal protection.
4. There is little use of geographical indications and designations of origin which could affect the differentiation and better positioning of agricultural exports and tourism sector and the productive chain.
5. Although the country is carrying out research on seeds, plant varieties records or trade secrets reflect that effort is wasted and the mechanism of protection for the commercial position of such agricultural improvements.

In regards to information and effectiveness of database IP query in Costa Rica:

1. Information obtained by the National Register was presented in a short time before the written request. However, you cannot even make online

inquiries on registration of IP in Costa Rica by several factors. On this point, the National Register is making significant efforts to ensure that such consultation may be the medium term. It is worth quoting in this regard, the National Registry and WIPO who have signed a project to create Centers of Support Technology and Innovation, which would provide advice nationally to those interested in patent search and receive expert advice.

2. The only database consulted to determine the volume of IP records nationwide, which is available online to users by the Ministry of Health, regarding the protection of test data and linkage of patent medicines.
3. While Patent Scope allows online searching of patents and PCT and is incorporated in Costa Rica, the national patent technical document is not available for consultation, unless personally go to RPI.
4. The inquiry terminals in the Register increased to meet demand with the opening of new facilities building IP in early 2012.
5. Due to consultation processes promoted to this diagnosis, RPI ordered consultation mechanism records of undisclosed information that originally did not exist. Currently you can check the number of secrets deposited, the year of application, the owner and the general title of secret keeping secret the contents thereof.
6. Access to IP information related to the State Phytosanitary Service is complex and required several communications that ultimately allowed the construction of the data regarding the protection of test data on chemicals, related to marketing authorizations.
7. There is no instance at public or private inventories which make innovations or initiatives nationwide that are eligible for IP protection.
8. Nor is there a single database to obtain an inventory of source IP records. As a corollary, there are no indicators of IP beyond the data obtained from the National Registry.

4. Conclusions

4.1. The Ideal Environment for Strengthening IP in Costa Rica

In Costa Rica there are successful initiatives in the field of IP protection which have contributed to the make the population aware of IP and a positive environment for the generation of public and private policies that promote innovation and development of property subject to the PI.

The experience gained has allowed grouping important academic initiatives that already exist in the country, aimed at different sectors, which shows that the country presents an IP academic offer permanent for constant update on the matter.

There is plenty to do in terms of education and training, mainly in initial levels of formal education and technical careers related to innovation and creativity, but certainly, there is already a path that allows the country a privileged position where there is qualified demand and supply for training in this area.

The knowledge possessed by the productive sector of IP requires an extra boost that allows them to recognize the importance of having internal IP strategies that include express protection of these rights and create guidelines to make them effective, starting from the promotion innovation to registration, licensing and exploitation of IP.

This requires continuing training processes and increase the focus on increasing innovation indicators in both the public and the private sector, enabling the transformation of national culture to a culture of protection and exploitation of IP.

4.2. The Growth of IP Serves as a Base for Knowledge and Development.

The awareness about IP should be transformed into a process of identifying the value that generates IP protection and return on investment that could lead to the record holder such intangible assets, which would allow the country to have clear indicators of the innovation that is generated locally, in order to guide policies and incentives to promote it.

There is a development of knowledge and innovation to the internal of the academy, which could allow universities and research centers to develop policies that promote flexible mechanisms for linking with the private sector and licensing structures for the production sector, which will promote competitiveness and development of national economy under the leadership of NEXO but with full coordination of actions with government and the productive sector.

It is important that the private sector and trade organizations promote the development of business strategies in the productive sector, that include IP as a mechanism for developing, promoting in turn the accounting valuation of intangibles, and systematic registration, oriented to contribute to national innovation indicators.

It should be identified the reasons why domestic companies with the PCT patent application in foreign markets are not interested in doing initially to the RPI, in order to define mechanisms that make it attractive and safe for the operator to start international registration process from Costa Rica.

It is necessary for national creative talent to understands the value of the registered protection of their creations and encourage their interest in registering the works, because most of them do not know the added value that has that record.

It is necessary to improve the supply and access to funding mechanisms that make IP available to micro and small entrepreneurs and researchers, to register their patentable inventions.

It is necessary to provide greater incentives to promote the creations of the Costa Rican cultural industry, and record such creations to the authorities, so that there is full assurance of recognition of IP generated in the country.

It is necessary to guide sectoral policies on IP to the strengthening of the strategic sectors identified.

4.3. Challenges that Need to be Faced by the System in Charge of Protecting IP in Costa Rica

The following challenges of the IP system protection in Costa Rica have been identified:

1. Educate the various stakeholders (generators, facilitators and users) on the production, benefits and protection of IP as a tool for development.
2. Improving understanding of the benefits of IP seen as a strategy for competitiveness.
3. Building a culture of respect and awareness and effective use of IP over sized stages, interested public and effective implementation of compliance processes.
4. Creating mechanisms for the identification, assessment and transfer of intangible assets of the productive sectors.
5. Implementing measures to strategic sectors that promote the protection and exchange of IP.
6. Creating conditions to increase confidence and certainty in the IP system.
7. Raising IP as a state policy and sector policies that allow developing sustainability and permanence.

4.4. Strengths and Weaknesses of the IP System

Strengths of the national IP system have been identified:

1. Institutional leadership of the governing body to coordinate and strengthen the IP system and promote dialogue among all stakeholders of IP.
2. Existence of the CIPPI as facilitator and coordinator of general policies in this area.
3. Existence of factors that position us in the region as a destination for FDI.
4. Interest of public and private sectors to boost competitiveness, promote innovation and support PYMES creative and technological base.
5. Infrastructure investment and public and private education.
6. Government's interest to strengthen the IP as an objective of the National Development Plan and include it as MLA of the Competitiveness Council.
7. Existence of link and link units in technical colleges, public universities and the productive sector.
8. Interest in government structures generating policies of the importance of IP.

As for the weaknesses of the IP national system, several have been identified:

1. Lack of educational programmes that instill a culture of respect for IP and lack of specific policy on IP teaching issues.
2. Little knowledge and awareness of the benefits and value of IP protection in all levels of production, cultural, professional, institutional and educational sector.

3. Lack of linkage between the processes of applied research and the needs of productive sectors.
4. Insufficient policies and incentives aimed for the IP in different productive sectors.
5. Insufficient incentives to create knowledge-based companies and the licensing of IP from academy to industry.
6. Little incentive to promote closer links between business and academy.
7. Low investment in infrastructure and scarce funding in science, technology and innovation compared to major competitors in Latin America.
8. Insufficient supply of public and private instruments to boost competitiveness, promote innovation and support entrepreneurship.
9. Lack of structures that facilitate the financial and accounting valuation of intangible assets that have IP protection.
10. Lack of experience in implementing effective IP enforcement processes.

Acknowledgements

I want to thank the University of Costa Rica, Western Branch, to facilitate a comprehensive learning law that allows the addressing of current issues such as intellectual property rights.

I want to express thanks to the Municipality of Upala for supporting me financially in the study of intellectual property rights.

Abbreviations

ACAM: Asociación de Compositores y Autores Musicales
ACT: Actividades científico tecnológicas
CONICIT: Consejo Nacional para Investigaciones Científicas y Tecnológicas
DO: Denominación de Origen
I+D: Investigación + Desarrollo
ICE: Instituto Costarricense de Electricidad
IG: Indicación geográfica
Innovación
MAG: Ministerio de Agricultura y Ganadería
MCJ: Ministerio de Cultura y Juventud
MICIT: Ministerio de Ciencia y Tecnología
OMPI: Organización Mundial de la Propiedad Intelectual
PCT: Tratado de Cooperación en Materia de Patentes
PND: Programa Nacional de Desarrollo
PROINNOVA: Unidad de Gestión y Transferencia de Conocimiento para la

PYMES: Peque as y Medianas Empresas
RDADC: Registro de Derechos de Autor y Derechos Conexos
RPI: Registro de Propiedad Industrial.

References

1. Aguilar, A. y Fernández, L. C. (2012). *La protección de los derechos de autor de obras musicales dentro de producciones cinematográficas. Análisis del montaje musical en Costa Rica.* Tesis de Licenciatura en Derecho: Universidad de Costa Rica.
2. Chaves, J. M. (2012). Tendencias recientes de la jurisprudencia de la Sala Primera en materia de propiedad intelectual. *Revista de la Sala Primera de la Corte Suprema de Justicia, 6*(1), 1-61.
3. Defensoría de los Habitantes de Costa Rica. (2004). *Criterio de la Defensoría en relación con el Proyecto de Ley de Adhesión al "Tratado de Budapest sobre el reconocimiento internacional del depósito de microorganismos a los fines del procedimiento en materia de patentes".* San José: Defensoría de los Habitantes de Costa Rica.
4. Ferraro, F. (12 de enero de 2012). Propiedad intelectual: política pública y academia. *La Nación*, pág. Editorial.
5. Hernández, A., Guilá, G., Álvarez, M. y Segura, R. (2010). *Manual para administradores de justicia sobre delitos de propiedad intelectual.* San José: Escuela Judicial Lic. Edgar Cervantez Villalta.
6. Hernández, R., Fernández, C. y Baptista, P. (2003). *Metodología de la investigación.* México: Mc Graw Hill Interamericana.
7. Kramarz, S. (2011). Propiedad intelectual y contrato de trabajo. *Revista de la Sala Segunda de la Corte Suprema de Justicia, 12*(2), 29-44.
8. Marín, A. y Villareal, O. (2010). *Inscripción de marcas sonoras y los derechos de propiedad industrial.* Tesis de Licenciatura en Derecho: Universidad de Costa Rica.
9. Ministerio de Justicia y Paz. (2012). *Estrategia Nacional de Propiedad Intelectual.* San José: World Intellectual Property Organization.
10. Miranda, G. (10 de mayo de 2012). La propiedad intelectual es un derecho humano. *La Nación*, pág. Editorial.
11. Montero, A. (2007). *Política de persecución criminal en delitos de Propiedad Intelectual.* Tesis de Licenciatura en Derecho: Universidad de Costa Rica.
12. Mora, S. (2007). Participación legislativa en la construcción de derechos de propiedad intelectual. *Revista de Ciencias Sociales de la Universidad de Costa Rica, 115*(1), 73-84.
13. Morales, J. P. (2010). *Propiedad intelectual sobre variedades vegetales en Costa Rica.* Tesis de Licenciatura en Derecho: Universidad de Costa Rica.

14. Sánchez, C. y Vanegas, L. M. (2008). Las obtenciones vegetales y los derechos de propiedad intelectual en Costa Rica. *Revista de Ciencias Económicas de la Universidad de Costa Rica, 26*(1), 335-347.

15. Valverde, S. (6 de enero de 2012). Nuevo Edificio de Propiedad Intelectual. *La Nación*, pág. Editorial.

Chapter 2

Innovation, Intellectual Property and Economic Impact on Developing Countries

*Farid Abd-Elreheim Badria**

Pharmacognosy Department, Faculty of Pharmacy, Mansoura University, Mansoura, 35516, Egypt

ABSTRACT

This study intends to share the wealth of knowledge, resources, and heritage among developing countries to accomplish advancement in science, to solve many health economic issues, and more over to bridge gaps and lessen political differences.

Enormous knowledge is hidden in the economics literature and in the ideas of corporate IP managers about the way companies have developed answers to these questions. Making such information available to top-level management will help lead intellectual property rights out of their shadowy existence in patent and legal departments and enable companies to tap into their strategic value.

Creation, protection and management of intellectual property (IP) were my key in successful knowledge management for applying forty-two (42) patents in the area of pharmaceuticals and medicine. In Egypt and other developing countries, where the economic growth of nations is driven increasingly by the creativity and knowledge of their people, effective IP systems, which provide incentives for innovation and create structures for sharing the results, are key to unlocking this human potential.

The economic impact of IP is to improve skills of human resources, utilize the available natural resources, mainly raw materials, in developing new therapeutic agents, bridge gaps between University, Industry, and community, and to emphasize the role of research and

* E-mail: faridbadria@gmail.com

innovation in improving economy, health, and welfare of society. Moreover the sustainability of research will be the positive outcomes of transferring basic knowledge into research, applied research and finally into helpful products with financial outcomes which will help sustain future research and make the cycle work efficiently.

Keywords: *Innovation, Intellectual property, Pharmaceuticals, Economic impact.*

1. Introduction

1.1. Creating and Sustaining Competitive Advantage

How can a company use intellectual property rights to gain and sustain competitive advantage?

How do IP rights affect the industry's structure?

What options do IP rights offer vis-à-vis competitors?

How can IP rights grant incumbency advantage and establish barriers to entry?

How can IP rights help the company gain vertical power along the value chain?

What organizational design accommodates an intellectual property strategy most effectively?

Intellectual property rights can help a company gain competitive advantage in various ways, but three are paramount:

i. They can provide a temporary technological lead (incumbency),
ii. protect brand names
iii. help form an industry standard.

Combinations of patents and trademarks can help to sustain IP-based competitive advantages. The use of patents to enjoy a short-term technological lead is the best-known way to create competitive advantage with IP rights, but it is fading in importance in many industries.

The outcomes of my concerted efforts in IP gained me a Gold Medalist award from the World Intellectual Property Organization (WIPO) in November 2011 as the best inventor in Egypt. Away from official channels we were able to bridge gaps in technology.

It is of utmost importance to participate in workshops that promote IP systems in Egypt. This will enable participants to derive maximum benefit from the IPR system and to address efficient utilisation of innovations and creativity. In Egypt and other countries as well, scientists and technologists can no longer plan and execute their researches without being adequately prepared with the state-of-the-art information driven strongly by IPR and thus need to have clear and sound understanding not only of the principles of IPR but also of the contemporary management strategies for its protection and exploitation.

Therefore, it is important to share these experiences in Science and Technology with different countries to provide national bodies with international best practices, and to discuss the mechanisms of sharing capabilities and experience of NAM and other developing countries; and more importantly, to discuss the core concept of a crucial issue on the role of IPR on sustainable development.

The following are some examples of how to establish a sustainable cooperation in Research, IPR and sustainable development regardless of political differences:

Innovate Sustainable facilities: *e.g.* An economic Mammalian Tissue Culture Lab (MTCL) which is essential for research on cells either for diagnostic or therapeutic purposes. The major components of this laboratory are:

1. Sterile area: Laminar flow hood equipped with UV lamp
2. Carbon dioxide incubator
3. Inverted microscope

2. The Impact on Scientific Research, Economy, and Development of Egypt

2.1. The Economic and Scientific Impact

The cost of the imported as shown below "Mammalian Tissue Culture Lab" is in the range of \$ 50,000 – 60,000 (300,000- 3,60,000 Egyptian Pounds). This cost may pose a big financial burden in many scientific institutions all over Egypt. Subsequently the lack of such facilities may represent an obstacle towards developing new pharmaceuticals and/or diagnostic kits.

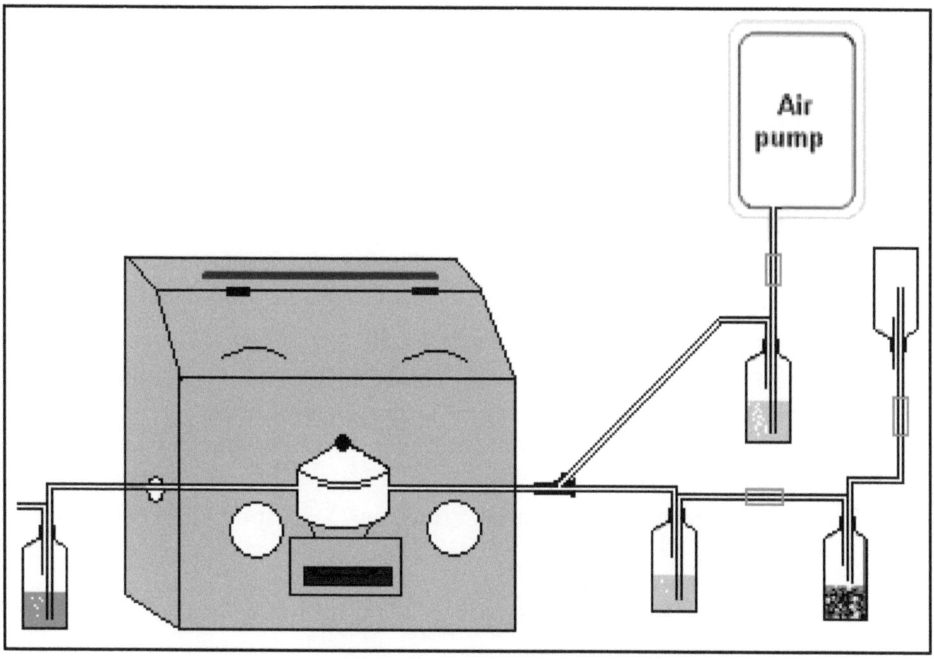

Figure 2.1: Diagramtic Sketch for a Laminar Flow Hood and Carbon Dioxide Incubator.

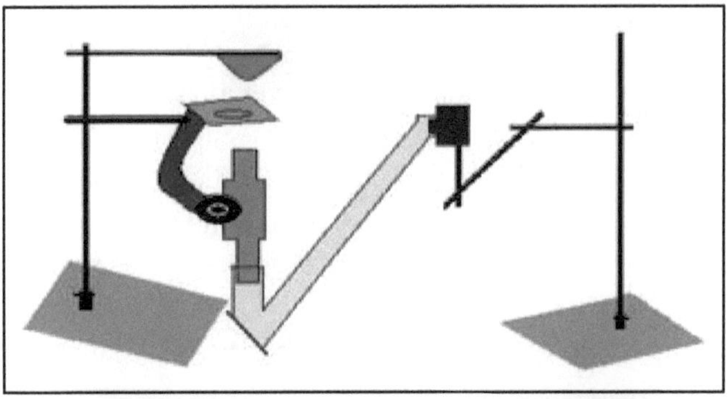

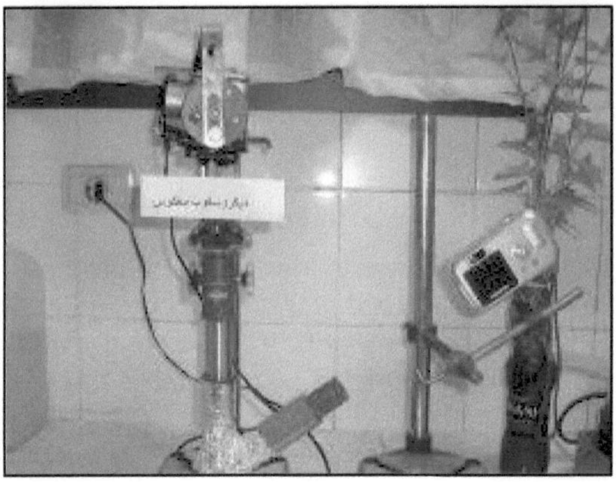

Figure 2.2: Diagramtic Sketch and Photo for the Invented Inverted Microscope.

2.2. Estimated Cost of Imported MTCL

1. Thermo Fisher Scientific Revco Ultima II Water-Jacketed CO2 Incubators, Thermo Fisher Scientific Scientific RTG5000D-9 Double Chamber 3-Gas Units

   List price $20,544.69 = Product CodeTH-BO-RTG5000D-9SKURTG5000D-
2. Inverted Microscope:

   Make: **Zeiss Invertoscope D** Price: **$5250**

   Zeiss Invertoscope D trinoccular Phase Contrast Inverted microscope with 8 MP camera system. Invertoscope D with Phase contrast condenser. pH 1-3 annuli installed. Additional lamp mounted PH 1 and PH 2 annuli also included Trinoccula
3. Laminar flow hood: Labconco® Protector® XStream™ High Performance Fume Hood **$ 15,000**

2.3. Estimated Cost for the Innovative MTCL ($ 600-7500)

1. CO_2 Incubators, : **$200-250**
2. Inverted Microscope: **$ 150-200** Plus an old light microscope
3. Laminar flow hood: **$ 250-300**

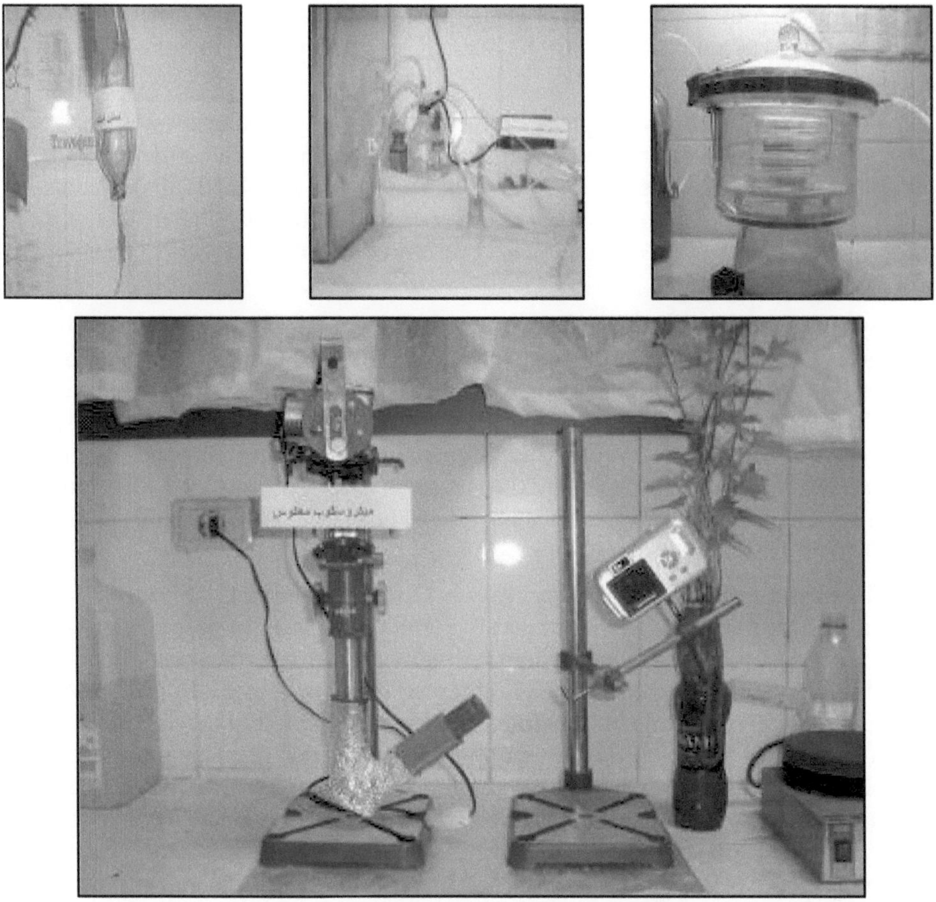

Figure 2.3: Innovation of MTCL (Mammalian Tissue Culture Lab).

The Laminar flow hood, CO2-incubator, and inverted microscope made work on cell culture possible for all students, faculty, and investigators.

Technology Transfer was from USA, Japan, Switzerland, Italy, Germany, Chile and France. We utilized extensive experience in the areas of Chemistry of Natural Products from the U. of Mansoura (Egypt), and Mississippi, USA, Biology (U of Minnesota, USA), Molecular biology (U. Mainz, Germany), and Medical and clinical (U. Roma, Italy) to develop potential agents and/or drugs to help fight endemic diseases among African community (*e.g.* Schistosomiasis, Hepatitis, fatty liver, parasites). We derived over 100 publications, several patents, and many innovative technique from these collaborations.

3. Recommendations

Under a new Egyptian IPR law, use of the protected product is permitted in all scientific activities without considering these activities as infringement. This is a very important provision since the pharmaceutical companies could use the protected pharmaceutical products to undertake research and analysis for better results (Balat and Loutfi 2004).

With the new IPR law in place, the above-mentioned situation will be totally changed. Patent protection will be available for any invention, whether products or processes, 'in all fields of technology' (as required by Art. 27 (1) of TRIPs). Moreover, patent rights will be enjoyed without discrimination in the field of technology. Accordingly, patent protection will also be granted for pharmaceutical products in addition to processes.

A product patent 'is the most desirable patent' for the pharmaceutical industry (Lewis, 1996). Without such patent protection, imitators would freely ride on the protected invention and duplicate the compound for a small fraction of the inventor's costs. In point of fact, imitation costs in pharmaceutical drugs are exceptionally low relative to the innovator's costs for discovering and developing a new compound. In addition, the protection term is for 20 years to be counted from the filing date of a patent application in Egypt (Art. 9 of the new IPR law). This Article corresponds to Art. 33 of the TRIPs Agreement.

The new Egyptian law, following the TRIPs Agreement, has no provisions dealing with the patentability of new uses of known substances or products, especially second or subsequent therapeutic uses for known pharmaceutical products, *i.e.* an anti-cancer drug with a new and widely accepted use for treating HIV/AIDS (Watal, 2001; Correa, 1998). It could be concluded that the second use of known substances, which are already in the public domain, should be excluded from patentability (new uses of old substances particularly second and subsequent medical uses of a known product are patentable subject matter under both the European Patents Convention (EPC) and the UK Patents Act, see Bently and Sherman, 2001. The search for newer and more effective treatment of diseases must, however, be taken into account. Therefore a balance between these two factors should be considered (Watal, 2001).

It is vital to highlight the increased importance of making use of inventions that have entered the public domain. The use of these inventions would be free of charge. To put such a suggestion into effect, it is necessary to know and recognize which patents have entered into the public domain. Accordingly, it is recommended that an authority, either governmental (such as the Patents Office) or non-governmental, be created or be given sufficient competence to search for expired patents and then declare that such patents are freely available to interested parties who would be able to use and exploit them. Such an authority should cooperate with other regional or international organizations (such as the World Health Organization) in order to achieve the greatest possible effect (Balat and Loutfi, 2004).

It is highly recommended that an on-going policy for R&D based on domestic raw materials and traditional plant varieties be adopted. In this regard, it is important to establish new scientific research centers with a view to taking part in modernizing the domestic drugs industry and in creating new pharmaceuticals to be available for the public at reasonable prices (Balat and Loutfi, 2004).

Conclusion

The economic impact of IP is to improve skills of human resources, utilize the available natural resources, mainly raw materials, in developing new therapeutic agents, bridge gaps between University, Industry, and community, and to emphasize the role of research and innovation in improving economy, health, and welfare of society. Moreover the sustainability of research will be the positive outcomes of transferring basic knowledge into research, applied research and finally into helpful products with financial outcomes which will help sustain future research and make the cycle work efficiently.

The new IPR law in Egypt presents a significant development in the search for an appropriate balance between the interests of IPR owners and pharmaceutical users. By providing protection to pharmaceuticals (seen as an incentive for R&D), the law does consider the interests of the rights holders. On the other hand, the interests of the users of protected products and the public generally are taken into account through the disclosure provisions, limitations and exceptions that are allowed under the law. The exact implications or impacts of the new patent protection for pharmaceutical products are difficult to predict. The new patent protection will have no impact or effect on existing drugs (understood as those which were marketed before the implementation of the TRIPs Agreement in Egypt).

References

1. Abbott, Frederick, (2002). 'Compulsory Licensing for Public Health Needs: The TRIPs Agenda at the WTO after the Doha Declaration on Public Health' Occasional Paper 9, available at: http://www.geneva.quno.info/pdf/OP9 per cent 20Abbott.pdf
2. Balat and Loutfi, The TRIPs Agreement and Developing Countries: A Legal Analysis of the Impact of the New Intellectual Property Rights Law on the Pharmaceutical Industry in Egypt, [2004] 2 Web JCLI(Web J. current legal issues)(1-25).
3. Bently, Lionel and Sherman, Brad (2001). Intellectual Property Law, (Oxford: OxfordUniversity Press).
4. Birairy, Mokhtar A. (2000) Commercial Transactions Law, Part I, (Cairo: Dar Al Nahda Al Arabia).
5. Correa, Carlos M. (2000). Intellectual Property Rights, the WTO and Developing Countries: The TRIPs Agreement and Policy Options, (London: Zed Books Ltd).
6. Correa, Carlos M. (1998). 'Patent Rights' in Carlos M. Correa and Abdulqwi A. Yusuf Intellectual Property and International Trade: The TRIPs Agreement (London: Kluwer Law International).
7. Lewis, Theresa Beeby, (1996). 'Patent Protection for the Pharmaceutical Industry: A Survey of the Patent Laws of Various Countries' 30 (4) The International Lawyer 835.

8. Mathews, Duncan, (2002). Globalising Intellectual Property Rights: The TRIPs Agreement (London: Routledge Publications).

9. Watal, Jayashree, (2001). Intellectual Property Rights in the WTO and Developing Countries, (The Hague: Kluwer Law International).

Chapter 3

The Promotion of Innovation and Creativity "The Dissemination of Global Developments"

*Nasser Galal Hasanin**

Professor of International Economics,
Higher Institute of Technology, Culture and Science Academy,
Cairo – Egypt

1. Introduction

The "Arab Regional Dialogue on Intellectual Property Rights, Innovation and Sustainable Development" organized by the UNCTAD, in June 2005, concerned the need to raise awareness about global initiatives in the area of open collaborative models, Creative Commons and access to knowledge and Technology in the Arab world.

WTO has set up an Advisory Committee on enforcement of IPR, which has initiated a new approach to enforcement. The approach is for the member countries to focus collectively on the real challenges that all countries (developed and developing) face in implementing practical procedure for enforcing rights. The Committee also investigates the best practices and procedures that could be used to effectively enforce industrial property rights, while keeping the time and cost burden at a minimum level.

* E-mail: nassergalal4@yahoo.com

In trade across borders, effective enforcement in each country requires coordinated international approach. Accordingly, enforcement agencies in each country are to increase cooperation for effective enforcement.

2. Objectives

The objective of the study is to examine the following two hypotheses:

- ✰ Enforcing IPR has a positive effect on the high-tech industries.
- ✰ The policies undertaken by the government in the process of combating piracy are efficient enough.

The study will stress on the role of formal and informal organizations to adopt an efficient enforcement policy against piracy, according to the methodology of the new institutional economics.

The study will discuss:

- ✰ The importance of the study, as it will shed some light on the need for IPR protection and how enforcing property rights will stimulate the rate of new creations in the industry, leading to growth and development.
- ✰ The theoretical framework of the study, by defining the concepts of "IPR" and "institutional economics", then by trying to show the link between establishing an efficient institutional system and the flourishing of high-tech industries using the methodology of the new institutional economics.

This study will only focus on the Intangible IPR which is known as "Intellectual property rights".

With this in mind, I would like to apply the new institutional economics to analyze the importance of IPR protection.

3. Methodology

This study follows the approach of the New Institutional Economics "NIE".

The methodology applied is more of a descriptive analysis, depending mainly on literature review and survey analysis. Some statistical measures will also be applied.

In order to achieve the above-mentioned objective, the research will provide a link between IPR enforcement and the flourishing of high-tech industries. The study will be utilizing the ideas of the new institutional economics to define the concept of property rights in general, and stress on the role of institutions and the importance of enforcement to unable the high-tech industries to flourish.

4- Theoretical Framework

The theoretical framework of the study is divided into two main sections.

The first section aims at tracing the different bodies of literature that deal with the issue of property rights. It will discuss briefly some of the approaches clarifying the emergence of property rights and its importance. Some important concepts for the study will be introduced, like transaction costs; institutions; and organizations.

The second section of the study will be mainly concerned with the concept of intellectual property, its protection instruments and its economic effects.

The theoretical framework of the study is built upon the ideas of the new institutional economics "NIE".

"NIE builds on, modifies and extends neo-classical theory to permit it to come to grips and deal with an entire range of issues heretofore beyond its ken." (John Harris, 1995)

It retains the neo-classical axioms of methodological individualism but rejects certain very restrictive assumptions. The neo-classical economists have implicitly assumed that institutions (political as well as economic) do not matter. They also treated the state as an exogenous actor.

5. Property Rights According to the New Institutional Economics

The classical intellectual-property doctrine, divides IPR into two branches:

- ☆ Industrial property
- ☆ Artistic property (Copyright and related rights).

This study focus on Industrial property, "IP can be thought of as creations of the human mind and intellect" (Watt, Richard, 2002).

This problem could arise from the public good nature of the IPR, which is accompanied by free-riding behavior. As a result, creations and product development will diminish and growth will be reduced.

Protecting property rights can be achieved through creating legal safeguards for protected materials and by enforcing these protective statues.

The law of IP in general attempts to protect the property right of creators in their creations, in order to encourage them.

In each country, the concept of protection is defined in the legislation.

It is widely recognized that without some sort of recognition and protection of IPR, economic systems would be significantly adversely affected, with the corresponding negative effects on economic growth of the whole economy in general (Watt, Richard, 2002).

In a world in which the wealth of nations and peoples is increasingly defined by their access to knowledge, intellectual property is of prime importance. Accordingly, it would be a national duty to protect IP and give incentives to its creators.

"There is no doubt, that there exists a strong relation between the development of an efficient economic system and the intellectual property it produces.

Efficient, in the sense that the system of property rights gives individuals incentives to innovate and produce and controversially inhibits those activities as pirating and other illegal actions, which lead to social and welfare problems related to the public good nature of the property rights" (North, Douglas C. and Robert Paul Thomas, 1973).

"Property rights are the rights individuals appropriate over their own labor and the goods and services they possess" (Douglas C. North, 1990).

Appropriation is a function of organizational forms, norms, legal rules, and enforcement – *i.e.* the institutional framework.

Any exchange involves positive transaction costs, in the absence of certainty and perfect information. A well-established system of property rights may reduce these transaction costs.

"Transaction costs can be defined as being the costs involved in protecting property rights, measuring what is being exchanged and in enforcing agreements." (North and Thomas, 1973).

Accordingly, any economic transaction involving the exchange of property rights will be very costly.

Transactions are costly, because of the various activities that accompanies any exchange of property rights, which are:

(a) The search for information regarding price and reliability of the contracting party.

(b) The negotiation and the formulation of a contract.

(c) The monitoring of the implementation of the contract.

(d) The enforcement of the contract (penalization of violations).

(e) The protection of property rights against infringements by other parties.

The existence of positive transaction cost and poorly defined property rights are the reasons behind the widening gap between social and private rates of return.

An efficient economic system will not occur, unless individuals are lured by incentives to undertake the socially desirable activities.

The gap between private and social benefits or costs means that some third party or parties, without their permission will receive some of the benefits or incur some of the costs. Such difference occurs when property rights are not well enforced.

If the private costs exceed the private benefits, individuals ordinarily will not be willing to undertake the activity even though it is socially desirable.

North and Thomas solved the problem of high transaction cost by simply suggesting the development of efficient institutions. But what is meant by efficient and what is meant by institutions?

Efficient in the sense that the system of PR gives incentives to create, innovate and deters the illegal actions against these rights as infringements for example.

The institutional environment that includes credible commitment entails the complex institutional framework of: formal rules, informal rules and enforcement, which together make possible low-cost transacting.

So to be able to enforce PR and to reduce TC, each country needs to develop its suitable efficient institutional system.

NIE starts from the reality that information is rarely complete, and that individuals have different ideas of the way in which the world about them works. Thus, there exists a positive transaction cost. (TC is the cost that accompanies any transaction activities).

Accordingly it could be said that the NIE is a development of neo-classical economics to include the role of transaction costs in exchange and so to take account of institutions as critical constraints on economic performance.

- ☆ The concept of Property rights in details will be introduced.
- ☆ The relation between Property rights and transaction costs will be analyzed.
- ☆ The enforcement of property rights and the role of third party enforcement will be discussed.

The NIE modifies and extends the neo-classical theory to permit it to deal with an entire range of issues beyond its ken (Harris, 1995).

The neo-classical theory has been a major contribution to knowledge. It is based on the fundamental assumption of scarcity and hence competition, however, it has implicitly assumed that institutions do not matter. This assumption is based upon its idea about the existence of a frictionless exchange process in which PRs are perfectly specified and information is likewise costless to acquire.

The NIE retains the neo-classical axioms of methodological individualism, as the fundamental assumptions of scarcity and hence competition. But it rejects certain very restrictive assumptions in the notion of "THE MARKET" that is central to the neo-classical economics.

The neo-classical theory defines a market as being an abstract area of impersonal economic exchange of homogenous goods by means of voluntary transactions on an equal basis between large numbers of autonomous, fully-informed entities with profit-maximizing behavioral motivations and able to enter and leave freely" (Harris-White, 1995).

The NIE argues that there exists a positive transaction cost that accompanies any exchange. An economic definition of transaction cost (TC) is the cost of measuring what is being exchanged and enforcing agreements.

In a larger context they are all costs involved in human interaction over time. They are the costs of:

- ☆ Finding out what the relative prices are:
- ☆ Negotiating contracts.
- ☆ Concluding contracts.
- ☆ Monitoring contracts
- ☆ Enforcing the agreements.

The fundamental ideas about transaction cost, by simply saying that they consist of the cost of arranging a contract ex ante and monitoring and enforcing it *ex post*, as opposed to production cost, which is the cost of executing a contract.

He has divided the costly activity that accompanies any exchange of PR into five main points, which are:

The search for information, regarding price and reliability of the contracting party:

- ☆ The negotiation and the formulation of a contract.
- ☆ The monitoring of the implementation of the contract.
- ☆ The enforcement of the contract.
- ☆ The protection of PR against infringements by other parties.

In a study, by North and Thomas (1973), TC is simply defined as being the costs involved in:

- ☆ Protecting PR
- ☆ Measuring what is been exchanged
- ☆ Enforcing the agreements
- ☆ Accordingly it could be said that the NIE is a development of the neo-classical theory to include the role of TC in exchange and so to take account of institutions as critical constraints on economic performance.

The NIE defines institutions as been socially devised constraints on individual actions (North, 1994).

Any institution results from a series of decisions by which a group of individuals determines how to conduct and regulate the interactions among members of the group.

So, it can be said that they are sets of rules that are recognized and frequently followed by members of the community, or more formally they are humanly-devised constraints that structure human interaction.

North argues that institutions are formed precisely to reduce uncertainty in human exchange. Broadly stated, they are defined as means of reducing TCs.

The institutional environment consists of:

- ☆ Informal constraints (conventions, norms of behaviour).
- ☆ Formal rules (statue law, common law, regulations).
- ☆ Enforcement characteristics of both.

Once property rights are specified and enforced, efficient resource allocation will result.

North and Thomas stated that the key to economic growth was and is the creation of an efficient economic system. It is the existence of economic and political institutions in a society (together with the technology employed) that determine the efficiency of an economic system.

Efficient, in the sense that the system of PRs gives individuals the right to produce and innovate, and in the mean time inhibits those activities that reduce individual incentives, such as theft or arbitrary confiscation.

It should be mentioned that institutions alone are not enough to guarantee efficiency. These institutions must interact with some organizations in order to enforce PRs. The ability of institutions to create and provide sufficient information at low cost is a necessary condition for the development of an efficient economic system. But a sufficient condition implies in addition that the contracts embodying the exchange process can be enforced by a third party at low cost.

Organizations, too, specify the constraints that structure human interaction inside the organization, but in addition they are action groups. They are composed of groups of individuals bound by a common purpose to achieve certain objectives. They include:

- ✰ Political bodies (political parties, the senate ...)
- ✰ Economic bodies (firms, trade unions.)
- ✰ Social bodies (churches, clubs...)
- ✰ Educational bodies (schools, colleges...)

6. The Emergence of Property Rights in Economic Literature

Property rights, in general are the rights individuals appropriate over their own labor and the goods and services they posses. Appropriation is a function of organizational forms, norms, legal rules, and enforcement. (North, 1990)

There are several examples of rights one can appropriate over his own property. These rights divided into three main categories, which are:

1. The right to use an asset
2. The right to derive income from an asset through contractual agreements with others.
3. The rights to transfer the ownership of an asset to others.

If any of these rights were restricted; the value of the asset will tend to diminish.

The emergence of property rights has often been explained in terms of behavioural regularities or equilibrium outcomes of recurrent, conflict interactions concerning the distribution of scarce resources (Schotter, 1981; Sugden, 1986).

Thus, according to this argument formal property rights evolve out of a spontaneous process of the emergence of informal or less identical social agents. The property rights literature that emerged in the 1960s (Alichan, 1965 and Demsetz, 1964) made it clear that the structure of property rights is crucial to economic efficiency and development. This literature has clarified to some extent the dimensions of individual rights. These are: the right to use, sell, destroy, modify, donate and transform property (Clague, 1997).

One of the main arguments of this literature is that a variety of property rights structures can be reasonably efficient, assuming that individuals are free to enter into contracts and that these contracts can be enforced by law. There were no barriers to efficiency as long as their rights can be traded. But they excluded situations in which such contracts are either prohibited by law or for other reasons are not enforceable in practice. These types of situations are considered inefficient by this literature.

Recent work in the economics of asymmetric information strongly qualified that the initial allocation of property rights does not have efficiency implications. According to this literature, the initial allocation of wealth has implications for the efficiency of resource allocation.

A private good can be differentiated from a public one, according to two main properties.

1. Rivalry Property: what is consumed by one can not be consumed by others.
2. Excludability Property: some agents have exclusive control over the good.

Private goods are rivalries and excludable, while public goods are not. Thus, it becomes very hard to force users to pay for the use of a public good. Accordingly, public goods are usually over consumed or under supplied.

Thus, they suggested that the problem of providing public goods can be solved through the creation of well defined property rights. (Weimar and Vining, 1989)

In the natural state, all goods are supposed to be public goods. No one can exclude anyone from consuming the scarce resources in the public domain, except by resorting to force.

For some goods to be called private goods, a society must establish property rights over these goods In other words, goods remain public as long as property rights over them have not been established.

Property rights are precisely what allow owners to exclude others from using the good.

Olson, 1965 saw that the concept of a public good could be applied to a great variety of group goals. But he was concerned about the cost of information and the rational ignorance of members of a large group. Accordingly, Olson developed his theory "The Theory of Collective Action", which was mainly concerned with how to make people with common interest, observe that interest and act to achieve it. This process could be easy if the number of individuals in the group is small, as they can communicate easily with one another. But large groups can only act collectively when political entrepreneurs create organizations that provide rewards to the entrepreneurs and incentives to the members. In other words, punishment or rewards that provide incentives for individuals to contribute to collective goals must be introduced.

Most people usually do not make large contributions to public goods unless there are enough private benefits from their actions to make it worthwhile. Large groups come into existence mainly through institutional devices that provide these private benefits.

Accordingly, public goods become private ones, when governments decide to protect the property rights of right holders over these goods (North, 1981).

In most cases property rights emerge when authorities take the initiative to:

- ✰ First: grant the rights.
- ✰ Second: enforce them.

Thus, the question of "how property rights emerged" can be restated by "how public goods become private goods".

The importance of establishing institutions that define and protect property rights in an environment that includes a law enforcing government was also a common idea among the different approaches through out the history of property rights.

Accordingly, it becomes obvious that without some sort of protection and enforcement of PRs, economic systems would be significantly adversely affected.

Enforcement means: make it obligatory or put it into force. This process embodies two main tasks:

1. Preventing their infringement by free-riders.
2. Chastising attempts by right-holders to extend them beyond the terms of the grant.

According to the NIE, property rights will be enforced, if each country develops its suitable efficient institutional system.

In the straightforward neo-classical theory, the gains from trade are realized with zero transaction cost, thus parties can exchange costless, knowing everything about each other and enforcement is perfect. In such a world of complete information, no institutions are necessary.

NIE starts from the fact that information is rarely complete, and that individuals have different ideas of the way in which the world about them works. Thus, there exists a positive transaction cost. The failure of neo-classical theories to develop adequate explanations from the emergence and evolutions of PR comes, primarily from neglecting this fact.

Each part of the general ideas expressed above needs to be clarified in order to understand the concept of property right protection and enforcement.

7. The Concept of Intellectual Property Rights (IPRs)

The emergence of new technologies and creations are considered key factors behind economic growth. The rights that protect these creations are the Intellectual property rights (IPRs).

It is frequently argued that relatively weak intellectual property rights protection in a country may lower the probability that multinational firms will invest there.

In other words IPR has become absolutely essential to make substantial investments in a country or to transfer advanced technology there. Thus IPRs protection plays a role in encouraging FDI and technology transfer.

Nowadays much of the advanced technology is wrapped up in a very simple package, which encourages its reproduction and dissemination. This process is known as intellectual theft.

These patterns are reflected in a growing demand for IPRs protection.

IPRs are an important component of any development programme. Implementing stronger IPRs as required by the TRIPS Agreement or in other policy initiatives will lead the developing countries to strike a balance between needs for technology acquisition, market access, and diffusion.

Accordingly, the concept of IPRs will be discussed in details, determining its branches, instruments, and its economic effects.

IPR can be defined as an asset, developed by inventive or creative work. It defines the extent to which the owners of the rights may exclude others from activities that violate or damage the property. Thus it protects the creative work of owners seeking to exploit the value of their creation.

Intellectual property (IP) is a field of law that deals with property rights in intangible property.

It refers to the creation of human mind and intellect. Rights to exclude its unauthorized use have been granted by law.

IP is mainly used as a business tool, but it also recognizes certain non-economic rights in creative works. These non-economic rights are also called moral rights. This sort of right is mainly implemented in the area of copyright.

Authors of a certain work may prevent actions that would harm their honor or reputation. In other words the authors will exercise certain types of control over their works. These non-economic rights include:

- ✰ The right to be known as the author.
- ✰ Prevent false attributions of authorship
- ✰ Prevent changes in certain types of work that would damage the author's reputation.

Economists consider IPRs a tool for creating legal monopolies, as it creates some market power. But it is more productive to consider them as as rules regulating the terms of static and dynamic competition.

It offers a way for promoting progress by protecting the rights of creators, and rewarding honest dealing by regulating certain features of business behaviour.

7.1 The Instruments Protecting IPRs

Different instruments to protect intellectual property have emerged over the path of history. These instruments differ in their subject matter, extent of protection, and field of application. These instruments reflect the society's objective to narrow the gap between creators and consumers interests for different types of intellectual works

The legal structure used to protect IP can be divided into five main groups:

- ✰ Patents
- ✰ Plant Breeder's Right
- ✰ Copyrights
- ✰ Trademarks
- ✰ Trade Secrets

7.2 The Economic Effects of IPRs

Intellectual property is used to promote economic development at on two levels:

- ✰ The Macroeconomic level
- ✰ The Microeconomic level

7.2.1 The Microeconomic Level

At the microeconomic level, IPRs make it possible to derive a private benefit from the innovation or creation of a new work.

Patents, copyright, and similar forms of IP provide a means by which innovators and investors can capture some of the economic benefit of their innovations.

The different forms of intellectual property provide a means by which innovators and investors can recover the investment of time and money needed to bring a new product to the market.

If there is no prospect of a reward, inventors may devote their efforts to some other activity than innovating or they may choose to keep their inventions secret. Incentives must be offered to the creator to encourage disclosure. Disclosure of new creative works is important because it permits new ideas to enter the public domain, to make it possible for others to begin building on them. Inventors and authors may choose to maintain their creation or work as "undisclosed information" if they choose to do so, but this will be of course against public interest.

7.2.2 The Macroeconomic Level

At the macroeconomic level, IP promotes economic development by encouraging innovation and foreign direct investment (FDI). FDI is considered a major source of technology transfer.

Prior studies have shown a positive relation between IPR and FDI. This relation however is not consistent for all sectors.

One of the most informative sources concerning the relation between IPRs and FDI is a study for the World Bank by Dr. Edwin Mansfield (1994).

Mansfield provides survey evidence of the importance of the strength of IPR systems in shaping the FDI decisions by firms.

He surveyed 100 major U.S firms in six manufacturing industries, to determine the impact of IP protection on the investment decisions undertaken by these firms.

He has provided a better understanding of the effect that a developing countries system of IPRs has on the transfer of technology to that country through FDI.

The responses of the firms toward the effect of IPRs protection on their investment decision can be divided into two different groups.

The first group of firms rules out substantial investments in countries affording weak protection.

These firms are particularly research-intensive firms, with products or processes easy to imitate.

The strength or weakness of a particular country's IP laws is highly important to such firms in determining their investment decisions in a country or in transferring technology there.

A computer executive states that although they have made investments in a large developing country, they have not implemented manufacturing operations there.

Manufacturing operations in such fields use the firms' highest level of technology and are highly important. In addition the firm has also limited the types of software being developed there due to the lack of adequate copyright protection.

The second group of firms regards IP protection as relatively unimportant in their Most of these firms are in many low-technology industries and some in very high-technology industries like electrical equipments.

The president of a firm producing machine tools stated that the strength and weakness of a particular country IPRs does not particularly influence their investment decision. He also said that unlike other industries it is very difficult for rivals in their industry to imitate a new product or technology without complementary inputs that are hard to obtain.

Mansfield's study (1994) makes it clear that the strength or weakness of a country's system of IP protection seems to have a substantial effect on the kinds of technology transferred by many U.S. firms to that country. Particularly in research-intensive firms which produce high-technology. Also, this factor seems to influence the composition and extent of U.S. direct investment there, the size of the effects will differ greatly from one country to another.

Especially firms with easily copied products, such as software and pharmaceutical products would be interested in the strength of intellectual property rights.

In Mansfield's study 20 per cent of firms reported that the strength of IPRs was a major consideration in decisions to invest in rudimentary production facilities, whereas about 80 per cent deemed it important for locating R&D facilities.

Thus the IP system creates a framework in which developing countries can participate jointly in the economic activities of the developed world.

The composition of FDI does matter when regarding the relative importance of IP protection among different countries. Many governments of developing countries realized that the amount of technology transferred to their firms depends on the types of investments made by foreign firms, and not just the dollar volume of such investments. Investments in facilities to make components or complete products are likely to increase the country's technological competence to a greater extent than other types of investments concerning sales and distribution outlets. Foreign firms tend to regard IP protection as important for the former than for the latter types of investment. Thus, a country's system of IP protection and enforcement may influence the composition of FDI transferred to the country, which will affect the country's overall technological competence and development.

Another important factor that should be taken into the consideration of developing countries is the age of transferred technologies to them. The age of a technology can be defined as being the difference between the year the technology was transferred and the year the technology was first used by the firm. It seems that U.S. firms transfer older technologies to countries with weak intellectual property protection than to those with strong protection.

In conclusion, the strength or weakness of a country's IP system seems to have substantial effect, particularly in high-technology industries, on the kinds of technology transferred and the composition and extent of FDI there. Thus, the absence of efficient institutions will inhibit large-scale investments and the extended.

Leafer's study (1991) makes it clear that weak intellectual property in developing countries is due to the absence of efficient governmental enforcement of law and the deficient coverage of intellectual property in the law itself.

8. Enforcing Property Rights (PR-Enforcement, Economic Development, and the Role of Governments)

Institutions alone are not enough, we are also in need for some organizations, which are going to implement these institutions and enforce the property rights. Institutions are just the rules of the game and organizations are the players.

Organizations may include political bodies (political parties, city council), economic bodies (firms, trade unions), and educational bodies (schools, colleges).

"Enforcement of PR embodies two tasks: preventing their infringement by free riders and disciplining attempts by the rights-holders to extend them beyond the terms of the grant" (Keith E. Maskus, 1997).

The verb enforcing means: make it obligatory, effective or put it into force.

Thus, "the enforcement of P.R. is undertaken by both owners (through security measures) and the state (Via the legal system and the state's coercive power)".

In the straightforward neoclassical story, the gains from trade are realized with zero transaction costs. Thus, parties can exchange costless, knowing every thing about each other and enforcement is perfect. In such a world of complete information, no institutions are necessary.

However, with incomplete information, cooperative solutions will breakdown unless institutions are created that provide sufficient information to police deviations.

To achieve this, the concept of punishment should be introduced. This implies the existence of a third party that should be responsible for:

- ☆ Enforcing the contracts carried by different parties
- ☆ Punishing (*i.e.* imposing a fine) the party, that violates the agreement (contract)
- ☆ The economics of innovation as a main instrument of IPR

All economies, both developed and developing, have an important dependence on innovation and creations in general.

The creative genius of the world is reflected in the flow from the imagination of the world's people. Thus, it becomes necessary to enforce PR to reward that creative genius and protect it against unauthorized exploitation.

The legal instruments are just one of the pieces that form a national system of PRs- protection. The institutions in charge of administrating the system and the organizations available for enforcing these rights are other crucial elements of the system's overall effectiveness.

Efficient enforcement of PRs is of primary importance to those engaged in innovative activities. Only recently has the legal environment noticed the relation between PR-enforcement and economic development.

Development economists have typically treated the state as an exogenous actor in the development process. North (1990), pointed out that the state can never be treated as an exogenous actor in development policy. He said that third-party enforcement represents the development of the state as a coercive force able to monitor property rights and enforce contracts effectively.

North stressed on the fact that PRs are classic public goods, because the marginal cost of copying them is low compared to the cost of discovering and developing them. Besides, as mentioned before, they are non-rival and non-excludable. Thus, with incomplete information, cooperative solutions will break down unless institutions are created. These institutions should provide sufficient information to the coercive power responsible for enforcing the rights.

To achieve this, the concept of third party enforcement should be introduced. This third party should be responsible for:

- ✰ Enforcing the contracts carried by different parties.
- ✰ Punishing the party, that violates the agreement.

Accordingly, an explanation of property right enforcement requires an understanding of the behavior of the state or government in some cases, which normally plays an important role in defining and enforcing PRs.

The enforcement of agreements in economic markets is ultimately a function of the political markets of economies. The political market imposes the polity that specifies the property rights and provides the instruments and resources to enforce the contract.

North and Thomas (1973), have reviewed the importance of property rights by saying that these rights played an important role in explaining the growth performance of western economies.

They also stated that the inability of societies to develop effective low-cost enforcement of contracts is the most important source of historical stagnation and contemporary underdevelopment in the third world. Nations, in which the power of the state is forced by the rule of the law to maintain property rights, are seen to grow faster than others.

Poorly developed legal systems prevent economies from developing, because without some sort of property rights enforcement, private agents will be discouraged to participate in any market activity. They will fear the expropriation of the proceeds of market activity by dishonest parties (pirates) to a contract. This will prevent the agents from receiving their full benefits. Accordingly weak property right enforcement is therefore likely to reduce incentives and opportunities for production, investment and innovation.

It should be mentioned, that talking about the development and enforcement of property rights (specially in ideas, inventions, and innovations which is the intellectual property), leads to a main conflict. This conflict is reflected in a widening gap between social and private rates of return.

The private rate of return is the sum of the net receipts which the economic unit receives from undertaking an activity. The social rate of return is the total net benefit (positive or negative) that a society receives from the same activity. Economists use the term "social return" to describe "the benefit from an investment received by a society as a whole, as opposed to a "private return" that may be achieved by the owner of the new work" (Moroney, 2003).

One public interest served by IP is to encourage the making and development of inventions.

Several studies have been conducted to measure the social return from innovations. A study conducted by Nathan Associates reported a social rate of return of 70 per cent, whereas the private rate of return was about less than half the social rate of return (Mansfield, 1977).

North (1996), made it clear that economic growth will not occur unless the existing economic organization is efficient. Efficient in the sense, those individuals must be lured by incentives, to undertake the socially desirable activities.

This disparity between private and social benefits or costs means, that some third party or parties, will receive some of the benefits or incur some of the costs without permission. Mansfield, 1977 found that imitators gain access to details concerning new products and processes rapidly, often within a year of their development.

The gap will occur whenever property rights are poorly defined or are not enforced.

If the private costs exceed the private benefits, individuals usually will not be willing to undertake the activity even though it is socially profitable. Some mechanism must be devised to bring social and private rates of return into closer parity.

The intellectual property system makes it possible to derive a private benefit from the innovation. Devices, like secrecy, rewards, prizes, copyrights, and patent laws are likely to narrow this existing gap. Intellectual property encourages the necessary investment of time and other resources by allowing innovators to capture some of the economic benefit of their innovations.

But, since creating, specifying, and enacting property rights are costly, it should be mainly the governments who take over the protection and enforcement of property rights. This is, because the government can do so at lower cost than any private volunteer groups and besides it has the authority and tools to do so.

Mansfield (1994) determined three areas of concern in assessing the strength of PRs in a country:

- ☆ The laws
- ☆ The legal infrastructure
- ☆ The willingness of governments to actively enforce property rights.

Thus, third party enforcement, presented mainly by the governments is of great importance, to narrow the gap between private and social rates of return, as to guarantee efficiency, and thus stimulate growth.

In the light of the above the NIE has added two major constrains to formal theories and especially to traditional neo-classical micro-economic theory:

1. Transaction costs.
2. The structure of property rights.

The importance of NIE approach stems in the fact that almost all economic and political activities in well-ordered societies are influenced and constrained by the structure of laws, rules and enforceable customs which are called in this case institutions- that are politically determined and enforced by the state. Different exchange processes via institutions that affect transaction cost and property rights, will have important implications for the economic behaviour of individuals, and hence for the overall performance of the economy. Economic growth will occur if property rights make it worthwhile to undertake socially productive activity. Gains from a market economy in terms of expanding private investments can be realized only if there exists an efficient system of institutions and government policies.

The intangible property describes the output of human knowledge and intellect. A person can practice property rights over his own creation or invention. This type of property is usually much harder to protect due to its intangible or cultural nature.

References

1. North D. and Thomas R., "The Rise of the Western World", Cambridge University Press, 1973.
2. Warren-Boulton F. and Baseman K., "The economics of intellectual property protection for software", paper prepared for a meeting of the American council on interoperable Systems in Washington D.C., June, 1994.
3. Theeuwes J., "Partial copyright high-tech industries", paper prepared for the WIPO meeting, Helsinky, 2002.
4. Varian H., "Intermediate Microeconomics", fourth edition.
5. North D., "Institutions, Institutional Change and Economic Performance", Cambridge University Press, 1990.
6. Clague C., "Institutions and Economic Development", Johns Hopkins University Press, 1997.

7. Harris J., Hunter J. and Lewis C., "The new institutional economics and third world development", Routledge, London and New York, 1995.
8. The Allen Consulting Group, "What should be measured?" Paper prepared for the WIPO meeting in Helsinki, July, 2002.
9. Picard R. and Toivonen T., "Methods of assessing the economic value of copyright", Paper prepared for the WIPO meeting in Helsinki, July 2002.
10. www.wipo.org
11. www.economist.org

Chapter 4

The Role of the Aripo Swakopmund Protocol in Salvaging Africa's Traditional Knowledge and Associated Genetic Resources: The Case of Ghana

*Sarah Norkor Anku**

Legal Practitioner and Intellectual Property Rights Consultant
Registrar General's Department
P. O. Box 118, Accra – Ghana

ABSTRACT

There is a systematic growth in the socio-economic value of Traditional Knowledge (TK) and associated genetic resources globally mainly as a result of the renaissance of the use of natural products. Exploitation of such TK and associated genetic resources can be utilized as one of the tools of poverty reduction and economic growth in Africa. Legal protection is one of the means to maximize the utilization and exploitation of the rights.

There has been global agitation for the protection of TK and its associated genetic resources. This global agitation has been attributed among others to misappropriation,

* E-mail: sarahnorkor.anku@gmail.com

misuse and lack of equitable benefit sharing with owners of TK and associated genetic resources. Internationally, some have argued for a *sui generis* protection of TK.

The African Regional Intellectual Property Organization on its part has adopted a Protocol known as "the Swakopmund Protocol on the Protection of Traditional Knowledge and Expressions of Folklore" which seeks to protect traditional knowledge and expressions of folklore. The Protocol recognizes among others, the inalienable rights of the African to traditional knowledge and the use of Africa's intangible assets for socio-economic development of the continent.

The main objective of this research is to analyze the provisions of the Swakopmund Protocol as it applies to traditional knowledge and associated genetic resources and to determine how to effectively implement the Protocol in Ghana.

The research comprises a desk research and a survey. The respondents in the survey ranged from Policy makers through holders of TK to the general users of TK in Ghana. The findings of this research indicate among others that, some provisions of the protocol conflict with some existing laws in Ghana, as such, implementation may require some amendments of these laws. It also indicates the interest of Ghanaians in the subject and the eagerness to participate in the effective implementation of the protocol.

Keywords: *Traditional knowledge, Genetic resources, Expressions of folklore, Swakopmund protocol, Ghana.*

1. Introduction

There has been a systematic growth in the socio-economic value of traditional knowledge (TK) over the years. Researchers have attributed this to the renaissance of the use of natural products as sources of new biochemical compounds for drugs, chemical and agro-product development by biotechnology, pharmaceutical and human health care industries (ARIPO website, 2010). Many of these natural products were first used by local people and the knowledge has been developed over the years. It has also been said to be an element in the commercialization of natural products. Paolo (2001) observed that the world market value of drugs, seeds, pesticides, healthcare products, cosmetics, ornamental plants species, plant extracts, perfumes and other products derived from genetic resources at the end of the 1990s was estimated to be within the range of 500 to 800 billion dollars a year. By 2020, it could reach 5 trillion dollars.

The agitation for the protection of traditional knowledge has been attributed to the lack of equitable benefit sharing with the owners of the traditional knowledge and associated genetic resources. For example, over a decade ago, as taken from Principe (1989), Possey and Dutfield (1996) suggested that, it is probably impossible to estimate the full market value of traditional knowledge due to its enormity which may increase as advances in biotechnology broaden the range of life forms containing such attributes. They also noted that by one estimate, the market value of plant-based medicines alone (many of which were used first by indigenous peoples) sold in developed countries amounted to $43 billion in 1985. However, only a tiny proportion of this (much less than 1 percent) has ever been returned to the source communities. In an interaction with Professor Laud Okine, the Director of the Mampong Centre for

Scientific Research into Plant Medicine, in March 2011, he revealed that, the Centre generated Ghc50,000 (US$33,333) in 2005 and has a potential of generating approximately Ghc100,000 (US$66,667) per annum or Ghc2,000 (US$1,333) per week yet the Centre has no policy on equitable benefit sharing with owners of the traditional knowledge from whom most of the plant-based medicines are derived. Advocates for the protection of traditional knowledge are generally of the opinion that adequate protection would ensure equitable benefit sharing with owners of the traditional knowledge and associated genetic resources from which such plant-based medicines and other TK related products are derived. Protection is also expected to curb misappropriation and misuse of TK and associated genetic resources.

The notion of the protection of traditional knowledge has been perceived in the global debate as one of the actions that could be taken to preserve, protect and promote the development of traditional knowledge.

There is currently a debate on the revision of Article 27.3(b) of the TRIPs Agreement which deals with the discretion of Members to exclude from patentability plants and animals other than micro-organisms, and essentially biological processes for the production of plants or animals other than non-biological and microbiological processes. The Article is said to control what is currently one of the most controversial areas regarding the patenting of life forms. There have been reports of large scale commercialization of traditional knowledge and the associated genetic materials owned by indigenous communities by trans-national corporations, meanwhile the Developing World is challenged with basic food security, medicine, and issues of equitable sharing of benefits derived from uses of the traditional knowledge and associated genetic resources.

A successful conclusion to this debate from the point of view of Developing Countries will involve the amendment of the TRIPs Agreement to include disclosure of the source of biological material and associated traditional knowledge in relevant patent applications. This process is expected to bring the TRIPs Agreement in conformity with the UN Convention on Biological Diversity as proposed under Paragraph 19 of the 2001 Doha Declaration (Doha Declaration, 2001), thus ensuring Prior Informed Consent of owners or holders of such knowledge and subsequent equitable benefit sharing with the owners involved.

Internationally, some have argued for a *sui generis* protection of traditional knowledge. The reasons proffered by advocates of such *sui generis* protection have included cross-cutting issues such as rights of indigenous populations to benefit from the use of their resources. Another issue of concern to the international community is the asymmetry between the benefits obtained by companies that exploit traditional knowledge-based products and the lack of benefit for the traditional knowledge holders. It is believed that the inclusion of disclosure of source of biological material and associated traditional knowledge would address the issue of equitable benefit sharing.

Currently, the Intergovernmental Committee (IGC) of the World Intellectual Property Organization (WIPO) is debating a probable internationally binding *sui generis* protection of traditional knowledge and traditional cultural expressions. At the end of the 21st Session of the IGC, held in February 2012, Draft Articles on the possible document for the protection of traditional knowledge was made public as a work in progress document (wipo_grtkf_ic_21_ref_facilitators_text.pdf).

The African Regional Intellectual Property Organization (ARIPO) is a Regional Inter-Governmental organization established under the Lusaka Agreement, an Agreement on the Creation of an Industrial Property Organization for English – Speaking Africa at Lusaka (Zambia) on December 9, 1976. The Agreement has been amended over the years and currently Membership is opened to all States: Members of the United Nations Economic Commission for Africa or the African Union (AU). There are currently eighteen (18) Member States, including Ghana and nine (9) Observer States. The Organization is mandated, among others, under Article III of the Agreement, to promote the harmonization and development of the intellectual property laws appropriate to the needs of its members and of the region as a whole. Given the rich biodiversity held by African countries and the alarming rate of bio-piracy, genetic erosion, the misappropriation and disappearance of traditional knowledge and folklore, ARIPO's mandate was extended in 2002, to cover the protection of genetic resources, traditional knowledge and expressions of folklore (ARIPO, 2011).

Over the past decade the Organization focused its work programme on traditional knowledge and expressions of folklore which led to the adoption of the Swakopmund Protocol in August 2010. The ARIPO Swakopmund Protocol on the Protection of Traditional Knowledge and Expressions of Folklore (the Swakopmund Protocol) is a Regional instrument aimed at protecting TK and enhancing the benefits of TK to the rightful owners/holders. Africa an economically challenged continent and Ghana in particular, stand to benefit greatly from adequate protection of TK and associated genetic resources.

As a medium term strategic plan, Ghana aims to enhance the creation of employment and income earning opportunities for rapid and sustained poverty reduction (GSGDA, 2010). Some have argued strongly that, protection of traditional knowledge is necessary to stimulate economic growth which, in turn, contributes to poverty reduction. Considering the depth of wealth of TK and the fact that TK is said to affect or is used, one way or the other, by all Ghanaians, it is believed that with appropriate protection, development and promotion of TK in Ghana, TK can be utilized as one of the effective tools for poverty reduction and help Ghana implement the provisions of the medium term development agenda – in particular, poverty reduction and economic growth.

1.1. Purpose of the Study

The purpose of this research is to highlight the benefits of the Swakopmund Protocol in protecting and promoting traditional knowledge and associated genetic resources in Africa, particularly in Ghana and highlight the possible challenges to the effective implementation of the protocol in Ghana as well as to recommend possible solutions.

2. Materials and Methods

The research comprised of a desk research and a survey. The respondents in the survey ranged from Policy makers through holders of TK to the general users of TK in Ghana.

The desk research covered the examination of secondary data which included among others, an analysis of the Swakopmund Protocol and laws and policies in Ghana that apply to traditional knowledge and associated genetic resources.

The survey related to both qualitative and quantitative primary data collection. The population covered TK holders/owners, Policy makers and Implementers of Policy, Researchers from two leading Universities in Ghana, as well as, Research Institutions and general users of TK.

Non-probability sampling methods were utilized. The non-probability sampling methods applied in this research are purposive and snowball sampling. The snowball sampling method is useful for sampling a population where access is difficult such as the vast stakeholders of TK. The task for the researcher was to establish who the critical or key informants are, with whom initial contact was to be made (Cohen *et al.*, 2003). There were also a few group interviews and focus group discussions.

The TK owners/holders included fifty (50) Chiefs from the National House of Chiefs. Chiefs in Ghana play significant role in the society. Their status in society is recognized by the 1992 constitution of the Republic of Ghana which defines chiefs under article 277 as follows:

A chief is a person, who, hailing from the appropriate family and lineage, has been validly nominated, elected or selected and enstooled, enskinned or installed as a chief or queenmother in accordance with the relevant customary law and usage.

Chiefs are custodians of some community-owned traditional knowledge in their traditional areas and are mandated by the constitution to undertake an evaluation of traditional customs and usages with the view of eliminating those customs and usages that are outmoded and socially harmful (Constitution 1992). Some chiefs are also Members of the Council of State. The Council of State is a Constitutional Advisory body to the President of Ghana (Constitution 1992).

The key informant among this group was the President of the National House of Chiefs who is also a member of the Council of State. He granted the researcher permission to address the National House of Chiefs on March 23, 2011. The House was unaware of the Swakopmund Protocol. However after a brief introduction of the subject matter and distribution of copies of the Protocol and synopsis of the research, the researcher had a fruitful interaction with the House as a group. Each Chief was given a questionnaire to fill. This was to elicit individual views as well as the views of the House as a group. Some Chiefs requested for a further one-on-one interview at their respective traditional areas before answering the questionnaire. This was a task which the researcher could not oblige due to time and financial constraints. Eighteen (18) questionnaires were analyzed from this group.

The next group consisted of Traditional Health Practitioners (THPs). This group has gained a lot of recognition in Ghana in recent times. THPs have a directorate under the Ministry of Health and an association (Association of Traditional Health Practitioners in Ghana). The group serves as a pressure group to lobby government and also educate and seek the welfare of their members. THPs are well organized and regulated by a code of ethics and standards of practice published in 2004. The key informant was the Registrar of Traditional Medicines at the Ministry of Health.

The researcher interviewed twenty (20) Lecturers and Researchers from two leading universities in Ghana, including the Vice Chancellors of the said universities. Researchers from the Council for Scientific and Industrial Research and the Nugouchi Memorial Institute were also interviewed.

It was equally important that the researcher sought the views of policy makers and implementers of policy to determine the gaps (if any) between these key stakeholders of traditional knowledge. The policy makers and implementers of policy constituted the flip side of the coin to the TK owners/holders/users. Their opinion or ideas from personal observation appear many times to differ from that of the beneficiaries of the policies/laws they make or implement, causing some of such policies/laws to be ineffective or inadequately enforced. It was therefore imperative to gather the views of such policy makers and implementers. In the process, three (3) Ministers of State and thirteen (13) Government officials were interviewed.

The researcher classified another group of respondents as general users of traditional knowledge. This group consisted of members of the general public selected at random from two cities in Ghana, namely, Accra and Cape Coast. Twenty-five (25) members of this group were also interviewed.

2.1. Data Collection and Procedures

The researcher conducted face-to-face interviews and telephone interviews with owners/holders of traditional knowledge, policy makers and implementers, Researchers from R&D Institutions and Universities and individuals from the general public. The interviews were semi-structured to prevent wide deviations on the part of the respondents. Being semi-structured, interview guides were developed for the exercise. The interview guide was based on information gathered from respondents of earlier interviews with the key informants. The initial questions were modified to capture questions that hitherto were not contemplated by the researcher but kept on recurring as issues among the key informants. Each in-depth interview lasted over an hour which gave an indication of the stakeholders' interest in the topic.

2.2. Data Analysis

The data collected were presented in a matrix indicating the preferred method of implementing the protocol. Analysis was descriptive in nature and figures were used for further explanation.

3. Results and Discussions

The matrix in Table 4.1 illustrates a summary of the findings of data collected from the field.

Table 4.1: A Matrix Indicating Consolidated Responses to the Three (3) Main Questions

Questions	*Categories of Respondents*			
	TK Holders/Owners (28 Respondents)	*Policy Makers/ Implementers (16 Respondents)*	*R&D Institutions (20Respondents)*	*General Users (25 Respondents)*
Are you aware of the ARIPO Swakopmund Protocol on the Protection of Traditional Knowledge and Expressions of Folklore?	None of the respondents had heard about the Protocol	Only 3 out of the 16 Respondents had heard about the Protocol Out of which Only 1 had seen the Protocol	None of the Respondents Had heard about The Protocol	None of the Respondents had heard about the Protocol
Should TK be protected in Ghana?	All the respondents said it is very important to protect TK but 3 said it should not be over protected so as not stifle the growth of TK	All the respondents said it is very important to protect TK but 1 said it should not be over protected	All the respondents said it is very important to protect TK but 6 said it should not be over protected	All the respondents said it is very important to protect TK but 7 said it should not be over protected
How can Ghana effectively implement the ARIPO Swakopmund Protocol?	Public education, documentation of TK, Competent Office and Laws	Laws, awareness creation regarding the rights and obligations under the laws, documentation of TK	Awareness creation, documentation of TK, laws	Awareness creation, documentation, laws

3.1. Data Analysis

The data collected was analyzed according to the four (4) categories of respondents and the three (3) consolidated questions. Table 4.1 indicates the categories of respondents and responses to the three main questions. The three (3) main questions were as follows:

1. Are you aware of the ARIPO Swakopmund Protocol?
2. Should TK be protected in Ghana?
3. How can Ghana effectively implement the ARIPO Swakopmund Protocol?

The results indicated that all the respondents believe that traditional knowledge has socio-economic value which can be enhanced by protection, development and promotion. All respondents except one (1) respondent from the general users category believed that it is important to protect TK in Ghana. However all the respondents except only one (1) of the policy makers and Implementers had not seen the Swakopmund Protocol. Only thirteen (13) of the total number of respondents, constituting 15 per cent of the total respondents even though agree that traditional knowledge should be protected also believed that it should not be over-protected since it has a potential to stifle the growth of the knowledge. There was a significant difference in the perception of the policy makers and Implementers on the one hand and other stakeholders on the other hand. While the policy makers and implementers believed that there is the need to enact laws as a precursor to the requisite protection of traditional knowledge, the other respondents believed that education and awareness creation on the value of TK and the need to protect TK in Ghana must precede the enactment of laws in order to make the laws effective and enforceable.

4. Analysis of Legislation and Policies Relating to TK in Ghana and the Swakopmund Protocol

Ghana is a signatory to the Swakopmund Protocol. Implementation of the Protocol will require an in-depth analysis of various laws and policies which impact on traditional knowledge in Ghana and an analysis of the ARIPO Swakopmund Protocol in relation to the current situation in Ghana. Legislations and Policies of relevance in this regard include the following:

1. The 1992 Republican Constitution of Ghana
2. The Copyright Act, 2005 (Act 690) of the Republic of Ghana
3. Traditional Medicine Practice Act, 2000 (ACT 575) of the Republic of Ghana
4. Republic of Ghana Treaty Manual
5. Policy and Administrative Guidelines on Complementary/Alternative Medicine Practices (2010) of the Republic of Ghana
6. Policy on Traditional Medicine Development (2003) of the Republic of Ghana
7. The Cultural Policy of Ghana (2004)
8. The Patents Act, 2003 (Act 657) of the Republic of Ghana

9. The Trade Marks Act, 2004 (Act 664)of the Republic of Ghana
10. The Industrial Designs Act, 2003 (Act 660) of the Republic of Ghana
11. The Geographical Indications Act, 2003 (Act 659) of the Republic of Ghana
12. The Layout Designs (Topographies) of Integrated Circuits Act, 2004 (Act 667) of the Republic of Ghana.
13. The Food and Drugs Act, 1992 (P.N.D.C. Law 305B) as amended of the Republic of Ghana
14. Council for Scientific and Industrial Research Act 1996 (Act 521)
15. The Council for Indigenous Business Associations Law, 1993 (Act 312)

5. Laws and Policies Which Impact on TK in Ghana

5.1. Laws

The 1992 Constitution is the supreme law of Ghana. The Constitution provides for fundamental human rights and freedoms. Even though the Constitution does not specifically provide for the protection of Intellectual Property Rights and TK, it recognizes the right of persons to own property either alone or in association with others.

The laws of Ghana as enshrined in the 1992 Constitution also include, enactments made by or under the authority of Parliament established by the said Constitution. Two of such enactments directly impact on traditional knowledge. These are the Traditional Medicine Practice Act, 2000 (Act 575) and the Copyright Act of 2005 (Act 690). There are other enactments which indirectly impact on the development, promotion and protection of traditional knowledge. These include the Intellectual Property Laws of Ghana, namely; the Patents Act, 2003 (Act 657), the Trade Marks Act, 2004 (Act 664), The Industrial Designs Act, 2003 (Act 660), the Geographical Indications Act, 2003 (Act 659) and the Layout Designs (Topographies) of Integrated Circuits Act, 2004 (Act 667). Other laws include the Food and Drugs Act, 1992 (P.N.D.C. Law 305B) as amended, Council for Scientific and Industrial Research Act 1996 (Act 521) and the Council for Indigenous Business Associations Law, 1993 (Act 312).

The Traditional Medicine Practice Act, 2000 (Act 575), mainly focuses on the regulation of traditional medicine practice in Ghana and the establishment of a Traditional Medicine Practice Council. Significantly curious, there are no provisions for the protection of traditional knowledge in traditional medicines and or practice.

The Copyright Act of 2005 (Act 690) on the other hand provides for the protection of folklore. The Act vests folklore in the state and protection is in perpetuity. There are no provisions for the protection of TK and associated genetic resources in the Act.

The IP laws of Ghana generally follow the traditional intellectual property rights systems with the incident limited duration of protection. However, the Geographical Indications Act, which provides for protection in perpetuity and the Trade Marks Act, which provides perpetual protection, subject to renewal may be utilized by the owners or holders of TK as marketing tools.

The Food and Drugs Act indirectly defines food and drugs to include traditional knowledge associated genetic resources. Therefore the regulatory provisions of the Act apply to such traditional knowledge.

The Council for Indigenous Business Associations Law, 1993 seeks to promote the interest of member associations. The member associations include traditional medical practitioners. Implementation of any law for the protection of traditional knowledge will indirectly impact on the law.

The Council for Scientific and Industrial Research Act 1996 (Act 521) governs scientific and industrial research in Ghana. The Council's mandate includes the implementation of government policies on scientific research and development and to advise the sector Minister on scientific and technological advances likely to be of importance to national development. The Plant Genetic Resources Research Institute (PGRRI), Crop Research Institute and the Animal Research Institute fall directly under the control of the governing Council. For that reason, any enactment for the protection of traditional knowledge and associated genetic resources will directly have an effect on the CSIR Act.

5.2. Policies

Ghana does not have a National Intellectual Property or Traditional Knowledge Policy. There is currently a development of a National IP Policy in progress. There are also some existing National Policies which deal with some aspects of TK. These include; the National Cultural Policy (2004), National Science, Technology and Innovation Policy, Ghana National Drug Policy (2004) and the National Trade Policy (2006).

5.2.1. National Cultural Policy (2004)

This policy document focuses mainly on traditional cultural expressions as against traditional knowledge *stricto sensu* and associated genetic resources. The policy provides for the documentation and promotion of Ghana's traditional cultural values while ensuring the growth and development of Ghana's cultural institutions and in the result making Ghana's cultural institutions relevant to human development, democratic governance and national integration. It provides for the enhancement of Ghanaian cultural life and development of cultural programmes to contribute to the nation's human development and material progress through:

- ☆ Heritage preservation, conservation and promotion
- ☆ Use of traditional modern arts and crafts to create wealth and alleviate poverty

5.2.2. National Science, Technology and Innovation Policy

This policy document does not specifically mention TK however it provides for facilitating the mastering of scientific and technological capabilities and providing the framework for inter-institutional efforts in developing Science, Technology and Innovation (STI) and programmes in all sectors of the economy to provide basic needs of the society. It also creates conditions for the improvement of scientific and technological infrastructure for research and development and innovation. With TK complimenting western science in Ghana, it is expected that any policy developed to improve science will have a rippling effect on TK and benefits to owners/holders of TK.

5.2.3. Ghana National Drug Policy (2004)

This policy document highlights concerns about impact of IP on access to drugs and public health. In this respect, the country also has a *Policy on Traditional Medicine Development (2003)* and a *Policy and Administrative Guidelines on Complementary/ Alternative Medicine Practices (2010).* These documents recognize the need to provide protection for the traditional herbal/medicine practitioners through appropriate existing Intellectual Property Rights laws. However the traditional IP tools have been found to be inadequate to protect TK including traditional medicines hence the *sui generis* protection provided by regional bodies, including ARIPO and some national laws.

5.2.4. National Trade Policy (2006)

The trade policy broadly deals with IPRs which can include TK when the protocol is implemented. The IPRs protection aspect of the national trade policy also provides that Governments must provide effective rules to protect IPRs, provide a coordination mechanism to ensure effective administration of copyright and industrial property rights and also design and implement awareness and education programmes on IPRs.

5.2.5. Ministry of Health Policy on Traditional Medicine Development (MoHPTMD) (July 2003)

This policy recognizes the lack of a well-defined legislation covering patenting traditional medicine products and processes. It also noted with concern the ignorance among practitioners of traditional medical practitioners about the meaning, implications and workings of patent laws and rights as well as the availability of trademark registers and protection. The policy acknowledges the lack of knowledge among Traditional Medicine Practitioners (TMPs) on the need for intellectual property protection. As a result, Traditional Medicine Practitioners do not disclose information about their knowledge (practice and products) giving the following as their reasons:

1. Lack of trust
2. Fear of losing their livelihood
3. Oath of secrecy
4. Maintenance of their status and reputation.

The Ministry has indicated the need to develop a generic system for TMP knowledge as well as guidelines for IPR. It has also identified the need to set up a system to facilitate the processes involved in gaining access to IPRs for traditional medicines and train TMPs on record keeping or documentation of efficacious traditional medicines.

The Policy also provides for the inclusion of Traditional Medicines in formal training. This provision was to address lack of adequate training among practitioners. Hitherto there were no established institutions of training of TMPs and the syllabi for training orthodox medical practitioners did not include traditional medicines. The policy recognizes the lack of motivation for orthodox practitioners to embark upon TMP training programs. With this Policy, training is expected to be provided for TMPs to improve upon their knowledge and skills of practice and to encourage allopathic health practitioners to study and practice Traditional Medicines. Currently, there is a degree programme on traditional medicines at the Faculty of Pharmacy, Kwame Nkrumah University of Science and Technology, a leading University in Ghana.

Even though the policy has been criticized as not comprehensive, it is a positive step. It is believed that a successful implementation of the Policy may serve as an example for protecting and developing traditional knowledge.

6. The Swakopmund Protocol on the Protection of Traditional Knowledge and Expressions of Folklore

The Swakopmund Protocol is designed to accommodate the characteristically holistic world view of African TK holders, and to provide legal certainty in the exercise and management of the inalienable rights of traditional knowledge and associated genetic resources. It empowers Member States to use TK for socio-economic and cultural development as well as wealth creation. It also makes provision for the registration of multicultural and trans-boundary TK and Expressions of Folklore to resolve uncertainties relating to ownership of this knowledge which may be held by more than one community within the same or neighbouring countries.

The Protocol seeks to help to curb bio-piracy and to prevent illicit claims being made in patent applications relating to TK-based inventions as has been reported in cases such as the appetite-suppressant Hoodia cactus used by the San tribe of Southern Africa.

The Protocol and its implementing instrument enable the registration of regional traditional knowledge and expressions of folklore. These are TK and expressions of folklore which are trans-boundary and multicultural in nature. It also has provisions on Access and Benefit Sharing (ABS) which has the potential of creating economic benefits to communities.

By and large, the Protocol recognizes the use of Africa's intangible assets for the socio-economic development of the continent and provides a framework for national legislative developments on the protection of these resources. The Protocol is flexible and enables Member States to draft their laws to suit their unique needs utilizing the Protocol as a model law.

The traditional knowledge database that would be created and kept by ARIPO will serve, among others, as an information bank for research.

7. Key Provisions of the Swakopmund Protocol on Traditional Knowledge and Associated Genetic Resources

The Swakopmund Protocol consists of four (4) parts, namely:

1. Preliminary provisions, which provides, among others, for the general purpose of the protocol;
2. Protection of Traditional Knowledge, which deals with the criteria for protection, the rights conferred, the duration of protection, the beneficiaries, administration, exceptions and limitations, enforcement and access to traditional knowledge associated with genetic resources, among others;
3. Protection of Expressions of Folklore, which also deals with the criteria for protection, the duration of protection, the beneficiaries, exceptions and limitations and the management of the rights in expressions of folklore among others; and
4. General provisions which focuses on sanctions, remedies and enforcement, regional protection measures as well as entry into force of the Protocol, among others.

The purpose of the Protocol is to protect traditional knowledge holders against any infringement of their rights and to protect expressions of folklore against misappropriation, misuse and unlawful exploitation beyond their traditional context.

The Protocol is currently not in force. It will come into force three months after six States have deposited their instruments of ratification or accession. So far only two States, namely; Zambia and Botswana have deposited their instruments of ratification, while Zimbabwe is in the process of ratification.

The Swakopmund Protocol would have to be ratified by an Act of Parliament or by a Resolution of Parliament before it can be enforced in Ghana. Whether it would involve the amendment of existing IP Laws in Ghana, to include the provisions of the Protocol or the development of a *sui generis* law will be a decision for the policy and law makers.

8. Benefits of the Protocol Respecting the Protection of Traditional Knowledge and Associated Genetic Resources in Ghana

The protocol generally covers all aspects of protecting TK while also allowing various States to craft their laws to suit the interest of their people and to interpret and enforce the protocol in a manner that would take into account the dynamic and evolving nature of traditional knowledge and the characteristic of traditional knowledge systems as framework of on going innovation.

The main benefit of the protocol to Ghana is the fact that the protocol will serve as a model law for the protection of TK in Ghana. The protocol also provides checks to the exploitation of TK, particularly, regarding Licences and Assignments. It provides that all access, authorizations, assignments or licences granted in respect of protected traditional knowledge shall be granted in writing and be approved by a National Competent Authority, failing which the document shall be void.

One area of protection that may not be of much interest to Ghana is the provision on trans-boundary TK. This is so because Ghana is surrounded by States that are not Members of ARIPO. It being so, it should be of utmost interest to Ghana, to fully participate in on-going discussions at the IGC of WIPO, since any treaty resulting from the negotiations will be binding on Ghana's neighbours and this will cover trans-boundary TK that affect Ghana.

Protection under the protocol is limited to the traditional knowledge associated with genetic resources and the genetic resources derived from traditional knowledge. By implication, Ghana will have to rely on other sources of legislation to protect genetic resources. Fortunately, Ghana is a signatory to the UN Convention on Biological Diversity which provides such protection and makes the necessary provisions for access - benefit sharing under the Nagoya Protocol to the Convention. It will be in the interest of Ghana to ratify both, the Convention and its Protocol as well as the Swakopmund Protocol.

9. Challenges of Implementing the Protocol in Ghana and Possible Solutions

The Swakopmund Protocol for the Protection of Traditional Knowledge and Expressions of Folklore addresses a subject matter of great interest to Ghanaians as a people.

The survey that was conducted indicated the following:

1. That there was a general lack of awareness of the ARIPO Swakopmund Protocol among respondents. Only one (1) of the sixteen (16) Policy makers and Implementers of Policy had seen the Protocol. It does appear from the results of the survey that implementation of the Protocol will be a daunting task for the policy makers and implementers of policy. Regrettably, thirteen (13) out of the sixteen (16) policy makers and implementers interviewed had never heard nor seen the Protocol. Of the three (3) who had knowledge about the Protocol, only one (1) had seen the Protocol. Ignorance about the Protocol was not peculiar to only this category but none of the remaining categories of respondents had any knowledge of the Protocol.

   Ignorance of the existence of the ARIPO Swakopmund Protocol could pose a challenge to its implementation. To overcome this challenge will require extensive awareness creation on the Protocol among all Ghanaians. Anything to the contrary will create inefficiencies in the implementation of the Protocol as beneficiaries will be unaware of their rights while users will flagrantly infringe on the rights.

2. Respondents believe that Traditional Knowledge must be protected however, 15 per cent of respondents believe that care must be taken to avoid overprotection in order not to stall the growth of TK.

   The 15 per cent of Respondents with this view have legitimate fears about the growth of TK in substance after all, TK is dynamic and any legislation that will seek to curb its growth must not be encouraged. Fortunately, the Protocol provides for exceptions and limitations to protection of TK. Section

11 of the Protocol is to the effect that, the protection of traditional knowledge under the protocol shall not be prejudicial to the continued availability of traditional knowledge for the practice, exchange, use and transmission of the knowledge by its holders within the traditional context. For Ghanaians with such legitimate fears, emphasis should be placed on this provision to assuage their fears.

3. There is a gap between the perception of Policy makers and implementers of Policy on the one hand and owners/holders of TK, researchers and General Users of TK on the other hand regarding the implementation of the Protocol.

   While Policy makers and implementers of Policy believe that as a precursor to the required protection, Ghana needs to enact laws to protect TK and by implication, the ratification of the Protocol, the owners/holders of TK, researchers and general users, on the other hand, believe that awareness creation prior to legislation would provide a better protection for the owners and users of TK.

   The reason proffered was that, education prior to legislation offers the rights' owners the opportunity to know their rights under the proposed law and be part of the law making process whilst creating awareness among users of TK to prevent infringement due to lack of awareness.

   About 18 per cent of respondents believe that both education and legislation must be pursued concurrently.

   The gap in perception of policy makers and beneficiaries of policies has often times resulted in ineffective laws. This seeming defect can be managed with public education on the subject prior to ratification, during and after ratification. To have the full effect of the benefits it would also be in the interest of Ghana if various stakeholders of TK are involved in the various stages of the implementation process.

Other challenges include the following:

1. The effect of the provisions of the Protocol on existing laws and policies in Ghana. After ratification the provisions of the protocol, in terms of hierarchy, will supersede that of existing statutes on the subject. There appears to be some conflicting provisions in some laws regarding the subject. Such provisions in the existing laws, particularly on expressions of folklore, may require amendments with the ratification of the protocol. Some of such laws include:

   (*i*) The Copyright Act, 2005 (Act 690): Section 6 of the Protocol deals with beneficiaries of protection of traditional knowledge. It is to the effect that, the owners of the rights shall be the holders of traditional knowledge, namely the local and traditional communities, and recognized individuals within such communities, who create, preserve and transmit knowledge in a traditional and intergenerational context. The traditional knowledge claimed must meet the requisite protection criteria in accordance with section 4 of the Protocol. Section 18 deals with the beneficiaries of protection of expressions of folklore. It is to the effect that, the owners of the rights in expressions of folklore are the local and traditional communities:

(*a*) To whom the custody and protection of the expressions of folklore are entrusted in accordance with the customary laws and practices of those communities; and

(*b*) Who maintain and use the expressions of folklore as a characteristic of their traditional cultural heritage.

In Ghana folklore is administered by the National Folklore Board for and on behalf of the Republic. Ownership therefore vests in the Republic, probably due to the definition of Folklore under the Copyright Act, 2005 (Act 690), no individual or group of persons can be identified as owners. Implementation of the Protocol will therefore require an amendment of the Copyright Act of Ghana.

(*ii*) The Copyright Act, 2005 (ACT 690) of Ghana defines folklore as *the literary, artistic and scientific expressions belonging to the cultural heritage of Ghana which are created, preserved and developed by ethnic communities of Ghana or by an unidentified Ghanaian author, and includes kente and adinkra designs, where the author of the designs are not known, and any similar work designated under the Copyright Act to be works of folklore*.

The main difference between Ghana's definition and that of the Protocol is the fact that, in Ghana the expressions of folklore must have been created, preserved and developed by an ethnic community or by an unidentified Ghanaian author whereas the Protocol does not limit it but broadly defines as any forms, whether tangible or intangible, in which traditional culture and knowledge are expressed.

Obviously implementation of the Protocol will require amending the definition as already exists in the Copyright Act of Ghana together with other relevant provisions that will be affected.

The Traditional Medicine Act, 2000 (Act 575) also defines traditional medicine as practices based on beliefs and ideas recognised by the community to provide healthcare by using herbs and other naturally occurring substances. This definition may not require any amendment.

2. ARIPO Member States recognize the need for protecting TK and the fact that protection must reflect the need to maintain an equitable balance between the rights and interests of those who develop, preserve and maintain traditional knowledge and expressions of folklore, and those who use and benefit from such knowledge and expressions of folklore. They emphasize that legal protection must be tailored to the specific characteristics of traditional knowledge and expressions of folklore, including their collective or community context, the intergenerational nature of their development, preservation and transmission, their link to a community's cultural and social identity, integrity, beliefs, spirituality and

values, and their constantly evolving character within the community concerned. The need for tailor made laws accords to the sovereignty of Member States. The issue then arises as to the flexibility of the Protocol to allow for the tailoring of it to suit the needs of Member States.

3. ARIPO has been mandated to create a Traditional Knowledge Digital Library. Ghana's contribution to the library may be limited considering the oral nature of TK in Ghana. As a national policy, the State may initiate the creation of a National Traditional Knowledge Digital Library for traditional knowledge that can be documented.
4. The Protocol provides for the creation of National Competent Authorities. Considering the cross-cutting nature of TK, a multi-disciplinary competent body may be established to supervise the work of the National Competent Authority.

10. Future of TK

The future of traditional knowledge in Ghana will depend on how Ghana is able to protect, promote and develop TK, starting with a successful implementation of the ARIPO Swakopmund Protocol.

Conclusions

It is concluded that, traditional knowledge and associated genetic resources can be utilized as a tool for socio-economic development in Africa. The Swakopmund Protocol can play a significant role in achieving this purpose when it comes into force. The Protocol will provide an appropriate legal regime for the protection, development and promotion of traditional knowledge in Africa, particularly in Ghana.

Recommendations

It is recommended that Member States of ARIPO should take the necessary legal steps to ratify or accede to the Protocol to ensure an early coming into force of the Protocol for the benefit of Africa as a continent. Ratification of the Protocol should be done concurrently with the accession or ratification of all other international treaties and protocols which positively impact on traditional knowledge and associated genetic resources.

Acknowledgements

I acknowledge with gratitude the support of the following individuals and institutions:

Mr. Ken Anku, Private Legal Practitioner; Mrs. Anatu Mahama, Lecturer, KNUST; Dr. Ben Kunbour, Minister for Justice; Mr. Joseph Kofi Harlley, Registrar-General of Ghana; Mr. Emmanuel Yoofi Sackey, Chief Examiner, ARIPO; Honourable Naa Professor Nabila, President of the National House of Chiefs and Member of the Council of State; the National house of Chiefs and the Ministry of Justice.

Abbreviations

ABS:	Access Benefit Sharing
ARIPO:	African Regional Intellectual Property Organization
CBD:	UN Convention on Biological Diversity
CSIR:	Council for Scientific and Industrial Research
GSGDA:	Ghana Shared Growth and Development Agenda
IGC:	Intergovernmental Committee of WIPO
IP:	Intellectual Property
IPRs:	Intellectual Property Rights
MoHPTMD:	Ministry of Health Policy on Traditional Medicine Development
TCEs:	Traditional Cultural Expressions
TK:	Traditional Knowledge
TMP:	Traditional Medical Practitioners
TRIPs:	Trade Related Aspects of Intellectual Property
WIPO:	World Intellectual Property Organization

References

1. ARIPO 2010. www.aripo.org
2. ARIPO/CM/XIII/6 November 4, 2011
3. Cohen, L., Manion, L. and Morrison, K. (2003). *Research Methods in Education* (5th Ed.). London: Routledge.
4. Constitution of the Republic of Ghana (1992).
5. Copyright Act, 2005 (Act 690) Republic of Ghana.
6. Council for Indigenous Business Associations Law, 1993 (Act 312) Republic of Ghana.
7. Council for Scientific and Industrial Research Act, 1996 (Act 521) Republic of Ghana.
8. Doha Declaration (2001). Doha WTO Ministerial 2001: Ministerial Declaration WT/MIN(01)/DEC/1November 20, 2001 (www.wto.org).
9. Food and Drugs Act, 1992 (P.N.D.C. Law 305B) as amended, Republic of Ghana.
10. Geographical Indications Act, 2003 (Act 659) Republic of Ghana.
11. Ghana National Drug Policy (2004). Republic of Ghana.
12. Ghana Shared Growth and Development Agenda (GSGDA) Costing Framework (2010-2013) Volume II, Costing and Financing of Policies and Strategies, National Development Planning Commission (December 2010), p. 2.
13. Lusaka Agreement on the Creation of the African Regional Intellectual Property Organization (1976) as amended.

14. Ministry of Health Policy on Traditional Medicine Development (MoHPTMD) (July 2003).
15. National Cultural Policy (2004). Republic of Ghana.
16. National Science, Technology and Innovation Policy.
17. National Trade Policy (2006). Republic of Ghana.
18. Paolo, B. (2001) cited in Ossy M J Kasilo (2006). *An overview of Intellectual Property Rights, Indigenous Knowledge and TRIPS in Africa* Regional Workshop on Regulatory Framework for the Protection of Intellectual Property Rights and Traditional Medical Knowledge, Brazzaville, 21–24 March 2006 (unpublished).
19. Posey D. and Dutfield G. (1996). *Beyond Intellectual Property Toward Traditional Resource Rights for Indigenous Peoples and Local Communities.* International Development Research Centre, Ottawa, p. 303.
20. Pricipe (1989) cited in Possey and Dutfield (1996). *Beyond Intellectual Property Toward Traditional Resource Rights for Indigenous Peoples and Local Communities.* International Development Research Centre, Ottawa, pp. 79-124.
21. Swakopmund Protocol on the Protection of Traditional Knowledge and Expressions of Folklore (2010).
22. Trade Marks Act, 2004 (Act 664) Republic of Ghana.
23. Traditional Medicine Practice Act, 2000 (Act 575) Republic of Ghana.
24. TRIPS Agreement (1994). Agreement on Trade-Related Aspects of Intellectual Property Rights.
25. UN Convention on Biological Diversity (1992).
26. wipo_grtkf_ic_21_ref_facilitators_text.pdf (2012) www.wipo.int.

Chapter 5

Intellectual Property Rights and Intellectual Property Center in Indonesia

*Budi Suharto**

Senior Staff of Legal Division,
Indonesian Institute of Sciences,
Jakarta-12710, Indonesia

1. Introduction

1.1. Understanding Intellectual Property Rights

Intellectual Property Rights are rights granted to the people for creations of the mind. Typically, they are exclusive rights granted to creators or inventors for a certain period. The creations of the mind refers to the product of human thought in the form of inventions, writings, artistic creations, symbols, names, images, and designs used in commercial activities.[1]

According to WIPO[2] (World Intellectual Property Organization), Intellectual Property Rights is in two categories, namely Industrial Property and Copyright.

1.2. Industrial Property

This category consists of the invention (Patent), Trademark, Industrial Designs and Geographical Indications.[3] Other types of intellectual property rights included

---

* E-mail: b_suharto@yahoo.com

1 http://www.wipo.int/about-ip/en/index.html (accessed 13 Jul.2012)

2 http://www.wipo.int/about-ip/en/ (accessed 13 Jul.2012)

3 *Ibid.*

in this category covered by the TRIPS Agreement are Undisclosed Information, including Trade Secrets and Layout Design (topographies) of Integrated Circuits.[4]

1.3. Copyright[5]

Copyright is a legal term that describes the rights given to creators of works of literature and arts. The main objective is to provide protection to such works, and to support and reward creative work. The works which are protected by Copyright are in the form of works of literature, such as; novels, poetry, performances, reference works, newspapers, computer programs, databases, films, musical compositions, and choreography or artistic works, such as; painting, drawing, photography and sculpture, architecture, advertising, maps and technical drawings, or rights related to copyright, including; artists who perform in a show, the producers of phonograms in the recording, and the broadcaster-announcer on radio and television programmes.

1.4. Patent[6]

Patents are exclusive rights, granted to protect inventions, in the form of: products or processes in general; a new way to make something; or offers a solution to a problem with a technique or a new way. Patents provide protection to the creators of the invention. Protection is granted for a period of 20 years.

1.5. Trademark[7]

A trademark is a certain sign, which is used to identify the goods or services produced or provided by a person or a particular company. Trademarks help consumers identify and purchase a product or service, based on the character and quality, which can be identified from a unique brand.

1.6. Industrial Design[8]

Industrial design is the ornamental or aesthetic aspect of an object. The design can be three-dimensional, such as shape or surface of an object or two-dimensional, such as patterns, lines or colors. Industrial design is used on various types of industrial products and handicrafts, such as technical and medical instruments, watches, jewellery and other luxury items, as well as household appliances and electronic equipment, vehicles and architectural structures, textile designs, as well as goods of entertainment. An industrial design is an aspect of aesthetic experience, and does not protect the technical features of the objects.

1.7. Geographical Indications[9]

A Geographical Indication is a sign used on goods that have a specific geographic authenticity and have the quality or reputation based on the place of origin. In general,

---

4 http://www.wto.org/english/thewto_e/whatis_e/tif_e/agrm7_e.htm (accessed 13 Jul.2012)

5 http://www.wipo.int/export/sites/www/about-ip/en/iprm/pdf/ch2.pdf. pp. 26-29 (accessed 13 Jul.2012)

6 *Ibid.* p.3-4.

7 *Ibid.* p.54.

8 *Ibid.* p.98-102.

9 *Ibid.* p.106-108.

Geographical Indications is the name of the place of origin of these items. For example, agricultural products usually have qualities that are formed from the place of production, and is influenced by local factors that are specific, such as climate and soil. Whether a sign is recognized as a geographical indication is a matter of national law. Geographical indications may be used for a wide variety of products, whether natural, agricultural or manufactured.

1.8. Trade Secrets[10]

Trade secrets and other types of other confidential information that have commercial value, can be protected from abuse or other activities that unlock the secrets of commercial practice. Reasonable steps must be taken in advance to protect such confidential information.

Tests on data submitted to the government as a step to gain approval to market pharmaceutical or agricultural products which have a new composition can also be protected from fraudulent trading.

1.9. Layout Design of Integrated Circuits[11]

Integrated Circuit is a form of finished products or semi-finished, in which there are various elements, at least one of these elements are active elements, which partially or wholly are inter-related, and formed an integrated manner, in a semi-conductor material that is intended to produce electronic functions. Layout Design is the creation of a groundbreaking three-dimensional design of various elements, at least one of these elements are active elements, as well as part or all of the interconnections in an integrated circuit and the setting up of three dimensions is intended for the preparation of Integrated Circuits.

2. Intellectual Property Rights in the Globalization Era

Knowledge is one important thing to trade, because ideas and knowledge can result in a creation that is traded. Therefore, intellectual property rights also touches aspects of the industry and commerce. Mostly, value is contained in new drugs and high-tech products, because of the amount of research activities, design and testing.

These products may have originally traded as low-tech goods, but, after idea, research and development, then these items may be items of high technology, so it will be possible to increase the sale value of such products. In terms of the creation of such products, the creator can be given the right to prevent others from using their inventions, designs or other works and creators can use this right to negotiate payment.

Development and implementation of the protection of intellectual property rights vary across the world. As awareness of the importance of intellectual property rights in trade increases, the perceptual differences between countries in the world become a source of debate in international economic relations.

---

10 http://www.wto.org/english/thewto_e/whatis_e/tif_e/agrm7_e.htm (accessed 13 Jul.2012)

11 http://www.wipo.int/export/sites/www/about-ip/en/iprm/pdf/ch2.pdf. *op.cit.* pp. 104-105 (accessed 13 Jul.2012)

The existence of internationally agreed trade rules, particularly regarding intellectual property rights is used as a way to keep order and maintain consistency, and to seek to resolve disputes in a more systematic manner.[12]

Recognizing the importance of intellectual property rights in international trade, then in the framework of the international trading system, agreements on Intellectual Property Rights (Agreement on Trade-Related Aspects of Intellectual Property Rights/ TRIPs) were negotiated for the first time in WTO negotiations, the Uruguay Round in 1986 - 1994.[13]

TRIPs agreement is the most comprehensive multilateral agreement on intellectual property rights. TRIPS is a minimum standards agreement, which allows WTO members to provide broader protection of intellectual property rights. Member States are free to determine the best methods possible to incorporate the TRIPs agreement into the legal systems in their respective countries.

3. Intellectual Property Rights in Indonesia and Problems

As a developing country, Indonesia has ratified the TRIPs Agreement with incidental consequences on the legal system of Indonesia, especially in the field of intellectual property rights and related matters. From the legal aspect, Indonesia already has a range of legislation that provides protection for intellectual property rights, but from the aspect of enforcement, Indonesia is one country that is weak and facing lot of problems. Therefore, Indonesia is still included in the list Watch Priority List by the United States of America.

Some of the problems faced by Indonesia, in the field of intellectual property rights, include:

1. The number of domestic patents are still low. Domestic patents filed by the Indonesia only 200-280 pieces per year, while patents filed by foreigners, directly, or within the framework of the PCT (Patent Cooperation Treaty) reaches 3000-4400.[14] Indonesia's domestic patent amounted to at least 10 per cent of the total number of patents in the country.
2. Law Enforcement is still weak. Increased violation of Intellectual Property laws. The problem has destroyed the State's economy, and society. Not only are the creators and inventors disadvantaged, but the state is also economically disadvantaged, particularly on the financial aspects of state revenue. Indeed, many countries that formerly belonged to a group of developing countries along with Indonesia, but today these countries have advanced in technology and economics. They are the developed countries in producing intellectual works. In contrast, Indonesia still survived as a developing country that has just a little invention, but a lot of piracy and counterfeiting Copyrights and Trademark violations areas of intellectual property rights.

---

12 http://www.wto.org/english/thewto_e/whatis_e/tif_e/agrm7_e.htm (accessed 13 Jul.2012)

13 *Ibid.*

14 http://nasional.kompas.com/read/2010/09/08/04351965/jumlah.p (accessed 13 Jul.2012)

3. Public understanding of Indonesia concerning intellectual property rights is still weak, and not well coordinated. Until now, many researchers in universities or at research and development institution do not understand what the intellectual property rights is.

4. Issue of Intellectual Property at Higher Education or Research and Development Institute

The results of research and development conducted by universities and research institutions are included within the scope of intellectual property rights, because they are the result of intellectual work. In doing research and development, researchers need support costs, energy, ideas, time and equipment to produce results.

Given that the results of research and development is the result of intellectual work that can solve a problem in a technical field, and is beneficial to human life, it would require the existence of a clear legal regime that can be appreciated by, the inventors creators, the holders of intellectual property and users of intellectual property rights. Holders of intellectual property rights have legal protection, in the form of special rights. For Copyright, special rights in the form of moral rights (moral rights) and economic (economic right). Economic rights is the right to obtain the economic benefits of the creation as well as products related rights.

The problem that then arises is who manages the Intellectual Property Rights? Universities and research institutions, as institutional elements in the National System of Research Development and Application of Science and Technology, have an obligation to seek information, disseminate results of research and development and own intellectual property while enhancing the importance of intellectual property protection.[15] The institutions are obliged to generate wealth and seek legal clarity regarding ownership of intellectual property rights especially for Government-funded innovations.

Furthermore, any intellectual property, especially, results of research and development, engineering and government and/or local government funded innovations, must be managed and utilized properly by universities and research institutions.[16] Therefore, the universities and institutes of research and development are required to manage intellectual property. This means, that in the universities and institutes of research and development, there needs to be an institution that specializes in intellectual property management business. The existence of institutions that manage intellectual property, more firmly determines that in order to improve the management of intellectual property, universities and research and development institutions should seek the establishment of a Center of Intellectual Property Rights, in accordance with their capacities and abilities.[17] The Center of Intellectual Property

---

15 Law Number 18 Year 2002 on National System of Research, Development, and Application of Science and Technology.

16 *Ibid.* Article 13(4).

17 *Ibid.* Article 13(3).

Rights is an institution that serves to manage and utilize intellectual property, as well as an information and service center for intellectual property rights, including market research results.

5. Intellectual Property Rights Center and Problems

According to Medy P. Sargo, in an article entitled 'Sentra HKI and Commercialization Issues',[18] the results of a study of the Ministry of Research and Technology in 2010, indicates that the commercialization of intellectual property in the Center of Intellectual Property Rights can not run smoothly. Only a few of Intellectual Property Rights Center carry out the commercialization of intellectual property rights. The number of it just a little. Amount of the Center of Intellectual Property Rights which exist today, about the 60's since Intellectual Property Rights Center was introduced Ministry of Research and Technology in 1999.

One of the obstacles faced by some Centers for Intellectual Property Rights, is the lack of capacity in the management of intellectual property rights, including the ability to organize activities in commercialization of Intellectual Property Rights, which supported its legal aspects. In fact, one purpose of the establishment of the Center of Intellectual Property Rights is to perform the function of commercialization of intellectual property rights. Therefore, the Center of Intellectual Property Rights should be able to be a marketer or at least an intermediator between owners and users of intellectual property rights, although it must be recognized that the reliability and industry recognition of domestic research results are still not conducive. As a result, they become an obstacle in the achievement of a business deal.

Center of Intellectual Property Rights should be better prepared as a mediator in the-commercialization activities of Intellectual Property Rights, whether by universities or research and development institutions, or better known as TLO (Technology Licensing Office), as developed in Japan or in other industrial countries.

According to Sabartua Tampubolon: 2012,[19] there are at least three factors that explain why the Center of Intellectual Property Rights were not functioning as the center for innovation, namely:

1. Centers of Intellectual Property Rights do not receive adequate support from the parent institution. In some colleges and institutes of research and development, there is lack of visible leadership commitment of the parent institution to make the Center of Intellectual Property an asset. Limited human resources, operational costs, as well as facilities and infrastructure, not only reduce the morale of the managers, but also makes the Center of Intellectual Property Rights not run properly.
2. Structure of Intellectual Property Rights Center: The Centres are not well coordinated. In addition to the lack of funds, human resources, facilities and infrastructure, the Center of Intellectual Property Rights is not well

18 http://17-08-1945.blogspot.com/2011/10/koran-digital-medy-p-sargo-sentra-hki.html (accessed 13 Jul.2012)

19 http://www.ristek.go.id/?module=News%20News&id=3213 (accessed 13 Jul.2012)

structured, such that there is no clear relationship with parent institutions. For example, in one institution,the Center of Intellectual Property Rights is under the Institute for Research and Community Service (LPPM), but the other, there is a place in the faculty. In research and development institutions, there is a place for non-structural unit (in the bureau or the handling of legal affairs), but the other, there is a place on the existing institutional structure. So, there are two unit to handle Intellectual Property Rights activities.

3. Centers of Intellectual Property Rights are likely to only deal with matters relating to registration of intellectual property rights to the researchers. In general, Centers of intellectual property rights that are institutionalized have gone well, however, they are still limited to the functions of providing information and related services of Intellectual Property Rights.

So far, by observation, no Center of Intellectual Property Rights has successfully marketed and pursued the process of industrialization and commercialization of any registered intellectual property rights.

Conclusion

The weaknesses of Intellectual Property Rights Centers, must be overcome or at least reduced. For that, at least three concrete steps must be taken, namely:

1. A more intensive information dissemination about the importance of the Intellectual Property Rights Centers. As an obligation under the Act Number 18 Year 2002, universities and research institutes must seek formation and development of such Centers, according to their capacity and ability. It takes consistent and persistent attitude to make the Centers of Intellectual Property Rights, the centers of innovation, rather than developing new innovation centers. An incentive system needs to be developed to encourage the establishment and strengthening of Intellectual Property Rights Center which had been previously established by the Ministry of Research and Technology.
2. Empowering the Center of Intellectual Property Rights to perform its functions. As an inter-agency mediation, the Center of Intellectual Property Rights is expected to be a door to connect universities and research institutions and the development of the industry. The Center of Intellectual Property Rights need to be involved in the planning of research and development activities, particularly with regard to capacity development, including choosing of researchers and partners and the diffusion of science and technology production system.

   Business and industry that may have experienced difficulty accessing information on product research and development, can resolve this by recognizing the Center of Intellectual Property Rights as the only entrance to universities and research institutions and development. Partnerships, more easily developed by the Center for Intellectual Property Rights, will be well established between universities and institutes of research and development and industry. Centers of Intellectual Property Rights will be able to do that, if given the authority and responsibility, through positive support from their parent institution.

3. Re-orientation of the functions of the Center of Intellectual Property Rights. As mentioned above, performance of the Center for Intellectual Property Rights is below expectation. The Centers of Intellectual Property Rights as centers of information and services incidental to intellectual property rights, are not proactive in marketing the results of research and development.

The functions of Intellectual Property Rights Center that will be developed, specialized in dissemination of intellectual property rights, registration of intellectual property rights, commercialization of results research and development of science and technology. There are at least four components introduced in the establishment of Intellectual Property Rights program, *i.e.* there must be a component of the management group, the legal group, technology group, and the components of the marketing experts for the benefit of science and technology commercialization.

Re-orientation should be in line with the implementation of research and development activities as a whole is very important. That means, if the leaders of institutions and researchers do not have the awareness to develop research and development acquired and have been pleased with the achievement of value for job administrative researcher only and absorption of the government budget alone, so until whenever the results of research and development activities, will not be developed and utilized by the industry, and ultimately will not have a significant impact on public welfare.

References

1. Indonesia, 2002. Law Number 18 Year 2002 on National System of Research, Development, and Application of Science and Technology.
2. World Intellectual Property Organization, 2012. About WIPO "What is Intellectual Property", Geneva, Switzerland. http://www.wipo.int/about-ip/en/index.html.
3. World Trade Organization, 2012. Understanding the WTO "Intellectual property: protection and enforcement", Geneva, Switzerland. http://www.wto.org/english/thewto_e/whatis_e/tif_e/agrm7_e.htm.
4. World Trade Organization, 2012. "Understanding Industrial Property", Geneva, Switzerland\ http://www.wipo.int/export/sites/www/about-ip/en/iprm/pdf/ch2.pdf.
5. PT Kompas Cyber Media, 2010. National News 8 September 2010 ed. "Jumlah Paten Indonesia Stagnan", Jakarta, Indonesia http://nasional.kompas.com/read/2010/09/08/04351965/jumlah.

6. Sargo, Medy P., 2011. "Sentra HKI dan Persoalan Komersialisasi", Jakarta. Indonesia. http://17-08-1945.blogspot.com/2011/10/koran-digital-medy-p-sargo-sentra-hki.html
7. Tampubolon, Sabartua., 2008. Artikel Iptek "Sentra HKI dan Peningkatan Inovasi", Jakarta, Indonesia http://www.ristek.go.id/?module=News per cent 20News and id = 3213

Chapter 6

The Intellectual Property Management Facilitation Process: As Strategy to Support Indonesia National Innovation System

*Alvini Pranoto**

Deputy Assistant (Director)
S&T Intellectual Property and Standardization Ministry of Research and Technology (MORT)
Republic of Indonesia

ABSTRACT

This paper discusses Indonesian Intellectual Property (IP) Policy management and National policy system of Innovation development. The level of Innovation Performance and number of patents from one country would become indicator of knowledge based activities to support economic growth. Problems related to IP management were highlighted in this paper, while facilitation program of management and protection of IP will be described in more detail. Programmes include incentive programme of IP Centre/Institution re-establishment 2010-2012, as part of performance contract of Ministry of Research and Technology to the President. The performance contract includes obligation to encourage patent growth and other IPR to support domestic industries activities. Parallel with this programme, MORT (Ministry of Research and Technology) also did policy analysis programme from monitoring and evaluation data status of 2002's IPR institution/centre both private and public. Another IP Management issue described in this paper is non-conventional model of facilitation process on management and protection on Genetic

* E-mail: alvini@ristek.go.id

Resources Traditional Knowledge and Folklore or Traditional Culture Expression (GRTKF/ TCE). The model is called Indonesian Genetic Resources and Traditional Knowledge or I-Grest. The I-Grest is a portal data or data base system which will be used as tool for GRTKF or communality IPR management and Protection system as defensive protection. Knowledge management is basic principle in the establishment of this system to form integrated data based system from various source as a portal data based.

Keywords: *Patent, GRTKF, IP Management facilitation process, IPR centre/IPR institution role.*

1. Introduction

1.1 Background

Intellectual Property (IP) Management is an interesting topic which could be connected to the development of technology and innovation performance for economic development. Many Countries protect their IP under Trade related Intellectual Property (TRIPS) agreement of World Trade Organization (WTO). In a holistic term, IP management usually used to describe the business processes of tracking IPR creation, licensing and usage. (See http://www.ndlrn.edu.au/verve/resources/managing_intellectual_property_rights.pd). Another definition stressing IP management to: IP development, IPR Protection, IPR exchange and market watch. IP development includes planning and implementation; conducive environment and staff motivation. Legal protection, trade secret and disciplinary are part of IPR protection. IPR exchange includes its acquisition and sale; spin offs and collaborative research projects.Finally the IP management activity in Market watches include measuring the opportunities as well as competitors and see the infringement of IPR. (See: http://www.1000ventures.com/business_guide/ipr/ipr_main. html)

Indonesia with population of more than 240 million (the 4th largest populated country) and ASEAN (Association of South East Asian Nation) countries are market destination for products from multinational companies (See Figure 6.1). These multinational companies bring Foreign Direct Investment (FDI), including Intellectual Capital *i.e.* Professional Human Resources and Technology. For Host country, this would stimulate and encourage domestic creative industry and make use of competitive environment to influence the establishment of domestic entrepreneurships to boost economic growth and encourage the national innovation system. Innovation is the driver of economic growth, and it requires an appropriate IPR system in place. Firms in US, Japan and EU manage their patent portfolios more actively. (see http://www.oecd. org/dataoecd/42/58/35213963.pdf).

The positive impact of trade and Foreign Direct Investment for development and innovations performances include: Strengthening competition and decreasing the market power of domestic producers, as well as improvement of total factor productivity as well as innovation power of related firms. Another positive impact is open access provide imported high technology especially to developing country. This intangible asset *i.e.* Knowledge, information, creativity and invention capability will replace and change traditional asset/tangible asset such as land, labor and capital as the major driving force of economic growth and social wellbeing. (See Fitzgerald and Fitzgerald, 2004).

However IP exploitation as the major driving force to Indonesia economic development still a problem for most R&D Institution, universities and other institutions. The reasons are Intellectual capital and capital budget for innovation activity are limited. Research lead to commercialization is expensive activity and requires enough financial support. Beside that in Indonesia IP management issue has not taken fully attention; to fully utilize its IP management system, Indonesia needs to set up a National IP strategy. WIPO National IP Strategy document shows that up to now there are 22 countries that have already set up their National IP Strategy, including India, Philippines, Japan and China. According to Directorate General of IP, as the Indonesian IP national vocal point, this kind of policy document now is in progress and supported by UNCTAD. According to WIPO,

> "National IP strategy is *an Intellectual Property Strategy referred to as Innovation or Science and Technology Strategy or Plans are in some cases called Research and Development Plans. An IP Strategy is a set of measures formulated and implemented by a government to encourage and facilitate effective creation, development and management of intellectual property …* An *IP Strategy may also be defined as a comprehensive national document which outlines how all the policy developments and implementation take place in a coordinated manner within a national framework.*" (See WIPO National IP Strategy http://www.wipo.int/ip-development/en/strategies/national_ip_strategies.html).

Indonesia have already had National Policy of S&T concept, and the development of Technology and Innovation system had been stated on the framework of Science and Technology (S&T) National Medium-term Development Planning (NMDP 2010 – 2014). The NMDP and National Research Agenda (NRA) have pointed out the expected direction of S and T Development within the context of Indonesian development. The priority of S&T development effort is to strengthen National Innovation System and to improve the quality of R&D and S&T application (See S& T Nation Policy, MORT 2010).

Indonesia inherited abundance genetic resources, traditional knowledge and folklore or traditional cultural expression (GRTKF/TCE) that can be further transformed into technology product as well as creative industry. The development of creative industry will help compete with western IP and technology. Currently, creative industries are mostly not protected by IPR, with local patent of only 7 per cent, and industrial design of only 5 per cent from total application. (Sinungan, Creative Industry in Indonesia and their potential, DGIP, 2009). According to Sukara (2010) Indonesia GRTKF should be well-managed because currently the management of GRTKF is done by individual institution or even by the researchers themselves, which in turn inhibits other to subscribe. Most people do not aware the importance of GRTKF. Most TCE have not even been documented yet, it is passed from generation to generation on word of mouth. GRTKF needs to be protected, especially since they have attracted the attention of international society such as WTO-TRIPS, Food and

Agriculture Organization (FAO), The United National Education, Scientific and Cultural Organization (UNESCO), United National Convention on Biodiversity (UN-CBD), International Treaty on Plant and Genetic Resources for Food and Agriculture (ITPGRFA), International Convention for the Safeguarding of Intangible Cultural Heritage (ICH) and Intergovernmental Committee (IGC)-GRTKF. (See Sukara, 2010 in Urgensy Data Based of GRTKF: Asset Management and Access to Bio/Cultural Diversity, in FGD of Facilitation Model on Management and Protection of Indonesia GRTKF, LIPI – Ristek, Jakarta, December 2011).

The fact above shows that we need good IP management system in order to support Technology and Innovation development, as well as growth of Patent and other IPR products. It is now up to MORT to generate good IP Policy Management System and National Innovation development from IP perspective.

1.2. Purpose

The purpose of this country paper is to give description of Indonesia IP management policy and activity especially from MORT policy perspective to support Indonesian National Innovation System. The purpose of this country report paper is also to share information about the contemporary IP management done by NAM and other developing countries.

1.3. Paper Framework and Methodology

This paper is prepared through desk review and from the result of MORT policy research and through expert interview. The framework paper consists of some general description of Indonesia IP system and policy especially from S&T policy Framework; secondly describes IP management Facilitation program or model construction for conventional IP development and nonconventional or communal IP management and protection system of GRTK. The following figure depicts the paper content while the detail description will be found in later pages of the paper.

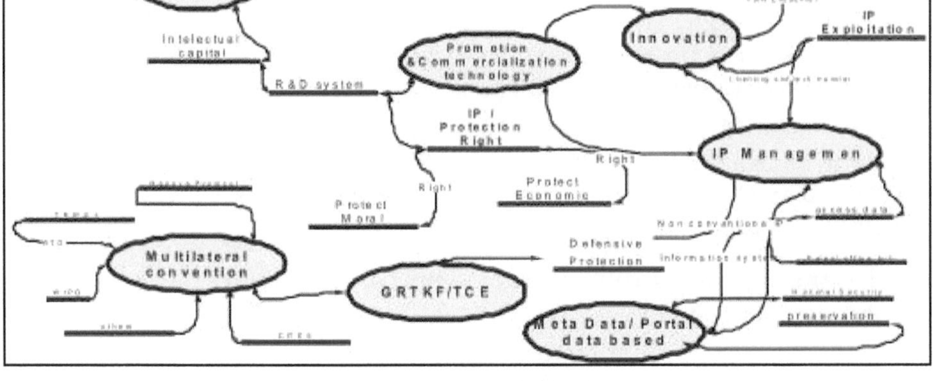

Figure 6.1: The Paper Framework.

***Source*: Alvini, 2012.**

2. Policy Framework

2.1. National S&T Development

The MORT Mandate is based on President Decree 97/2009, *i.e.*, Formulating S&T Policy; coordinating and synchronizing S&T policies Implementation.

Act No. 18/2002 is about National System of Research, Development and Application of Science and Technology. In Act No. 18/2002 MORT has a task to formulate National Strategic policy on Science and Technology. Two Articles related to IP and IP management, *i.e.*:

Article 13(3)

In an effort to manage intellectual properties, university and research and development institutions shall be obliged to arrange for the esthablishment of Intellectual Property institute acoording to their respective capacities and abilities.

Article 23(1)

The goverment shall ensure the protection of intellectual property rights held by any individuals or institutions in accordance with the prevailing law and regulations.

Article 23(2)

The goverment shall ensure the protection of Local/Traditional Knowledge, Traditional Culture Expression/Folklore, Biodiversity and non natural Property.

The Ministry Regulation No. 193/M/KP/IV/2010 about S&T National Strategy Policy Development 2010–14, states four government Regulation as fundamental basic source derivative from Act No 18/2002 *i.e.* Government Regulation No. 20/2002, No. 35/2007, No. 41/2006 and No. 48/2009.

Government Regulation No. 20 year 2002 about Technology Transfer of Intellectual Property and research productivity of Universities and R&D Institutions distributed widely in order to enhance socio ability in S&T utilization and development.

Government Regulation No. 35 year 2007 states the revenue allocation element of business institutions for engineering development capability, Innovation and technology diffusion. This regulation encourages collaboration or partnership between R&D Institution, Universities and Business sector.

Government Institution No. 41 year 2006 states R&D activities of foreign university, foreign R&D institution, foreign Business and foreigner. This government regulation aims to avoid the utilization of natural Indonesian property (biodiversity and others), Artifact, Treasure.

2.2. Technology and Innovation System Development

The National S&T development policy and direction of Research and Technology Minister is stressing to the importance of National Innovation System (NIS) development within 5 years. In the National Policy of S&T development, Technology and Innovation system had also been stated and can be seen in the framework of S&T National Medium-term Development Planning (NMDP 2010–14). The NMDP and

National Research Agenda (NRA) have identified the targeted direction of S and T Development in the context of Indonesian development. The priority of S&T development effort is to strengthen National Innovation System and to improve the quality of R&D and S&T application.

The development priorities in strengthening National Innovation System is focusing on S&T Institution, S&T Resources and S&T Network. There are 2 main goals in Improving R&D and application of S&T with 7 National Research Agenda (NRA) and 10 development focus. The first goal is to increase National capacity in R&D and application of S&T *i.e.* publication, patent, technology services, prototype, technology entrepreneur. The second goal is to improve the relevance of Research activities with the real issues and needs, accompanied by S&T Society Awareness Development (See Figure 6.2).

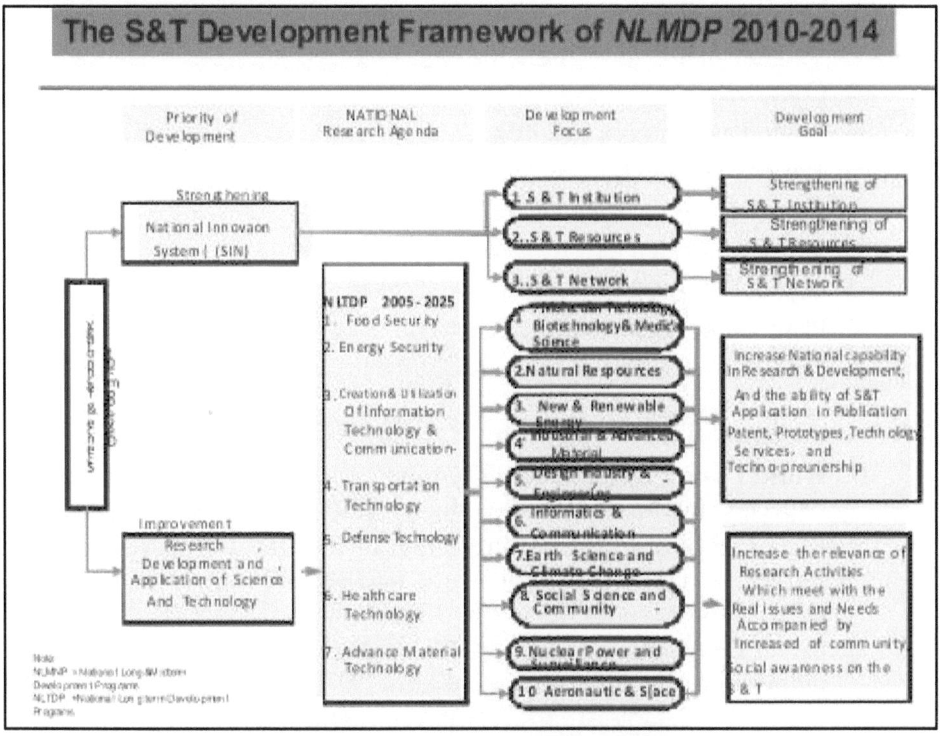

Figure 6.2: The Framework of NLMDP.
***Source*: Ristek, LIPI 2010.**

3. Intellectual Property Domain and Regulation

3.1. Intellectual Property Rights Domain

IPR Domain Consist of Copyright/Author Right and Industrial Property. Copyright/ Author Right Consist of

1. Artistic Works

2. Literary Works
3. Science Works
4. Neighbouring Rights

Industrial Property Rights are

1. Patent
2. Trade Marks
3. Industrial Design
4. Lay Out Design of IC
5. Trade Secret
6. Plant Variety

3.2. Law which Administering

- ☆ Copyright Law (*Law No. 19/2002*)
- ☆ Patent Law (*Law No. 14/2001*)
- ☆ Trademark Law (*Law No. 15/2001*)
- ☆ Trade Secret Law (*Law No. 30/2000*)
- ☆ Industrial Design Law (*Law No. 31/2000*)
- ☆ Layout Design of IC Law (*Law No. 32/2000*)
- ☆ Plant Variety Law (*Law No. 29/2000*)
- ☆ Unfair Competition Law (*Law No. 5/1995*)

3.3. International Treaties and the Ratification

1. **World Trade Organization** (WTO) and Agreement TRIPs (Trade-Related Aspects of Intellectual Property Rights) ratified by law No. 7 of 1994;
2. **Paris Convention** for the Protection of Industrial Property, and the Agreement Establishing the World Intellectual Property Organization (1883-last amended 1979), ratified by Presidential Decree No. 15 of 1997;
3. **Patent Cooperation Treaty** (PCT) and Regulation under the PCT 1970, ratified by Presidential Decree No. 16 of 1997;
4. **Trademark Law Treaty** 1994 (TLT), ratified by Presidential Decree No. 17 of 1997;
5. **Berne Convention** for the Protection of Literary and Artistic Works (1886-Last amended 1979), ratified by Presidential Decree No. 18 of 1997;
6. **WIPO Copyright Treaty** 1996 (WCT), ratified by Presidential Decree No. 19 of 1997;
7. **WIPO Performances and Phonograms Treaty** 1996 (WPPT), ratified by the Presidential Decree No. 74 of 2004.
8. Indonesia is also 'considering' joining the **Madrid Protocol** for International Registration of Marks.

4. IP Performance and National Competitiveness

Table 6.1: Patent in Some ASEAN Countries

Sl.No.	Country	International Patent		Patent Domestic	
		2009	2010	2009	2010
1	Indonesia	7	15	662	760
2	Singapore	593	637	627	892
3	Malaysia	224	302	1234	1275
4	Philippines	21	15	668	746

Source: DGIP 2011.

Indonesia and the other ASEAN countries are members of Patent Cooperation Treaty (PCT). By joining PCT, these countries could have the right in their own IP on territorial bases, in consequences that they have to register the IPR/Patent in the countries related to their business. In 2009 patent international was 7 and become twice in 2010. This figure can assume that the Indonesia investment condition in 2010 better than 2009. Meanwhile Indonesia domestic Patent has growth in 14 per cent. Only Philippine experience by negative patent growth 28 per cent in 2009 to 2010 of International Patent, but for domestic patent steady growth in 11 per cent.

Table 6.2: Patent Application/Registration

Sl.No.	Year	Patent				Simple Patent		Total
		PCT		Non-PCT		In Country/ Domestic	Foreign	
		In Country/ Domestic	Foreign	In Country/ Domestic	Foreign			
1.	1991-2000	1	4.628	749	23.872	782	465	30 497
2.	2001	4	2.901	208	813	197	24	4147
3.	2002	6	2.976	228	633	157	48	4048
4.	2003	-	2.620	201	479	163	29	3492
5.	2004	1	2.989	226	452	177	32	3877
6.	2005	1	3.536	234	533	163	32	4498
7.	2006	6	3.805	282	519	242	26	4880
8.	2007	5	4.357	279	493	209	34	5377
9.	2008	12	4.278	375	469	214	34	5382
10.	2009	2	3.761	413	342	247	38	4803
11.	2010	11	4.596	497	401	251	38	5794
12	2011	8	4.839	533	458	236	56	6130
	Jumlah	57	45.286	4.225	29.464	3.038	856	82925

Source: DGIP, 2011.

Singapore has the high number both in 2009 as well as 2010 for international patent as well as their domestic patent among ASEAN 4. The patent performance of Malaysia from ASEAN 4 is the second level number of patent growth. The growth of International patent in Malaysia is 34 per cent. Then the Domestic patent is 3 per cent growth in 2009 to 2010.

The Table 6.2 is about Indonesia patent applicant number *i.e.* in 1991 – 2011 not many domestic PCT and this figure was much different from foreign PCT. This could be happen because the activities of international trade mean that Indonesia is attractive countries for investment. Patent domestic non PCT before 2007 was up and down and become more stable in growth in 12 per cent average from 2008 until present.

Table 6.3: Patent Granted (2009 - 2011)

Sl.No.	*Year*	*Patent*		*Patent Simple*		*Total*
		Domestic/ In Country	*Foreign*	*Domestic/ In Country*	*Foreign*	
1.	2009	102	2282	81	25	2490
2.	2010	119	2357	75	10	2561
3.	2011	200	2197	58	11	2466

Source: DGIP, 2011.

Table 6.3 shows Indonesia patent granted consist of patent and patent simple. The Patent simple was different from patent because patent was having complexity of product inventions characteristic. The patent simple, has shortly life protection *i.e.* 10 year base, while patent have varied from 15 year to 20 years and after that become public domain and people will free to use without worries to license. From 2009 – 2011 the patent granted performance of foreign more higher than the domestic. Moreover the simple patent showed opposite one. Then the interesting number from the table of patent simple was slight down both domestic as well as foreign granted from 2009–11. This matter could be there some treat in the process from patent register – granted. One factor could be the quality in patent drafting. So it's really important that beside the researcher and engineer is also the management or support factor like inventors would better just focus on their duty.

As a World Trade Organization (WTO) member country, Indonesia has already ratified the Agreement of Trade Relates Aspect of Intellectual Property Rights (TRIPS) through Act No. 7 year 1994. While complying with various international regulation associated with global Intellectual Property rights, Indonesia is also expected to pursue and utilize its IP in productive and innovative approaches and to compete with other countries. in 2009 of the WEF global index despite Indonesia's 10 point better position than the previous year (*i.e.* 44 from 54), Its position was 2 points down in 2011 (46). The Intellectual Property Rights, especially patent, has been commonly used as indicators for country technological achievement.

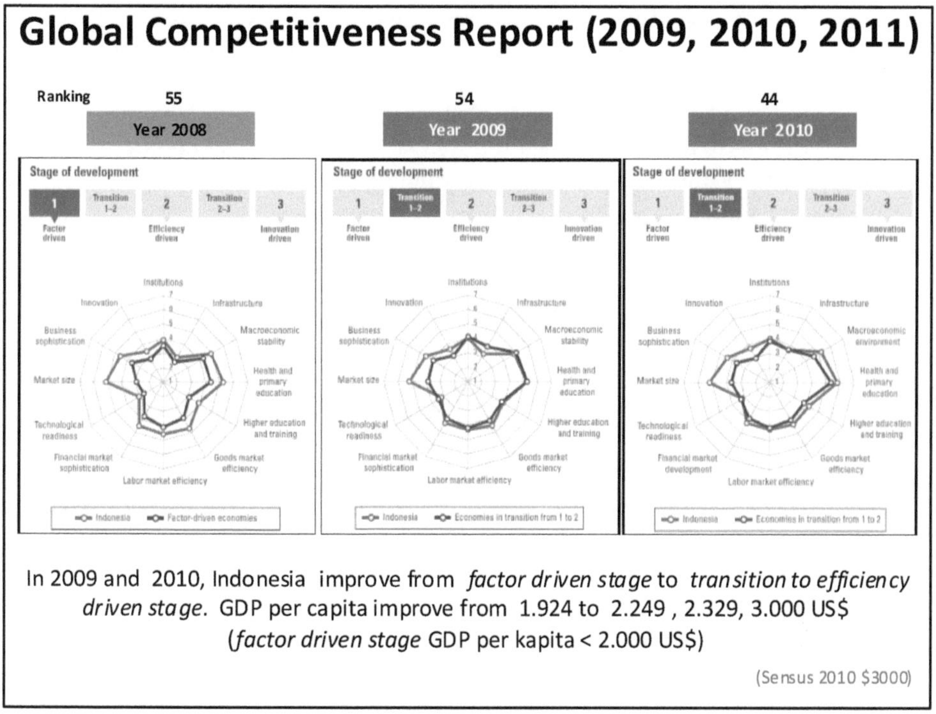

Figure 6.3: Indonesia Ranking on Global Competitive Report.
(*Sources*: Menristek, 2010)

5. MORT Policy Study and Evaluation Programme on IP Facilitation Management

5.1. Study of the Role of Indonesian IPR Centre/Institution 2010-11

The establishment and strengthening of IPR centers that have been mandated by Law No. 18 of 2002 on the National System of Research, Development and Application of Science and Technology, is expected to encourage the acquisition of IPRs in the R&D Institutes and Universities with respect to their closely related main functions. Various constraints have been identified, including inadequacy of institutional support that affects the intensity of human resources management, unsynchronized work procedures, and the vagueness of the operational cost that hinder the sustainability of the existing centers for IPR management, although its formation has been facilitated by the government.

This study was designed to find and provide list of facts regarding the existence and the information, the implementation of IPR management in accordance with the provisions of the Law No. 18 of 2002 on the National System of Research, Development and Application of Science and Technology, and to analyze data and information on various regulations that exist in the management of IPR in R&D Institutes and Universities.

The scope of this study includes the assessment on various provisions of legislation related to intellectual property and the results of intellectual property reports, development of database on reporting and management of R&D results in R&D Institutes and Universities. The study was conducted through literature study and direct surveys to the Universities and R&D Institutes and stakeholders. Further analysis of primary and the secondary data obtained were performed.

In 2002, the Ministry of Research and Technology noted there were 96 centers for IPR in R&D Institutes and Universities in all over Indonesia. In this study, data from these centers were used to explore IPR information and to confirm their presence. Some other data were drawn from list of universities in Indonesia. Of the 132 returned questionnaires, there were only 62 respondents that meet the criteria as center for IPR previously defined which are targeted as subject of the study and also become respondents in this study. These respondents only represented less than 10 per cent of around the 3000 R&D Institutes and Universities in Indonesia. The demographic distribution of Center for IPR respondents in the current study are not much different from the 2002 center for IPR data, which are located in the Central and Western Indonesia where the population of respondents found the highest concentration in the area of Java. From the respondents data there were also obtained information regarding the new IPR Center that was not recorded in the 2002 data. They were located in the province of the Bangka Belitung Islands, Central Kalimantan, South Kalimantan, South East Sulawesi, East Nusa Tenggara and Papua. Based on this documents finding, it can be observed that these centers for IPR are newly established institutions that have not or were not recorded in the previous data. The existence of Center for IPR should be assisted to align with the development of Regional Innovation System (RIS) concept. RIS is interpreted as the existence of a dynamic relationship and knowledge transfer between technology generating institutions, policy makers, business entity and society.

Regarding to IPR productivity, from 44 respondents reported that Patent and Copyright dominate the IPR registration *i.e.*, 915 and 778, respectively. Followed by the registration of Plant Variety Protection (PVP) and Brand Name as many as 232 and 282, respectively. The rest of the IPR consist of Industrial Design which accounted to only 43 registrations. The majority of respondent did not focus on Industrial Design and PVP due to their nature of research activities or have not achieved a potential to generate Industrial Design yet nor associated with PVP. The highest patent productivity achieved by the Center for Innovation LIPI which filed 199 patents. Meanwhile, the greatest productivity on Copyright is achieved by State University of Surabaya as many as 569 registrations. Further elaboration regarding productivity magnitude of Copyrights need because Copyright protection occurs at the time of publication of a creation with/without registration. For example, the Center for Innovation – the Indonesian Institute of Sciences (LIPI) issued a policy not to register creations unless fixed in the form of computer software, audio visual and prototypes that are considered significant and required written documents of authenticity. In the field of Plant Variety Protection, Ministry of Agriculture is the largest contributor with total of 229 registrations. However,study showed that other institutions that have resources like Ministry of Agriculture have potential to do so but they did not use the opportunity. This is due to the intensity of socialization in the field of PVP that is not well perceived as other IPR socialization so that not many respondents understand the substance and procedures for the acquisition of PVP.

Law No. 18 of 2002 on the National System of Research, Development and Application of Science and Technology requires that all IPRs produced using the state budget are owned by the state and managed by the institutes. The results of respondents' answers regarding how the ownership of IPR is managed are very diverse. Only 4.26 per cent of respondents reported that only the institute's managed the IPR, 13.82 per cent of respondents reported that intellectual property rights were managed as private property, 16.58 per cent of respondents reported that IPR were managed as common property, 10.52 per cent of respondents managed IPR as joint ownership, and the 54.83 per cent of respondents did not answer. This information is very important to investigate the existing legal relationship between the parent institute that has the Center for IPR and the individual demand. The absence of legal relationship will lead to uncertainty on the management of IPR funded by the state budget. On the other hand, this data strongly indicate lack of understanding regarding the status of publicly funded IPR.Most of respondents understood the basic knowledge that should be owned by the management of IPR such as knowledge of licensing, marketing practices and commercialization of R&D but most of them do not have the experience to perform marketing functions and establish partnership within the framework of IPR commercialization. This condition should be noted in order to provide guidance to Center for IPR in the future. IPR management unit needs assistance to commercialize R&D results and further acts as the driving force for the National Innovation System (NIS).

The results of this study do not provide the actual number of the existing IPR Management Unit in Indonesia based on the number of R&D Institutes and Universities. There are two main constraints in determining the population of IPR Management Unit: The first constraint is the absence of data which reveal the portion of research oriented R&D Institutes and Universities from the total 3,000 institutions. The second constraint is the lack of information on the presence of IPR Unit in those with research-oriented institutions. In closer observation, the majority of institutional respondents that have IPR Management Unit are universities. Unfortunately, there is no exact data on research-oriented universities, so forecasting the potential productivity of IPR, particularly patents, from universities can not be done properly. This fact should urge action plan that focuses on two important points: first, assisting the university respondents that are currently managing IPR; second, stimulating IPRs productivity by managing their results in other research oriented universities. The compositions of these types of institutions in more detail are: 72 per cent of respondents from universities, 14 per cent of R&D institutions, and 14 per cent of respondents from other government institutions.

The results of this study showed that majority of respondents are directing their IPR Management Unit towards commercialization of R&D results. On the other hand, most respondents that did not experience in commercialization, show asymmetric of information and inconsistency. The success of the IPR management Unit in carrying out the functions of IPR commercialization is a key importance in the National

Innovation System (NIS) cycle. In many countries around the world, the commercialization function, commonly known as technology transfer (licensing technology), is always shown by the initiation and intensive interaction with the user community. Indications of lack of capacity and capability to carry out the functions of technology transfer occur in the majority of the respondents. Capacity and capability to carry out the functions of technology transfer is a prerequisite for managing IPR Management Unit.

The commitment of IPR management Unit of the parent organization to implement the IPR obligations as mandated by the Law No. 18 of 2002 on the National System of Research, Development and Application of Science and Technology, can be observed through the planning and other administrative actions in establishing and managing the activity of IPR Management Unit. In addition to the implementation of constitutive obligations of the law, the parent organization commitment also affects the overall performance of IPR management Unit. Several factors that indicate the management commitment will be discussed in more detail below.

Based on questionnaires, it is revealed that in general most of the respondents have been supported by legal basis for their Center for IPR establishment. Although more than half of respondents already have the legal basis for establishment, the number of respondents who do not yet have a legal basis for the establishment is quite significant. Based on patent productivity, it is observed that the respondents who do not have a legal basis for the establishment, donot produce any patent. Nevertheless, these data are not sufficient to prove a correlation between the lacks of legitimacy of the establishment with patent productivity. The most common form of legitimacy is the decision of the parent organization leaders. Another form is the regulation of parent organization head, especially that of the IPR Management Unit of the institutions.

In line with the legal establishment, the linkage between organizational status and the performance becomes an important indication to see the direction of IPR Management Unit. It is worth noting that results of this study shows that the productivity of intellectual properties, particularly patents, are much better in the respondents with organic status compared with other categories of institutional status. In addition to the formality factors of the institution there are still other factors that significantly influence the performance of the IPR management Unit. There is a strong presumption that most of the IPR management units are established due to a strong commitment of the volunteers/activists who have conducted IPR related activities. These same people also bring the issue of a better IPR management system to the top level to obtain legitimacy of the movement in order to be more structured, focused and in line with the goal of their parent institute. In some cases, changes are also found in the governance of IPR management within the organizations, including change in the organizational status of IPR management Unit, from previously *ad hoc* into organic. Examples of such practices are found in Bogor Agricultural Institutes (IPB) and the National Atomic Energy Institute (BATAN). Presumably, this is taken as a compromise step in order to obtain authorized funding for their IPR management activities while still keep the state finance disbursement rules intact.

In the context of IPR management, complexities are found not only financial issues for example institutional formality, authority, performance and ownership of IPR. Ideally, an IPR management unit that serves as the Technology Licensing Office (TLO) has an independent source of funding received from the transfer of technology activities. However, financial independency of IPR Management Unit in Indonesia is still far from the expected due to low commercialization activities. Financial funding for management of IPR found in this study varied from designated state budget, Incentives from certain ministries, Private, and Cooperation. The amounts of funds used also vary from less than Rp. 10 million to more than Rp. 100 millions. Other sources of financial support may be obtained from Incentives research scheme and IPR establishment scheme which are offered by the Ministry of Research and Technology. However, not all of IPR management unit able to win the scheme since the requirements and selection proceed are quite competitive.

To support the activities of IPR management unit it is important to strengthen the supporting infrastructure, including conducive policies, facilities, and skilled human resources. The most fundamental national policy is regarding legal or licensed computer software. Although the majority of respondents have noticed this isuue, but 39.21 per cent of respondents still needs to be warned about its use in daily works because they may lead to serious violations of IPR. Other internal policies that require attention is the application of the material transfer agreement (MTA). This agreement is very crucial especially when the material to be transferred in the form of genetic resources or germ plasma. Recently only 17.8 per cent of respondents claimed to have implemented MTA. Lastly, Internal policy of the amount of royalty to encourage creativity of inventors is also important. There are 48.41 per cent of respondents knew the existence of such arrangements which are embedded in their organization regulation.

Not all units surveyed have the infrastructure for supporting IP management activities which is supporting facilities include work space, computer, phone/fax, Internet networks, and online sites (WEB). However, this fact has no direct effect on their productivity. Data showed that the legitimacy and institutional formality reflect the seriousness of the corresponding organization in understanding the important role of IPR management Unit.

The success of IPR management unit is depended upon the capacity of the managers and the policies that put them at strategic positions. The majority of human resources involve in IPR management unit comprise less than 10 people. This amount is thought to be related to the needs in the field and the existing workload. Judging from the level of education, the human resources involve in the IPR management unit are relatively well-educated, with majority of them are university graduates or higher. Quantitatively, this figure is adequate. However, to be able to manage IPR properly, these human resources must be equipped with managerial and business interaction skills so that the commercialization of R&D target can be achieved. Another problem found in the human resource management is the lack of funding guaranteed by the management of IPR to conduct routine activities, particularly those who do not have a permanent funding source. As a result, many IPR managers do not focus on IP business management objectives and choosing to have additional work elsewhere.

Another consequence is the high frequency of turnover in the human resources involved in IPR management Unit which had seriously impacted on the Unit performances.

The existence of intellectual property rights management unit in R&D institutes and universities in this study do not reflect the central role of IPR as expected by Law No. 18 of 2002 on the National System of Research, Development and Application of Science and Technology. The majority of corresponding organization has not given a strong commitment to make the centers for IPR as an important part of the corporate entity, resulting in lack of endorsement of the management of Center for IPR in achieving organizational goals.

IPR management function has not been implemented in exercising programmes and activities that employ IPRs to support economic growth and improvement of public welfare, because the majority of the centers for IPR do not have the insight and capacity that are adequate to carry out these functions.

To support the implementation of IPR management in R&D Institutes and Universities, breakthrough on operational policies are needed, so that the centers for IPR can function optimally. R&D Institutes and Universities that do not yet have their own IPR can start performing their functions by utilizing technology results of other R&D institutions that meet the aspect of "freedom to operate", especially those that can take advantage of local commodities. The existence of a Center for IPR is ideally a complement to the concept of RIS that facilitates knowledge transfer between technology producing academic institutions, policy makers, businesses people and communities, in dynamic way.

Leadership in the Research Institutes and Universities is required to provide care in the management of IPR in their institution, as the success of R&D Institutes and Universities is indicated by the number and quality of the outcome IPR. A piloting of successful IPR management, starting from IPR registration to commercialization and distribution of the incentives to inventors and administrators of the Center for IPR management unit, needs to be established to induce motivation and awareness of the importance of IPR for researchers and the Government.

The implementation of reward and punishment to the parent organization of R&D Institutes and Universities needs to consider IPR elements in the achievement of organizational goals. Reward may be in the form of IPR incentives affirmations by the government, while the punishment may be implemented in the form of public announcement in the media for R&D Institutes and Universities that do not contribute to the development of IPR.

To support the implementation of IPR management in R&D Institutes and Universities, it requires preparations of regulatory and operational policies, especially in the field of Licensing Regulation, Government Regulation on Royalty. What is most needed today is an operational technical policy that is legalized by the Ministry of Finance. The approved direct use of income generated by R&D commercialization for funding research and development activities will stimulate and encourage research cooperation between R&D Institute – Universities and industries.

To strengthen the management of IPR in R&D Institutes and Universities, a more in-depth study that would become the milestone policy of Center for IPR in accordance with the mandate of Law No. 18 of 2002 on the National System of Research, Development and Application of Science and Technology, is needed. The S&T National Capacity for strengthening the NIS through its element or pillars include S&T Institution, S&T Resources and S&T Network, S&T relevance and productivity as well as S&T Utilization. The activities of each NIS elements called subprogramme activities. The activity of subprogram on strengthening of S&T resources include the strengthening the capacity of S&T Infrastructure and facility, S&T investment, S&T development of data and Information, and finally strengthening Intellectual Property and Standardization (See: MORT, Policy Research, 2011).

5.2. GRTKF/Non Conventional IPR Facilitation Model Protection and Management

Genetic Resources, Traditional Knowledge and Folklore (GRTKF), translated in bahasa as "Pengetahuan Tradisional, Ekspresi Budaya Tradisional dan Sumberdaya Hayati" have become prominent issue of WIPO. This communal IPR is property that needs to be protected and managed well by the owner countries in order to utilize for the people prosperity. Mostly, the owner of GRTKF is developing countries, and are keen and hopeful that the GRTKF protection system be separated and differentiated from the Conventional IPR regime, that covers protection to copy right and related right, patent, merk/brand, industry desain, integrated circuit, trade secret and plant variety. WIPO had taken this important role in bridging the communication between countries of GRTKF owner (mostly developing countries) and countries which oppose GRTKF special protection (Suis Generis).

Recently, many industries have actively promoted traditional culture and knowledge to the commercial world. This also happens in genetic resources materials. The commercialization of Traditional Knowledge and Genetic resources becomes problems because they did it without asking permit to the owner countries/ community who owns those TK or GR.

Since the beginning in 2000's, MORT has been prepare to copewith this problems, and have done some action in responding to the issues of GRTKF. At the end of 2004 to early of 2005 MORT have proposed that GRTKF issues be discussedin the Asia Afrika conference in Bandung, which was held on April 2005. The Departement of Foreign Affair together with Department of Law and Human Rights through its Director General of Intellectual Property and Ministry of Environment (KLH) and several other Department, had agreed that the GRTKF issue is to be proposed as one of main issues for Conference Agenda. As a result, the GRTKF resolution was accomodated in article 7 and 9 of Asia Africa Conference. For that same reason, the Department of Foreign Affair and DGIP of Minister Law and Human Rights together with WIPO, had carried out Asian African Forum on Intelectual Property and Tradiotional Cultural Expression, Traditional Knowledge and Genetic Resources.

Through this forum, participant had learnt that the quickest way to protect the GRTKF is by documenting it in a data base system in order topreserve the properties well. The data base will be very useful when other party misuse and misappropriate

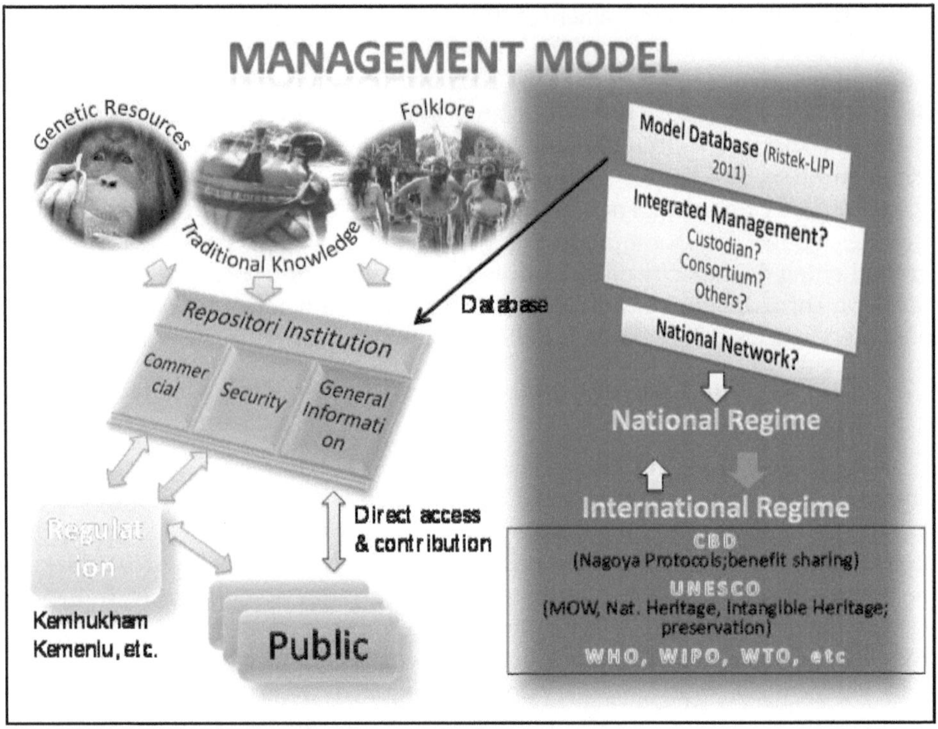

Figure 6.4. Model of Indonesia GRTKF Management and Protection (Ristek-LIPI)
***Source*: Model of Indonesia GRTKF Management, Ristek – LIPI, 2011.**

use or unfair use of Indonesian resource GRTKF. The arise question now is who should do the documentations. The answer is of course all Indonesian GRTKF stakeholders, including community and regional government. In 2005 MORT had been conducting incentive programmes so called"perlindungan pengetahuan tradisional (LINTRAD)" or TK Protection programme or incentive programme competition. The program produced a data base called "Seri Pelestarian Budaya Bangsa" or national culture preservation serial, consist of medicine plant name, "khasiat" and its main bioactive ingredient (See Ristek-LIPI, 2010).

This effort needs to be continued in wider scale after it was discontinued in 2006. This was the main reason MORT studied the status of stakeholders in data base development in 2010. From mapping activity in 2010, it is found that there are some stakeholders who actively develop data base related to GR, such as KLH. While Ministry of Culture and Tourism produced a data base for TK and Folklore or Traditional Culture Expression (TCE). MORT assumed that if other Indonesia Minister or Institution or even within community follow suit, it will become a strategic effort and could be an effective way in creating data bases, just like it is done in India with its Traditional Knowledge Digital Library (TKDL) or the Republic of China. The creation of data base can be managed together by all stakeholder through one agreed system. Discontinued of LINTRAD project, which had previously yielded good data base, should be followed up by a new and innovate system. Now, the GRTKF data are still spread out within the stakeholder and most of the raw data is still in the researcher or individual person files. Another phenomena showed that the source of GRTKF, especially within community which is still not documented and passed through from generation to generation, could be missing or even claimed by other nation country, as most Indonesian cultures are ill-documented cultures. Database that is already existed but in separate management, could not be accessed openly (for disclosure data) via internet by other GTKF stakeholder or community, even though these data were managed by them in many years. MORT sees that a kind of integrated data system with limited access and utility in a integrated format, is needed.

Base on the above discussion, a model of knowledge management needs to be developed. This model should be able to store, manage, provide as well as to be able to integrate the data and information of GRTKF which is already existed, using interoperability system. This model is expected to connect research institution, decision maker, security department/institution (Customs and Policy), and could also could be end the commercialization/sale which is related to GR (for CITES checking system aims connected to Trade in endanger species) mechanism. So in the future this model could be also customized for several aims of multilateral convention compliance, such as CITES. The pilot test model will be conducted using data base in LIPI (Indonesian Institute of Sciences) and MORT/LINTRAD.

The model design is for two years (2011-12), and is currently still in progress, athough no pilot is tested using real data. In 2011, the team finished identification process, data collection and initial model, and prototype model and the guideline would be produced in 2012. The methodology of model uses "Soft System Methodology (SSM) model. SSM is selected because the team is using complex system approach to solve complex problem condition, unstructured and base on holistic analysis and system thinking. SSM is also a participatory method that can help various stakeholders in understanding their different perspectives. Data and information to support the model was obtained from desk study, identification to several research institution and community, focus group discussion and in-depth interview to various government institutions and ministry offices.

To depict the model, the team created a prototype portal interoperability namely Indonesian Genetic Resources and Traditional Knowledge (I-Grest). To bring the model and the prototype into real policy, the work needs to be followed up. A detail master plan is needed in the form of management architecture, system and information technology within a management system of Indonesian GR and TK. Through I-Grest portal, it is hoped that the mapping of GRTK Indonesian property would become Indonesia's defensive protection facility for Indonesia property, which protect GRTK claim from other parties/countries who are not a legal own, and to serve as a facility for decision maker related to policy decision for IPR communality/GRTK and as facility of policy related to the future GRTK as well as GRTKF management (See: Ristek – LIPI, 2011).

6. Enclosing

Summary and Recommendation

- Intellectual Property (IP) Management is important and covers many aspects. It is not just IP Institution role to support the development numbers and publications, but IP management related to the International trade development as well. The free competition as the consequence of globalization and regionalization has positive impact for better Indonesian IP management and Innovation domestic programme.
- Policy for Domestic industry should be targeted to create domestic market for more than 240 million populations. The role of Innovation as the driver to economic growth and stimulus innovation requires an appropriate IPR system. Patent portfolios actively manage by Firms are common in US, Japan and EU.
- The IP and Innovation as well as Patent are used as an indicator of competitive index in certain country by WEF (World Economic Forum). Indonesian Patent should be stimulated not only by MORT policies but synergy with other policy especially Industry Policy for Innovation. Financial Policy to support innovation and IP management development are also important to utilize IP (IP exploitation from technology transfer activity).
- To make use of IP or IP utilization as a major driving forces for Indonesia economic growth still a problem for most government funded R&D Institutions, as well as universities and others. The reason is investment for innovation activity still low which requires a breakthrough policy. Research activity for commercialization is expensive and need enough financial support.
- In 2010–011 monitoring studied, showed that IP management function of government funded IP institions were mostly ineffective. The problems identified include inadequacy of institutional support for maintenance of IP institution/centre activity, unsynchronized work procedures, and the lack of the operational cost prevent the sustainability of the existing centers.
- The establishment and strengthening of IPR centers/Institution for IP management in Universities and R&D Institutions have been mandated by Law No. 18 of 2002 in articles 13(3) and 21(1). The scope of IP centre study includes the assessment on various legislations related to intellectual property and the results of intellectual property reports, development of data base on R&D output and management within R&D Institutes and Universities.
- In 2002, the Ministry of Research and Technology reported e 96 centers for IPR in R&D Institutes and Universities spread all over Indonesia. From 132 questionnaires which resulted in 62 respondents to met the criteria as IPR center that previously defined. These respondents are only representing less than 10 per cent of the 3000 R&D Institutes and Universities in Indonesia.

- ☆ The demographic distribution of Center for IPR respondents in the current study is not much different from the 2002 center of IPR data where mostly located in Java. Some new IPR Center recorded from some provinces in Sumatra, Kalimantan, Sulawesi, East Nusa Tenggara and Papua. Ideally Center for IPR should be directed to align with the development of the concept of Regional Innovation System (RIS).
- ☆ From 44 respondents it is noted that Patent and Copyright dominate the IPR registration *i.e.*, 915 and 778, respectively, followed by the registration of Plant Variety Protection (PVP) and Brand Name which are 232 and 282, respectively. The rest of the IPR registration consist of Industrial Design for 43 registrations. The majority of respondents did not focus on Industrial Design and PVP due to the nature of research activities or the respondents have not achieved a potential to generate or not associated with the corresponding IPR. The highest patent productivity achieved by the Center for Innovation of LIPI which filed 199 patents. Meanwhile, the greatest productivity on Copyright is achieved by State University of Surabaya with 569 registrations.
- ☆ National Security issue has arises along with the Indonesian IP task force effort to set up National Regime to protect and manage Indonesian GRTKF or Genetic Resources, Traditional Knowledge and Traditional Culture Expression or folklore from misuse and other misappropriate conducts. National security system creates a data base system called defensive protection.
- ☆ The pilot system was develop through knowledge management, such interoperability database system for commonalty IPR or Genetic Resources Traditional Knowledge and Folklore/Traditional Culture expression (GRTKF) protection. Since 2011 MORT and Indonesian Institute of Sciences (LIPI) conduct a joint activity to develop model data base called I-Res (Indonesian Genetic Resources and Folklore) using dummy data and I-Grest (Indonesian Genetic Resources and Traditional Knowledge) using the output of 2012. The pilot test of I-Grest will use real data. I-Grest prepared not only for GRTKF WIPO but can customize compliance with other Conventions such as CBD, CITES.

Acknowledgements

Dr. Mulyanto – Minister Secretary of MORT

Prof. Dr. Fredy P Zen – Deputy Minister for S&T Resources MORT

Prof Amin Subandrio – Deputy Minister for S&T Network MORT

Dr. Subiyatno and Mr Yoga Edie – Centre for Innovation LIPI

Mr. Razilu. Mrs Dede Mia Yusanti - Directorate General IPR

Mrs Nada Marsudi and Staff – Director International S&T Network

Dr. Sabartua and all colleague – Deputy Assistant S&T IP and Standardization

Dr. Ira Djarot – Evaluation Division, Deputy Assistant for Program Relevance

References

1. Akil *et al.*, 2011, Study on the Status Science and Technology Development in Indonesia, LIPI, Jakarta
2. Act No. 18 year 2002, The System of National Research, Devekopment and S&T Application, Jakarta
3. Fitzgerald, Anne and Brian Fitzgerald, 2004, Intellectual Property in Principle, Thomson, Law Book Co, NSW
4. Greenhalgh, C and Mark Rogers, 2010, Innovation, Intellectual Property and Economic Growth, Princenton University Press.
5. Idris, Kamil, 2003: Intellectual Property – A power Tool for Economic Growth, 2nd Ed. WIPO Publication No. 888.1.
6. MORT, 2010, Innovation for Social Prosperity (Inovasi untuk Kesejahteraan Masyarakat) Jakarta.
7. OECD, 2012, Innovation for Development Project, A discussion of The Issues and An Overview of The OECD Directorate for Science, technology and Industry. Access on 11 June 2012.
8. Purba, A.Z. Umar, 2011, Perjanjian TRIPS dan beberapa Isu Strategis, Alumni, Jakarta.
9. Pierson, Kim D, 2011, Importance of Intellectual Property Management, http://ezinearticles.com/?Importance-of-Intellectual-Property-Management&id=6540227, access in June 2012.
10. Menristek, 2010, Peningkatan Effectivitas Riset Secara Sinergi antara Perguruan Tinggi dengan Lembaga Litbang, Universitas Lambung Mangkurat, 15 Desember 2010.
11. Sinungan, A, 2009, Creative Industry in Indonesia and their Economic Potential, DGIP.

Websites

12. http://www.oecd.org/dataoecd/42/58/35213963.pdf, 2005, Conference on IP as an Economic asset: Key issues in Valuation and Exploitation (30 June- 1 July 2005), Berlin. access in June 2012.
13. http://www.ndlrn.edu.au/verve/_resources/managing_intellectual_property_rights.pd, access in June 2012.
14. http://www.1000ventures.com/business_guide/ipr/ipr_main. html, access in June 2012.
15. WIPO National IP Strategy: http://www.wipo.int/ip-development/en/strategies/national_ip _strategies.html), access in 2012.

Technical Report (unpublished)

16. MORT, 2010, Report on Policy Research on Formulation of IPR Management in R&D Centre and Universities, Jakarta.

17. MORT, 2011, Report on Policy Research on Formulation of Private IPR Management in R&D Centre and Universities, Jakarta.
18. MORT, 2011, Report on Facilitation Model on Protection and Management of Intellectual Property Communality or GRTKF, Jakarta.
19. Sukara, Endang, 2011, Urgensy Data based of GRTKF: Asset Management and Access to Bio/Cultural Diversity, in FGD of Facilitation Model on Management and Protection of Indonesia GRTKF, Ristek, Jakarta, December.

Chapter 7

Jordan and Intellectual Property Rights Issues

*Nasri J. Rabadi**

University of Jordan
Amman, Jordan

ABSTRACT

Intellectual property rights (IPR) protection is a powerful tool for economic growth of countries. In Jordan, for example, recent intellectual property reforms have greatly benefited the country's economy in general and in particular, its pharmaceutical sector which has gained new export markets and has started to engage in innovative research that advanced it to new level of development. New health sectors, such as contract clinical research, have emerged, and health-sector employment has grown as well.

It was not that long ago since Jordanians started to believe that having a proper IP system would enhance the overall business environment in Jordan; and that it would allow Jordan a more comprehensive approach to bettering its business environment. Part of this approach is to recognize that there are some types of investments that are more sensitive to the level of IP protection than others and that higher standards of IP protection could generate more investments in certain industries. Furthermore, the absence of a certain level of IP protection could be a major impediment in the face of investment to developing these industries.

In this paper development of the IPR protection in Jordan will be highlighted, outlining areas of positive developments, and concerns, in the areas of legislative compliance in copyright, trademarks, patents, and data protection. Light will be shed on the already achieved progress and the closely foreseen progress in IPR in Jordan.

A report prepared by the USAID stated that Jordan has not been listed on the United States Trade Representative (USTR) Watch Lists since 2000 and has continued to show steady progress in adopting progressive laws and policies over the past several years.

---

* E-mail: ag2jordan@gmail.com

1. Introduction

There has been considerable debate worldwide about the importance of intellectual property (IP) laws in encouraging investment, in particular foreign direct investment (FDI.) Understanding the relationship between IP and investment requires a comprehensive analysis, however this issue is beyond the scope of this work since it needs evaluation of the correlative capacity of each of the two factors toward each other.

The main beneficiaries of higher standards of IP protection are those industries that depend on IP to boost their development. Pharmaceuticals and chemicals, information and communication technologies (ICT), and integrated circuits' designs are examples of business activities in Jordan that are highly affected by the level of IP protection. Even within the same industry there are certain activities that seem to be more sensitive to IP protection than others. For example, in the pharmaceutical sector research and development (R&D) seems to receive more attention than sales and distribution. It is expected, therefore, that any investor in the afore-mentioned areas would expect a certain level of IP protection in order to start his own business in a given country.

In establishing a sound investment environment that includes IP protection three considerations should be kept in mind. The first is that it is not enough to have IP laws and regulations without having a proper enforcement system. In other words it is important to introduce an IP system that is efficient in its three components; legislation, administration, and enforcement. The second is that it is not enough to have a strong IP system in order to attract investments. The investment climate consists of a wide range of economic, political, social, and legal elements and all these should be consistent and attractive to investors. The third consideration is related to other industries which are seemingly immune to the level of IP protection such as textiles. These industries do not seem to be bothered with the level of IP protection as it is not a major element in their production.

2. Progress in IPR

Jordan's legislative effort over the past several years has led to the adoption of numerous intellectual property laws dealing with standards of protection outlined in the World Trade Organization (WTO) Agreement on Trade Related Intellectual Property Rights (TRIPS) which Jordan joined in the year 2000, becoming its 136th member. In 2001 it entered the Jordan-US Free Trade Agreement (JUSFTA), the first of such agreement between the United States and an Arab trading partner. JUSFTA agreement signaled the beginning of a new round of legislative reform to comply with its intellectual property obligations in the fields of patents, copyright, trademarks, data protection and IPR enforcement. The government of Jordan, intrigued by those agreements, continued a process of comprehensive economic reforms that had been underway for more than a decade. In fact, Jordan passed several IPR laws prior to joining WTO (Table 7.1).

Table 7.1: IP laws in Jordan

Patent Law No. 32 of 1999 and its amendments.	The Law of Unfair Competition and Trade Secrets No. 15 of 2000.
Trademarks law No. 33 of 1952 and its amendments.	The Geographical Indications Law No. 8 of 2000.
The Protection of layout designs of Integrated Circuits No. 10 of 2000.	Copyright Law No. 22 of 1992 and its Amendments.
The Industrial Designs and Models Law No. 14 of 2000.	The Protection of New varieties of Plants Law No. 24 of 2000.
Goods Marks Law No. 19 of 1953.	Trade Names Law No. 22 of 2003.

Laws consistent with the WTO Agreement on Trade-Related Aspects of Intellectual Property Rights (TRIPS) now protect trade secrets, plant varieties, and semiconductor chip designs in Jordan. Registration of copyrights, patents, and trademarks is required. Copyrights are registered at the National Library and patents are registered with the Registrar of Patents and Trademarks, which is part of Jordan's Ministry of Industry and Trade. Jordan has signed the Patent Cooperation Treaty and the protocol relating to the Madrid Agreement concerning the registration of marks. Jordan has also acceded to the World Intellectual Property Organization (WIPO) treaties on copyrights (WCT) and performances and phonograms (WPPT).

The following list some of Jordan's latest achievements in the field of IPR:

- ☆ A new draft amendment to the Copyright Law has been introduced by the Government and is currently progressing through the constitutional stages. The main aim of these amendments is to ensure full compliance with JUSFTA.
- ☆ Customs Department plans to introduce a draft amendment to Article 41 of the Customs Law to enhance for *ex officio* border measures and prosecution.
- ☆ Introduction of new amendments to Jordan Institute of Standards and Metrology (JISM) Law regarding administrative *ex officio* trademark enforcement.
- ☆ *Ex officio* enforcement actions by National Library continued to be show serious efforts by the Government of Jordan to combat piracy.
- ☆ Introduction of new amendments to the Public Health Law that incriminates and imposes high fines on traders and manufacturers of counterfeit medicines.
- ☆ A new amendment to the Trademark Law was developed in 2008 to ensure further compliance with JUSFTA, including raising fines from JOD 3,000 to JOD 6,000.
- ☆ Finally, American Chamber and Jordan Intellectual Property Association (JIPA) recommend that the Government of Jordan take the following steps to ensure more effective IPR enforcement:
  - Take more stringent actions against piracy (particularly audiovisual and optical piracy) against known locations and traders in downtown

Amman, Zarqa and Irbid that has negatively affected legitimate business.

- Expedite the adoption of the proposed amendments to Article 41 of the Customs Law.
- Assign specialized judges trained on IPR issues to deal with IPR cases to ensure better implementation of the IPR Laws.

3. Procedure for Registration of IPR

Procedure for registration of IPR is thoroughly explained in Abu Ghazaleh Intellectual Property (AGIP) Handbook, 2011. The following is a summary of the procedures for registering patents, copy rights, and trademarks.

3.1. Patents

Although Jordan is a member of the Paris Convention for the Protection of Intellectual Property, the International Patent Classification is not observed in Jordan. Applications for the grant of a patent are filed with the Patent Office, which examines the applications for compliance with formalities and patentiability under the Jordanian Patents and Design Law and may require amendments to applications to achieve conformity. Appeals by applicants against the requirements of the Patent Office as decided by the Registrar of Patents are made by petition to the High Court of Justice within thirty days of the Registrar of Patents' decision.

Approved applications are published in the Official Gazette. The period during which any interested party may file an opposition is two months from the date of publication. If no opposition is filed, or if the registrar or a court rejects the filed oppositions, a decision granting the patent is issued.

Patents are valid for a period of sixteen years from the date of filing provided that registration fees are paid along with the decision to grant the patent and that renewal fees are paid every four years during the patent term.

Patent rights are freely transferrable; however, notice of the transfer must be published in the Official Gazette and properly registered with the Patent Office so that they may become valid vis à vis third parties.

Under the Patents and Design Law, patents are not granted for chemical products relating to medical drugs, pharmaceutical compositions and food. The methods and processes used in the preparations of such products, however, may be the subject of a patent. The Patents and Design Law requires that the owner of a patent use the patented product or process in Jordan within three years of the date the patent was granted; if this requirement is not satisfied, the law provides for compulsory licensing of the patent. The Patents and Design Law provides penalties for infringement of patents.

3.2. Trademarks

The international classification of goods regarding trademarks is observed in Jordan although the Trademarks Law does not adopt the classification for service marks that are recognized worldwide. Applications for registration of a trademark are filed with the Registrar of Trademarks. The Registrar conducts an examination of the application, and, if accepted, the trademark application is published in the Official Gazette. Any interested party may file an opposition within three months of publication.

Oppositions which are not settled by the Registrar or appeals based on the Registrar's decision, are brought to the High Court of Justice. If no opposition has been filed or if the Registrar or a court rejects the already filed oppositions, a decision granting the trademark is granted and the appropriate certificate is issued.

Trademark registration is valid for a period of seven years beginning on the day the application was filed and is renewable for additional periods of fourteen years each.

Trademarks are freely transferable, but in order for them to be valid vis à vis third parties, notice of the transfer must be published in the Official Gazette and properly registered with the Registrar of Trademarks.

The Trademarks Law requires actual use of the trademarks registered. Trademarks of which there was no bona fide use or which have not been actually used for a period of two years immediately prior to the submission of an application for cancellation may be canceled. Unauthorized use or imitation of a trademark registered in Jordan is punishable by law. Currently, an amendment to the Trademarks Law is pending before the Jordanian Parliament. Among the more important changes proposed is the introduction of the international classification for services.

3.3. Copyright

In 1992, the Copyright Protection Law No. 22 was enacted. The Copyright Law grants copyright protection to original works of literature, art and science of any type, purpose or importance. It covers works of art as may be expressed in writing, sound, drawing, photography and motion pictures, including books, speeches, plays, musical compositions, films, applied art, three-dimensional works and computer software.

Copyright registration is filed at the Ministry of Culture. The work protected must be original and involve personal innovation and arrangement. The protection period, for both Jordanians and foreigners, is fifty years after the death of the author. Ministry of Culture may publish or republish a work subject to copyright protection if the author or the author's heirs have not published or republished the work within six months of the date the Ministry has given notice that the work is to be so published or republished. In the event of publication or republication by the Ministry of Culture, the author or author's heirs are entitled to fair remuneration.

The Copyright Law provides penalties for infringement. Enforcement of the Copyright Law is in the jurisdiction of the civil courts, however, the implementing regulations relating to the law have not yet been promulgated. Amendments to the Copyright Law which are supposed to make enforcement more effective are currently pending before the Jordanian Parliament.

4. Problems and Obstacles

It should be noted that the current standards of IP protection in Jordan might be problematic in some areas. The rush to adopt these laws and accelerate their maturation to levels found in developed countries raises a series of questions regarding their effects on vital sectors such as public health and education. Another forensic issue is whether developing countries should adopt standards of IP protection consistent with their level of economic and technological development and to gradually improve alongside their economic capacity. This point of view should be taken seriously by Jordanian policy makers in any further steps to increase the level of IP protection.

Another serious issue would be the cost of enforcing IP laws. It is widely accepted that enforcing such laws is a costly process that requires huge financial and human resources. This could only be justified if the economy can achieve benefits that would outweigh these costs.

Conclusion

A quick review to the intellectual property rights legislated and enforced is shown. Jordan has improved noticeably during the last twenty years. However, the country still has not done enough at least from the point view of the foreign investors. The economic status of the general public and the cost the government has to carry by enforcing IPRs are serious obstacles to reaching an acceptable level of protecting the intellectual rights whether for local inventors or international ones.

References

1. USAID, "Progress of Intellectual Property Rights Legislation and Enforcement in Jordan vis-à-vis the Special 301 Report for 2009, Final Report," Feb., 2009.
2. Keith E. Maskus, "The Role of Intellectual Property Rights in Encouraging Foreign Direct Investment and Technology Transfer," Duke Jr. of Comparative and International Law, Vol. 9:109, 1998.
3. Jordan Investment Board website, article titled "Intellectual Property Law,"http://www.jordaninvestment.com/BusinessandInvestment/Taxation/IntellectualPropertyLaw/tabid/116/language/en-US/Default.aspx
4. http://www.infoprod.co.il/country/jordan2e.htm
5. http://www.agip.com, "Abu Ghazaleh Intellectual Property Hand Book, 2011."
6. Ferris K. Nesheiwat, "The Adoption of Intellectual Property Standards beyond TRIPS - Is It a Misguided Legal and Economic Obsession by Developing Countries," 32 Loy. L.A. Int'l and Comp. L. Rev. 361 (2010). http://digitalcommons.lmu.edu/ilr/vol32/iss3/2.

Chapter 8

Management of Intellectual Property in Kenya

*David M. Ngigi**

National Council for Science and Technology
Nairobi, Kenya

ABSTRACT

Intellectual property is perhaps one of the less appreciated rights in Kenya. This law covers creative works such as trademarks, copyrights, trade secrets, and patents among others. Kenya has legislative policies that govern the right to ownership of material classified under intellectual property, but adherence to these legal parameters is almost non-existent. Furthermore, some policies are almost obsolete considering the dynamic changes in the world that lead to inventions and ideas that require protection from intellectual property theft. From an international perspective, some countries especially in Europe and American states shield authors, inventors, and owners from adverse effects of presenting their innovations to the market. These countries know that owners may not have the mechanisms to follow their works all over the world in order to prevent copyright theft. In such countries, new works undergo scrutiny before getting protection through intellectual property law. However, such products could flock the Kenyan market where the lenient penalties and laws provide a halfway house for intellectual property infringement. Nevertheless, Kenya has made steps towards eliminating pirated material from the market. Enactment of the Anti-Counterfeit Act 2008 brought into effect a ban on trade in counterfeit products. This hopes to prevent importation of counterfeit products or manufacture of the same in Kenya. The biggest hurdle in Kenya's move towards protecting intellectual property is getting the human resource to track infringement of the legal acts that protect owners and inventors. This workforce must understand the rights they intend to protect, which means there is

---

* E-mail: ngigimd@yahoo.com, ngigi@ncst.go.ke

need for public awareness about intellectual property rights. It also requires extensive analysis of content already in the market to create a standardized procedure towards a counterfeit free nation.

Keywords: *Intellectual Property Rights, Copyright, Intellectual Property in Kenya, Copyright law, Counterfeit, Copyright act, Intellectual Property law.*

1. Introduction

Intellectual property (IP) is a collective term for the work of inventors, artists, authors, and designers among others. It loosely translates to original works credited to a specific creator. There are different types of IP, but they fall under two categories: industrial property and copyright. Industrial property includes patents, trademarks, industrial designs, trade secrets and geographical indications, while copyright covers literary creations such books, music, film and video, pictures, artefacts and architectural blueprints among others (World Intellectual Property Organisation n.d). Vaidhyanathan, explains that a patent protects an invention, idea behind the invention and the process involved in the invention. There are different types of patents such as utility patents, which inventors use to get rights to a new invention, machinery, formula and the production process. This patent can also cater for improvements on previous works. The second type of patent covers design and the overall pattern of an item. The least frequently issued type of patent are plant patents normally granted for any asexually or sexually reproducible plants and may include cultivating different types of plants to create mutants or hybrids and also newly found seedlings. This type of patent protects the owner by protecting creation of the similar type of plant or profiting from the plant for at least 20 years. (Vaidhyanathan 2001).

Trademarks refer to logos, designs, packaging, brands, or other unique identity that a company or product enjoys in the market. Therefore, intellectual property law protects a company's exclusive right to use a trademark. This creates a level playing field in the commercial platform where companies can trade fairly with each other (Vaidhyanathan 2001). Copyright on the other hand, ensures creators or authors get ownership of intangible rights arising from the works. According to the World Intellectual Property Organisation (World Intellectual Property Organisation, n.d), these rights require protection as the only way to ensure subsequent inventions or creations advance concepts stated in the previous work instead of imitating or copying what the world knows already.

2. Intellectual Property in Kenya

IP rights in Kenya are governed by various Acts and laws. For instance, the Industrial Property Act caters for patents, industrial designs, utility models, and technovations. Copyright is covered under the Copyright Act, while trademarks fall in the Trade Mark Act. Seeds and Plant Varieties Act protects plant breeders' rights (Ombija, 2011).

2.1 Industrial Property Act

This Act caters for arts, machinery, and processes among other things that are either new inventions or improvements to existing inventions. Items in this category include basic essentials like food; textile products, operations used in the manufacturing sector and electricity. However, this Act strikes out concepts used in science or mathematics, treatment methods and gaming rules among others (Patents 2011). An application for patent under the Industrial Property Act Cap 509 requires a descriptive request that includes drawings of the invention where possible. A request should expound one method of using the invention and indicate why an applicant wants it patented. In addition, a request should have an abstract explaining the technical aspects of the invention ("Industrial Property Act" 2011).

2.2 Copyright Law in Kenya

Prior to 2001, Kenya was operating within the Copyright Act Cap 130 of 1966. One year into the new millennium, Kenya got her first copyright policy that lead to the Copyright Act, 2001 ("History of Copyright" 2011). The 1966 Act had a number of loopholes such as trivial penalties, classification of breach of this legal provision under civil law, and it lacked a defined implementation structure. Additionally, this Act did not cater for ICT sector concepts and products like software and computer programs. The new Act of 2001 lists violations of the Copyright Act as criminal and civil crimes. Its enactment also led to establishment of the Kenya Copyright Board. Moreover, the new Act empowered law enforcers to assist in adherence to copyright laws through inspections, seizures and arrests of offenders. Unlike the previous Act, the 2001 law has severe penalties with fines of up to shs.100,000 and a two-year jail term (Otike 2005).

This Act also lists works that qualify for copyright protection. They include literary, musical, artistic, sound recordings and broadcast works. Nevertheless, this Act has some restrictive clauses that control how works qualify for copyright protection. For instance, broadcast copyrights cover works aired on broadcast services while literary, artistic or musical works must have proof of inventors' overall contribution in making the work unique. The work must be available in a medium such as in recorded form or otherwise ("The Copyright Act" 2011).

2.3 Anti Counterfeit Act, 2008

This Act outlines offences that lead to counterfeit action against an offender. For instance, it justifies litigation for people found with counterfeit products, accused of manufacturing or producing fake goods, or offenders accused of distributing fake goods for commercial purposes. Imports of counterfeit goods and exhibition of the same also leads to legal penalties. An owner of intellectual property can file a complaint under this Act, upon gathering sufficient information about the offence. Penalties resulting from infringement of provisions in this Act for a first time offence can lead to about five years in jail, or a fine that is about three times the cost of the product. A second time offender can get a sentence of about 15 years imprisonment, or a fine that is five times the cost of the commodity ("Anti-Counterfeit Act" 2008).

3. Institutions Charged with Legislation of IP in Kenya

Major agencies that protect IP rights owners, inventors, and artists are Kenya Industrial Property Institute, Kenya Plant Health Inspectorate Services, and Kenya Copyright Board (Ombija 2011).

3.1 Kenya Industrial Property Institute (KIPI)

Kenya Industrial Property Institute (KIPI) is a Government parastatal under the Ministry of Trade and Industry. This parastatal arose from ratification of the Industrial Property Act 2001. Previously the Institute existed as Kenya Industrial Property Office (KIPO), which was established in February 1990 after enactment of the Industrial Property Act, CAP 509 of the Laws of Kenya. The institute main responsibility include administering industrial property rights through; protection, provision of information and training and promotion of inventive and innovative activities for social economic development ("About KIPI" 2011).

3.2 Kenya Plant Health Inspectorate Services

The plant breeders' rights fall under this body. Its purpose is protecting breeders of new varieties of plants from infringement of intellectual property pertaining to their discoveries and products. An IP owner can use such discoveries for commercial purpose by producing the plant without fear of imitations of the plant varieties by competitors. The rights holder gets exclusive rights to license producers who want to use the plant for commercial gains. These rights work the same way as patents since an owner can sell or assign them to other parties ("Plant Variety Protection" n.d).

3.3 Kenya Copyright Board

It evolved from the Copyright Act, 2001 ("Background," 2011).This board oversees the managerial process of copyright registration in the country. Hence, owners and inventors must register through this board to copyright their work as required under the Copyright Act 2011. Kenya Copyright Board also trains law enforcers to assist in apprehending IP rights offenders. Owners with substantial proof of copyright violations can seek legal assistance by reporting crimes to this board ("Our Services" 2011). It consists of key players in different industries catered for by the copyright law. They include individuals from the public and the private sector ("The Board" 2011). Other bodies and agencies that help in protection of intellectual property include.

3.4 Anti-Counterfeit Agency (ACA)

Its mandate arose from the Anti Counterfeit Act of 2008. It is responsible for public education and controlling the proliferation of fake goods in the Kenyan market. ACA also conducts research and consumer education programs ("About ACA" n.d).

3.5 The Music Copyright Society of Kenya (MCSK)

The Kenya Copyright Board has a number of organisations under it that help in propagating information about copyright. MCSK is one of them. Its membership extends to the music fraternity, from individuals in production, composition to artists.

It collects and distributes royalties resulting from purchase and use of artistic content covered by this organisation (Murunga 2009 and Mbote 2005).

4. Penalties for Infringement of Intellectual Property in Kenya

Every Act or law protecting owners and inventors of any work, has stipulated procedures for seeking legal redress. They vary with the gravity of the infringement, type of offence as well as the type of offender. This means that a first time offence can have lower legal repercussions unlike a second or third offence. The major remedies for copyright infringement in Kenya are injunctions, payment of damages, seizures, and account of profits made from the sale of infringing goods. For criminal infringement, the offender gets sanctions, fines and imprisonment. It gets worse for a person who possesses or imports copyrighted works for personal use since the fine can go as high as Shs. 400,000 or about 10 years in jail (Sihanya n.d). The Industrial Property Act Section 109 specifies penalties for infringement of patent, utility models or designs. It specifies fines not beyond shs.50,000 and/or 5 years in jail ("The Copyright Act" 2011).

5. The State of Intellectual Property in Kenya

The development of Intellectual property management and innovations are fundamental to economic growth, especially in newly emerging economies which normally are endowed with vast reserves of natural resources and human knowledge that remain unprotected. Taplin and Nowak (2010) list Acts and laws amended in Kenya over the last few years to advance the management of IP. These amendments such as in the Industrial Property Act, Trademarks Act, and Trade Descriptions Act 2002 provide a chance for Kenya to attain international intellectual property protection standards. For instance, the present Trade Descriptions Act complies with international trade policies such as Trade Related Aspects of Intellectual Property Rights.

The TRIPS Agreement provides protection for copyright and artistic works, trademarks, geographical indication, trade secrets and patents among others ("Overview: The TRIPS Agreement" 2012). These amendments have aligned Kenya's present IP laws to the changes in the market. However, there are still many challenges that the legal framework needs to act on so that intellectual property in Kenya gets maximum protection.

One of the striking challenges under the copyright Act is piracy. Despite the presence of strict penalties for offenders, the state of piracy in relation to music and other artistic compositions is alarming. This menace results from importation of machines and systems that mass-produce the products of underground piracy houses. Kenya Revenue Authority alleges that the piracy market diverts about Shs.10 billion annually ("Formulation of an EAC Policy on Anti-Counterfeiting…," 2009). Moreover, the Kenya Publishers Association claims that it experiences an annual loss of about Sh.2 billion resulting from pirated copies of books (Ohito and Odongo 2012).

These statistics present the ugly inefficiency of existing legislation. Another factor that stands out is the slow speed of prosecuting offenders. It translates to lack of appropriate official mechanisms meaning offenders can walk away without any legal repercussions for their actions. For instance, a case presented by the Kenya Publishers Association had 13 years of court proceedings (Ohito and Odongo 2012).

According to Justice Ombija there are particular tribunals charged with hearing cases about intellectual property infringement. These tribunals cater for specific violations depending with the IP offence. They include industrial property, trademarks, seeds and plant varieties, copyright, and the industrial designs, utility models and technovations tribunals. These committees consist of scholars, intellectuals with understanding of the IP law in Kenya (Ombija 2011). Matters resolved by these committees assist judges and other legal professionals who may not have sound knowledge of IP. Nevertheless, there are particular challenges facing these tribunals. Even though they are established by an Act of Parliament, they lack resources to operate independently and fully. Justice Ombija also points out that inability to find qualified personnel to serve in these tribunals also affects its effectiveness.

Prof. Sihanya echoes similar sentiments since government officials do not have sufficient machinery to handle copyright infringement. He says that these officers lack information, resources, and the desire to protect copyright as IPR. It makes IPR offences trivial amongst other cases that require legal attention. Bodies and agencies charged with protection of IP rights also lack skilled personnel who can combat these offences despite the changing face of IP theft in the world (Sihanya n.d, pp. 15-17).

6. Benefits of Better IP Law in Kenya

The most significant loss resulting from inefficient IP policies is the loss of foreign investors. Companies do not invest in regions that pose potential danger to their patents, trademarks and copyrights especially if such intellectual property rights are the differentiation factors that the company uses to fight competitors. Taplin and Nowak(2010) reported that Kenya's former Attorney General mentioned counterfeits and pirated materials as causing losses of about $420 m annually to Kenya. He said that protection of IPR is an important incentive to direct investment where lack of protection have irreversible damage on the local front. Africa's margins of registered patents has been shown to averagely rise from 26 in 1998 to 398 in 2000 (Mbote, 2005, p. 2). Kenya can push this margin higher, by ensuring owners, inventors, and the public understands that respect and protection of intellectual property harnesses a country's potential. Globalisation also calls for watertight policies to match guidelines offered by major trade organisations in which Kenya has membership. This reflects on the fact that IP is receiving an international approach where all countries operate from the same platform. It presents the advantage of bilateral trade without some countries infringing on the rights of others (Mazonde, and Thomas 2007).

Conclusion

Intellectual Property in Kenya is anchored in various Acts and laws. Rights included in these groups are patents, trademarks, copyrights and trade secrets among others. These rights are essential in protecting and rewarding owners and inventors. Legislators in Kenya have amended previous laws and Acts to present better laws that can assist the country in the modern age. The major rights protection fall under the Copyright Act 2001, Industrial Property Act and the Anti- counterfeit Act 2008. The laws cover works under different intellectual property categories and the penalties resulting from infringement accruing from rights. Furthermore, Acts and laws stipulate the legal framework for filing cases when right holders have evidence of potential violations. Institutions charged with ensuring adherence to these laws include Kenya Industrial Property Institute and Kenya Copyright Board.

Matters arising from ineffective IPRs policies range from lack of public awareness strategies to educate citizens and inventors about intellectual property in Kenya. Further, institutions and agencies lack technical and operational skills to enhance application of various IP laws. The most rampant effect of lapses in these legal mechanisms is increased piracy of copyright material. The available laws have tough penalties, but the only way to enforce them is by strengthening relevant institutions to oversee cases of IP infringement. More investments in creating public awareness is need to help in reducing cases of IP infringement.

Abbreviations

IP: Intellectual property
US: United States of America
TRIPS: Trade Related Aspects of Intellectual Property Rights
ACA: Anti Counterfeit Agency
MCSK: The Music Copyright Society
KIPI: Kenya Industrial Property Institute
USPTO: The United States Patent and Trademark Office

References

1. Abode Amnesty Campaign, 2012, Kenya Copyright Board. http://www.copyright.go.ke/?q=node/50 (Accessed 7 Aug. 2012)
2. About ACA, 2012. Anti Counterfeit Agency. http://www.aca.go.ke/index.php?option=com_content&view=category&layout=blog&id=85&Itemid=495 (Accessed 7 Aug. 2012)
3. About KIPI, 2011. Kenya Industrial Property Institute. http://www.kipi.go.ke/index.php/about
4. Anti Counterfeit Act 2008 http://infojustice.org/wp-content/uploads/2012/04/Kenya-AC2008.pdf (Accessed 7 Aug. 2012)
5. Background, 2011. Kenya Copyright Board. http://www.copyright.go.ke/?q=node/22 (Accessed 7 Aug. 2012)
6. Buscaglia, E. and Long, C., 1997. U.S Foreign Policy and Intellectual Property Rights in Latin America. Hoover Institution Press. Stanford, California. pp 2-8. http://books.google.co.ke/books?id=3fjR2E1sHD0C&printsec=frontcover&dq=intellectual+property+in+latin+america&source=bl&ots=x7Su4V HniZ&sig=ilR0Ze_kX8tmdH3BqLc30KkjvuA&hl=en&sa=X&ei=-hUhUO noFsO1hAf_

9YH4BA&redir_esc=y#v=on epage&q=intellectual%20 property%20in%20 latin%20america&f=false

7. Formulation of an EAC Policy on Anti-Counterfeiting, Anti-Piracy, and Other Intellectual Property Rights Violations, 2009.The EAC Community. http://www.google.co.ke/url?sa=t&rct=j&q=&esrc=s&source=web&cd=5&ved=0CGoQFjAE&url=http%3A%2F%2Fwww.iccwb o.org%2FWorkArea%2FDownloadAsset.aspx%3Fid %3D2147490043&ei=PsUg UL3iHcamhAe_zoGwDA&usg=AFQjCNEKscWt_dAHDnq_c9y-rYaCTWRoPg (Accessed 7 Aug. 2012)
8. History of Copyright, 2011. Kenya Copyright Board. http://www.copyright.go.ke/?q=node/38 (Accessed 7 Aug. 2012)
9. Industrial Property Act, 2011. Laws of Kenya. pp. 23-24 http://www.law.co.ke/klr/fileadmin/pdfdownloads/Acts/IndustrialPropertyActCap509.pdf (Accessed 7 Aug. 2012)
10. Institutional Framework for Intellectual Property and Technology Transfer, n.d. Intellectual Property Management Office (IPMO), University of Nairobi. http://www.uonbi.ac.ke/ip/?q=node/20 (Accessed 7 Aug. 2012)
11. Intellectual Property Law and Policy, 2011. USPTO Gov. http://www.uspto.gov/ip/index.jsp (Accessed 7 Aug. 2012)
12. Laws of Kenya: Industrial Property Act, Chapter 509, 2010, pp.23-24. http://www.law.co.ke/klr/fileadmin/pdfdownloads/Acts/IndustrialPropertyAct Cap509.pdf (Accessed 7 Aug. 2012)
13. Mazonde, N. I., and Thomas, P., 2007. Indigenous Knowledge Systems and Intellectual; Property in the Twenty-First Century. University of Botswana and the World Association for Christian Communication. http://books.google.co.ke/books?id=dLW6dZm9LskC&printsec=frontcover&dq=intellectual+property +in+Africa&source=bl&ots=7YT7u_SOZg&sig=yUd9TO5H9a OH600ZwFZLyer83-I&hl=en&sa=X&ei=pqQgUMuVIKek0QWKroHQBw&r edir_esc=y#v= onepage&q=intellectual%20property%20in%20Africa&f=false
14. Mbote, K. P., 2005. Intellectual Property Protection in Africa: An Assessment of International Environmental Law Research Centre. http://www.ielrc.org/content/w0502.pdf (Accessed 7 Aug. 2012)http://books.google.co.ke/books?id=aonxxWg4u4cC&pg=PA108&lpg=PA108&dq=is+ the+internet+a+free+world&source=bl&ots =w8540mGuaa&sig=59x4fO56akIL Wq26yPHV5 Gh-i3s&hl=en&sa=X&ei=KQEhUI3IIqWs0QWGvIHgAg& redir_esc=y#v=one page&q=is%20th e%20internet%20a%20free%20world&f =false (Accessed 7 Aug. 2012)
15. Murunga, B., 2009. Emerging Trends in Copyright. http://www.simba-advocates.com/downloads/copyright.pdf (Accessed 7 Aug. 2012)
16. Namusyule, S., 2011. Consumer Awareness Critical in Fighting Counterfeits in the Region: Ministry of Industrialization. http://www.industrialization.go.ke/index.php?option=com_content&view=article&id=269:consumer-awareness-

critical-in-fighting-counterfeits-in-the-region&catid=52:press-releases&Itemid=200 (Accessed 7 Aug. 2012)

17. Ohito, D. and Odongo, D., 2012. Publishers Lose Sh. 2 Billion to Pirates. Business Weekly. http://www.standardmedia.co.ke/?id=2000055903&cid=457&articleID=2000055903 (Accessed 7 Aug. 2012)
18. Ombija, R, N., 2011. Case Study of Kenya's Specialized Intellectual Property Rights Court Regime. Kenya Law Reports. http://www.kenyalaw.org/klr/index.php?id=978 (Accessed 7 Aug. 2012)
19. Otike, J., 2005. Intellectual Property Rights in Kenya with Particular Reference to Copyright. Moi University. http://www.mu.ac.ke/sis/images/PDF/copyrightpaper9.pdf (Accessed 7 Aug. 2012)
20. Our Services, 2011. Kenya Copyright Board. http://www.copyright.go.ke/?q=node/26 (Accessed 7 Aug. 2012)
21. Overview: The TRIPS Agreement, 2012. World Trade Organisation http://www.wto.org/english/tratop_e/trips_e/intel2_e.htm (Accessed 7 Aug. 2012)
22. Patents, 2011, Kenya Industrial Property Institute. http://www.kipi.go.ke/index.php/patents (Accessed 7 Aug. 2012)
23. Plant Variety Protection: Plant Breeders Rights Legislation, n.d. Kenya Plant Health Inspectorate Service. http://www.kephis.org/index.php?option=com_content&view=article&id=22&Itemid=43 (Accessed 7 Aug. 2012)
24. Sihanya, B., n.d. Copyright Law in Kenya. http://www.innovativelawyering.com/attachments/article/26/Copyright%20Law%20in%20Kenya%20-%20Prof%20Ben%20Sihanya.pdf (Accessed 7 Aug. 2012)
25. Sponsored Software Helps Artists Profit From BitTorrent, 2012. BBC NEWS. http://www.bbc.co.uk/news/technology-18981491 (Accessed 7 Aug. 2012)
26. Taplin, R. and Nowak, Z. A., 2010. Intellectual Property, Innovation and Management in emerging Economies. Routledge: New York. http://books.google.co.ke/books?id=lt2OIY50slYC&pg=PA49& lpg=PA49&dq=intellectual +property+in+kenya&source =bl&ots=LnE 1XRPqCE&sig=b65EHPvrpzFT CEASNj gIOBlnUV8&hl=en&sa=X&ei= CKUgUILvOIa X0QXp xIDYBA&redir_esc=y# v=onepage&q=intellectual% 20property%20in%20kenya&f=false (Accessed 7 Aug. 2012)
27. The Board, 2011. Kenya Copyright Board. http://www.copyright.go.ke/?q=the%20board (Accessed 7 Aug. 2012)
28. The Copyright Act, 2011. http://portal.unesco.org/culture/en/files/30229/11416612103ke_copyright_2001_en.pdf/ke_copyright_2001_en.pdf (Accessed 7 Aug. 2012)
29. Vaidhyanathan Siva, 2001, Copyrights and Copywrongs: The Rise of Intellectual Property and How it Threatens Creativity. New York University Press, New York. http://books.google.co.ke/books?id=sGjSY0rRC _wC&printsec=frontcover&dq=w hat+is+intellectual+property&sou rce=bl&ots=rQDNc

jpEYL&sig=zjSitlzm_TUcCR WOmaOYYz8e9ZM&hl=en&sa= X&ei= tY4fUOTUKsTPhA eWuYDIDQ&redir_esc=y#v=onep age&q=what% 20is%20intellectua l%20property&f=false

30. World Intellectual Property Organisation, n.d. What is Intellectual Property? WIPO Publication Switzerland, No. 450(E), pp. 2-3. http://books.google.co.ke/ books?id=ELtc_o_5-38C&printsec=frontcover&dq=what+is+intellectual+ property&source=bl&ots=8WZWfiQCqA&sig=scN4YYIn8 4jxqBJq8lsgrDaoLok &hl=en&sa=X&ei=tY4fUOTUKsTPhAeWu YDIDQ&redir_esc=y#v= onepage &q= what%20is%20intellectual% 20property& f=false

Chapter 9

Tecnológico de Monterrey (ITESM) Strategies to Develop New Patents in our Communities

J.R.A. Romero J., D.V. Pi ón and A. Zanatta A.*

Dean of the Graduate School,
Innovation and Entrepreneurship Tecnologico De Monterrey
Puebla, Pue, Mexico

ABSTRACT

Since the industrial revolution, technological development has been characterized by change and knowing how to use innovation to replace the energy provided by human or animal efforts. According to the economic growth model of R.M. Solow, technological progress increases the efficiency of labor and in conjunction with globalization, allows consumers to access products and services more quickly and safely. This works as a cycle of progress, and guiding companies to be in pursuit of innovation to be competitive in this global environment. Thus, innovation and competitiveness are keys to maintaining the progress of countries and that currently the main growth factor that is sought is the management and use of knowledge expressed in human capital.

Keywords: *Technological parks, Development, Innovations, Incubation, Patents, Technology Transfer, Economy.*

---

* E-mail: alejandro.romero@itesm.mx

1. Introduction

Since the industrial revolution, technological development has been characterized by change and knowing how to use innovation to replace the energy provided by human or animal efforts.

Thus, the technological change processes become important and these are generated, by focusing on the relationship between change and economic growth. According to the economic growth model of R.M. Solow, technological progress increases the efficiency of labor and in conjunction with globalization, it allows consumers to access products and services more quickly and safely. This ultimately works as a cycle of progress, and guides companies to be in pursuit of innovation and to improve their production processes, to maintain market share and therefore to be competitive in this global environment.

The innovation and competitiveness are keys to maintain the progress of countries and currently the main growth factor that is sought is the management and use of knowledge expressed in human capital.

2. Tecnológico de Monterrey

The Tecnológico de Monterrey is an academic institution founded in 1943, which focuses primarily on its students. Promoting the innovator and entrepreneur spirit, this target is achieved based on its strategic goals and mission 2015; that says: "promoting international competitiveness of enterprises of knowledge, innovation, technological and sustainable development.

Also, this institution promotes knowledge management, facilitates the formation of a culture of innovation among its 90,000 actual students and its 250,000 graduates in its 31 campuses all over Mexico; it is focused on establishing a link between businesses and knowledge-generating institutions, such as: universities, research centers and technology transfer centers. In this environment, the concept of technological parks has been extended and used to prove that they are an effective mechanism for innovation, facilitating the transfer and therefore the growth of the region.

Overall, Technology Parks are areas of excellence in innovation and strategic points of relationship between universities, research centers and companies. They act as drivers of industrial and economic development, through the exploitation of technology, in the territory where they are located.

As indicated by Arturo M. in 2012 *"A way to Promote Economic Development in Mexico"*, a Technology Park seeks to increase the wealth of the community by promoting the culture of innovation and competitiveness of its members, and promoting the growth of research and marketing technology. Certainly, these parks have a high physical quality environment aimed at creating a synergistic effect between the transfer and exchange of knowledge and generating new business, incorporating research and technological development and technology-based companies and services.

The Tecnológico de Monterrey has developed its own strategy, with models based on the idiosyncrasies of the different regions of Mexico, focusing its research and development in scientific and technological areas to support the country's competitiveness. These models are able to bring great value to the Institute's vision aligned with regional needs, seeking to create a linkage between business and knowledge through interaction programs and activities, consultancies, academic affiliation, business and government, etc.

The Tecnológico de Monterrey initiative for the creation of technology parks in Mexico starting from the first decade of the 21st century was according to the natural, economic, demographic, social and policies in the region of interest. In Puebla it is defined under a model, mainly for the attraction and business development, and serves as an incubator, offering consultancy services, technology management, but mostly it is based as a landing center with a capacity to house between 40 and 60 companies wishing to start operations in the region, providing the facilities required so that they become established in a more agile and secure environment.

Therefore, the three basic services offered by the Technology Park are: incubation, acceleration and landing. The incubation model of Tecnológico de Monterrey is currently certified by the Ministry of Economy and works as a support to entrepreneurs for the creation and consolidation of companies (start-up and spin off), contributing to job creation, innovation and community development.

Acceleration process, seeks to optimize the execution speed of different business/ companies functions, commercial, administrative, financial, technological and/or human resources, in order to align their objectives and strategies in a specific period. Obtaining at the end of acceleration, 20 per cent increase in sales, and 20 per cent increase in employment. Here the Federal Government through the Ministry of Economy provides financial support to pay for the acceleration.

Finally, the landing program is one that focuses exclusively on helping international companies to establish their operations and grow more rapidly in Mexico or local companies looking to settle in the park in order to internationalize. For this last point, the institute has 13 offices around the world in places like Vancouver, Boston, Paris, Madrid, Brussels, Shanghai, Beijing, Guangzhou for academic purposes; and one devoted entirely to attract foreign investment in México, and is located in TEDA, Tianjin China.

At Puebla´s Technology Park "CIT" (Center for Innovation and Transfer) there are 20 national and foreign companies integrated, dedicated primarily to the area of Information and Communication Technologies as well as some focused on sustainable energy, among these companies are Probayes, Vision IT, Flexway, MoviT, Orcius, Technit Solutions, Cleantech Cluster, and a lab created in conjunction with T-Systems, a legal center and offices of Corporate Arbitration and overall credit union. Several local newspapers (Synthesis, URB Economic, El Universal) state that the economy spills that can be generated by this technology park in this part of the region of the country is around 15 millions dollars, which plans to integrate clusters in areas such as automotive and auto parts, textiles, software and information technologies, as well as family businesses (Figure 9.1).

Figure 9.1: Technological Park - Campus Puebla.

Thus, the Tecnológico de Monterrey based on its mission 2015, is committed to contributing to society, building people of integrity, entrepreneurial and high capacity for innovation, and providing adequate tools for the creation of ecosystems to generate beneficial knowledge. Currently, the technology and science parks are a figure of System R+D+i^2 of Tecnológico de Monterrey, which seeks to promote the progress based on knowledge, and in turn these parks create a management model based on the protection of intellectual property and technological transfer, which serves as the main promoter of this culture of innovation throughout the southern region of Mexico and finally established as the Office of Technology Transfer.

Offices of Technology Transfer (OTT) born under a strategic management for a synergy between scientific research and technological, academic and business, where the main objective is to transform tacit knowledge into tangible application by the Intellectual Property (IP) to generate technological resources, human resources, sustainable resources and financial resources to complete the circle of innovation. Figure 9.2.

The creation and development of OTT was born under the great interest of many international universities, with emphasis on this work in Latin American universities because they have different abilities that allow them to conduct research and innovation, which occur within the university environment. The universities also develop solutions to engineering problems arising in various industrial enterprises located in an industrial area (Cluster), creating new lines of research and technological development, leading to scientific and technological growth for the benefit of society.

Mexican universities do not have a culture of protection of technological developments, *i.e.*, obtaining patents to protect the know-how and otherwise transfer this technology to a third party (company) to transform this knowledge into a tangible process to derive monetary gain. For this reason, a central body has been created to help manage and identify areas of opportunity for companies in technological developments.

The OTT is a bridge that connect the necessities of a industrial corporation with the academy, the last one has the target to create technology that solve the problem of the industrial corporation and the OTT manages all the Intellectual Property Process to protect the innovation and later sell the technology to other companies.

The Tecnológico de Monterrey system has been operating a network of OTT in each system stewardship in this particular case will discuss the strategic management for application processes to develop Intellectual Property Patent of Campus Puebla.

The management system of OTT Campus Puebla born under the mission: To transform the management of human resources in knowledge of scientific and technological innovation to help solve problems that occur in our industry with a sustainable approach and to promote intellectual development, linked to the business sector to increase economic and cultural development of our country.

The OTT's duties lie in being a moderator and inclusive office between the triple helix (Academia, Business and Government), performing the tasks of identifying clusters with a business to provide a high economic impact in the region are: Metalworking industry, medical industry, sustainability and the ceramic industry.

Once the identification of these clusters was made, there were signs of growing rapprochement with the leaders to promote the OTT services. These services are:

- ☆ New Industrial creations. (Patents, Utility Models, Industrial Design)
- ☆ Trademarks.
- ☆ Copyright.
- ☆ Technology Transfer.
- ☆ Research.

Knowing the needs of a company, the next step is to identify the process to follow, if the company has a Research and Development (R+D+i) Departments, the OTT rests with the management and consulting for the protection of new technology by writing a patent provided that the new product is innovative, industrially applicable and generate monetary resources, if the company doesn't have a Research department, the OTT will link up with an academic expert to found a innovative solution.

Otherwise, if the company does not have an R&D department (R+D+i) the OTT is responsible for the academic focus depending on the area of knowledge to solve technological problems affecting the company, improve production processes, minimize resources and maximize productive results, perform design and validation of new products. This is a competitive advantage for the company, because in Mexico there is no culture of innovation and development; and often the company does not allocate resources for the creation of this department. This process ensures that from the companies that are in Mexico to restructure, the approach to be consumer companies and manufacturing companies of foreign technologies, but will also be competitive in terms of developing new technologies and products, transforming and increasing the value chain of business processes, always managed by the intellectual protection provided by the OTT.

Another factor to be considered are the innovations generated by independent inventors who lack the support of an institution to support the projects they made in Mexico. In 2011 were registered a total of 14.055 patents (International and National Patents) before the Instituto Mexicano de la Propiedad Industrial (IMPI).

The only 7.5 per cent of patents were registered by Mexican companies, Mexican universities, Mexican research centers and Independent researchers of Mexico, the last one, increased 54 per cent respect to the past year (2010). This is an opportunity to for the OTT to promote the advisory and consulting services for the protection of Mexican innovations.

Data from educational institutions, particularly the Tecnológico de Monterrey system indicate that for the sixth consecutive year, is the university that has applied for more patents in Mexico. In 2011 the university applied for 47 patents. This was followed by the National University of Mexico UNAM and in third place was the National Polytechnic Institute IPN. It is observed that the number of registered patents is low, because in previous years there was only an office manager who took care of the system of patenting and facilitated the drafting and administrative process of the same. Management of information was not adequate, thus presenting a serious problem for inventors. The long administrative process necessitated the creation of an OTT with well-trained people in IP, to efficiently manage the patenting process. This ensured the gradual increase in patent applications, not only in the Tecnológico de Monterrey system but also in the community.

Averagely, it takes approximately five (5) years for the Mexican Institute for Industrial Property (IMPI) to process a patent application (another reason to discourage an inventor cannot protect your invention). There is an emerging problem for inventors, specifically regarding the issue of licensing and manufacturing technology. The inventors do not have the resources to exploit their patents. It has been observed that, only one (1) out of every ten (10) patents in Mexico is exploited commercially. Thus the focus of the OTT is to manage IP, particularly, to create an enabling environment for transfer or exploitation of technology resulting in the creation of business opportunities internationally and a cycle of innovation.

The collection of talent management is displayed in the triple helix mentioned above, where the OTT is responsible for regulating and integrating these groups to obtain a continuous improvement process innovation can be seen in the Figure 9.2.

The Figure 9.2 it a circular pattern and inclusive of the main clusters in the state of Puebla, which based on the networking opportunities with leaders of these important industrial areas and the regulatory activity of the OTT is channeled to the academy to identify areas of opportunity. An analysis of what has been and is to be achieved through the application of scientific innovation is performed based on the engineering knowledge that is reflected in a developing industrially applicable technology. This process will result in the ownership of copyright in articles, books, conference participation and obtaining Patents in technologies that can be commercialized, for example, licensed to third parties interested in commercial exploitation of innovation.

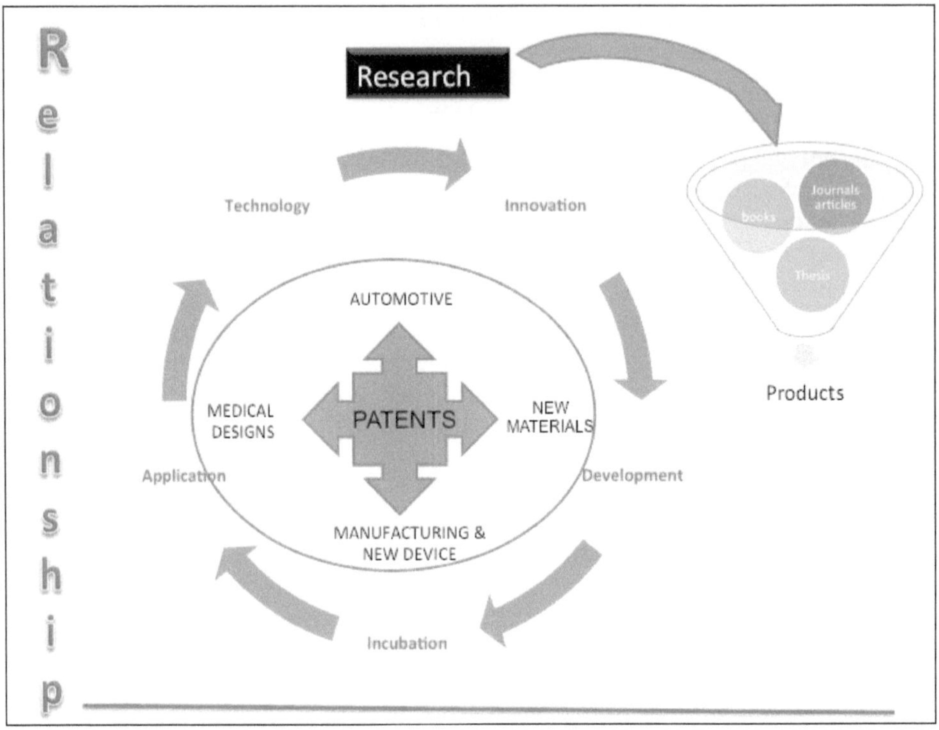

Figure 9.2: Model of Research and Innovation for the OTT Campus Puebla.

This process has no end, because it must constantly be restructured with the contribution of new knowledge, for updating and developing new technologies to ensure the growth of a society. These are all managed by OTT services to facilitate the management of intellectual property rights, resulting in enhanced human, social and financial resources.

In addition, Tecnológico de Monterrey in conjunction with the state government is implementing strategies to increase the number of patent applications in Mexico and to offer incentives as part of the Scheme of Input and Output Strategy shown in Figure 9.3.

The IO strategy is premised on the fact that Science Technology Parks as landing, acceleration and incubation centers, functions as the initiator point of the process, by offering a variety of business services in one place, for example, many of the best inventions to be patented, or trademarks and industrial designs obtained originates in the business incubator.

It's important to know that exist an element that function as a mediator that establishes a link between business and the academic institute. This linkage is achieved through the Technology Transfer Office, which specializes in Intellectual Property Rights and has standardized processes of records, providing a major efficiency in the proceedings.

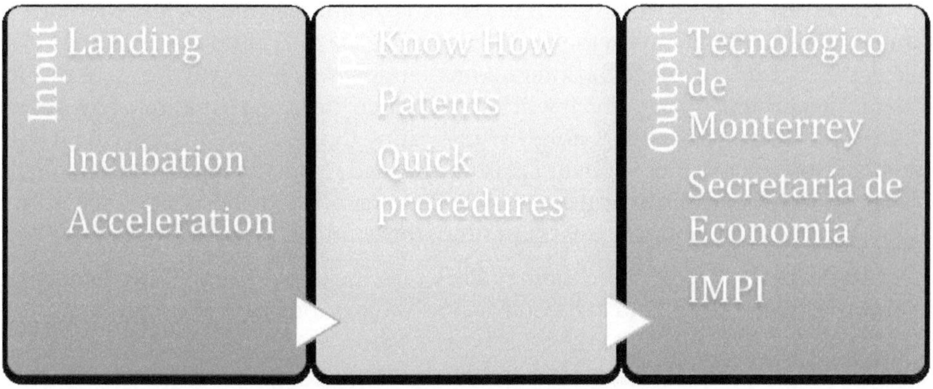

Figure 9.3: Scheme of IO Strategy.

Finally there is the lead agency that controls the processes of industrial property registration and determines titles to be awarded. Given this, the Secretariat of Economy, through the IMPI has implemented a driving strategy that involves offering more facilities to universities and research centers to increase the number of patents applied for during the year. These facilities are geared to positive intervention in all patentable projects from each institution, engaging from start to finish in the patenting process. This ensures that the process is carried out effectively so that there is more titles are awarded.

Another incentive offered by the institute is that the universities, the Micro or small businesses and individuals are granted a 50 per cent discount on the cost of the application, either to patents, utility models, trademarks, industrial designs.

Finally, from 2009 to date, all the combined efforts have resulted in application for 14 patents, 5 industrial designs and 8 trademarks and 5 more patents registered this year. This works as an indicator of the viability of the technology transfer office, because as discussed above, by providing more facilities to the creators of new technologies, to patent their inventions, particularly, students and teachers of the Institute, it persuades and encourages such creators to continue inventing and exploiting their products.

Conclusions

The importance of innovation in national and local economies has increased steadily since the late 80's with the development of knowledge-based economy, globalization and international competitive pressure. In recent years, Mexico has steadily lost places in competitiveness, as stated by recognized international indices such as the World Economic Forum and the International Monetary Fund.

To reverse this trend, it is necessary for Mexico, and implement structural reforms, increase investment in research and technological development as it only invests about 0.5 per cent in this category, compared to members of the Organization for Economic Cooperation and Development Economic, performing an average investment of over 2 per cent.

The future is being designed in the short term and Tecnológico de Monterrey Campus Puebla mainly, with the creation of an Office of Technology Transfer. The role of the OTT is to manage the integration of industrial clusters in the academy, in order to create joint works, which will be reflected in the transformation of the value chain of products. This will be done by integrating the research process which will add value to the industries in obtaining products made from raw material technology and patented Mexican inventions which guarantee the development scientific, technological, social and financial support of the country.

But the real value of a Technology Park is in the joining and strengthening of relations between key actors in the science-technology-business in a region.

Acknowledgements

The authors would like to thank Tecnológico de Monterrey -Campus-Puebla for their assistance.

References

1. Molina, A. De Lizardi, C. Santillán, M. (2012). "A NEW WAY TO PROMOTE ECONOMIC DEVELOPMENT IN MEXICO: The Technology Parks of the Tecnológico de Monterrey". Pp 41.
2. Solow, R. (2007). "GROWTH THEORY: An Exposition". Illustrated, p. 190.
3. D. V. Pi ón (2012). "Informe de operaciones Parque Tecnológico CIT, Campus Puebla" pp 25.
4. ITESM (2009). Definition of Technology Park, online: http://www.itesm.edu/wps/portal?WCM_GLOBAL_CONTEXT=/migration/ITESMv22/Tecnol_gico+de+Monterrey/Emprendimiento/Red+de+Parques+Tecnol_gicos/Qu_+es+un+parque+tecnol_gico
5. Molina, A.; Romero, D. Ramírez, B. (2008). "Estrategias del I + D + i2 en el Tecnológico de Monterrey para Impulsar el Desarrollo Competitivo Regional de México".
6. OMPI. "Practical guide to create and management a Technology Transfer Office".
7. Robles, S. "Model of Innovation and Research".
8. IMPI. (2012). "Cifras desde 1993".
9. Ortiz, A (2012). "Es el Tecnológico de Monterrey líder en patentes por sexto a o consecutivo".

Chapter 10

Status of Intellectual Property Rights Management Systems in Nepal

Chiranjivi Regmi

Nepal Academy of Science and Technology,
P.O. Box-3323, Kathmandu, Nepal

ABSTRACT

Nepal has been a member of the World Intellectual Property Organisation (WIPO) since February 4, 1997. It signed the Paris Convention in 2001 and the Berne Convention in 2006. There are many obligations and commitments of Nepal in this regard. In this context Nepal had to build up capability in terms of infrastructure, legislative, human resources and management for the protection of IPR. Similarly Nepal became a member of the World Trade Organisation (WTO) in 2004, and had to fulfil its, obligations regarding the implementation of TRIPs. Efforts are being made by the Government of Nepal, in this line although very slow. The paper will discuss the current status of management of IPR *i.e.* copyrights and industrial property rights including protection of plant variety rights.

Keywords: *Intellectual Property Rights, Legislation, Protection, Copyrights, Patent, Trademarks.*

1. Introduction

Nepal has more than 75 years history of legalization and protection of Intellectual Property Rights (IPR), starting from 1935 (BS 1993) with the promulgation of Patent, design and Trade Mark Act. Two and half decades later, Copy Right Act was also

* E-mail: info@nast.org.np, planning@nast.org.np

promulgated in 1963. These Acts were replaced by Patent Design and Trademark Act, 1963 and Copyright Act, 2003, respectively (Acharya, 2000).

Nepal became member of the World Intellectual Property Organisation (WIPO) in February 4, 1997. It signed the Paris Convention on June 22, 2001 and the Berne Convention on January 11, 2006. It also signed the Convention on Biodiversity (CBD) on June 12, 1992. Nepal became a member of World Trade Organisation in 2004. In accordance with Trade Related Aspects of Intellectual Property Rights (TRIPS), all WTO members are required to meet certain minimum standards for protection of Intellectual Property. The term 'Intellectual Property' refers to a design, technology or product invented by a person or corporation and 'Rights' refers to the recognition that the inventor should be granted a reward such as the exclusive right to use it or to earn royalties renting out its use. Under TRIPS, such rights are conferred by provisions related to patents, copyright, trademarks, geographical indications, industrial designs, and layout-designs of integrated circuits and protection of undisclosed information.

Nepal considers the protection and promotion of intellectual property as a dynamic tool for socio-economic development. Accordingly, the policy for intellectual property is to provide effective and adequate protection for all categories of Intellectual Property Rights in conformity with the TRIPS Agreement.

2. Organizational Structure

At present there are two main government offices with designated responsibilities for IPR protection.

2.1. Nepal Copyright Registrar's Office (NCRO)

Major functions of this office are:

Registration, Certify, monitor and control copyrights

Establish royalty collection institutions

Hear petitions of unsatisfied parties in royalty

Inform the society about copyrights and coordinate GOs and NGOs.

2.2. Department of Industries (DOI)

Major functions and duties of DOI are limited to Industrial Property Rights; patents, trademarks and industrial designs. They are:

Examination of proposals regarding IP registration

Registration of patent design and trademarks

Formulate rules and regulations

Punish and compensate the violators as per quasi judicial power,

Work as the focal point of WIPO

The responsibilities of management of IPR protection are given to different offices under different ministries.

- ☆ **Copyrights:** Nepal Copyright Registrar's Office is in the Ministry of Culture, Tourism and Civil Aviation

- **Patents:** Department of Industry, Ministry of Industry
- **Trademarks:** Department of Industry, Ministry of Industry
- **Biodiversity:** Department of Plant Resources and Department of Wild Life Conservation, Ministry of Forest and Soil Conservation
- **Plant Breeders and Farmers rights:** Nepal Agriculture Research Council, Ministry of Agriculture

There is a need for a separate IPR office under the Government of Nepal with all the facilities in terms of infrastructure, and trained human resources capable of doing necessary activities for the protection, regulation/monitoring and management of all types of IPRs in an integrated manner.

2.3. Legislation

There has not been any separate policy for the protection of IPR so far in Nepal. The legislation and enforcement arrangements which are effective today are as follows.

- Patent, Design and Trademark Act 1965
- Copyright Act, 2002
- Copyright Rules 2004

Efforts have been made time to time to bring out a new Patent Design Act and Trademarks Act in line with TRIPS requirement and for better protection of IPR, but could not materialise due to political reasons. Similarly there are neither any ACTs nor legislative regulations for the protection of IPRs such as Geographical indication, Trade secret and Layout design of Integrated circuits, Plant variety protection, and traditional knowledge (Regmi, 2012).

3. Protection of Patent

3.1. Registration Procedure

Applications for exclusive rights over and an invention are registered in the Department of Industry (DOI). The DOI conducts investigation to assess whether the subject matter mentioned in the application is an invention. A formality examination is made to determine whether the application fulfills the necessary procedural and formal requirements. An invitation to correct is made where necessary documents are missing. Substantive examination is carried out by the examiners, who will decide whether or not the claimed invention should be patented. It will be thoroughly checked whether:

- The claimed invention is patentable subject matter or not.
- The claimed invention is novel, an invention is new if it is not anticipated by the prior art.
- It can be applied for practical purposes for its utility or the industrial applicability.
- The existence of inventive step or not, there must be a clearly identifiable difference between the state of the art and claimed invention.

- ✰ The invention is sufficiently disclosed in the application or not. The application must disclose the invention in a manner sufficiently clear for the invention to be carried out by a person skilled in the art.

Upon completion of formality examination, DOI shall conduct substantive examination. Patents are available for all kinds of products and processes without discrimination as to the technological field.Normally it takes six months to one and a half years for filing to registration of Patent. Patent rights are protected for 7 years with a possibility of two renewal periods of 7 years. The patent holder has the exclusive right to transfer or licence a patent and to request the third person to stop infringement, and may claim compensation in case of infringement.

4. Protection of Industrial Design

In Nepal, effective protection of Design is properly secured only by registration. The creation of Design rights under Nepal Law is also 'first to file within the jurisdiction'. Application to protect the design of any article is made to the DOI, which will register the design in the name of the applicant and issue a certificate. Registration is denied if the design harms the prestige of any individual or institution, or adversely affects public conduct or morality, or undermines the national interest or in case such design had already been registered in the name of any other person.

4.1. Registration Procedure

Upon receipt of application, DOI shall conduct formality examination. Substantive examination is carried out by the examiners and it is thoroughly checked whether;

- ✰ The claimed design is protectable subject matter or not.
- ✰ The claimed design has novelty and originality concept. The words new or original involve the idea of novelty either in the pattern, shape or ornament itself or in the way in which an old pattern shape or ornament is to be applied to some special subject matter.
- ✰ Design can be applied to articles or not. An article to which the design is to be applied must be something which is to be delivered to the purchasers as a finished article.
- ✰ Design has eye appeal or not. There must be a special, peculiar, distinctive, significant or striking appearance something catches the eye.
- ✰ It can be applied for practical purposes for its utility or the industrial applicability.

Registration of industrial designs is for five years, renewable for two more terms of five years.

5. Protection of Trademark Rights

In Nepal, a trademark can be protected on the basis of its registration; no one can claim trademark right on the basis of use within the territory. Full trademark protection is properly secured only by registration. The creation of trademark rights under Nepal Law is 'first to file within the jurisdiction'.

5.1. Protection of Well-known Trademark

Though Nepal is a member country of Paris Convention, it is obliged to protect the well-known trademark in its territory; however, Nepal Law is silent on the provisions of well known trademark and its recognition along with to demarcation between well-known trademark and others. No basic facts or bases are stated in Nepal Law to recognize as a well-known trademark.

In order to protect the well-known trademark, at least, Nepal law has provided that if it is felt that proposed trademark may hurt the prestige of any individual or institution or adversely affect the public conduct or morality or undermine the national interest or the reputation of the trademark of any other person, or if such trademark found to have already been registered in the name of another person, it shall not be registered.

5.2. Registration Procedure

Upon receipt of application, DOI shall conduct formality examination. A formality examination will be made to determine whether the application fulfills the necessary procedural and formal requirements. An invitation to correct will be made where necessary documents are missing. Upon completion of formality examination, DOI shall conduct substantive examination. DOI examines the sample mark submitted under the class to ascertain similarity and Trademark shall be examined for absolute and relative grounds for refusal, that is, whether they are sufficiently distinctive, not deceptive, not immoral etc. such an examination is highly desirable in the interest of consumer protection but for competitors too, and for the trade in general, if the submitted mark is found to be distinctly different, a decision to grant publication for pre opposition is made. The period of pre-opposition is 90 days and if there is no opposition within prescribed time schedule, the decision will be made for registration.

6. Protection of Copyright

Registration of Copyright is not mandatory in Nepal. In accordance with the Copyright Act 2002, and the Copyright regulation 2004, registration is not required for Copyright protection. However, the registration of copyright provides to enter into any licensing, agreement with others in order to full enjoy of exclusive right of copyright.

The Office of Copyright Registrar is in the Ministry of Culture, Tourism and Civil Aviation. It is the authorized agency for royalty collection, administration of royalty collection societies. Punishment for Copyright infringement may take the form of a fine of NRs 10,000-100,000 imprisonment for a maximum of 6 months or both. For repeated infringement the fine is raised to NRs 20,000-200,000 and imprisonment to a maximum of one year. Persons importing unauthorized copies of any work are punished with a fine of NRs. 10,000-100,000 and unauthorized copies are seized. For any other Copyright infringement, punishment is a fine of NRs. 5,000-50,000. In all cases Compensation must be provided to the right holder.

7. Protectable Subject Matters

Literary book, pamphlet, article, thesis lectures, and computer programmes etc

Artistic – Architectural design, photography, painting, sculpture, woodcarving, lithography, work of applied art, illustration, map, plan, etc.

Musical- Musical notation, with or without words, sound recording, etc.

Dramatic- Drama, dramatic music, dumb show, performance etc.

7.1. Registration Procedure

Any owner of the work, sound recording, performance or broadcasting who desires to register any work, sound recording, performance or broadcasting have to submit an application to the Registrar in the prescribed format with specified his/her evidence. Upon receipt of application, Registrar examines it whether

1. The fixation of material/permanent form of work, if there is no fixation, no copyright. In order to protect the work under copyright law, idea should be in physical form or tangible form.
2. The work is original or not, and others

If the Registrar is satisfied on those grounds, he/she shall register such a work, sound recording, performance or broadcasting in the applicant's name on the basis of submitted documents.

Conclusion

Existing IPR protection system is far from being satisfactory in Nepal. It is seen that the inventive and innovative activities are lacking resulting in low productivity and competitiveness. There are rampant infringements of copyright and trademarks. Patents and industrial designs are very few. The implementation and monitoring of the provisions of IPR related acts and rules are weak. The awareness level of general public about IPR is very low. Nepalese laws do not provide for the protection of many types of IPRs such as Geographical indication, Trade secret, and Layout design of Integrated circuits, Plant variety protection, and traditional knowledge. The organizational structure for the protection of IPR is fragmented and weak and the coordination among these organizations are lacking. The human resource development aspects on IPR are also not satisfactory.

Acknowledgement

I am very much grateful to Prof. Dr. Surendra Raj Kafle, Vice Chancellor, NAST, for his guidance and cooperation. Similarly I am also very much grateful to NAM S&T Center and its Director Prof. Dr. Arun Kulshreshtha for organizing the training course on IPR and giving me opportunity to present the paper. Many thanks to my colleagues at NAST for their cooperation in the preparation of this paper.

References

1. Acharya, B.P. 2000. Intellectual Property Rights in the context of Nepal. Proc. Nat. Workshop on IPR in the Nepalese context, NAST, pp. 1-4
2. Copyright Act, 2004. Ministry of Law and Justice, Nepal.

3. Patent, Design and Trademark Act, 1963. Ministry of Law and Justice, Nepal.
4. Regmi, C., 2012. Status of Intellectual Property Rights (IPR) with reference to Genetic Resources in Nepal. Intellectual Property Rights Management in Developing Countries, NAM S&T Center, New Delhi, pp. 158-166.

Chapter 11

An Overview of the Nigerian Patent System

*Davies Olufolake Sola**

Intellectual Property and Technology Transfer Office Coordinator,
Federal Institute of Industrial Research,
Oshodi, Lagos, Nigeria

ABSTRACT

The Patent system facilitates the availability of information by sharing the protected knowledge in an invention. This helps to stimulate the discovery of new technologies in the society. The rationale of the patent system is to encourage technological development while safeguarding the inventor's rights for a limited period of time during which the inventor may have recouped his investments in the development of the technology, and also made profit. In order words, patents serve as an incentive for innovation. A viable patent system can aid in the economic growth and in the improvement of the standard of living of a developing country.

This paper is about the patent system in Nigeria. Nigeria, like many other developing countries is just beginning to take action in improving the patent system, in order to reap the economic and social benefits. Patents are granted in Nigeria under the Patents and Design Act of 1970, Cap 344 of Laws of the Federation of Nigeria 1990. Patents are granted by The Trademarks, Patents and Designs Registry under the Federal Ministry of Trade and Investment. Nigeria is party to the Paris Convention for the Protection of Industrial Property (Accession, 1963), and the Patent Cooperation Treaty (PCT) (Accession, 2005). The stakeholders in the Nigeria patent system include researchers, university, research institutes, industry, and the public at large.

This paper gives a brief history of patents in Nigeria, and the process by which patents are granted. The impact of the patent system and the challenges to the effectiveness of the

* E-mail: folawole2001@yahoo.com

patent system are discussed. Lack of awareness on patents, inadequate human capacity, limited resources, and a lack of institutional capacity to address intellectual property rights issues are some of these challenges.

Government efforts in improving the patent system are highlighted. Recommendations are made on how the patent system in Nigeria can be improved. Creation of awareness on intellectual property rights, human capacity development, improvement of Nigeria patent laws are some of the recommendations of the paper.

Keywords: *Intellectual property rights, Patents, Nigeria, Paris Convention, PCT, Technology.*

1. Introduction

Intellectual property is intangible property which results from individual or collective creativity and inventiveness. The rationale behind the protection of intellectual property is two-fold: One is to give statutory expression to the moral and economic rights of creators in their creations and the rights of the public to access those creations. The second is to promote, as a deliberate act of Government policy, creativity and the dissemination and application of its results and to encourage fair trading which would contribute to economic and social development (WIPO, 2004). The Federal Government of Nigeria (2011) recognizes the need to 'protect Intellectual Property Rights (IPR) and give recognition to creative Nigerians in order to stimulate the development of inventions as well as create wealth for IP owners and country'.

Intellectual property rights are in two categories: Industrial property, which includes inventions (patents), trademarks, industrial designs, and geographic indications of source; and Copyright, which includes literary and artistic works such as novels, paintings, sculptures, etc.

A patent is an exclusive right, granted by the Government to an inventor for his invention for a limited period of time, during which he has the right to prevent others from making, using, selling, or distributing the patented invention without his permission. The World Intellectual Property Organization (WIPO) defines a patent as 'an exclusive right granted for an invention, which is a product or a process that provides, in general, a new way of doing something, or offers a new technical solution to a problem.' A patent is a government-granted property right in an invention.

The patent system has two functions: Protection, which is territorial, *i.e.* by country or by region wherein the patent owner has the exclusive right, during the term of the patent, to 'exploit' the patented invention, including the right to make, hire, sell, use or import the invention, and/or authorise another person to do so usually for a period of 20 years from the date of filing the application. The second function is disclosure. A patent application must contain all of the information necessary to practice or implement the invention. When the patent is published, this information becomes available to the public. This information is technical in nature and is freely available, not bound by territory or time. This means one can learn from patent information disclosed anywhere in the world to promote innovation in the society. Patent information helps to avoid re-inventing the wheel and is a unique source of technical information not found anywhere else.

A patent is a powerful business tool for companies to gain exclusivity over a new product or process, develop a strong market position and earn additional revenues through licensing (WIPO, 2006). Patents promote research and development by enabling the researcher/inventor/investor to re-coup investments and also make profit from his invention. The patent system has attributes which can be of immense benefit especially for developing countries. It enables developing countries to incorporate processes: both the most advanced technology of the industrialized countries and the technology most suitable for the needs of the development process; it encourages inventiveness in developing countries so that, in time, they will also be able to compete in those fields on the international technology market; and also the patent is a source from which valuable information can be obtained (Nasir, 2008).

A strong patent system encourages innovation and economic growth. Patents are a general characteristic of an industrialized society, and the indicator of the highest level of technological development (Ituku, 2011).

This paper will give an overview of the Nigerian patent system. It presents a brief history of the patent system, examines the challenges that exist within the system, and makes recommendations to overcome them.

2. History of Patents in Nigeria

Patents in Nigeria date back to the colonial era. The first patent legislation enacted in Nigeria was the Patents Ordinance No. 17 of 1900 and the Patents Proclamation Ordinance No. 27 of 1900 which both applied to the Colony of Lagos and the Southern Protectorate; and the Patents Proclamation Ordinance No. 12 of 1902 which applied to the Northern Protectorate. These laws paved the way for the patents administration system in Nigeria. Later on, after the amalgamation of the Southern and Northern protectorates, these statutes were replaced by the Patents Ordinance of 1916 later renamed and re-enacted as the Registration of United Kingdom Patents Ordinance of 1925 (Cap 182 Laws of the Federation of Nigeria and Lagos 1958).

Whereas, the 1900 ordinances provided for an independent patent system; the 1925 ordinance merely extended the validity of patents granted in the UK to Nigeria, provided an application to register the same was made to the registrar of patents in Nigeria within 3 years of the grant of the patent in the United Kingdom. Thus the independent patenting system provided for under the 1900 ordinances was terminated, and Nigeria became an extension of the territory of application of a United Kingdom patent.

This situation remained until 1970, when the Patents and Designs Decree No. 60 (now Patents and Designs Act) was enacted. This Act created a Nigerian patent system and administration and was published as chapter 344 of the Laws of Federation of Nigeria 1990.

3. Legal Framework for Patent Protection

In Nigeria, Patent can be obtained at the national and international level. The patent protection is governed by the Nigerian Patents and Designs Act of 1990 which is being implemented by the Trademarks, Patents and Designs Registry currently under the Federal Ministry of Trade and Investment. Nigeria has also concluded some multilateral treaties in the field of patents and which are effective to-date. These include the 1883 Paris Convention on Industrial Property; the 1970 Patent Cooperation Treaty (PCT); the 1971 Strasbourg Agreement concerning International Patent Classification; the 1979 Budapest Treaty on the Deposit of Micro-organisms and the 1994 Agreement on Trade Related aspects of Intellectual Property (TRIPS).

3.1 Conditions for Patentability

According to the Nigerian Patents and Designs Act of 1990, an Invention is patentable in Nigeria if

a. It is new, results from and inventive activity and is capable of industrial application; or
b. It constitutes an improvement upon a patented invention and also is new, results from inventive activity and is capable of industrial application.

An invention is capable of industrial application if can be manufactured in any kind of industry including agriculture.

Patents cannot be obtained in respect of

- Plant or animal varieties or essentially biological processes for the production of plants or animals (except microbiological processes and their processes)
- Inventions, the publication or exploitation of which would be contrary to public order or morality; or
- Principles and discoveries of a scientific nature.

3.2 Rights Conferred, Scope and Exceptions

The right to a patent in respect of an invention is vested in the person, who, whether or not he is the true inventor, is the first to file an application, or the first to validly claim a foreign priority for an application, in respect of the invention. A patent is granted for a period of 20 years form the date of filing of the patent application.

Section 6(1) of the act stipulates the rights conferred upon a patentee:

A patent confers upon the patentee the right to preclude any other person from doing any of the following acts:

(a) Where the patent has been granted in respect of a product, the act of making, importing selling or using the product, or stocking it for the purpose of sale or use; and

(b) Where the patent has been granted in respect of a process, the art of applying the process or doing, in respect of a product obtained directly by means of the process, any of the acts mentioned in paragraph (a) of this subsection.

Section 6(2) deals with the scope of protection, while 6(3) lays down the exceptions to the patent rights.

(2) The scope of the protection conferred by a patent shall be determined by the terms of the claims; and the description (and the plans and drawings, if any) included in the patent shall be used to interpret the claims.

(3) The rights under a patent.

(a) shall extend only to acts done for industrial or commercial purposes only; and

(b) Shall not extend to acts done in respect of a product covered by the patent after the product has been lawfully sold in Nigeria, except insofar as the patent makes provision for a special application of the product, in which case the special application shall continue to be reserved to the patentee notwithstanding this paragraph.

3.3 Patent Examination

Patents are granted without substantive examination by the Registrar. Examination is only to confirm that the requirements of formal registration are met, and not to establish whether the subject of the application is patentable, or whether the description and claims satisfy the requirements, or whether a prior application has been made, or patent granted as a result of such an application.

Section 4 of the Patent and Designs Act provides that:

The registrar shall examine the application, and if he is satisfied that all the documents which are required to be submitted with the application have been submitted, shall grant the patent without enquiring into the questions

(a) Whether the subject of the application is patentable under section 1.

(b) Whether the description of the invention and claims made comply with the requirement that they must be sufficiently clear and complete as to enable a person skilled in the art or field of knowledge to which the invention relate be able to put it into effect.

(c) Whether there is a prior application or a prior grant of a patent for the same invention has been made in Nigeria.

Thus the Nigerian patent system is called the "Deposit" system of patenting. Section 4(4) of the Patent and Design act states that Patents are granted at the risk of the patentee and without guarantee of their validity.

3.4 Patent Application Procedure

3.4.1 Filing

To obtain a patent for an invention in Nigeria, an application is filed to the Registrar, Patents and Trademark Registry. The formal requirements for a patent application are set out in section 3 of the Patent and Designs Act, which provides that every patent application

(a) Shall be made to the Registrar and shall contain

(i) The applicant's full name and address and if that address is outside Nigeria, an address for service in Nigeria,

(ii) A description of the relevant invention with any appropriate plans and drawings,

(iii) A claim or claims, and

(iv) Such other matter as maybe prescribed; and

(b) The application will be accompanied by

(i) The prescribed fee of 15,000 for local (Non-convention), and 25,000 for overseas (Convention) patent applications.

(ii) where appropriate, a declaration signed by the true inventor requesting that he be mentioned as such in the patent and giving his name and address, and

(iii) If the application is made by an agent, a signed power of attorney

The description of the invention shall disclose the relevant invention in a manner sufficiently clear and complete for the invention to be put into effect by a person skilled in the art in the field of knowledge to which the invention relates. Also the claim(s) shall state the protection being sought within the limit of the description.

A patent application shall relate to only one invention, but may include in connection with that invention

(a) Claims

(i) For any number of products

(ii) For any number of manufacturing processes for those products, and

(iii) For any number of applications of those products; and

(b) Claims

(i) For any number of processes, and

(ii) For the means of working those processes, for the resulting product or products and for the application of those products.

(c) Foreign Priority

If an applicant seeks to claim a foreign priority for an earlier application made in a country outside Nigeria, he shall append in the application submitted at the Patent Office, the date and number of the foreign application, the country where the foreign application was made, and the name of the person who made the foreign application. Also within three months of submission of the application in the Nigerian Patent Office, the applicant is expected to furnish the Registrar with a copy of the earlier application certified by the Industrial Property Office (or its equivalent) in the country where the application was made.

3.4.2 Examination Phase

After the submission of the application, the Registrar will examine the application to ensure it conforms to the formal requirements.

☆ Where the formal requirements are not met, the application shall be rejected by the Registrar.

- Where a patent application relates to more than one invention, the Registrar will not reject the application as a result of this. Instead, he shall invite the applicant to restrict the application to one invention as required by law for the application to be qualified for approval.
- Where the necessary procedures are not followed in respect of foreign priority, the Registrar shall disregard the request.

3.4.3 Grant of Patent

Where a patent application satisfies the formal requirements as provided in the Patents and Designs Act, the patent shall be granted as applied for without further examination as to the conditions of patentability, full disclosure of the description and the requirements of foreign priority. This is because at the moment, the Patent Act in Nigeria does not provide for substantive examination. Where the requirements of foreign priority are met, when the patent is granted the foreign priority claimed shall be mentioned in the patent.

Patent is granted and registered by the Registrar by the issue to the patentee of a document containing the following:

(a) the number of the patent in order of grant;

(b) the name and address of the patentee and, if that address is outside Nigeria, an address for service in Nigeria;

(c) the dates of the patent application and the grant;

(d) if foreign priority is claimed–

(i) an indication of the fact, and

(ii) the number and date of the application on which the claim is based and the name of the country where it was made.

(iii) the description of the invention (with any relevant plans and drawings) and the claims, and

(iv) where appropriate, the name and address of the true inventor.

3.4.4 Registration and Publication of Patent after Grant

Upon the grant of the patent, the Registrar shall maintain a register of patents which consists of duplicates of the documents issued to the patentee and all other important information with respect to the patent. The Registrar shall also publish a notification of the grant containing detailed information on the patent except the description

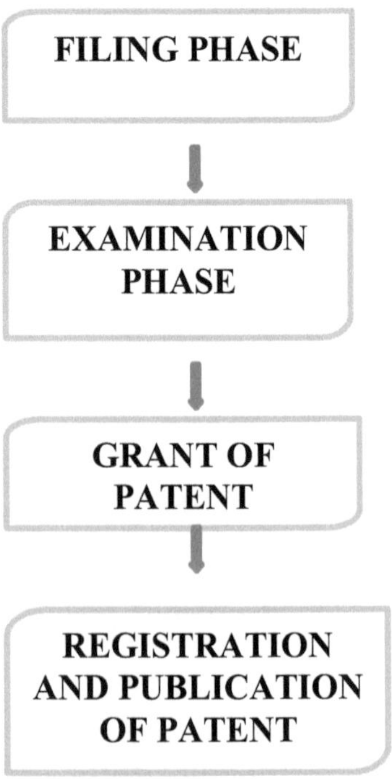

Figure 11.1: Patent Application Procedure.

and the plans and drawings, if any; or if a summary form of notification is prescribed, a notification in that form.

3.5 Licensing

A patent needs to be exploited effectively for it to be of benefit to its owner. This depends on the commercial success of a product which is based on the patent. One of the ways in which an inventor may choose to exploit his invention is by granting licenses to interested parties to use a patent in exchange for royalty. The Nigerian Patent Law provides for the granting of licenses, specifically for the working of patented inventions by other persons. Sections 10 and 23 of the 1990 Act deal with voluntary licences, licences of right and Contractual licences respectively while Section 11 and schedule 1 relate to non-voluntary licences *i.e.* compulsory licences and the use of patented inventions for the service of Government Agencies.

3.6 Enforcement of Patents

3.6.1 Infringement of Rights

Patent rights give the owner the opportunity prevent or stop competitors from copying products of his invention. Infringement or the violation of the rights under a patent is dealt with in Section 25 of the 1990 Act. The onus lies on the patent owner to identify and take action against infringers. Section 25(2) of the Patent and Designs Act of Nigeria provides that

"An infringement of the rights of a patentee or design owner shall be actionable at the suit of the patentee or design owner in question; and in any action for such an infringement all such relief by way of damages, injunction, accounts or otherwise shall be available to the plaintiff as is available in any corresponding proceedings in respect of the infringement of other proprietary rights".

3.6.2 Legal Proceedings

There are various civil remedies available to compensate aggrieved patent owners. Section 26 of the Patent and Designs Act deals with the subject of legal proceedings. It provides that the provisions of the Trade Marks Act applicable to legal proceedings shall apply with necessary modifications to legal proceeding under this Act. Jurisdiction of legal proceedings with respect to patent rights is vested in the Federal High Court.

4. Agencies Responsible for the Registration, Administration and Promotion of the Patent System in Nigeria

4.1 Trademarks, Patents and Designs Registry

The Trademarks, Patents and Designs Registry, under the Federal Ministry of Trade and Investment is the administrative body for the protection of patents in Nigeria.

4.2 National Office for Technology Acquisition and Promotion (NOTAP)

The National Office for Technology Acquisition and Promotion (NOTAP) under the Federal Ministry of Science and Technology plays a vital role in assisting researchers from tertiary institutions and research institutes to patent their inventions. NOTAP was established in 1979, when the government recognized that the transfer of technology had become a viable instrument for accelerated development of enterprises and countries with transnational movement of technology benefiting both suppliers and donors of technology (Nasir, 2008).

The roles of NOTAP in this regard are two folds. First, bearing in mind that the patent law does not make provision for substantive examination of patents and patents are only granted based on satisfying the formal requirements; NOTAP assists researchers to assess their inventions and add technical value to them before the inventions are filed at the Patent Registry for the grant of patent. Secondly, NOTAP pays the filing fees for patent applications filed by the Office on behalf of Nigerian inventors. NOTAP plays these roles in pursuance of its mandates in facilitating the acquisition of foreign technology and promoting the development of indigenous technology in Nigeria.

Table 11.1 shows the patent submitted to the Patent Registry over a nine-year period. Between 1999 and 2008 September, 233 patent applications were submitted through NOTAP, and 61 of these were granted.

Table 11.1: Summary of R&D Results/Inventions Submitted to NOTAP for Assistance to File Application for Patent January,1999–September, 2008

Year	*Number of Inventions Submitted to NOTAP*	*No. of Patents Filed by NOTAP at the Patent Registry*	*No. of Patent Applications Pending (Under evaluation/ awaiting response from inventor)*	*No. of Patent Applications Granted by the Registry*
1999	2	1	1	1
2000	32	14	18	9
2001	14	8	6	3
2002	17	2	15	3
2003	8	0	8	0
2004	27	12	15	7
2005	41	14	27	18
2006	24	16	8	14
2007	28	13	15	4
2008 Sept.	40	6	3	2
TOTAL	233	86	147	61

Source: Ibigbami and Orji (2009)

4.2.1 Patent Information Documentation Centre (PIDC)

NOTAP also maintains the PIDC which is a network of information that links the National Office with other Patent Information Centres in the world. It is an avenue through which information on industrial property are sought globally. The PIDC enables NOTAP to have access to technology information contained in patent documents and these are made available to interested users such as researchers, patent attorneys, private investors, and entrepreneurs.

4.2.2 Establishment of Intellectual Property and Technology Transfer Offices (IPTTO)

As at 2012, NOTAP has established over thirty Intellectual Property and Technology Transfer Offices (IPTTOs) in Universities, Polytechnics and Research Institutions in Nigeria, to promote interaction and strengthen the linkage between University/Research Institutions and Industries.

The IPTTOs are designed to develop a robust intellectual Property Rights portfolio through patenting, copyright, technology licensing; to support the Institutions' initiative in developing patent culture. The IPTTOs also set into motion the formal system of incentives and reward that encourages individual researchers to be involved in partnerships.

One of such IPTTOs was established in 2007 at the Federal Institute of Industrial Research, Oshodi. The activities at the office include, creation of awareness of Intellectual Property, to which end, a weekly bulletin named 'IP Awareness' is published; patent searches, and patent drafting. The office also facilitates collaboration between the Institute and Industry. The first Intellectual Policy for the Institute has been drafted.

5. Challenges to the Nigerian Patent System

The patent system has not had any significant impact on the Nigerian society. The patent system was basically conceived as an important tool to stimulate indigenous technological development, promote domestic inventive activity and enhance the exploitation (Mengistie, 2003). However, Nigeria is still struggling to benefit from its efforts at utilizing the patent system. This situation can be attributed to several factors:

5.1 Low Level of Awareness of Patents

One of the major challenges of the Nigerian patent system is the low level of awareness of the intellectual Property system in general and the patent system in particular. Oyewale (2006) noted that "patent education is poor in Nigerian institutions and researchers were not informed about patent issues".

5.2 Low Patent Culture

The Intellectual Property System in Nigeria is characterized by a low patent culture. Very little inventions emanating from the tertiary and research institutions are patentable (Owoseni, 2012). Essien (2011) catalogues the experience of Nigerian Inventors in filing and working inventions. Some of the challenges experienced are low inventive activities and poor education of the Nigerian inventor on the patentability criteria of invention especially novelty and non-obviousness. He also notes that Nigeria patents are considered weak by potential licensors because they are not given substantive examination and are at risk to the inventor. Ibigbami and

Orji (2008) also noted that "the low turnout of patents in Nigeria is as a result of lack of IP culture in the tertiary and research institutes' environment and the society in its entirety. Most of the patents granted by the Patent Registry are Foreign owned. Table 11.2 shows that between 1998 and 2007, a total of 2398 foreign patents were granted, while only 318 local patents were granted. Analysis of the samples of patents registered in Nigeria in 2010 shows that 10 per cent of the patents registered are local patents (Owoseni, 2012). The remaining 90 per cent are foreign patents. This low level of evolution of patents is also a reflection of current level of technological development, using patent as one of the indices or determinants of economic growth.

Table 11.2: No. of Patent Applications Filed and Granted in Nigeria from 2000 to 2007

Years	*Foreign Patents (Conventional)*		*Local Patents (Non-conventional)*	
	No. Filed	*No. Granted*	*No. Filed*	*No. Granted*
2000	473	351	49	42
2001	476	142	34	13
2002	466	62	36	3
2003	450	179	55	15
2004	425	421	88	40
2005	297	316	81	64
2006	255	212	95	87
2007	565	218	84	33
TOTAL	4257	2398	566	318

Source: NOTAP.

5.3 Research-Industry Linkages

There is little or no linkage between the research institutions and the industry in Nigeria. The institutions and the industry are working at cross purposes. Most researchers in the research institutions carry out research activities for publication to earn their promotion. Therefore the research results emanating from the institutions are not meeting the needs of the industry (Owoseni, 2011). In a study conducted by Oyewale (2005), it was observed that "Because of information gap between the Nigerian academia and industrial firms, utilisation of the inventions/research results by industrial firms was low, and such were probably for resolution of problems, rather than commercialising new inventions. Research and development outputs of Nigeria's institutions/institutes were not satisfactory enough to the firms, possibly because over 50 per cent of the researchers studied conducted knowledge-driven researches, while about just 38 per cent conducted market-driven researches, which may be relevant to industrial needs." The industrialists depend solely on research centres in their parent companies abroad. This lack of linkages hampers the development of research activities and patentable inventions.

5.4 Premature Disclosure of Inventions

Premature disclosure of inventions is rampant in universities and research institutions because of the 'publish or perish' syndrome. This is corroborated by Oyewale (2006). In his study, he discovered that 50 per cent of a group of researchers had published their research findings in journals, and therefore could not patent. He stated that "the university system is tilted against patents as universities give papers higher priority than they do patents. Therefore, researchers prefer to publish papers".

5.5 Inadequate Human Capacity

Technical skills and capabilities required to carry out intensive innovative and inventive activities have not been fully developed, and for cases in which research works which require low technical know-how are carried out to the final, they lack the finesse required to make them meet up with international standards. In addition to this, there are few patent practitioners who specialize in drafting patent applications, and firms which offer such services. Therefore, patent drafting is very expensive.

5.6 Poor Infrastructure

Poor infrastructures such as irregular power and water supply, lack of good access roads, poor telecommunications system all impact on development of creative and inventive works and consequently hamper the development of intellectual property rights system.

It is interesting to note that the Trademarks, Patents and Designs Registry has no computerized databases for conducting searches on national patents. Patent searches take too long compared to developed countries, where a detailed report takes a few days to at most a couple of weeks.

5.7 Lack of Institutional Capacity and Ineffective Enforcement of Patent Right

Nigerian patent law is ineffectively enforced against the action of infringers. Patent enforcement is weak, and judicial procedures are slow. Government's lack of institutional capacity to address IPR issues is a major constraint to enforcement. Infringement actions such as court injunctions, payment of damages, court order, are either not followed or the implementation processes are cumbersome and thereby discouraging. The reasons for this are sometimes attributable to lack of required capabilities on the part of the law enforcement agents such as the Police, Patent Attorneys and Judges handling the intellectual property cases.

6. Recommendations

In order to induce rapid technological advances within the context of the overall economic development of a country, it is important for a nation to create the necessary enabling environment. The following are suggestions which are essential to the creation of this desired environment:

6.1 Creation of Awareness Program on Intellectual Property Rights

Government needs to intensify its efforts in increasing the level of awareness on intellectual property at all educational levels, through special programmes, and incorporation of the teaching of IPRs in the curricula of tertiary institutions and secondary schools. The level of awareness and understanding of IP among all stakeholders can be increased through organization of Workshops and sensitization programmes on IP, and the dissemination of the technology information contained in patent documents to researchers and scientists.

6.2 Capacity Building

Human capacity should be enhanced at three levels:

- ✰ Training of IP professionals to enable them conduct substantive examination of inventions in line with international standards. Empowerment of the patent registry officials to conduct substantive examination, in order to have patents which measure up to international standards.
- ✰ Building local capacities for local inventors and intellectual property managers to promote demand-driven R& D and stimulate transfer of technology.
- ✰ Developing the capability of professional IP service providers Patent Attorneys and Judges to handle IP cases efficiently and timely.

6.3. Improvement of infrastructure

As at the time of writing this paper, the Nigerian Trademarks, Patents and Designs Registry has no presence on the Internet. There is an urgent need to launch a website to provide information on Nigerian intellectual property to the world; also in order to facilitate access to patent information; Government needs to upgrade the facilities at the Trademarks, Patents and Designs Registry by computerizing Nigerian patent data, so that interested parties can conduct searches on national patents.

6.4 Promotion of Research-Industry Linkages

Universities and research institutions should establish linkages with industrial firms, such that the inventions generated during the course of their research can be utilized. There is a need to study the challenges in this present system of linking Universities and Research Institutes' with Industry, and explore best practises in linkages, emulating success stories in developed countries. Patents can serve as bridges between research and industry, whereby industrial firms acquire and exploit patents emanating from universities and research institutes (Oyewale, 2005).

6.5 Review of Intellectual Property Laws

The importance of an appropriate patent legislation that creates the necessary enabling environment cannot be over-emphasized. Government needs to review and update the Patent Law to meet international standards.

6.6 Enforcement of Intellectual Property Law

The existence of an appropriate mechanism for the enforcement of patent rights is vital to the improvement of the patent system. The enforcement of Nigerian patent laws should be strengthened, to serve as deterrents to infringers. In order to reap the benefits of patent protection it is vital that patents be enforced in a timely and cost effective manner. Ineffective patent enforcement will discourage inventors and ultimately hinder economic growth. A judicial system free from political influence and free from corruption is necessary to ensure proper enforcement of IPRs. The judges should be familiar with the legal aspect of IPRs and have understanding of science and technology.

Conclusion

In order to improve the Nigerian Patent System, the first line of action is to foster a patent culture in the society through creation of awareness of the patent system, trainings, and capacity building on intellectual property protection in various sectors. The patent law also needs to be amended to incorporate substantive examination in the granting of patents, to minimize the granting of 'weak patents' at the risk of inventors. Linkages need to be promoted between Universities and Research Institutions, and Industry, such that research will be conducted to meet industry needs, and not just to meet publication target for promotion. Instead, patents should be criteria for promotion.

Lastly, enforcement of patents should be strengthened such that inventors would be encouraged to bring their inventions forward for patenting without fear of their rights being infringed with impunity.

Acknowledgements

Many thanks to Mrs. Caroline T. Owoseni of NOTAP, for her valuable suggestions and information in writing this paper.

References

1. Essien, Okon E., 2011. The experiences of Nigerian inventors in filing and working patents in Nigeria. Paper Presented at the WIPO Workshop on Patent Information-Patent Search Strategies and Techniques, Abuja, July 13-15, 2011.
2. Federal Government of Nigeria, 2011. Science and Techology and Innovation (STI) Policy. http://www.fmst.gov.ng/uploadfil/sti_policy2011.pdf (Accessed 3 March 2012)
3. Getachew, Mengistie, 2003. Impact of the international patent system on developing countries. Assemblies of the member states of WIPO, 39th Series of Meetings, Geneva, September 22-October 1, 2003.http://www.wipo.int/edocs/mdocs/govbody/en/a_39/a_39_13_add_1.pdf(Accessed 10 June, 2012)
4. Ibigbami, Victor M. and Orji, Christopher U. (2009). A review of the Nigerian system of intellectual property. In: CAS-IP NPI. 2009. Institutionalization of Intellectual Property Management: Case Studies from Four Agricultural Research Institutions in Developing Countries. CAS-IP, Rome, Italy.

5. Ituku, Elangi B., 2011. Promotion of innovation: Usefulness and value of patent information for public and private sectors. Paper Presented at the WIPO Workshop on Patent Information- Patent Search Strategies and Techniques, Abuja, July 13-15, 2011.
6. La Flame Jr. Michael., 2010. The European patent system: an overview and critique. Houston Journal of International Law, 23(3), pp. 608-634. *www.hjil.org/ArticleFiles/LaFlame.pdf (Accessed 30 May, 2012)*
7. Nasir, J.M., 2007. The legal regime for the protection and promotion of patents in Nigeria. The Advocate: A Journal of Contemporary Legal Issues, Vol. 11.,pp.103-128. http://dspace.unijos.edu.ng/bitstream/10485/362/1/103-128.pdf *(Accessed June 1, 2012)*
8. Nasir, J.M., 2008. Patents and transfer of technology in Nigeria's development. The Advocate: A Journal of Contemporary Legal Issues, 12(12), pp. 31-71. http://dspace.unijos.edu.ng/bitstream/10485/342/1/31-71.pdf *(Accessed June 1, 2012)*
9. Nigeria Patents and Designs Act. http://www.nigeria-law.org/Patents per cent 20and per cent 20Designs per cent 20Act.htm (Accessed 30 May, 2012)
10. Okongwu, D.A., 2006. Highlights of the conclusions and recommendations of Nigeria's intellectual property audit. Paper Presented at the WIPO-NOTAP Workshop on Developing a National Intellectual Property Strategy. Abuja, August 28-29, 2006.
11. Owoseni, C.T. and Akinkunmi Y.O., 2011. Status and Challenges of Intellectual Property Rights in West African Countries. Unpublished Paper.
12. Owoseni, C.T., 2011. Procedures for filing and grant of patent in Nigeria. Unpublished paper
13. Owoseni, Caroline T., 2001. New developments and challenges in the protection of intellectual property rights. A Nigerian perspective. Paper Presented at the International Conference on Intellectual Property, the Internet, Electronic Commerce and Traditional Knowledge. Sofia, Bulgaria, May 29-31, 2001. http://portal.unesco.org/en/files/11610/10515189411sof01_2_7.pdf/sof01_2_7.pdf (Accessed 1 June, 2012)
14. Oyewale, A.A., 2005. Addressing the research-industry linkage impasse in Nigeria: the critical issues and implementation strategies. Paper Presented at the Third International Globelics Conference – Africa 2005, Organized by the Global Network for the Economics of Learning, Innovation and Competence (Globelics),Tshwane University of Technology, Tshwane, South Africa, October 31-November 4, 2005. http://www.globelics2005africa.org.za/papers/p0032/Globelics2005_Adesina per cent 20Ayobami per cent 20Oyewale.pdf (Accessed 1 June, 2012)
15. Oyewale, A.A. 2006. Nigeria's research system and the culture of patenting. D.I.M.E. Conference on Intellectual Property Rights for Business and Society, London, September 14-15 2006. http://www.dime-eu.org/files/active/0/Oyewale.pdf (Accessed 1 June, 2012)

16. Umahi, Okechukwu Timothy.2011. Access to Medicines: The Colonial Impacts on Patent Law of Nigeria. http://ssrn.com/abstract=1975928 or http://dx.doi.org/10.2139/ssrn.1975928 (Accessed 2 June 2012)
17. Umar, Muhammad, 2011. Development of innovation and MSMEs in Nigeria: challenges for local innovators. Paper Presented at the WIPO Workshop on Patent Information- Patent Search Strategies and Techniques, Abuja, July 13-15, 2011.
18. WIPO(2004). WIPO Intellectual Property Handbook: Policy, Law and Use. Geneva.
19. WIPO (2006). Inventing the future: an introduction to patents for small and medium sized enterprises. Intellectual Property for Business Series No. 3.
20. Yoshikazu, Tani 2003. Overview of the Japanese Patent System.http://www.taniabe.co.jp/J/information/main-eng005.pdf (Accessed 10 June 2012)

Chapter 12

Copyright Awareness in Nigeria's Film Industry: Empirical Evidence

*Adelowo Caleb M.**

Senior Research Officer, National Centre for Technology Management,
(Federal Ministry of Science and Technology)
PMB 012, Obafemi Awolowo University,
Ile-Ife, Nigeria

ABSTRACT

Piracy, illegal distribution of copyrighted works and lack of motivation for creativities are the resultant effects of inadequate promotion and awareness of intellectual property right in the creative industry. This paper assesses the level awareness of copyright in the creative industry in Nigeria using Nollywood as a case study. Nollywood is the film industry in Nigeria which attracts a lot of interested parties both within and outside the country due essentially to how the industry evolved over time. The industry is marred by various activities ranging from illegal distribution of works to piracy which has denied several authors and actors of their royalties. Questionnaire method was adopted to assess the awareness of copyright among the actors within the industry. Out of 100 questionnaires administered, 54 per cent were returned and analysed. The result shows that over 90 per cent of the actors in the industry are not aware of the property rights in the works. Therefore, it is imperative at this time to sensitise the public through various means to address the issue. Also, there is the need to assess the contribution of copyright to the economy so as to design robust policy to promote the sector.

***Keywords**: Nollywood, Copyright, Piracy, Creative industry, Nigeria.*

---

* E-mail: caleb.adelowo@nacetem.org and calebakinrinade@yahoo.com

1. Introduction

Copyright is a branch of intellectual property which confers exclusive right on authors of literary and artistic works.[1] The legal protection flows from the fact that an author independently creates the work and that his or her "expression" of an original work is owned by him/her contrary to the novelty standard in patents which focuses on the newness of a useful idea or concept as opposed to the expression of that idea. Copyright extends only to the expression of ideas and concepts and not to the ideas or concepts themselves (Kamil, 2004).

Thus, in practice, copyright protection has been extended to works that a layman might consider neither literary nor artistic works. Examples are computer software and technical documentation. It is essential to note that copyright may subsist in an article, product or process with other Intellectual Property Rights (IPRs). For instance, in computer software, industrial design and trade secret protection may co-exist with copyright. It should be noted as well that copyright does not require any formality for its protection except in some jurisdictions like the USA where fixation and deposit of a copy is a prerequisite. This means that a copy of the work has to be deposited in the national library for registration.

The economic implication of copyright has brought justification to the time, energy and other resources committed to its generation. Nigeria's film industry generated over US $200 million in export sales between 1992 and 2005. The industry provides job opportunities for many and serves as wealth creation sources for the creators in the industry. It turns out more than 1,000 film titles per annum (Nigeria Copyright Commission, 2005).

Despite the huge potentials of this industry, one of the critical challenges facing Nigerian film industry (Nollywood) is low awareness of copyright which has made the industry become a haven of pirates thereby denying the nation of the income which would have accrued through taxation and other socio-economic benefit like employment and improved standard of living, especially to actors, producers and government. Therefore, this paper assesses the level of copyright awareness in the film industry (Nollywood) and provides policy suggestions to promote copyright awareness among the players to curb illegal copy and distribution of copyrighted works. The paper also bridges the literature gap on Nigeria's copyright matters.

2. Literature Review on Copyright Protection in Nigeria

The primary legislation is the Nigerian Copyright Act Cap. C.28, Laws of the Federation of Nigeria 2004, initially passed in 1988, amended in 1992 and 1999 and re-codified in 2004.

The other laws pertaining to anti-piracy measures and copyright enforcement are:

- Copyright (Collecting Societies) Regulations 1993;
- Copyright (Video Rental) Regulations 1999;

---

1 Article 9 (1), Berne Convention

- Copyright (Security Devices) Regulations 1999;
- Copyright (Optical Discs Plants) Regulation 2006; and
- Copyright (Collective Management Organisation Regulation, 2007).

Nigeria is a signatory to several international treaties for the protection of copyright and related rights of which cannot be binding except they are ratified by law maker and are incorporated into the local legislation. The copyright related conventions to which Nigeria is signatory include:

- Universal Copyright Convention (UCC),
- International Convention for the Protection of Performers, Producers of Phonograms and Broadcasting Organisations (Rome Convention),
- Berne Convention for the Protection of Literary and Artistic Works (Berne Convention),
- Convention Establishing the World Intellectual Property Organization (WIPO Convention),
- Agreement on Trade Related Aspect of Intellectual Property Rights (TRIPS) within the Framework of GATT,
- WIPO Performances and Phonograms Treaty; and
- WIPO Copyright Treaty[2].

The last two are called internet treaties as it empowers the country to protect the works on the internet and allow the use of rights management system.

2.1. The Nigerian Copyright Commission (NCC)

Copyright protection in Nigeria is enshrined in chapter 68 of the Law of Federal Republic of Nigeria 1990 as amended, where provision is made for both copyright and related rights.

In the analysis of the law, it was discovered that the proper provision has been made for the administration of works in the country but not until 1989 copyright council was established to manage the works in the creative industries. By virtue of the increasing responsibilities of the council, in 1996, the Council was upgraded to the status of a Commission. The Nigerian Copyright Act has subsequently been amended in 1992 and 1999 and now incorporated as Copyright Act CAP C28 Laws of the Federation of Nigeria 2004 to cope with increasing national and international responsibilities within the copyright system.

At present, the Commission is an Agency of the Federal Government of Nigeria under the Federal Ministry of Justice, responsible for all copyright matters in Nigeria, with an expanded mandate for the administration of copyright; enforcement of copyright; regulation of Copyright-based Industries (CRI); and promotion of copyright in Nigeria.

---

2 Ibigbami V. M. and Christopher U. O (2009), A Review of the Nigerian System of Intellectual Property: A Case Study *under NABDA/CAS-IP NPI Collaboration Project.*

The duties of the agency are well spelt out in its mandate which involves keeping of databank of works and their respective authors in order to monitor the rights and for the authors to benefit maximally from their efforts. Various initiatives and policies are developed to ensure that the Agency lives up to expectation in terms of rights administration in the country. One of these initiatives is Strategic Action against Piracy (STRAP) which so far has been effective but not enough to tackle the menace of piracy in the country. STRAP was introduced by The Nigerian Copyright Commission as the national anti-piracy campaign for effective protection against piracy and all forms of intellectual property theft in 2005.

The aims of the initiative are to combat all forms of piracy of music, film, software, books and all other protected works, create a conducive environment for copyright protection for all categories of works, empower local industries, create opportunities for legitimate distribution of protected works and attract foreign investment and through a sustained campaign, restore the image of Nigeria as a country that upholds the ideals of creativity (NCC, 2010).

The commission also under the STRAP carries out an enlightenment programme to create awareness of copyright and educate the public on the dangers of piracy to the right holders and the economy at large. Likewise, the Commission in its enlightenment campaign claimed that it has put in place a means to intensify efforts to enforce rights through Copyright Litigation, Assistance and Mediation Programme (CLAMP). Over the year, the number of copyright cases handled by the commission has not been made public, while several raids have been carried out to curb illegal rental clubs operating almost at every corners of the country.

The Copyright Video Rental and the Copyright Security Devices Regulations is a cushion to the Commission's enforcement drive. This was introduced to sanitise the activities in the film and music sub-sectors primarily for the benefit of film producers, artistes, musicians and investors to usher in the use of authorised rental copies for use by video rental operators in the film sub-sector, and a security device affixed to genuine works (hologram) in the music sub-sector. These measures promise to protect the economic interest of right holders. In order to further enhance the earnings of right owners, the Commission encourages the formation of collecting societies pursuant to Section 32(b) of the Nigerian Copyright Act. Accordingly, whereas the Performing and Mechanical Rights Society of Nigeria, (PMRS) and more recently, Musical Copyright Society of Nigeria (MCSN) have been approved as collecting societies for musical works, the Reproduction Rights Society of Nigeria (REPRONIG) has been authorised to handle rights in the literary works.

A collecting society is an association of copyright owners, which has as its objectives the negotiating, and granting of licenses, collection and distribution of royalties in respect of copyrighted works of its members.

In addition, the Commission through its Monitoring Unit monitors the broadcasts of local television, cable and satellite stations to check the occurrence of infringement of rights in the broadcasting industry. Defaulting broadcasting stations are formally notified to pay royalties to author(s) whose works are used or face the option of prosecution in the law court. Some of the achievements made so far by the agencies are discussed hereunder.

From May 2005 to May 2007, STRAP activities resulted in the inspections of plants and outlets for CD, optical disc and video productions and rentals all over the country to verify that they operated within the law. In addition, over 115 operations were carried out against book, music, film, software and broadcast counterfeiters. The outcomes reveals that 373 suspects arrested, 8,346,815 pirated works were seized, 15 new copyright cases brought to court, resulting, so far, in four convictions: two in the Federal High Court of Maiduguri for counterfeiting books and two in Federal High Court of Calabar for broadcast piracy, the public destruction (burning) of seized counterfeit products with an estimated market value of N1,263,000,000 (US$10,710,000) and 15 optical disc plants were brought under regulation through the new Optical Discs Plant Regulation issued in December 2006 (WIPO, 2008, NCC, 2010).

STRAP attributed a huge part of its success to coordinated inter-agency collaboration among enforcement agencies such as the police, customs service, the Standards Organisation of Nigeria, the National Food and Drug Administration and Control (NAFDAC) and the Economic and Financial Crimes Commission (EFCC) as well as the industry players.

2.2. The National Film Video Censors Board

The National Film and Video Censors Board is the regulatory body set up by Act No.85 of 1993 to regulate the film and video industry in Nigeria. The Board is empowered by law to classify all films and videos whether imported or produced locally. It is also the duty of the Board to register all films and video outlets[3] across the country and to keep a register of such registered outlets among other functions; to license to a person to exhibit films and video works and premises for the purposes of exhibiting films and video works. The establishment of the Board therefore empowers it to assess, classify and register films and video works and the film outlets across the country and monitor the films and film outlets.

It is clear from the mandate of the Board that most of their activities are directed to ensure that films that are released into circulation meet the standard quality and societal moral standards. The question of rights management and collecting societies for the right-owners in the industry are catered for through certifying the rental outlets of the works in the industry and registering the films which are produced from the industry.

Having considered the two key organisations that are responsible for the administration of rights in the film industry in Nigeria, it is very important to evaluate and assess their performances over the year in terms of effectiveness and efficiency. This will help the nation to understand the gap in the sector and provide requisite solutions in order to harness the values that abound in the industry. At this point, it is important to look at the evolution of film industry in Nigeria (Nollywood).

---

3 There are hundreds of thousands of such film retail and rental shop across the country.

2.3. Film Making and Protection

Full-length motion pictures are marketed, according to a specific schedule, allowing for maximisation of profit potential at each level. The first phase is theatrical exhibition[4], where the experience involves a large screen, amplified sound, and sharing with others. Separate income figures are maintained for this. The next phase is the home video market, where videograms, or, lately, digital versatile disc (DVD) devices are purchased or rented for viewing in the privacy of the home. The next phase is the release in the cable and satellite television markets, a private circuit for which consumers generally pay a subscription fee. This can be initiated by pay-per-view and is followed by general dissemination as part of regular cable or satellite programming. Around this time a niche-marketing effort to specific audiences, such as passengers on planes and boats, occurs. The final phase of the life of an audio-visual production is usually free television. However, the introduction of new technology, such as DVD, can often revive an otherwise dormant asset and produce considerable income revenue by virtue of creating a new market and new consumers for pre-existing works. Copyright laws apply expressly to audio-visual or cinematographic works. However, because the costs and number of parties associated with creating audio-visual works are much greater than those for writing a song or a book, special rules have developed as to who is the rightful owner of an audio-visual production. In some countries, it is the producer, that is, the one who produces the financing. In other countries, it is the persons who make contributions to the work, such as the writer of the underlying literary material, the director, producer, actors, or photographer. This is why ownership of audio-visual works is a matter of national legislation.

The Rome Convention (1961) was the first international instrument to focus on and grant protection to performers. However, viewed from today's perspective, the instrument contains provisions that do not adequately protect audio-visual performers, as technology and the economy have changed radically since its adoption. In an effort to find consensus as to protection for performers in audio-visual productions, WIPO hosted the Diplomatic Conference on the Protection of Audio-visual Performances from December 7 to 20, 2000. The conference came very close to adopting a new instrument, which could have been viewed as a follow-up to the WIPO Performances and Phonograms Treaty (WPPT), which deals only with performers of audio phonograms. However, consensus was lacking, although 19 out of 20 articles of the audio-visual treaty were approved.

2.4. Film Making in Nigeria

It is clear from the forgoing that the Nigerian film industry of today is completely different from the operations of other film industries in the world, in that films are produced right into CDs within few weeks of shooting and are made available in the market. In the 70's, films were shown in the cinemas where most producers or financiers were able to monitor the rights in the works, but still film making was a

---

4 This was prevalent in the western world and in Nigeria during 70s and 80s.

difficult task in terms of equipment for the shooting. During that period, there were really limited forms of piracy activities in the industry unlike we have today.

Moreover, film production in the country can be said to be insufficient as per title released to the market, for example; the production of say 12 million copies of a popular film for a population of over 160 milion people may be inadequate and when the demand is far beyond the supply in the market instead of allowing the price to go up, people tend to dub or burn more disks to keep their market. This is exactly the argument of some marketers and distributors that were interviewed.

3. Research Methodology

The area of the study was Lagos State. Lagos was chosen because the popularity of Nollywood is believed to have emanated from there, and most practitioners of the industry are concentrated within Lagos. Only 54 per cent of the 100 questionnaires that was administered were returned and analysed to ascertain the level of awareness of copyright among the film producers, distributors and marketer. To ensure that needed information was extracted from the respondents, they were visited during their working hours so as to actually interact with them on their attitudes towards intentional copying of protected works.

4. Data Analysis and Discussion

It is revealed from the Table 12.1 that larger percentage of the respondents possessed O'level (51.9 per cent), ordinary national diploma/National Certificate in Education (35.2 per cent) and few of them possessed first degree (11.1 per cent) and Masters (1.9 per cent) in their respective discipline. This is an indication to some extent of the low awareness of property rights in the works they are dealing in. The inference is made because at this level of education, the issue of copyright or intellectual property is not part of the curriculum in the country.

Table 12.1: Background Information

Academic Status	*Per cent (N=54)*
O'Level	51.9
OND/NCE	35.2
B.Sc./BA.	11.1
M.Sc/MA.	1.9

Source: Field survey, 2010.

There may be an argument that the level of education is not a prerequisite for the awareness rights in the works, but it is important to understand that level of education usually influences the understanding of certain issues particularly where protection of rights are involved.

Table 12.2 reflects the types of business concern operating in the sector where only few firms are into the film production (18.5 per cent) while the service[5] and commercial[6] cover larger part of the market (81.5 per cent). The film producers invest heavily into the making of the films and considering the nature of Nigeria's financial system, limited copies may be produced at first which obviously will pave ways for further reproduction in case of future increase in demand. But the sad news is that as the films are released into the market, upon high demand, some rental shops opt for dubbing while in some cases, marketers are involved. This is evident in the response of the operators as depicted in Table 12.3.

Table 12.2: Types of Business

Sector	*Per cent (N=54)*
Producer	18.5
Service	14.8
Commercial	66.7

Source: Field Survey, 2010.

Table 12.3: Assessment of Operators Activities

	Do you Burn more Disks when you are Out of Stock?	
	Yes	*No*
Commercial	7	8
Service	11	17
Producer	6	5
Total	24	30

Source: Field Survey, 2010.

Table 12.3 illustrates that the operators lack awareness and do not respect the rights in the copies of CDs they sell or rent out to people (Customers). To corroborate this, some respondents (Service) also affirmed that some of their customers include individuals and film displaying centres. These film displaying centres are not the conventional film theatre but make more money at times than the rental shops and marketers. In this case, the question of business registration comes to mind in order to assist the authors reap the benefit of their creativity.

---

5 These are firms concerned with the renting out copies of films on CDs for commercial purposes.

6 Firms that sell CDs, they mostly get their orders from the producers and they are also referred to as independent marketers.

Moreover, the operators are not aware of any collecting society in the sector though majority of them are aware of the Musical Society of Nigeria, a society charged with the responsibility of monitoring the right of musicians for proper collection and distribution of their royalties.

5. Summary and Conclusion

This paper has considered and looked critically at the management of copyright in the film industry in Nigeria, especially Nollywood. The film industry in Nigeria is flourishing, and the major challenges of the industry have been low awareness of IPRs in the works resulting in piracy, which has in fact, eaten deep into the fabric of the industry. There is therefore the need to take giant steps to tackle the menace. A closer study of the operations of actors in the industry need to be undertaken so as to profer accurate solution to that effect.

Also, this paper looks at the various legal frameworks available in the country to ensure adequate protection and enforcement of rights in the sector which is not devoid of many lacunas. First, the law is due for review to accommodate the current pace of information technology to ensure that rights management is enshrined in the law. Second, continuous capacity building and awareness promotion is critical at this time to nip the menace in the bud. Law enforcement agencies must equally be brought on board to speed up the process of prosecuting the offenders to deter further infringement.

The low level of copyright awareness in the industry accounts for the burning of discs by the operators, when they are out of stock. This also borders on enforcement which must be strengthened to ensure that creators are motivated and their investments secure. In the same vein, it is sad to see that there is no collecting society in the industry to monitor and collect royalties for the author of the works in the film industry and this is responsible for the various illegal activities of copying, dubbing and burning of films into CDs and DVDs.

It is noteworthy that the law allows the administrative organ of copyright (NCC) to establish or certify interested organisation to carry out the roles of collective right management in order to provide incentives for the right owners, but to date none has been established.

In conclusion, it is important for the country to provide adequate measure that will safeguard the interest of the right owners in the film industry. Adequate attention needed to be paid to the recommendations below to move the industry forward and enhance the level of socio-economic contributions of the industry.

6. Policy Recommendations

Every successful economy is driven by well-articulated and robust policy. Here, it is important for the country through the NCC to design robust policy that will facilitate the development of the industry in the first instance and ensure that rights are protected, respected and enforced as quickly as possible in order to provide adequate incentives for the creators in the industry.

Also, the intervention of rights management organisation in the industry is needed as an intermediary between the owners of the works and the users to allow the owners benefit from their creative works. Here, the use of right management information to prevent unauthorised copying of protected works should be allowed in the industry.

The issue of registration of the operators in the industry is highly essential to the industry, therefore, to monitor the operations of the players and to combat piracy, every operator must be mandated to register their business and this should be coupled with an identification number. Identification number will facilitate the monitoring of the operations in the industry. Another important step to be taken is the complete overhaul of the industry through frequent sensitisation workshops or seminars for the operators. This will rid the industry of illegal activities. There is the need to conduct impact assessment of film industry on national economies to provide a baseline data for planning and decision making in the industry.

Acknowledgement

I am particularly grateful for the scholarship offered by the World Intellectual Property Organisation, Geneva, ARIPO and Africa University which gave birth to this paper. I am also very grateful to the entire management and staff of NACETEM for their cooperation and support during the programme and for useful comments made during the seminar presentation. I cannot but extend my appreciation to my supervisors Dr. (Mrs) Pamela Machakanja of Africa University, Zimbabwe and Dr. (Mrs) Gao Hang of WIPO, Geneva.

References

1. Adebambo A. (2009), Copyright Earns Nigeria N1.2tr annually, Comment made on *Friday, September 18, 2009.*
2. Adelowo *et al* (2010), Management of copyright in the creative industry in Nigeria: Nollywood experience. Being a paper presented at GLOBELICS 2010, Kuala Lumpur, Malaysia.
3. Adewopo A. (2009), Framework for Copyright Registration: a Case Study of the Copyright Notification Scheme of the Nigerian Copyright Commission (NCC), A paper submitted by the Director General, Nigerian Copyright Commission to the National Biotechnology Development Agency as part of the Case Study on the System of IP, Nigeria.
4. Alikhan S. and Mashelker R. (2004), *Intellectual property and competitive strategies in the 21st century*, Kluwer Law International.
5. Berne convention for the protection of literary and artistic work 1883.
6. Burama K. (2005). *Strengthening local creative industries and developing cultural capacity for poverty alleviation,* A paper presented at the *sixth annual conference held between 17-20 November 2005 in Dakar, Senegal.*
7. Idris K. (2004), *Intellectual Property: A power tools for economic growth* WIPO Publication, Geneva, Switzerland No. 888, page 190.

8. Guide on Surveying the Economic Contribution of the Copyright-Based Industries, WIPO, 2003.
9. John O.A. (2004), Nigeria *copyright law and practice,* Nigeria copyright commission (Publication), Abuja, Nigeria.
10. Melville B.N and David N. Nimmer on copyright (New York: Matthew Bender and company, 2000) 2-6; 2-30. See also Articles 2(1) and 2(2) of Berne convention and 9(2) TRIPS Agreement.
11. Sallie A. et al (2007), Flattening ontologies of globalisation: the Nollywood case, March, 2007, Vol.4, No 1, pp. 45-63.
12. WIPO Publication (2002), National studies on the assessment of the economic contribution of Copyright-based industries series to development series Number one.
13. WIPO guide on the survey of economic contribution of copyright-based industries to development.
14. Copyright industries in US economy: The 2000 report (Washington DC international intellectual property alliance, 2000).
15. Nigeria surpasses Hollywood as world's second largest film producer – UN, United Nations.2009-05-05. http://www.un.org/apps//news/story.asp?NewsID=30707&Cr=nigeria&Cr1=. Retrieved 2009-09-30
16. Gbemisola A. (2007), Nollywood and Literary/Performance Studies in Nigerian Universities: A Case for School-to-Street Connection- a Paper for the 5th Globelics Conference, Saratov, Russia 19th – 23rd September, 2007.
17. Kamil I. (2004), Intellectual Property a power tool for economic growth WIPO Publication No. 888, page 190.
18. WIPO guide on the survey of economic contribution of copyright-based industries to development.
19. Guide on Surveying the Economic Contribution of the Copyright-Based Industries, WIPO, 2003.
20. Copyright industries in US economy: The 2000 report (Washington DC international intellectual property alliance, 2000).
21. National study in assessing the economic contribution of copyright-based industries series Number 1.
22. WIPO, Basic Notions of Copyright and Related Rights *Document prepared by the International Bureau of WIPO.*
23. WIPO (2008), STRAP and CLAMP, Nigeria Copyright Commission in Action, September Edition, 2008. Also available at http://www.wipo.int/wipo_magazine/en/2008/05/article_0009.html
24. See Berne Convention Articles 2(1) and 14 bis.
25. See Berne Convention Articles 14bis (2) and (3).

Chapter 13

Global Competitiveness, Innovation and Patents: The Case of the Philippines

*Gilbert R. Arbon**

Provincial S&T Director,
Department of Science and Technology-Region 7, Philippines

ABSTRACT

For many years the Philippines has been lagging behind many other developing countries in terms of global competitiveness, including technological innovation as manifested in number of patent filings. In order to catch up technologically, the Philippine government has responded in several ways. One was by formulating jointly with the private sector a four-pronged national innovation strategy called "FILIPINNOVATION." Another way was by legislation—the enactment of the Technology Transfer Act of 2009. This law allows research and development institutes to own intellectual assets and, together with researchers, share in the revenues from commercialization of R&D results. Still another way was by administrative action on the part of the Intellectual Property Office of the Philippines (IP Phl). IP Phl made its services more accessible to the general public by establishing IP Satellite Offices (IPSOs) and Innovation and Technology Support Offices (ITSOs), *i.e.* patent libraries, in different parts the country.

Keywords: *Global competitiveness, Innovation, Patent, Intellectual property, Strategy.*

1. Introduction

The contemporary intellectual property (IP) regime in the Philippines was built on the country's colonial legacy, as explained by Cabilo (2009) and Santiago (2006).

---

* E-mail: grarbon@yahoo.com

Protection of IP rights formally began after Spain colonized the islands in the 16th century. The Spanish Law on Intellectual Property of 1879 and the Spanish Patent Law of 1888 were enforced in the Philippines. The Treaty of Paris of 1898 sought to secure patents acquired by Spaniards in the Philippines. Under American rule, the Philippine Legislature in 1919 passed Act No. 2793 otherwise known as the "Patent Law" (basically a copy of the US patent law). IPR promotion and protection was enshrined as State policy in the 1935 Constitution, then in the 1973 Constitution, and finally in the 1987 Constitution. Landmark IP laws were passed in the post-American period, including Republic Act (RA) No. 165 (Patent Law) and RA No. 166 (Trademark Law) in 1947, and Presidential Decree (PD) No. 49 (Copyright Law) and PD No. 285 (Compulsory licensing of foreign books) in 1972. Some of these and other laws were repealed in 1998 by RA No. 8293 (Intellectual Property Code of the Philippines). This change in the IP regime was a necessary consequence of the country's accession to the General Agreement on Tariffs and Trade-World Trade Organization (GATT-WTO) in 1995. The Philippines had to make its IP system compliant to the Trade-Related Aspects on Intellectual Property Rights (TRIPs) Agreement.

Having chosen to be integrated in the global knowledge-based economy, the Philippines is feeling the pressure to cope with the relentless competition for markets for the country's products and services. But even as it struggles up the path of progress, the country remains hobbled by inherent weaknesses, such as chronic poverty and vulnerability to natural disasters. To go faster, the Philippines must rely more and more on technological innovation. But this option is not without its problems—technological innovation does not happen by accident.

2. Literature Review

Selective research (desk) involving the review of relevant literature (from both electronic and physical sources) has yielded adequate information to paint a picture of the Philippines.

2.1. State of Philippine Competitiveness and Innovation System

The World Economic Forum (WEF) counts technological innovation as the ultimate of 12 pillars of economic competitiveness. One measure of such innovation is the number of utility patents (*i.e.* patents for inventions) granted per million population.

In the WEF's 2010-2011 Global Competitiveness Index (GCI), the Philippines garnered an overall score of 4.0 (highest is 7), ending up 85th among 139 countries. However, with respect to innovation, the country lagged even more—it ranked 111th, with a score of only 2.7.

A year later, the country unexpectedly moved up 10 notches. The 2011-12 GCI showed the Philippines now at 75th place (among 142 countries), with a higher score of 4.1. The country's innovation ranking rose to 108 while its score increased to 2.8.

While the feat seems impressive, the fact remains that in the 2007-08 GCI, the Philippines ranked 71 (out of 138 countries), and it ranked 79 in the area of innovation.

In effect, the Philippines has only managed to regain some advantage it lost as it slipped in overall competitiveness since 2007. This is clearly shown in the Table 13.1.

Table 13.1: Comparative Performance of the Philippines in the World Economic Forum Global Competitiveness Index for the Period 2007-12

Years Covered	*No. of Countries*	*Overall*		*Innovation*	
		Ranking	*Score*	*Ranking*	*Score*
2007-08	131	71	4.0	79	n.d.a.
2008-09	134	71	4.1	76	3.0
2009-10	133	87	3.9	99	2.8
2010-11	139	85	4.0	111	2.7
2011-12	142	75	4.1	108	2.8

Source: World Economic Forum Global Competitiveness Reports.

n.d.a = no data accessible by the author

This slippage appears to correlate with statistics from the Intellectual Property Office of the Philippines (IPO Phil). The data show the following facts for the period 2005-11:

- ✰ The average annual number of patent filings was 3,229, of which 3,029 (94 per cent) were by non-residents and only about 200 (6 per cent) were by residents.
- ✰ The average annual number of invention patent grants was 1,347, of which about 1,334 (99 per cent) went to non-residents while only 13 (1 per cent) went to residents
- ✰ The average annual number of utility model filings was about 556, of which 34 (6 per cent) were by non-residents and 522 (94 per cent) were by residents.
- ✰ The average annual number of utility model registrations was about 425, of which 43 (10 per cent) were to non-residents and 382 (90 per cent) were to residents.

In comparison, Thailand for the same period averaged 5,123 invention patent filings, of which 929 (18 per cent) were by Thais and 4,194 (82 per cent) were by foreigners. Thailand ranked 39 and scored 4.5 in the 2011-12 GCI. It ranked 54 and scored 3.3 in terms of innovation. So, not only did Thailand have more invention patent filings than the Philippines, it also had more filings by its citizens.

The Philippines' national innovation system has, in fact, been diagnosed to be suffering from several infirmities. Patalinghug (2003) noted, for example, the practically non-existent university-industry collaboration.

He also cited the poor private sector participation in research and development (R&D), despite the availability of R&D-related incentives offered by the Board of Investments (BOI). As far as the firms were concerned, R&D was not an attractive undertaking. R&D was equated to uncertainty, risk, and high cost—a shortsighted view which Patalinghug thought was partly rooted in the businessmen's lack of risk-taking skills and knowledge about the company's products, markets, production processes and opportunities.

On the other hand, non-R&D incentives (*i.e.* tariff reduction) were more generous. Moreover, the firms also lacked R&D capability, having relatively few technical personnel. This in turn can be traced to the firms' reluctance to invest in extensive worker training.

Incidentally, in the 2012 Investment Priorities Plan prepared by the BOI and approved by the President, R&D continues to be a priority sector.

Patalinghug thus proposed a catch-up type framework for the National Innovation System. This comprehensive response would address such needs as the following: to establish institutions and promote institutional innovations; to let government invest more in start-up costs of R&D institutions; to make universities work closely with industry and government; and to increase the capability of educational and training system to produce more quality S&T personnel, with companies sharing the burden.

Former DOST Secretary William Padolina (2004), in an international conference on innovation systems, pointed out that several components of the Philippine innovation system are in place but these are beset by many constraints. These constraints include: (1) high external debt, which reduces government R&D investments; (2) declining productivity; (3) exports are low value-added products; (4) declining quality of education at all levels; (5) weak S&T infrastructure (*i.e.* laboratories); and (6) small number of highly trained R&D personnel.

Noting the difficulty in the implementation of the National Science and Technology Plan (NSTP), Padolina stressed the need for a comprehensive National Agri-Industrial Development Plan that would provide the framework for medium- and long-term interventions under the NSTP.

Gonzales, *et al.* (2010), in their study of the determinants of locating R&D activity in the country, found out that only 50 out of 205 manufacturing firms surveyed in CALABARZON (an acronym for a cluster of provinces in the northern island of Luzon) engaged in R&D. Eight of the 50 were foreign-owned, 17 were joint ventures, and 25 were local companies. The study cited the top three obstacles to industrial upgrading or innovation, namely: (1) lack of R&D supporting industry; (2) high cost of R&D support services available; and (3) high tariffs on equipment for innovation. On the other hand, the following enabling factors entice foreign firms to locate R&D in the country: (1) low cost of doing business; (2) good physical and communication infrastructure; (3) legal system; and (4) availability of R&D support services. The Philippines, however, has no specific policy measures targeting the promotion of R&D from abroad.

The same study cited Paderanga (2009), who ascribed the Philippines' chronic underinvestment in R&D (the least in the ASEAN) to the following causes: (1) general weakness in the country's public institutions; (2) inadequate labor pool, especially R&D personnel; and (3) lack of S&T awareness beyond more progressive regions in the country.

Gonzale, *et al.*, recommended for the government to focus more on the development of policy instruments that can offer better support for R&D activities (*i.e.* ways to include local and indigenous materials in product development). Also, the government can start and support joint R&D efforts among firms in a specific sector to take advantage of spillover effects.

The national government, of course, has long recognized the need to accelerate technology transfer and commercialization. In 1987, the President issued Executive Order (EO) No. 128, "Reorganizing the National Science and Technology Authority" into the Department of Science and Technology (DOST). By virtue of this EO, the Technology Application and Promotion Institute (TAPI) was created as one of DOST's service agencies. TAPI was charged primarily to promote the commercialization of technologies (including intellectual property protection) and to market the services of DOST's other operating units.

3. TAPI's Intellectual Property Rights Assistance Programme

In 1995, TAPI set up the Intellectual Property Rights Assistance Programme (IPRAP) and started providing free consultancy services on IP protection and patent/ utility model registration practice. The programme was expanded in 1999 to cover financial assistance for a complete package of patenting/utility model registration

Table 13.2: Number of Technologies Supported by TAPI's IPR Assistance Programme for the Period 2004-11

Year	*Category*			*Status*			
	Invention	*Utility Model*	*Not Catego-rized*	*Filed/ Notice of Publication*	*Request for Extension*	*Under Prosecution*	*Completed/ Certificate Obtained*
2004	0	3	7	0	0	0	7
2005	1	11	0	0	0	1 (as of 2008)	10
2006	4	14	0	0	0	1 (as of 2010)	14
						3 (as of 2011)	
2007	10	12	0	0	3 (as of 2012)	1 (as of 2007) 1 (as of 2008) 2 (as of 2009) 1 (as of 2020)	11
2008	5	5	0	0	4 (as of 2012)	1 (as of 2011)	5
2009	4	11	0	2 Filed (2009) 2 Notice (2012)	1 (as of 2012)	5 (as of 2010)	5
2010	0	2	0	0	0	0	2
2011	1	7	0	2 Filed (2012)	0	3 (as of 2012)	3

Source: Javate, Manolita (2009). Assessment of the TAPI's Intellectual Property Rights Assistance Program to RDIs.

assistance through the services of the Philippine Association of Certified Patent Agents or other Intellectual Property Office (IPO)-recognized patent attorneys/agents, including payment of professional, filing examination, issuance and publication fees. Currently, the program aims to hasten the commercialization of the technologies generated by DOST-Research and Development Institutes (RDIs), the academe, and other private inventors. TAPI's effort in helping obtain IP protection for locally developed technologies is indicated in the Table 13.2.

As the Table 13.2 shows, TAPI's track record in securing IP protection for technologies is quite mixed. Javate (2009), in a study of TAPI's IPRAP, made several findings: (1) The program lacks human resources, which delays the selection of technologies for assistance; (2) It was not proactive in attracting more clients to avail of the funding assistance; (3) It lacks a standardized periodic monitoring system to check the progress or status of the technologies that have received assistance, whether or not these have achieved the objective in acquiring IP protection in the facilitation of assignment/licensing and availing of incentives.

4. Filipinnovation

In 2007, the Philippine national government launched the National Innovation Strategy called *Filipinnovation*—"innovation by the Filipino for the Philippines and the global community." This was in response to the call of the President then to make technology the foundation of future economic development. Consequently, the DOST spearheaded the effort to craft the strategy jointly with the Intellectual Property Office of the Philippines (IP PHL), the Asian Institute of Management Policy Center, and IBM, and in consultation with other stakeholders.

Through *Filipinnovation*, the stakeholders hoped to achieve the vision of "a Filipino nation having a competitive and multidisciplinary workforce competent in producing value-added knowledge-based products and services of global standards; competitive local firms driven by constant innovations brought about by or borne out of increased research and development; and a public policy environment that ensures continuous innovation not only through executive, legislative and judiciary initiatives but through local government programmes as well."

As described by its proponents, Filipinnovation as a national strategy for innovation aims to achieve the following by 2010:

- ✰ A competitive and multidisciplinary work force competent in producing value-added knowledge based services of global standards.
- ✰ Competitive local firms driven by or borne out of constant innovations brought about by increased research and development.
- ✰ A public policy environment that ensures continuous innovation not only through executive, legislative and judiciary initiatives but through local government programs as well.

It is hoped that such achievement "brings forward a distinct brand for the Philippines as an Asian innovation hub, different yet as competitive as its Asian neighbors and striving to be at par with leading innovation regions such as North America and Europe.

The strategies under *Filipinnovation* fall under four categories: (1) Strengthening Human Capital—bolstering competencies of Filipinos to make them globally competitive; (2) Supporting Business Incubation and Acceleration Efforts—increasing industry productivity through innovation at the industry level; (3) Regenerating the Innovation Environment—at the public policy level, ensuring the flourishing of an innovative environment across all levels; and (4) Upgrading the Filipino Mindset—effecting a paradigm shift in the national mindset to bolster the competitive innovation agenda.

With regard to intellectual property, *Filipinnovation* laid out two strategies: (1) Leveling the playing field by setting a policy environment that supports competition (*i.e.* a sound IP regime) (under the category "Regenerating the Innovation Environment"); and (2) Having an Intellectual Property Regime that is neither restrictive nor regulatory but rather serving as depository of innovative ideas which can inspire others to innovate competitively as well (under the category "Upgrading the Filipino mindset").

5. Technology Transfer Act of 2009

In March 2010, the President signed into law Republic Act No. 10055, otherwise known as "Technology Transfer Act of 2009." The statute took effect on May 8, 2010.

The objective of the law is "to promote and facilitate the transfer, dissemination, and effective use, management, and commercialization of intellectual property, technology and knowledge resulting from R&D funded by the government for the benefit of national economy and taxpayers."

The law covers all government-funded R&D implemented by public and private R&D institutes and institutions (RDIs), as well as all intellectual property rights derived from such R&D activities.

Under the law, RDIs generally own the IPs and IPRs derived and generated from government-funded R&D, unless they have agreed in writing to share, limit, waive, or assign these in favor of the government-funding agency (GFA). The RDIs are required, under the research funding agreement with the GFA, to manage and protect the IPs and pursue their commercialization, even to the extent of creating spin-off companies. The RDIs are thus encouraged to set up their own Technology Licensing Offices and/or Technology Business Development Offices and to adopt their own policies on IP management and technology transfer.

Revenues consequently generated accrue to the RDIs. However, the revenues may be shared with the GFAs (based on the research funding agreement) and with the researchers (as per employer-employee contract). In the case of public RDIs, the law authorizes them to use their share of the revenues as a revolving fund for operational costs and expenses (*i.e.* for IP management) except salaries and allowances.

For the researchers, the law allows them to directly benefit from IP commercialization in meritorious cases. They may create, own, control, or manage a company or spin-off firm undertaking commercialization, or otherwise be hired as an officer, employee, or consultant in such firm (but a researcher-employee must take a leave of absence for one year, renewable for another year). A researcher of a public RDI may opt to be seconded or detailed to the private sector.

The GFAs are tasked to protect the government's interest in the IPs and IPRs via the research funding agreements. They have to ensure that the RDIs perform their obligation of securing IP protection and pursuing IP commercialization. The GFAs are mandated to assume ownership of potential IPRs in case of national emergency or other concerns of extreme urgency, or where the public interest requires, and in particular concerns for national security, nutrition, health, or the development of other vital sectors of the national economy.

6. IP PHL, IPSOs and ITSOs

The State agency in charge of managing and administering the country's intellectual property system is the Intellectual Property Office of the Philippines (IPO Phil or IP PHL). It was created in 1998 by Republic Act 8293, known as the Intellectual Property Code of the Philippines. IP PHL thus implements the State policy set in the Constitution that -

> "An effective intellectual property system is vital to the development of domestic and creative activity, facilitates transfer of technology, attracts foreign investments, and ensures market access for our products. Thus, the State shall protect and secure the exclusive rights of scientists, inventors, artists and gifted citizens to their intellectual property and creations, particularly when beneficial to the people, for such periods as provided in this Act."

To expand its geographical reach beyond the National Capital Region where it remains currently based, IP PHL established IP Satellite Offices (IPSOs) across the archipelago. In 2008, IPSOs were set up in the key cities of Cebu (central Philippines) and Davao (southern Philippines). Four more IPSOs were established in other cities in 2009.

These moves increased IP PHL's accessibility, and allowed IP PHL to get closer towards its vision of "an Intellectual Property Conscious Philippines in a demystified, development-oriented and democratized IP System by 2020." IP PHL has made it its mission to be a "knowledge-driven government organization that works towards economic, technological and socio-cultural development by communicating, enabling and ensuring the effective use of the IP system in all levels of society for the creation, protection, utilization and enforcement of IP." Establishing satellite offices was not enough.

Consequently, in late 2011, IP PHL started establishing a network of Innovation and Technology Support Offices (patent libraries) in areas and institutions with high potential for patent activity, such as usage of patent information, filing of patents and commercialization of patented inventions. IP PHL crafted the ITSO to be the institutional mechanism to demystify and democratize the patent system so that it can be an effective tool to propel technological development.

The ITSO may be hosted by any eligible cooperating institution, such as a university or research and development institute. So far, ITSOs have been established in 41 host institutions. Of this number, 32 are universities and colleges, seven (7) are government offices and institutes, and two (2) are private or non-government organizations. (A complete list of the ITSO host institutions is found in the annex.)

An important component of IP PHL's ITSO programme is the Patent Protection Incentive Package (PPIP), otherwise called "Juan's Thousand Inventions." As per Office Order No. 73, Series of 2012, IP PHL "shall waive its fees for the first 1,000 patent applications/registrations subject to the Rules for eligibility/qualification."

7. Discussion

Technological innovation may indeed be a pillar of competitiveness, as the World Economic Forum sees it. However, the reliance on the relative number of patent grants as indicative of the relative strength of a country's technological innovation capacity focuses on quantity, not quality. This approach is practical, but it may tend to gloss over peculiarities in the creative potential of individual nations. Some countries may be strong in R&D-based inventions because they already have a strong industrial base. Others may lack industries, so they strive to be innovative in other ways, such as in software services (which need not be patented).

Nevertheless, as a crude yardstick for comparing technological innovativeness among countries, the patents-per-million-population measure will probably suffice.

The comparison between the Philippines and Thailand in the area of patent filings highlights the important role of a national culture or system of innovation, especially in a developing country. A weak national innovation system or culture manifests itself in many ways, such as the lack of patent filings. Conversely, a thriving or robust one may not only lead to a rise in patent filings, it may also offset the preponderance of filings by foreigners.

Unfortunately, based on the studies and expert opinions cited, there does not appear to be a sufficiently dynamic system of innovation in the Philippines. If there is such, it is not geographically widespread. The national innovation system appears to be concentrated only in a relatively few areas, most especially in the National Capital Region (NCR) where major academic and research institutions are located.

It is, of course, unrealistic to expect the national innovation system to pervade equally all throughout the Philippine archipelago. Not all provinces have cities. Not all cities have universities. Not all universities have R&D laboratories. Where scientific and technological resources are rather scarce, it makes economic sense not to spread these resources so evenly.

Yet it is quite clear that the *status quo* is becoming, or has even become, untenable. Given the country's laggard performance in the area of technological innovation, something has to be done to energize the national innovation system.

That is why recent IP-related State initiatives such as *Filipinnovation* and ITSOs should be viewed as encouraging signs of positive intellectual ferment, starting at the policy level. While these initiatives impliedly acknowledge the shortcomings in the existing national innovation system, they also indicate that the government is at least working to improve the situation, to infuse dynamism into an otherwise sluggish innovation system.

Consider the proliferation of IP Satellite Offices (IPSOs) and Innovation and Technology Support Offices (ITSOs). As far as the rest of the country is concerned, *i.e.* the regions outside the National Capital Region, the decentralization of IP PHL's services and its active networking with academe and other institutional partners in establishing patent libraries are indeed a timely and welcome development. This branching out by IP PHL is expected to heighten public awareness of IP and possibly induce more demand for IP services such as patent search and prosecution.

IP PHL's "Juan's Thousand Inventions," *i.e.* its scheme to lure more inventors to file patent applications by removing the filing fees, is another significant step in the right direction. This assumes, of course, that there will be enough creative individuals to respond to the economic incentive.

Under a more liberal IP regime fostered by the recently enacted Technology Transfer Act of 2009, there is reason to suppose that more IPs will be generated by RDIs and universities. Researchers from these institutions will likely comprise the first beneficiaries of IP PHL's PPIP.

Filipinnovation should also help address this concern about where to get the inventors. Among other things, Filipinnovation aims to "upgrade the Filipino mindset." This is a huge undertaking. It could mean encouraging not only scientists and engineers to be inventive but also students, farmers, factory workers, housewives, and other ordinary citizens to think like inventors, *i.e.* to be continually searching for technical solutions to practical problems. It could even mean empowering people to play the role of producers instead of being just mere consumers of technology.

Such paradigm shift, if successful, could have a profound impact on the Philippines' innovation capacity. A grassroots culture of innovation would constitute the fertile soil in which more advanced innovations can take root and grow. More locally invented products and processes would then proliferate. This in turn would lead to more patent filings.

All these positive prospects, however, need to be tempered with the realization that they all involve a change in people's attitudes and behaviour. That kind of change does not come automatically. University teachers and students will not necessarily start producing inventions and innovations just because more patent libraries have been established, or because they have the opportunity to profit from their R&D work. Farmers will not necessarily start devising creative ways to grow crops, or fishermen start developing innovative methods to catch fish, just because the government and the media aggressively promote the message of *Filipinnovation*. Even if these people know why and how they should change their mindset, they still might lack the motivation to do so.

Filipinnovation and other IP-related initiatives may improve the conditions for stimulating widespread creativity that eventually results in more patent filings; they may not per se produce the inventions. In short, these initiatives do not necessarily guarantee IP creation.

Conclusions

The government-initiated responses to the challenge of stimulating innovation nationwide would depend greatly on the ability of the stakeholders concerned to translate lofty goals into concrete results at the ground level, given the limited resources available. This is therefore a case of change management on a large scale.

Given the magnitude of the change envisioned, it would be prudent for the government and other concerned stakeholders to begin taking stock of the situation. A review or evaluation of the following would thus be in order:

- ✰ The initial results of the implementation of the Filipinnovation strategy, the Technology Transfer Act of 2009, the IP Phl's IPSO and ITSO, and other related government-sponsored interventions, whether these indicate success or not; and
- ✰ The underlying assumptions and risks associated with the above-mentioned interventions, whether these are still valid or not vis a vis changed or changing realities.

Such a review-cum-reality check would be useful in proposing necessary adjustments in strategies or tactics, or otherwise avoiding needless waste of time and resources.

Acknowledgements

The author gratefully acknowledges the support given by the Department of Science and Technology with regard to the author's participation in the training course. The author also acknowledges the cooperation extended by personnel of the Technology Application and Promotion Institute and the Intellectual Property Office regarding the sharing of information and advice.

References

1. Alabastro, Estrella (2008). National Innovation Strategy. Retrieved from http://filipinnovation.dost.gov.ph/presentation/EFA_National_Innovation_Strategy.pdf, 1 June 2012.
2. Cabilo, Zuraida Mae (2009). Philippine Intellectual Property Rights under the World Trade Organization, 1995-2005: Implementing the Flexibilities under a TRIPs-Plus Commitment. Retrieved from http://journals.upd.edu.ph/index.php/kasarinlan/article/download/2054/1974, 15 July 2013.
3. Gonzales, K., Macasaquit, M. and Yap, J. (2010). Determinants of Locating R&D Activity in the Philippines: Policy Implications. Philippine Institute for Development Studies. Retrieved from http://dirp4.pids.gov.ph/ris/dps/pidsdps1007.pdf, 30 June 2012.
4. Filipinnovation: The Philippine National Innovation Strategy (2009). Retrieved from http://www.iranscap.com/wp-content/uploads/2011/12/filipinnovation.pdf, 30 June 2012.
5. Intellectual Property Code of the Philippines and Other Laws (1998 7th Ed). Central Book Supply, Inc.

6. IP Philippines (2012). ITSO Patent Libraries. Retrieved from http://www.ipophil.gov.ph/main.php?contentid=60, 30 June 2012.

7. IP Philippines (2012). ITSO Host Institutions.

8. IP Philippines (2012). Office Order No. 73, Series of 2012: Establishment of IPOPhl's Patent Protection Incentive Package (PPIP), Also Known as the "Juan's Thousand Inventions".

9. IP Philippines (2012). IP Statistics. Retrieved from http://www. ipophil.gov.ph/81c0d873_IPStatistics2005-2012Apr2012.xls, 14 June 2012.

10. IP Thailand. Statistics of Patent Application. Retrieved from http://www.ipthailand.go.th/ipthailand/index.php?option=com_docman&task=cat_view&gid=191&Itemid=81.

11. Javate, Manolita (2009). Assessment of the TAPI's Intellectual Property Rights Assistance Program to RDIs.

12. Padolina, William (2004). The National Innovation System of the Philippines: Challenges and Opportunities. Retrieved from http://publications.apec.org/file-download.php?filename=SessionB_04_ist__innovation.pdf&id=452_toc, 1 July 2012.

13. Patalinghug, Epictetus (2003). The Philippine Innovation System: Structure and Characteristics. Philippine Institute for Development Studies, Research Paper Series No. 2003-04. Retrieved from http://dirp4.pids.gov.ph/ris/rps/pidsrp0304.pdf.

14. Republic Act No. 10055 ("Philippine Technology Transfer Act of 2009"). Retrieved from http://www.dost.gov.ph/index.php?option=com_content&view=article&id=859:philippine-technology-transfer-act-of-2009#, 2 September 2012.

15. Santiago, Josephine (2006). Making the IP System More Accessible to Universities and R&D Institutions: Challenges and Opportunities.

16. Schwab, Klaus, ed. World Economic Forum (2011). The Global Competitiveness Report 2011-2012. Retrieved from http://www3.weforum.org/docs/WEF_GCR_Report_2011-12.pdf, 1 July 2012.

17. Schwab, Klaus, ed. World Economic Forum (2010). The Global Competitiveness Report 2010-2011. Retrieved from http://www3.weforum.org/docs/WEF_GlobalCompetitivenessReport _2010-11.pdf, 14 June 2012.

18. Schwab, Klaus, ed. M. World Economic Forum (2009). The Global Competitiveness Report 2009-2010. Retrieved from http://members.weforum.org/pdf/GCR09/GCR20092010fullreport.pdf, 2 July 2012.

19. Schwab, K. and Porter, M. Co-Directors. World Economic Forum (2008). The Global Competitiveness Report 2008-2009. Retrieved from http://members.weforum.org/pdf/GCR09/GCR20092010fullreport.pdf, 2 July 2012.

20. The Official Gazette (2012). Investment Priorities Plan 2012 (2012). Retrieved from http://www.gov.ph/2012/06/13/investment-priorities-plan-2012/1 July 2012.

Annex

ITSO Host Institutions

Universities

1. University of Sto. Tomas (UST)
2. De la Salle University (DLSU)
3. University of the Philippines Manila (UP Manila).
4. Mapua Institute of Technology (MIT)
5. Adamson University (AdU)
6. Ateneo de Manila University (ADMU)
7. Don Bosco Technical College/Don Bosco Communications and Information Training Institute (CITI)
8. Benguet State University (BSU)
9. Bicol Universty (BU)
10. Lyceum of the Philippines University (Lyceum)
11. Eulogio Amang Rodriguez Institute of Science and Technology (EARIST)
12. Polytechnic University of the Philippines (PUP)
13. Technological Institute of the Philippines (TIP)
14. Technological University of the Philippines (TUP)
15. Angeles University Foundation (AUF)
16. Cebu Institute of Technology (CIT)
17. University of Cebu (UC)
18. University of San Caros (USC)
19. University of San Jose Recoletos (USJ-R)
20. University of the Philippines in the Visayas-Cebu College (UPVCC)
21. Western Visayas College of Science and Technology (WVCST)
22. Visayas State University (VSU)
23. Mindanao University of Science and Technology (MUST)
24. University of Southeastern Philippines (USEP)
25. Teehankee Center for Rule of Law of the Ateneo Law School
26. University of the Philippines Diliman (UP Diliman)
27. University of the Philippines (UP)
28. Samar State University (SSU)
29. Iligan Institute of Technology of the Mindanao State University (IITMSU)
30. University of the Philippines Los Ba os (UP Los Ba os)
31. Central Luzon State University (CLSU)
32. Bataan Peninsula State University (BPSU)

Other Institutions

33. Ayala Foundation, Inc. (AFI)
34. Technology Application and Promotion Institute (DOST-TAPI)
35. Department of Science and Technology-NCR (DOST-NCR)
36. Department of Trade and Industry-Cebu Provincial Office
37. Cebu Chamber of Commerce and Industry (CCCI)
38. Technology Resource Center (TRC)
39. Product Development and Design Center of the Philippines (PDDCP)
40. National Museum of the Philippines (NMP)
41. Philippine Rice Research Institute (PhilRice)

Chapter 14

The South African Intellectual Property from Publicly Financed Research and Development Act No. 51 of 2008: The Role of the National Intellectual Property Management Office in its Implementation

*Thabang Jase**

Technology Transfer Specialist,
The National Intellectual Property Management Office
Department of Science and Technology, South Africa

ABSTRACT

The South African Government through the Department of Science and Technology introduced a legislation governing management of Intellectual Property (IP) emanating from Publicly Financed Research and Development Institutions (PFRDIs) in 2010. Through this legislation, IP from PFRDIs are identified, protected, utilised and commercialised for the benefits of all South Africans, economically, socially, militarily and otherwise.

---

* E-mail: Thabang.Jase@nipmo.org.za

It is hoped that the introduction of this legislation will bring about positive spin offs for South Africa and as a result contribute to economic development. The International Property Rights Index (in Nyatlo et al, 2010) acknowledges this and further indicates:

South Africa was ranked 24th in a study that shows that countries that protect the physical and intellectual property of their people enjoy nearly nine times higher GDP per capita than countries ranking lowest in property rights protection......The underlying assumption is....the correlation between having an effective property rights regime and its significant impact on the economic performance of a country" (Nyatlo et al., 2010, p.11).

Since this legislation was introduced, the National Intellectual Property Management Office (NIPMO) was set up to ensure the effective implementation of the legislation and adherence of its provisions by its target stakeholders.

Keywords: *Intellectual Property, Legislation, Offices of Technology Transfer, Commercialisation.*

1. Introduction

An innovation chasm was identified in South Africa as a gap that exists between research and the market. Research outputs do not make it to the market place despite increased research and development investments in South Africa. The South African government spent ZAR 6.4 bn in 2008/09 and ZAR9.1 bn in 2009/10 on research and development (R&D) The bulk of the amount was spent higher education institutions (Figure 14.1).

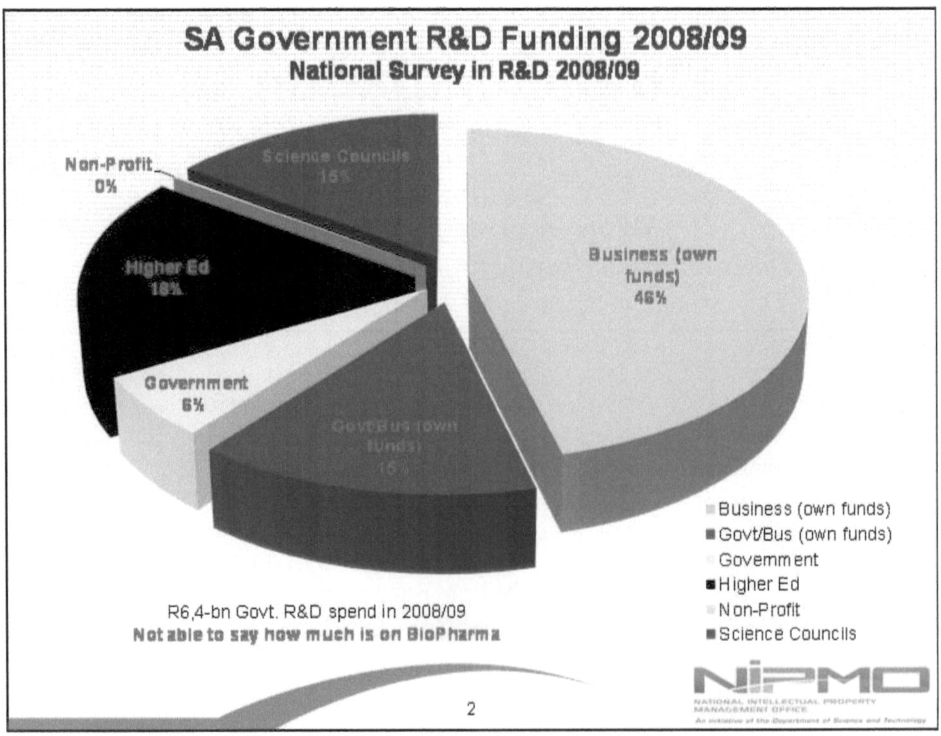

Figure 14.1: South African Government R&D Funding of Institutions.

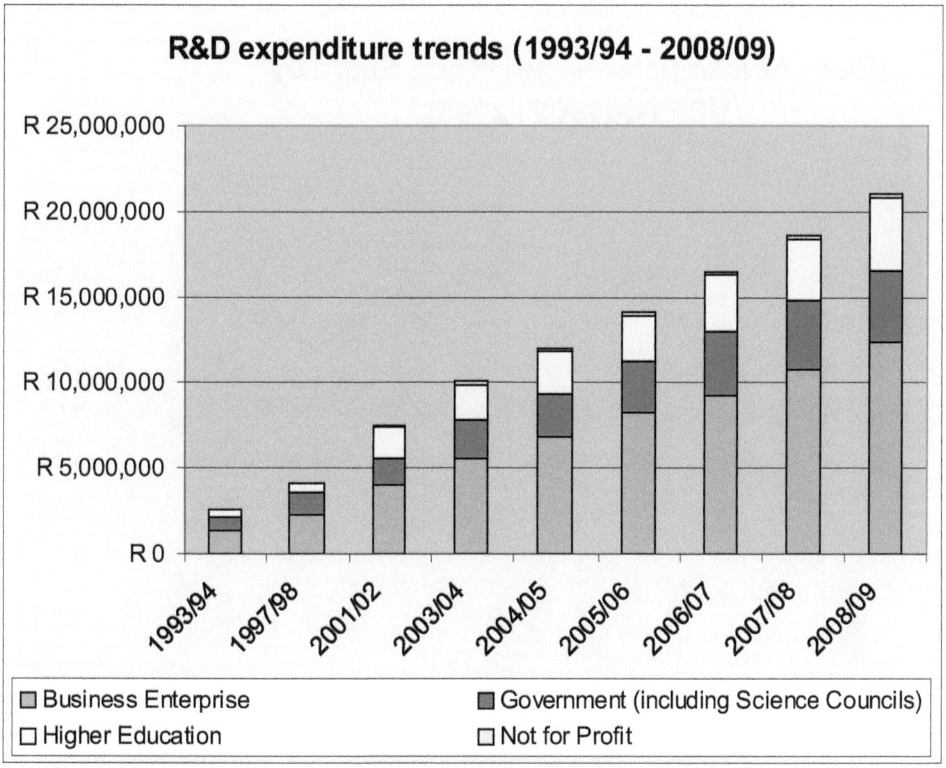

Figure 14.2: South African R&D Expenditure (1993 – 2009)
***Source*: NACI 2010, South African Science and Technology Indicators.**

Recent research indicates that South Africa (SA) has not substantially improved its performance in local or international patenting over the last decade. More particularly, the patent patterns for SA show very low levels of patenting by Publicly Financed Research and Development Institutions (PFRDIs) (Figure 14.3).

In recognition of this imperative and response to these challenges, Government passed the Intellectual Property Rights from Publicly Financed Research and Development Act, 2008 (Act 51 of 2008) ("the IPR- PFRD- PFRD Act"), to provide a regulatory framework for management of such IP.

"Intellectual Property Rights (IPRs) encourages innovation and creates a favourable environment for foreign direct investment and international trade in goods and services. IPRs perform an important development function in providing a basis for the transfer of technology and the development of local industry" (Journal of the ICC IP Roadmap, 2012, p. 73).

IP exploitation is recognised globally as bringing about significant improvement in the lives of people from the resultant economic benefits. It is however important to note that it is not everyone that recognises the importance that IP plays in bringing about economic benefits. This may be due to a number of factors such as the period it takes for IP to create positive spin offs in the economy and the fact that majority of

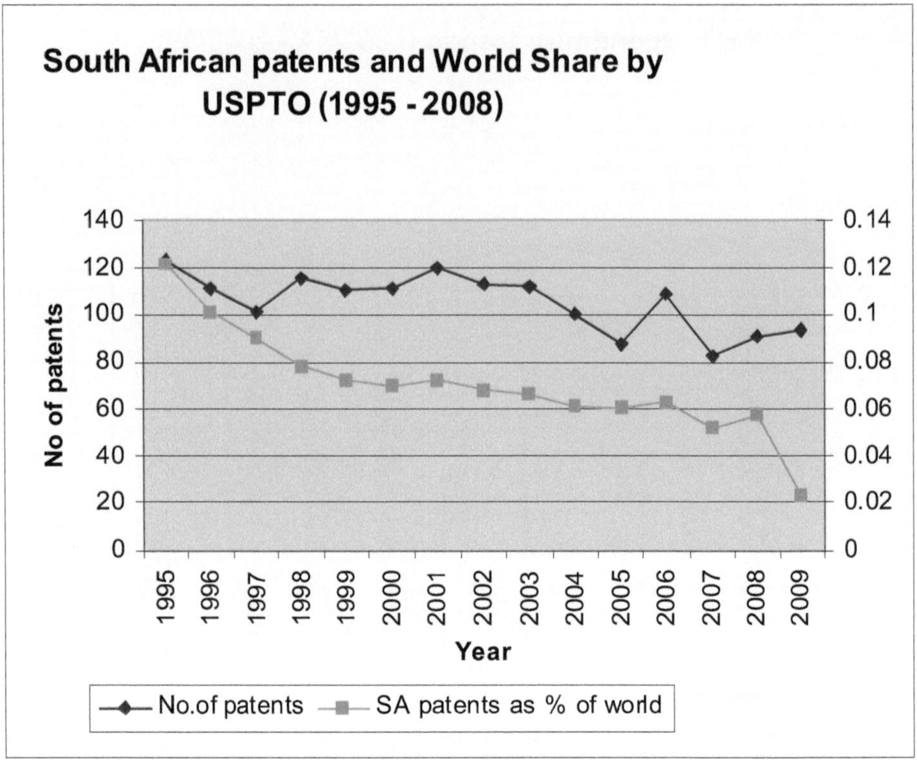

Figure 14.3: SA Patents and World Share per cent by USPTO.
***Source*: NACI 2010, South African Science and Technology Indicators.**

South Africans may not be fully conversant with the subject since it is new to them. Some SAs regard IP as a complex subject that is reserved only for professors and other learned people within academia. Research also indicates that most developing countries experience a similar scenario. The Journal of the ICC IP Roadmap supports this notion and has this to say;

"The role that IP plays in economic growth and development is not, however, fully realised or appreciated in some sectors and in some countries – in particular in some developing countries. This is due to a low awareness of the importance of innovation and IP rights in business and academic communities, as well as government" (The ICC IP Roadmap, 2012, p. 73).

There is also a need to increase the number and quality of the innovative industry practitioners in critical skills that will make it possible for people to innovate. The Department of Science and Technology (the custodian of the IPR PFRD Act) is committed to ensuring that critical skills are developed in the area of science, engineering and technology (SET).

The DST Ten-Year plan for South Africa (2008-18), emphasizes that the NSI must be more focused on long-range objectives, including confronting SA's failure to

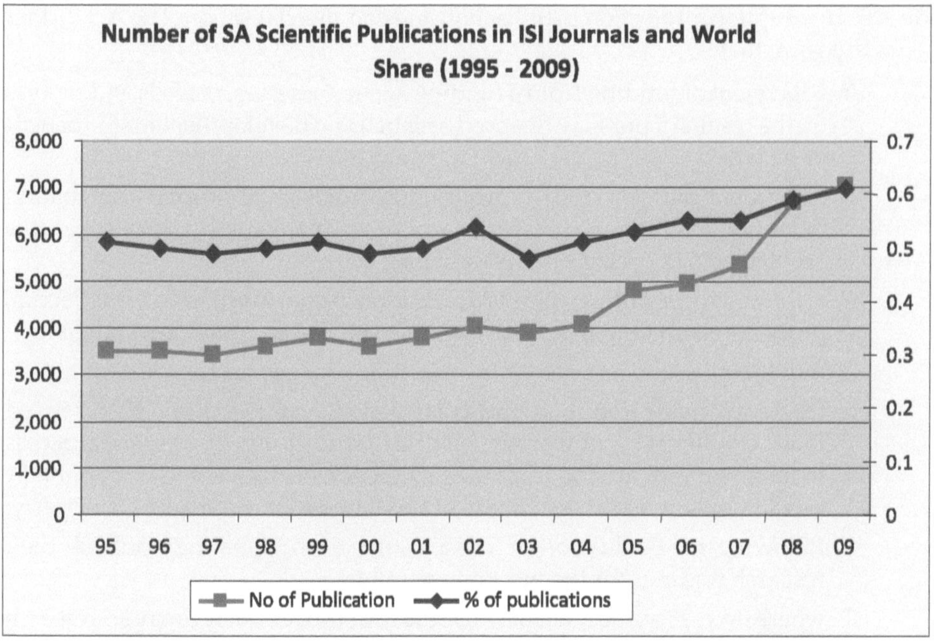

Figure 14.4: Number of SA Publications in ISI Journals (1995–2009).

commercialise the results of scientific and technological research. Furthermore, the inadequate production (in both a qualitative and quantitative sense) of knowledge workers capable of effectively contributing to the building of globally competitive knowledge economy is another area which needs addressing (The DST Innovation Enabling Skills Framework, 2008, p. 6).

Through this legislation, Offices of Technology Transfer (OTTs) or a function thereof, have been set up within PFRDIs. The OTTs' main objective is to ensure that researchers within PFRDIs are assisted in taking their noble ideas from inception to protection, to utilisation and commercialisation.

It is hoped that this and many other efforts will have a desired effect in the future and that SA will finally realise a huge return on the investment that all the people of the Republic will benefit from. The knowledge produced in universities and science councils should be transferred and used in industry so as to contribute to economic growth, development and improvement in standards of living.

2. IPR-PFRD Act and NIPMO Set Up/Mandate

The IPR- PFRD Act stipulates that a National Intellectual Property Management Office ("NIPMO") be established as an office within the Department of Science and Technology (DST) to provide for its effective implementation. NIPMO provides support and advisory services to PFRDIs by helping PERDI to set up and capacitate Offices of Technology Transfer (OTTs) which in turn assist researchers to manage their research ideas from inception, protection to utilisation and commercialisation. The Act further seeks to ensure that:

- a recipient of funding from a funding agency assesses, records and reports on the results of publicly financed research and development for the benefit of society;
- a recipient protects from appropriation, intellectual property emanating from publicly financed research and development and ensures that it is accessible to the people of the Republic;
- a recipient identifies commercialisation opportunities for intellectual property emanating from publicly financed research and development;
- human ingenuity and creativity are acknowledged and rewarded;
- the people of the Republic, particularly small enterprises and Broad Based Black Economic Empowerment (BBBEE) entities, have preferential access to opportunities arising from the production of knowledge from publicly financed research and development and the attendant intellectual property;
- following the evaluation of a disclosure, researchers may publish their research findings for the public good; and
- where necessary, the State may use the results of publicly financed research and development and the attendant intellectual property in the interest of the people of the Republic.

NIPMO implements various initiatives to ensure that stakeholders affected by the legislation are aware of the legislation and its implications, understand as well as comply with the provisions the Act. In addition, NIPMO has the following functions:

- provides assistance to institutions with:
    a) the establishment of offices of technology transfer and related capacity-building;
    b) intellectual property transactions;
    c) commercialisation of intellectual property; and
    d) any other matter provided for in the Act;
- provides appropriate standards and best practices in consultation with recipients of public funds for R&D purposes;
- develops guidelines for intellectual property transactions involving non-South African entities and persons, and manages the implementation of such guidelines; and
- monitors, evaluates and reviews obligations of recipients of public funds for R&D purposes in terms of the IPR-PFRD Act.
- considers and deals with any intellectual property referred to it by a recipient in terms of the IPR-PFRD Act;
- liaises with the recipients or any other party it deems fit to determine the viability of—

a) obtaining statutory protection for the intellectual property referred to it, if it is in the national interest;

b) concluding any intellectual property transactions; or

c) Commercialisation of such intellectual property.

- manages information in respect of intellectual property contemplated in the IPR-PFRD Act, including data concerning the recipients;
- provides incentives to recipients who create intellectual property, rewards them for proactively securing protection for the intellectual property, commercialising the IP and, generally, for promoting innovation.

In addition to its other functions, NIPMO may do anything necessary to meet the objects of this Act even though these may not be prescribed in the Act and as long as these conform to the law. Any administrative decision of NIPMO that adversely affects a recipient must be dealt with in terms of the Promotion of Administrative Justice Act, 2000 (Act No. 3 of 2000).

3. NIPMO Initiatives

NIPMO constantly reaches out to all stakeholders through meetings, conferences, NIPMO website among others. The objective of these efforts is to ensure that all stakeholders are educated about the IPR – PFRD Act, NIPMO and its functions as well as about IP in general.

3.1 Human Capacity Building Strategy (Technology Transfer Professionalisation)

In its Human Capacity Development (HCD) strategy the NIPMO explores various ways to develop the skills of professionals within Offices of Technology Transfer (OTTs). It is acknowledged that the implementation of the IPR- PFRD Act will require specialized set of skills and suitably trained technology transfer professionals.

A major challenge for technology transfer professionals in SA is the lack of formal education on technology transfer. Although some institutions offer post graduate courses such as the Bachelor of Science's Honors Degree in Technology Management and Masters Degree in Innovation Management; these programmes are not specifically for technology transfer Professionalisation. Other short courses relating to technology transfer exist as offered by organisations such as the Southern African Research and Innovation Managers Association (SARIMA) and Licensing Executives Society (LES) but are not accredited through the qualifications authority of South Africa.

NIPMO seeks to co-ordinate technology transfer and IP management Human Capacity Development initiatives in the national systems of innovation country-wide extensively, particularly for publicly financed research organisations' OTTs.

NIPMO's HCD strategy focuses on programmes that can do the following:

- Have relevance to practical issues in IP management and technology transfer
- Provide avenues for OTT professionals to obtain formal qualifications

- Improve skills of OTT professionals
- Provide methods for OTT professionals to be more effective in conducting their IP management and technology transfer procedures
- Offer constant professional development
- Keep up to date with current trends in IP management and technology transfer

3.2. Residence in Training

NIPMO through formal agreements with international institutions involved in technology transfer organised two international residences in training internships. These entailed technology transfer professionals spending 2-6 weeks in the hosting institution's OTT and learning best practices in technology transfer. The two international partners where the individuals were sent for training are:

- ISIS Innovation, UK: a wholly-owned subsidiary of the University of Oxford, managing technology transfer and academic consulting for Oxford, and providing consulting advice to clients around the world.
- Waikatolink, New Zealand: a commercialisation and technology transfer company of the University of Waikato. A wholly-owned subsidiary of The University of Waikato.

Overall, technology transfer training through financial assistance from NIPMO has been done through partnerships with the above-mentioned institutions. Moving forward the possibility of training individuals in other international OTT organisations could be explored. There is also the possibility of taking this approach within local OTTs.

3.3 Other HCD Initiatives

Other HCD initiatives to assist NIPMO achieve its objectives are:

- WIPO Summer School on IP
- Advocacy and Awareness/*IP Wise*™
- AUTM Webinars
- NIPMO OTT Framework
- NIPMO IP Chair at UNISA

3.3.1 World Intellectual Property Organization (WIPO) Summer School on IP

The NIPMO interim office through the Department of Science and Technology has established a relationship with the World Intellectual Property Organisation (WIPO), a specialised agency of United Nations which focuses on the development of a balanced and accessible global Intellectual Property (IP) system that provides incentives for creativity; stimulates innovation and drives economic development whilst safeguarding the public interest; to implement the South African WIPO Summer School on IP.

The objective of the Summer School is to provide an opportunity for senior students and young professionals to acquire deeper knowledge of IP, and to gain appreciation of IP as a tool for economic, social, cultural and technological development and the role WIPO plays in the global administration of IP.

Through its Academy founded in 1998 and in response to demand for knowledge and skills in IP training, teaching and research, WIPO offers a wide and growing range of general and specialised courses on all aspects of IP and its management. The Academy's rich portfolio of interdisciplinary courses caters to a wide range of IP educational needs including:

- ☆ Students from a range of disciplines (*i.e.* law, engineering, business) can grasp the fundamentals of the IP system;
- ☆ Policymakers and diplomats can examine and discuss the pivotal importance of IP for development and economic growth;
- ☆ Administrators can explore best practices to improve the delivery of IP services back home;
- ☆ Academics can widen their understanding of emerging trends in IP; and
- ☆ Legal professionals can hone their practical IP skills and knowledge.

The Department of Science and Technology/NIPMO in collaboration with WIPO has successfully hosted three summer schools (2009, 2010 and 2011) on IP and a fourth Summer School in 2012 will be focusing on IP and Technology Transfer.

3.3.2 Advocacy and Awareness/IP Wise™

The NIPMO initiated an Advocacy and Awareness programme termed *IP Wise*™ earmarked at encouraging researchers and research managers to protect their intellectual property and exploit it through commercialisation thereby generating revenues for the institution or enhancing local economic growth through start-up company creation.

The current mantra within institutions is "publish or perish" which encourages researchers to put their research results onto the public platform prior to protection. This mindset needs to be changed to "patent and thrive" that embraces technology transfer through IP protection and exploitation.

3.3.3 Association for University Technology Managers (AUTM) Webinars

Online professional development courses were identified for capacity development by NIPMO. The courses termed Web based seminars (Webinars) on technology transfer were distributed amongst OTTs as cost effective and readily available resources for OTTs. These webinars include question and answer sessions to allow full participation between the audience and the presenters.

3.3.4 NIPMO OTT Framework

Although some institutions (universities and science councils) already had OTTs or a designated person/structure to undertake the responsibilities of the OTT in South Africa, prior to the IPR-PFRD Act, research indicates that institutional OTTs are a relatively new development in South African universities and research organisations and are not yet found in all research institutions. While some efforts were made to promote technology transfer activities as early as the 1980s, it was not until the late 1990s that a handful of institutions set up Offices of Technology Transfer (Wolson, 2007).

While in the process of creating and operating OTTs, publicly financed institutions in South Africa need to bear in mind that understanding the OTT life cycle is essential as this would help OTT professionals to encourage academics to participate in technology transfer. This would help maintain support when returns seem slow. The longer the OTT operates the better would be its cumulative results and performance outputs. Technology transfer practitioners suggest that it typically takes five or more years for technology that is licensed to an industry partner to result in a marketable product. Thus, according to these practitioners, OTTs require seven to ten years to be successful, regardless of how one chooses to measure success. At times it can be more than twenty years before real success is seen.

3.3.5 Chair on IP Management

The NIPMO/UNISA IP Chair was implemented to commence duties on developing a post graduate diploma in IP management. This course will be offered mainly to technology transfer professionals though other individuals will be admitted, such as personnel from the legal professions, private sector, government departments and researchers in Southern Africa. This course will be designed for professionals who already have knowledge on Intellectual Property with practical experience and wish to strengthen and expand their future role in the field. The focus will be on effective management of intellectual assets. The course will empower managers of IP in publicly financed institutions to approach the exploitation of Intellectual Property rights effectively.

This qualification will also allow for the stakeholders to have access to a formal qualification in IP management which currently does not exist in SA. A post-graduate qualification in technology transfer is being brandied about in view of the fear that the other diploma may not necessarily cover all aspects of technology transfer. This could either be a 6 months certificate or one year post graduate diploma. This qualification should be able to cover the various aspects of technology transfer including IP management, technology commercialisation and technology development. It should attract individuals from a science/engineering, legal and commerce backgrounds.

3.4 Future Initiatives

Other initiatives which NIPMO has identified as part of its future plans to capacitate professionals within OTTs as well as others in IP arena include the following:

- Certified Licensing Professionals
- WIPO online courses
- Technology Transfer workshops

3.4.1 Certified Licensing Professionals

The Certified Licensing Professionals, Inc. administers the Certified Licensing Professional (CLP) programme for professionals in technology transfer. This certification is a credential that distinguishes professionals that have demonstrated experience, proficiency, knowledge, and understanding of licensing and commercialisation of intellectual property through involvement in patenting, marketing, negotiation, legal and intellectual asset management. The NIPMO interim office can elect to sponsor a minimum of 3 candidates in the 2012/13 financial year to take the CLP examination. This would allow the local OTT community to have some professionals who are at par with international standards.

3.4.2 WIPO online courses

WIPO through its Academy offers a wide range of distance learning courses. These entail on-line teaching techniques that utilise the Internet for teaching and training purposes. Distance learning courses bring teachers specialising in intellectual property issues closer to students and other interested parties in all corners of the world through virtual means. This method allows students to follow a range of educational programs in intellectual property at their own convenience.

3.4.3 Technology transfer workshops

The NIPMO interim office would look into the possibility of hosting at least one workshop a year where international experts are invited to give a talk on technology transfer to local stakeholders.

4. Achievements

A number of achievements have been recorded since the IPR-PFRD Act was introduced and implemented towards the end of 2010; it is hoped that all South Africans would benefit from an abundance of highly skilled resources existing at universities and science councils. Industry would benefit from innovations arising from these institutions by setting up companies to commercialise. Small, Medium and Micro Enterprises (SMMEs) will be set up, while community projects will also be created to provide jobs and skills (especially in rural areas). Some of the notable achievements are:

- ✰ NIPMO has been established, staffed and capacity building of staff is a continuous process which is meant to prepare staff for much bigger roles and responsibilities within NIPMO. The following directorates currently exist at NIPMO:

Regulatory and Compliance directorate which is responsible for:

- ✰ Monitoring, reviewing, and enforcing Government's rights to such IP Central registry for all IP derived from publicly financed R&D
- ✰ Managing and approving Full Cost Matrices, and international licensing approvals
- ✰ Providing Policy Guidelines toward advancements of publicly funded home-grown discoveries and technologies

Advisory and Support Services Directorate is responsible for:

- Providing guidelines for OTT capacity building for identification, disclosure, protection and use of IP from PFRD.
- Promoting human capital and infrastructure development.
- Developing critical IP management capacity through Offices of Technology and Transfer (OTT) in local institutions.
- Creating advocacy and awareness of IPR-PFRD Act and NIPMO.

Operations and Special Projects directorate is responsible for:

- Managing special projects
- Providing Secretariat for the Advisory Board and Dispute Panel
- Managing the IP Fund, and the Patent Incentive Fund
- Cultivating appropriate international partnerships aimed at translating IP from PFRD into tangible products and services
- Managing and Reporting on Social Benefits

There are currently 33 academic, research and development institutions in South Africa; a total of 21 Offices of Technology Transfer (OTTs) are in operation at various institutions and 2 Regional-OTTs have been set up in KwaZulu Natal (anchoring 4 universities) and Eastern Cape (anchoring 4 universities) Provinces. The OTTs have been set up through NIPMO assistance; in instances where the OTT is not yet available, an OTT function exists. OTTs are an important aspect not only in the identification and protection of, but also the successful commercialisation of intellectual property emanating from publicly financed research. They form an integral part of a well regulated and enabling environment necessary to increase the rate and quality of such commercialisation activities. These OTTs are expected to become self sufficient with time. This is also supported by Waikatolink in their international survey of OTTs Funding Models and Benefit Sharing Policies done in February 2011 when they stated that:

> *"Although the goal of many OTTs is to generate enough revenue from retained earnings to become self-sufficient, it is widely agreed that this takes time to achieve. OTTs generally go through a series of phases from being heavily dependent on the parent institution, through to recovering costs and eventually becoming self-sufficient and generating surplus revenue".*

NIPMO Advisory Board (AB) was set up to advice NIPMO on performance of its functions, the exercise of its powers and execution of its duties as well as providing guidance and assistance. The AB is characterised by the following:

- Advisory Board (A/B) appointed by the Minister and comprises between 5-9 members;
- Chairperson is appointed by the Minister for presiding;
- Appointment to the AB does not exceed 4 years, but may serve a second term by reappointment by the Minister;

- Head of NIPMO is an *ex-officio* member of the AB;
- The AB is accountable to the Minister and reports annually to her;
- Collectively, the AB has a balance of experience and expertise in research, research management, Higher Education Institutional (HEI) environment, IP protection and management, technology licensing and commercialization, technology transfer and business;
- It constitutes and maintains expert committees and seeks expert advices where required;
- NIPMO provides administrative and secretarial support to the AB.

The NIPMO Dispute Panel (DP) has been established by the Minister to hear and determine disputes relating to administrative decisions made by NIPMO.

A NIPMO IP Fund has been established to:

- provide financial support to institutions for statutory protection and maintenance of IP (including novelty searches, etc.);
- finance NIPMO costs for statutory protection.

Conclusion

Loss of revenue resulting from IP that is used and managed out of SA for many years signifies that SA has an abundance of skilled people who, if properly supported and managed, could bring about much-needed economic empowerment to the country. Governement has introduced relevant legislation in the form of the IPR PFRD Act to ensure that SA benefits from IP that is derived from public institutions mainly; universities and science councils.

The Department of Science and Technology has set up NIPMO to bring about change in the way in which IP emanating from publicly financed R&D was managed in the past. Significant progress has been made to ensure that the Act is understood and accepted by its stakeholders, it should however be acknowledged that the Act is still in its early stages and there is still a huge amount of work to be done in terms of institutional buy in. People are accustomed to the way in which they have been operating and once change is introduced, it is not easy for some to embrace.

Much work still needs to be done in order to ensure that the IPR PFRD Act is not only well received by researchers and research managers, but that it is adhered to all the time. Engaging these stakeholders on a continuous basis is therefore a key factor with which much progress would be realised.

Economic benefits resulting from the results of IP usage and commercialisation normally take much longer to be realised. SA as a developing country would benefit a great deal when all IP from public institutions is commercialised through various ways such as through the creation of spin-off companies as well as ensuring that IP is utilised for social good.

References

1. Caballero C, Fernando M.A.M., Nyatlo S.M., 2012. Intellectual Property Rights Management in Developing Countries.
2. Gumbi, S., 2009. A Review of Performance Standards to Monitor, Evaluate and Assess the Impact of Technology Transfer Offices.
3. Intellectual Property Rights Act, 2008 (Act No. 51 of 2008).
4. *IP Wise*™ Report; 2011.
5. Mapping the Resources, Processes and Stages required for Technology Transfer Offices to successfully commercialise Intellectual Property through Spin-out Companies; The DST Study.
6. Montobbio, F. Intellectual Property Rights and Knowledge Transfer from Public Research to Industry in the US and Europe: Which Lessons for Innovation Systems in Developing Countries?
7. Nyatlo, S.M., 2010. Office of Technology Transfer Survey Report.
8. Policy and Procedures for Measurement of Research Output of Public Higher Education Institutions; Ministry of Education 2003.
9. Technology Transfer Baseline Assessment Report: Department of Science and Technology; 2011.
10. Technology Transfer Office Funding Models and Benefit Sharing Policies, An international Survey; Waikatolink 2011.
11. The ICC Intellectual Property Roadmap; 2012.
12. White, K.J., 2012. Technology Transfer.Taking the High Road? University Technology Transfer.
13. Wolson, R., 2007. Technology Transfer in South African Public Research Institutions.

Chapter 15

Negotiation Skills for a Successful Technology Transfer

Renuka Jayatilleke*

Institute Secretary, Industrial Technology Institute (ITI), Colombo, Sri Lanka

ABSTRACT

The person who owns Intellectual property (IP) has to share it with the rest of the world not only to derive an income but also for the development of industries and betterment of humanity. Sharing of IP should be pursuant to negotiations, which needs skill and commitment as transfer of IP involves substantial real or potential value.

In licensing of IP the provider is referred to as the 'Licensor" who is the "legitimate owner of the IP" and the receiver is referred to as the "Licensee" who hopes to exploit the IP.- Negotiations play a major role in bringing these two segments whose interests differ, together.

As the matter being licensed is "IP" or "Technology" or "Knowledge" when transferring, the parties involved will require protection available under law with regard to confidentiality as it would enable them to work together in sharing information of value in confidence. This requirement brings the necessity of adopting Preliminary Agreements between the parties.

Even if a Negotiation for a technology transfer does not end up in an Agreement, still the parties should be in a position to walk away as friends. If an Agreement is reached it should result in a "win – win" situation which would provide the environment for the parties to develop a lifelong relationship.

Negotiations have to be carried out by an interdisciplinary Team of Experts whose differences in the inputs should be regarded as "strengths" and not as "threats". Pre-negotiation discussion among the team members is vital.

---

* E-mail: rjayatilleke@gmail.com; renuka@iti.lk

As good negotiators are made and not born the skills needed to carry out a negotiation have to be acquired.

The two Negotiating teams should build a mutual trust among each other since a successful Technology Transfer is an ongoing relationship between parties that is built on trust and confidence and not merely a relationship based on terms in a License Agreement.

Keywords: *Intellectual Property, Negotiations, Technology Transfer, Non Disclosure Agreements, Licensing, Term Sheet.*

1. Introduction

"Let Us Never Negotiate Out Of Fear-But Let Us Never Fear To Negotiate".

—John F Kennedy

In the past quarter century a great deal of effort was devoted to develop Negotiation theory and practice in order to move beyond competitive negotiation and to pave the way for real problem solving. With problem solving or interest based bargaining, parties look at their underlying interests rather than positions. Together they search for solutions to address underlying interests while making concessions with their own needs and concerns.

Negotiating is a day to day affair and therefore cannot be avoided. We negotiate with our spouses, superiors, co workers, grocery seller, and the list goes on. Negotiating prior to finalizing a transaction is vital as otherwise the parties will not know what is expected from the other.

As a negotiation is a process where solutions are looked for jointly by two different teams it has to be noted that those teams involved have to recognize that needs and interests differ and reflect different values, concerns and motives. Such differences allow the negotiation to become an inquiry to find differing needs and the solutions that will fulfill those needs. As money is a factor to be dealt with in most negotiations, it can become one element of a solution that has many other aspects.

Negotiation is a side by side dialogue where parties can trade on their differences and not battle over a limited resource.

Almost every transaction on earth is negotiable and what we finally achieve may not be what we wanted or what we deserved but what we negotiated for. Hence there is a necessity in acquiring skills for a negotiating to be a success.

Negotiation is an art that every one of us have to acquire through sheer determination and practice, as none can be born as a "good negotiator."

World economy is changing. It is changing towards an economy based on knowledge. In Sri Lanka much is spoken of "Knowledge-Based Economy" and Sri Lanka aspiring to be the "Knowledge Hub" in Asia.

In a Knowledge- based economy, much effort must be taken for protecting "knowledge" since such an economy would treat Knowledge as valuable intangible property or Intellectual property as it would generate wealth.

In the recently concluded Budget speech of the Government of Sri Lanka (GOSL), much emphasis was made on the need for private enterprises to exploit the research and technology developed in State research institutions such as the Industrial Technology Institute (ITI) to which I belong. In order to ensure that this vision of the GOSL becomes a reality an attractive tax concession was introduced to the private sector ensuring that the R&D institutions are armed with an additional tool when participating in negotiations concerning technology transfer. In other words the GOSL has made R&D institutions a stronger party in the process of negotiating.

Passing Knowledge from the public sector to the private sector, from research institutions to Industry can take place only by Technology Transfers (TT) which involves Licensing. Transferring a Technology is not pushing technology out for the rest of the world to grab; it is about the rest of the world wanting to pull it in. Marketing a technology is not merely advertising or selling but a multistage process that addresses the who, what, why, where and when of an invention. Therefore, the people who are involved in marketing inventions should use a systematic approach, which is much more complicated than marketing a product. In technology transfer, we have to keep in mind that the relationships established after a successful negotiation, are not short term but are lifetime commitments.

For any company, private or public, Technology is vital for survival in today's competitive world.

Therefore it has now become necessary that effective negotiations take place prior to any Technology Transfer since the mechanism for a successful Technology Transfer is only by "negotiations" and not by merely "demand".

2. Negotiation Stratergy

Talking is an effective method the human being is gifted with for expressing views. Letting the other person know what we really need and what we can give, is the basis for "negotiating".

How can we acquire Technology or IP, which is a vital tool for development if we do not have it with us? The only way is by acquiring it from another party who already has it, provided the other person is prepared to share it. Although we want the best deal when purchasing knowledge it is also necessary that we negotiate the deal fairly. Negotiation is a process that cannot be ignored if we are to acquire what we need for what we can afford.

The person, who owns the IP, has a legal right to prevent the others from using it. Therefore, unless one obtains the consent of the owner to use his IP for exchange of money or something else in value, which can take place through assignments, transfer, joint ventures or spin-offs, protected IP cannot be used by any other during the period of IP protection. In order to conclude an IP license or other forms of transferring IP successfully we cannot avoid "talking to one another" in a "business manner" which is called "Negotiating".

Unlike purchasing commodities, purchase of Technology cannot be concluded only by the buyer paying the agreed price to the seller. Technology Transfers do not happen that way. In purchasing Technology, you may not exactly know if you will be able to successfully use and exploit the technology you bought. Both the seller and the buyer will have to be "partners" for a long time and may be forever. Either party will have to depend on the other. Therefore, in purchasing Technology, Negotiating the sale plays a major role.

When buying Technology the parties have to ensure that both the seller and the buyer end up in a "win-win" situation as a "win lose" will result in a "Lose- Lose" situation.

In negotiations the following underlying principles have to be kept in mind:

- what we get may not be what we deserve but what we were able to negotiate
- everything is negotiable

A negotiation will bring together individuals with different backgrounds and experiences as it is a team work.

The experts who participate in a negotiation should keep in mind that once a technology transfer is agreed, what is transferred to the other party cannot be withdrawn as what the other party receives is an intangible property. Unlike movable or immovable property, technology if once given can be enjoyed by many even by the whole world at the same time.

It would be a mistake to approach a negotiation as a casual encounter without prior preparation and forethought as such meetings would be "just another get together" without any focus. An organised meeting with specific goals would be proactive and result oriented. Lack of planning often appears at the negotiation table as too much reliance on demands and an ineffective attempt to persuade the opponent.

As Negotiation is a discussion intended to produce an Agreement the following elements should be kept in mind.

2.1. Preparation or Planning

What is meant by "preparation" is "advanced preparation". As the Negotiating team would consist of people with different disciplines, it is of much importance that the team members prepare themselves for the forthcoming negotiation by finding answers to a series of questions such as the business reason for licensing? What does the other party want? And what is the time frame? These questions must be answered whether the party is the licensor of the licensee. Preparations are important to avoid doubts among the team members and to face the negotiations with confidence.

The key issues for a Technology license can be in a form of a Term Sheet. A Term Sheet is a short outline of key terms of the license concentrating on the "business terms". It has an internal version and an external version. The internal version is for in house use only and the external version could be given to the other party as an aid to reaching the License Agreement.

A Term Sheet is not the same as a Letter of Intent or a Memorandum of Understanding. A Term Sheet is also not a short Agreement. It is a list of the key terms with a tentative statement of your requirements written under each key term and can have many important functions.

The most important task of a Term Sheet is to help sort through the many complex issues in a technology license and make sure that you don't miss any. It helps to spot problems. A Term Sheet can also help to communicate within the team so that constant positions are taken, avoiding the embarrassing experience of having different team members saying different things in the negotiation session. It is also a valuable tool in communicating with the legal counsel if he is not present in the negotiation. It is used to make sure that the positions that you plan to take are in fact authorized and practically feasible. Finally it helps the team keeping a track of the objectives of the negotiation.

The Term Sheet could be circulated internally on confidential basis to persons who must be consulted to obtain internal clearances, inputs and approval. It could be shown to the Legal consultant for edits and comments.

Listed below are some of the questions that could be incorporated in a Term Sheet.

(*i*) Subject matter (specifications, technical descriptions, patent numbers, name of a work, trademark, etc.)

(*ii*) Ownership

(*iii*) Related Agreements (development, consulting, training, purchase, investment, service etc)

(*iv*) Development (is the technology completed, functional? If not who will complete development, do further research?)

(*v*) Scope of license (What rights are being licensed? Non-exclusive or exclusive, make, sell, use, store, make copies, distribute)

(*vi*) Derivative works, improvements (whether the licensee has the right to change the technology or make new products based on the technology)

(*vii*) Geographical limitations

(*viii*) Financial (down payments, royalties, stage payments, caps on royalties, calculation of royalty)

(*ix*) Term

(*x*) Obligations (due payments, testing, quality standards, setting up factories)

(*xi*) Post transfer technical support

(*xii*) Dispute resolution and applicable law.

In order to obtain answers to the above, the members of the intended Negotiating team and the Negotiator should not only circulate the Term Sheet internally as stated above, also prepare themselves for the forthcoming negotiation by answering the Term Sheet.

Preparation before negotiation can lead to better confidence at the negotiation table and a plan of action for uncovering factual data, interests and priorities of the parties that can be used to draft the Agreement with the best possible solutions.

The Negotiating team should ideally consist of experts in business strategy, marketing, legal, science and technology, regulatory, production, finance and a senior person empowered to take decisions.

Preparation for a Negotiation is based on the following factors:

(*a*) **Decide Interests on Priority basis and Rank them:** Each party can initially decide on their priority goals for the sessions. What are the underlying interests for the demands already made? Is it only the money? Is it a continuing relationship with the other side? Is it the recognition? Is it a harm caused by the other side? After identifying its goals, each party should determine the priority of these items. Negotiating after all, is a matter for both parties conceding and reaching a solution.

(*b*) **Assess the other side's priorities:** Each party to a negotiation should spend some time in the other party's shoes, imagining what the other party might want to achieve. The more one can understand the values, needs and issues from the perspective of the other, each party will have a better chance of guessing at what the priority needs are of the other side.

(*c*) **Money represents other needs:** Money is often a substitute for other human needs. Lawsuits will offer damages, penalties and may be in some instances injunctive relief. In a negotiation it is vital to look into as to what extent the money would matter to the other side and to look into ways to satisfy those needs more productively.

(*d*) **Plan money moves based on objective principles:** Money will almost always arise as a component of the negotiated solution. The better the monetary matters are handled the better the outcome. Working on agreed formulae, rationale are other effective techniques for handling money phases in a negotiation.

The first move of any negotiation sets the tone for the entire process. Among Negotiators resolving the same problem, the first negotiator to make the more ambitious offer that does not undersell its claims and leaves room for concessions will get a superior result. A reasonable balanced offer or demand will help avoid the possibility of a conflict spiral that may result when a negotiator make outlandish demands. A reasonable offer is more likely to be appealing to the other side and will induce reasonable counteroffers in return.

2.2. Discussing

The discussions among and with the researchers, the accountant, the auditor, the lawyer and the negotiator prior to the negotiation commences are important.

The presence of an Accountant should not be under estimated as a costing should be carried out in order to ensure that the efforts of the researchers are sufficiently compensated. As for a Government institution such as ITI, the role of an Auditor to be involved/consulted cannot be overlooked as there is a requirement to comply with the applicable circulars, approved procedures and regulations.

2.3. Proposing

Proposing the technology or a process developed by one party clearly and effectively is important as the other party should understand what is offered and on what terms. Proposing the technology in a Negotiation should be in the form of a discussion and not a demanding session. Proposing the value too plays a major role.

2.4. Bargaining

This is mostly 'what you get and for how much" situation. To bargain freely, there should be a cordial relationship maintained by both parties. Bargaining is the most difficult situation to deal with in a negotiation. There is a general belief that the Research and Development (R&D) institutions should cater either free of charge or at a nominal fee to industry as technology is for the development of the country. At the same time the R&D institutions, like any other organisation, are expected to generate their own income and remunerate their researchers adequately in order to retain their services. Those requirements of research institutions should not be overlooked by the industry.

2.5. Time Frames

When the broad details are negotiated, a time frame for signing the License Agreement should be determined. The following events could be considered in determining the execution of License Agreement:

(*i*) A product Launch

(*ii*) A press release

(*iii*) A conference

(*iv*) If it's a joint research, then at the beginning or at the end

3. Interim Agreements

3.1. Preliminary Agreements

Non Disclosure Agreements (NDA) are often important to protect business and technical disclosures, scientific information and the know-how that are discussed during the negotiation. The NDA is ideally signed prior to the negotiations take place.

NDAs are also known as Confidentiality Agreements (CA), Confidential Disclosure Agreements (CDA), Proprietary Information Agreement (PIA) or Secrecy Agreement. Whatever the name used they are legally binding and are signed by the parties to a negotiation in order to protect confidential information.

When sharing knowledge or ideas with another party who wishes to make use of those for business purposes it should be kept in mind that there should be mutual trust. It is to ensure that mutual trust is maintained that parties enter into a NDA. It allows the parties to a negotiation to be at ease when sharing certain information which should be known only by persons who have the "need to know" and therefore should not be disclosed to outside parties. A NDA also imposes penalties on the persons who violate those secrecy terms contained therein. A NDA would function as an Agreement that would protect NON PUBLIC business and Technical information.

The confidentiality agreement would allow the parties to examine the technology that is considered for licensing and thereby enable interested parties to make judgements about its specific nature, functions, performance and value. With the existence of a NDA the parties will feel freer to exchange business information. Nevertheless parties to a technology transfer should keep in mind that being too free, even with a NDA, is not prudent.

For a NDA to be in force there should be more than one party (individuals, companies or other types of business ventures such as partnerships, joint ventures, etc) who have agreed with the terms of the NDA by placing their signatures thereto. A NDA should also specify the period of protection afforded, the IP that is protected, penalties for violation and any other obligation of the parties.

A sample of a NDA is attached as "Appendix A" for guidance.

3.2. Interim Agreements, Feasibility Agreements and Prototype Agreements

These Agreements are sometimes useful when you need more information in order to ensure whether a technology license would be a good idea. The key terms of these Agreements are generally, that each side will bear its own expenses, or that one side or the other will pay certain expenses or provide equipment or data, who owns or will own the IP used or created, who will do what work, prototype creation or testing, confidentiality, and that the Agreement will end by a certain date, which is a short term. These should not be used as substitutes for Technology License Agreements.

Letters of Intent and Memoranda of Understanding should be avoided as those are vague documents and merely statements of undertakings which may not have a sound legal binding.

Standstill Agreements or Agreements to negotiate only on an exclusive basis are not desirable and generally should be avoided. These Agreements can give an undue advantage to one side and remove the option of turning into an alternative if negotiation is not successful.

4. Venue for Negotiations

Negotiations that are interrupted and then carried on by correspondence tend to be protracted. An in-person negotiation in which both sides agree on terms, goals and deadlines works most effectively to get closure.

The location should be comfortable, close to eating and toilet facilities. It is useful to have a computer in the room for taking notes, to consult the Term Sheet and eventually the contract document. It is important to have access to material the members of the team have collected.

The surroundings to a negotiation and the seating arrangements can play a role, although not critically. It is recommended that parties to a Negotiation sit face to face at the negotiating table and avoid one party being seated in an elevated position.

A very effective place is used by The International Development Law Organization (IDLO), Rome as their venue for Negotiations the large conference room facing the beautiful Vatican City which I had the privilege of visiting while participating in a workshop on IP. Such surroundings would create a "peace of Mind" and "God is watching you" feeling for the parties involved in the negotiation.

My office at ITI is facing the Criminal Investigation Department (CID) in Colombo. I wonder how a negotiating team would feel if the venue is facing the CID!

5. Elements for a Successful Negotiation

Given below are eight necessary elements for a successful negotiation:

5.1. Best Alternative to a Negotiated Agreement (BATNA)

The Wikipedia describes BATNA as the **best alternative to a negotiated Agreement** or **BATNA** can also be understood as the course of action that will be taken by a party if the current negotiations fail and an agreement cannot be reached. In a broader sense BATNA should be the "bottom line", or the key driving force behind a negotiation. A party should not accept a solution worse than its BATNA.

It would be advisable not only to know your BATNA but also the BATNA of the other party. When the strength of one's BATNA is greater, then the walk away possibilities are also stronger, although BATNA should not be confused as your walk away possibility. Therefore your approach to a negotiation and the attitude towards the negotiation process has to change depending on the strength of your BATNA.

5.2. Meets Both Parties Interests

Interests are your underlying needs. They are your expectations, your goals and real needs. They are the reasons for anyone to be at a Negotiation. It is also necessary that the Interests are prioritised before a Negotiation.

5.3. Positions

One's position should not be a factor at a Negotiation. Positions are questions of pride, fixed approaches that do not relate to your real needs. "Do or Die" attitude and "All or Nothing" attitude are results of being concerned only of the Positions and not Interests.

It should never be 'my position against your position". It should be "You and I together Vs. the Problem". Positions are ego driven where you want the other side to lose for you to win.

5.4. Utilising Options

All different varieties of possibilities available to the parties should be considered.

5.5. Legitimacy

Are we doing what is legally permitted? The laws relevant have to be referred, international best practises, the existing common practices and precedents created have to be kept in mind. The Agreement finally reached should be not only fair by both parties but also in compliance with the applicable laws and practices.

5.6. Relationship

The Negotiation process should improve the relationship between the parties involved or at least not damage it.

5.7. Communication

Communication should be clear and constructive as the "message given is the Message received".

5.8. Commitments

Commitments are what a party will do and will not do. Commitments have to be specific, realistic, clear, firm and implementable.

6. Closing the Deal

If the parties have worked with a Term Sheet and have recorded tentative agreements, the drafting of the necessary Agreement, in theory, should not be difficult. Agreements should be specific, not contain clauses where you agree to enter into an agreement in future.

Agreements have to be signed by both parties as otherwise it would not be a valid document. A Licensing Agreement would establish, in written form, the rules of an ongoing relationship. The success of Licensing will not depend only on the terms of the License Agreement but also on the confidence and trust that is established between the parties which can be more powerful than a well drafted License Agreement.

Once the Agreements are signed it would be ideal to have a celebration as it would be the starting point for a business relationship. The Agreement is only the beginning. The Agreement should not be in a locked file where the key is thrown away. The Agreement provides an important guide to what should happen, who should do what in a complex relationship such as technology transfer. Technology Transfer Agreements are complex and often impose important conditions where violation of which can create legal liability and business mistrust.

It is necessary to have ongoing attention and reference to the Agreement once signed. It is advisable to review the Agreement to identify such terms and to assign responsibility for tracking each one.

7. Failure in Negotiation

Failure in a Negotiation can sometimes be construed as a success! When the key interests in both sides conflict, the best outcome in a negotiation would be to withdraw, leaving room for an alternative solution. Withdrawing from a negotiation does not necessarily mean a failure. The negotiation team may make a decision that the negotiations cannot succeed except with the sacrifice of the important objectives and bottom line interests of the negotiating team and the entity and therefore agree to terminate the discussion. Such a considered decision must be deemed a business success rather than a negotiation failure. It would be a failure if an Agreement is concluded because of personal involvements or commitments of the Negotiator even if the interests of the parties are not well met.

Conclusion

In a Negotiation you have to be mindful of what you say and how you say it, especially at the beginning of a Negotiation. It is said that the first impression is vital even in a marriage proposal or at an interview. It applies in negotiations as well.

You have to set your tone and not be aggressive or authoritative. Time has to be spent on building rapport with the other party. A casual function before the Negotiation taking place can be an ideal time to develop a relationship. It is also important to remember the elements of a negotiation when engaged in the process.

When an Agreement is signed, the executives and managers who work with both parties should be aware of the License Agreement and the terms thereto. Agreements have important dates that must be recalled. It is also important to keep a track on the deadlines given in Agreements.

Disagreeing during a negotiation should not lead to personal attacks but clearly focussed on the issue. The focus should not be on the differences between the sides but towards the interests that are common to both sides. The attitude of the parties should be "this is the problem and this is how we are going to solve it jointly". Therefore the parties should act as partners in solving a problem. It is only then that the parties will build a mutual trust among themselves and conclude a License Agreement for the benefit of both the inventor and the investor.

Acknowledgements

This Manuscript would not have been possible without the guidance and assistance rendered by Prof. Vijaya Kumar, the Chairman of ITI.

I am grateful to Dr. A.M. Mubarak, Director/CEO and my colleagues at ITI for their encouragement which enabled me to participate in the workshop titled "International Advanced Training Course on "Contemporary Management Strategies in Intellectual Property Rights (IPR) relevant to NAM and Other Developing Countries" 16-20 July 2012 resulting in compilation of this Manuscript.

I thank Ms. Gunaseeli Edirisuriyage, Personal Assistant/Secretary, Chairman's office, ITI for her time and expertise in formatting and completing this document in line with the guidelines.

I also thank my family members for their support in reading the draft Manuscript many times prior to finalization enabling me to minimize possible errors.

References

1. A. Krattiger, R.T. Mahony, L Nelson *et al.*, IP Management in Health And Agricultural Innovation : A hand book of Best Practices. Negotiating an Agreement: Skills Tactics and Best Practice, p. 1155-63.
2. WIPO Publication No 903 E. Asset Management Series, Successful Technology Licensing, pp. 11-14 and 38 -50.
3. IDLO, Rome, Italy Publication "Technology Transfer and IP Licensing" Dos and Don'ts, 10–20 May 2010. Presentation by Giulio Zanetti, Director, Strategic Networks Department International Development Law Organization (IDLO).

4. Intellectual Property Act No 36 of 2003. The Democratic Socialist Republic of Sri Lanka PART IV, Chapter XI, pp. 49-72.
5. http://www.1000ventures.com/technology_transfer/tt_negotiations_unido.html. An article on Negotiating Transfer of Technology (Partially adapted from the "Training Manual on Technology Transfer", by United Nations Industrial Development Organization (UNIDO).
6. http://en.wikipedia.org/wiki/Non-disclosure_agreement. An Article on "Non-disclosure agreement" from Wikipedia, the free encyclopedia.
7. A report on "Key Implications and Best Practices for Technology Transfer Managers". Site Guide for Technology Transfer Managers http://www.iphandbook.org/handbook/siteguides/techtransfermanagers/.

Appendix A: Sample Non Disclosure Agreement

THIS AGREEMENT (the "**Agreement**") is entered into on this ____ day of ___________ Year Two Thousand and Twelve (2012) by and between .... of .... (hereinafter referred to as the "**Disclosing Party" or "...........**") which term shall where the context so requires and admits mean and include the said .... its successors and assignees)

AND

.................................a company duly incorporated under the provision of .... having its registered office at .... (hereinafter referred to as (the "**Recipient**" or the "**Receiving Party"** or........................**"**) which term shall where the context so requires and admits mean and include the said "**...............................**" and its successors and permitted assignees.

WHEREAS the Recipient hereto has already participated and/or desires to participate in discussions regarding Technology and the knowhow in the production/process for production called and known as "..." (hereinafter collectively called and referred to as "..............................." or the "said products") developed by the disclosing party and certain other services from the "disclosing party" as described below for the production of the said "..................................." (hereinafter referred to as the "**Transaction**").

AND WHEREAS during these discussions, Disclosing Party may share certain proprietary information with the Recipient. Therefore, in consideration of the mutual promises and covenants contained in this Agreement, and other good and valuable consideration, the receipt and sufficiency of which is hereby acknowledged, the parties hereto agree as follows:

1.1. Definition of Confidential Information

(a) For purposes of this Agreement, "Confidential Information" means any data or information that is proprietary to the Disclosing Party regarding Technology and the knowhow in the production called and known as "..........................." and not generally known to the public, whether in tangible or intangible form, whenever and however disclosed, including, but not limited to: (i) any marketing strategies, plans, financial information, or projections, operations, sales estimates, business plans and performance results relating to the past, present or future business activities of such party, its affiliates, subsidiaries and affiliated companies; (ii) plans for products or services, and customer or supplier lists; (iii) any scientific or technical information, invention, design, process, procedure, formula, improvement, technology or method; (iv) any concepts, reports, data, know-how, works-in-progress, designs, development tools, specifications, computer software, source code, object code, flow charts, databases, inventions, information and trade secrets; and (v) any other information that should reasonably be recognized as confidential information of the Disclosing Party. Confidential Information need not be novel, unique, patentable, copyrightable or constitute a trade secret in order to be designated Confidential Information. The Receiving Party acknowledges that the Confidential Information is proprietary to the Disclosing Party, has been developed and obtained through great efforts by the Disclosing Party and that Disclosing Party regards all of its Confidential Information as trade secrets

(b) Notwithstanding anything in the foregoing to the contrary, Confidential Information shall not include information which: (i) was known by the Receiving Party prior to receiving the Confidential Information from the Disclosing Party; (b) becomes rightfully known to the Receiving Party from a third-party source not known (after diligent inquiry) by the Receiving Party to be under an obligation to Disclosing Party to maintain confidentiality; (c) is or becomes publicly available through no fault of or failure to act by the Receiving Party in breach of this Agreement; (d) is required to be disclosed in a judicial or administrative proceeding, or is otherwise requested or required to be disclosed by law or regulation, although the requirements of paragraph 4 hereof shall apply prior to any disclosure being made; and (e) is or has been independently developed by employees, consultants or agents of the Receiving Party without violation of the terms of this Agreement or reference or access to any Confidential Information.

1.2. Disclosure of Confidential Information

From time to time, the Disclosing Party may disclose Confidential Information to the Receiving Party. The Receiving Party will: (a) limit disclosure of any Confidential Information to its directors, officers, employees, agents or representatives (collectively "Representatives") who have a need to know such Confidential Information in connection with the current or contemplated business relationship between the parties to which this Agreement relates, and only for that purpose; (b) advise its Representatives and Employees of the proprietary nature of the Confidential Information and of the obligations set forth in this Agreement and require such Representatives to keep the Confidential Information confidential and obtain necessary documents/agreements and undertakings from its employees in order to ensure that the confidential information regarding this transaction is kept confidential; (c) shall keep all Confidential Information strictly confidential by using a reasonable degree of care, but not less than the degree of care used by it in safeguarding its own confidential information; and (d) not disclose any Confidential Information received by it to any third parties (except as otherwise provided for herein).

Each party shall be responsible for any breach of this Agreement by any of their respective Representatives.

1.3. Use of Confidential Information

The Receiving Party agrees to use the Confidential Information solely in connection with the current or contemplated business relationship between the parties and not for any purpose other than as authorized by this Agreement and the Technology Transfer Agreement executed between the parties, without the prior written consent of an authorized representative of the Disclosing Party. No other right or license, whether expressed or implied, in the Confidential Information is granted to the Receiving Party hereunder. Title to the Confidential Information will remain solely in the Disclosing Party. All use of Confidential Information by the Receiving Party shall be for the benefit of the Disclosing Party and any modifications and improvements thereof by the Receiving Party shall be the sole property of the Disclosing Party.

1.4. Term

This Agreement shall remain in effect during the period of the Technology Transfer Agreement executed between the parties hereto and shall survive the termination of the said Agreement in respect of the Receiving party.

Therefore the Disclosing party may share the confidential information with third parties upon expiration or termination of the said Technology Transfer Agreement.

The Receiving party shall hold in confidence the Confidential Information that was disclosed during term of the said Technology Transfer agreement and shall continue to keep such information as confidential information indefinitely.

1.5. Remedies

Both parties acknowledge that the Confidential Information to be disclosed hereunder is of a unique and valuable character, and that the unauthorized dissemination of the Confidential Information would destroy or diminish the value of such information. The damages to Disclosing Party that would result from the unauthorized dissemination of the Confidential Information would be impossible to calculate. Therefore, both parties hereby agree that the Disclosing Party shall be entitled to injunctive relief preventing the dissemination of any Confidential Information in violation of the terms hereof. Such injunctive relief shall be in addition to any other remedies available hereunder, whether at law or in equity. Disclosing Party shall be entitled to recover its costs and fees, including reasonable attorneys' fees, incurred in obtaining any such relief.

1.6. Return of Confidential Information

Receiving Party shall immediately return and redeliver to the other all tangible material embodying the Confidential Information provided hereunder and all notes, summaries, memoranda, drawings, manuals, records, excerpts or information deriving there from and all other documents or materials ("Notes") (and all copies of any of the foregoing, including "copies" that have been converted to computerized media in the form of image, data or word processing files either manually or by image capture) based on or including any Confidential Information, in whatever form of storage or retrieval, upon the earlier of (i) the completion or termination of the dealings between the parties contemplated hereunder upon expiration or termination of the Technology Transfer Agreement between the parties hereto; (ii) the termination of this Agreement; or (iii) at such time as the Disclosing Party may so request; provided however that the Receiving Party may retain such of its documents as is necessary to enable it to comply with its document retention policies. Alternatively, the Receiving Party, with the written consent of the Disclosing Party may (or in the case of Notes, at the Receiving Party's option) immediately destroy any of the foregoing embodying Confidential Information (or the reasonably nonrecoverable data erasure of computerized data) and, upon request, certify in writing such destruction by an authorized officer of the Receiving Party supervising the destruction.

1.7. Notice of Breach

Receiving Party shall notify the Disclosing Party immediately upon discovery of any unauthorized use or disclosure of Confidential Information by Receiving Party or its Representatives, or any other breach of this Agreement by Receiving Party or its Representatives, and will cooperate with efforts of the Disclosing Party to help the Disclosing Party regain possession of Confidential Information and prevent its further unauthorized use.

1.8. Warranty

The Disclosing Party warrants that it has the right to make the disclosures under this Agreement. The parties acknowledge that although they shall each endeavor to include in the Confidential Information all information that they each believe relevant for the purpose of the evaluation of a Transaction, the parties understand that no representation or warranty as to the accuracy or completeness of the Confidential Information is being made by either party. Further, The Disclosing Party is not under any obligation under this Agreement to disclose any Confidential Information it chooses not to disclose.

1.9. Miscellaneous

(a) This Agreement constitutes the entire understanding between the parties and supersedes any and all prior or contemporaneous understandings and agreements, whether oral or written, between the parties, with respect to the subject matter hereof. This Agreement can only be modified by a written amendment signed by the party against whom enforcement of such modification is sought.

(b) The validity, construction and performance of this Agreement shall be governed and construed in accordance with the laws of ....

(c) Any failure by either party to enforce the other party's strict performance of any provision of this Agreement will not constitute a waiver of its right to subsequently enforce such provision or any other provision of this Agreement.

(d) Although the restrictions contained in this Agreement are considered by the parties to be reasonable for the purpose of protecting the Confidential Information, if any such restriction is found by a court of competent jurisdiction to be unenforceable, such provision will be modified, rewritten or interpreted to include as much of its nature and scope as will render it enforceable. If it cannot be so modified, rewritten or interpreted to be enforceable in any respect, it will not be given effect, and the remainder of the Agreement will be enforced as if such provision was not included.

(e) Any notices or communications required or permitted to be given hereunder may be delivered by hand or sent under registered cover to the address of the other party first indicated above (or such other addressee as may be furnished by a party in writing to the other party).

(f) This Agreement is personal in nature, and neither party may directly or indirectly assign or transfer it by operation of law or otherwise without the prior written consent of the other party, which consent will not be unreasonably withheld. All obligations contained in this Agreement shall extend to and be binding upon the parties to this Agreement and their respective successors and assigns.

(g) Paragraph headings used in this Agreement are for reference only and shall not be used or relied upon in the interpretation of this Agreement.

IN WITNESS WHEREOF, the parties hereto have executed this Agreement as of the date first above written.

(Note: This draft NDA is provided on "as is" basis for guidance without warranty of any kind and reliance on it is at your own risk.)

Chapter 16

The Use of the Patent System by Inventors in Tanzania

*Georges S. Shemdoe and Dugushilu Mafunda**

Tanzania Commission for Science and Technology, P.O. Box 4302, Dare es-salaam, Tanzania

ABSTRACT

In the current knowledge-led economy, Intellectual Property (IP) has become an integral part of world business and a major source for wealth creation and economic growth. Unfortunately, developing countries particularly, Tanzania has not yet made effective use of IP for socio-economic development. In a study conducted to find out the status of utilization of the IP system among Tanzanian researchers it was revealed that there is a low level of utilization of the patent system. This leads to duplication of research work and improper utilization of the little research resources available in the country. It further revealed that Tanzanian researchers do not know the importance of protecting their innovation neither do they utilize the available patents and patent information available. The study involved seventy one (71) institutions whereby five hundred and fifty questionnaires were distributed to the researchers. Among the reasons for the low patent information utilization is lack of awareness and access to patent documentation. There are some initiatives which have been taken in Tanzania to reverse this situation. These include among others the establishment of the Tanzania Intellectual Property Advisory Services and Information Centre (TIPASIC), which is currently being upgraded to Technology and Innovations Support Centre. This paper discusses the patent system as a part of intellectual property system that creates a depository of vital technical information, utilization of patent information in Tanzania, initiatives to foster usage of patent information and finally make conclusions and recommendations.

Keywords: *Intellectual property, Intellectual property rights, Patent system, Patent information, TIPASIC, TISC, Tanzania.*

---

* E-mail: dmafunda@costech.or.tz, djmafunda@yahoo.co.in

1. Introduction

In the current knowledge led economy, Intellectual Property (IP) has become an integral part of world business and a major source for wealth creation and economic growth (ARIPO, 2002). The current debate on the role of Intellectual Property Rights (IPR) and economic development generally, as well as implications on research capabilities and capacities, is linked to the fundamental changes that have taken place in international IPR system following the implementation of the Trade-related Intellectual Property Rights (TRIPS) Agreement.

A Patent is one of the forms of intellectual property protection. The patent system has two major functions. One is the "monopoly" function, which encourages creativity and innovations and the other is the "information function", which adds knowledge and contributes to the promotion of further creativity and innovation (Grabowski and Vernon, 2000; Morris, 2002; and Cullet, 2003).

A study was conducted aiming at establishing the status of use of the patent system and the TRIPS research exemption as well as identifying opportunities and constraints being faced by Universities and Research and Development (R&D) institutions both public and private in Tanzania in developing their research capability and capacity.

Results from the study revealed that there is a low level of utilization of the Intellectual Property Rights System among Tanzanian researchers. This has led to the national R&D institutions in Tanzania to "re-invent the wheel" and hence making inefficient use of scarce research resources. It further revealed that lack of institutional intellectual property policies is also a major factor hindering the use of the patent system in Tanzania.

2. Intellectual Property Rights

Intellectual property is mainly divided into two major categories: Industrial property and copyrights. Industrial property comprises of patents, utility models, trade and service marks, industrial designs, geographical indications and trade secrets.

There are two schools of thought on the theory of Intellectual Property Rights (IPR): The utilitarian and the non-utilitarian theory. The utilitarian theorists have a view that the creation of IPR fosters innovation. The utilitarian theorists further argue that, patent protection duration should be reasonablely minimal so as to be in the public domain for public economic and socialwelfare. The non-utilitarian theorists put emphasis on the creators' moral rights to control their work (Menell, 1999). Menell (1999) explains further that the principal value of the utilitarian works lies principally, if not exclusively, in their ability to perform tasks *i.e.* IPRs provide incentives to turn inventions into useful products, which enrich a society's culture and knowledge and improve its welfare. On one hand, the Patent law, benefits from utilitarian theory as patent is given for a specific time from which the patent could thereafter be in the public domain for public use. On the other hand, the Copyright law, which implicates a broader interest of the creator than patent law, benefits from the utilitarian framework to the extent that society seeks the production and diffusion of literary and artistic works. Intellectual Property Rights (IPRs) emerged during the early mercantilist period for the states to unify and increase their power and wealth through development of manufacturing and the establishment of foreign trading monopolies (Menell, 1999).

Economic theory suggests that a society without intellectual property protection at all would certainly not be allocating resources to inventions and creations at optimal level. But equally a society that overprotects would certainly incur costs that exceed the benefit (Drahos, 2005).

2.1 Patent System

The patent system is based on the fundamental principle of granting an inventor a temporary exclusive right in return for the public disclosure of his/her invention/innovation. Patent therefore is an arrangement between the State and the inventor whereby the State assures the inventor that no one will copy his/her invention without his/her consent after disclosing and publicizing his/her invention (Salazar, 1998; Gupta, 2002). Historically, the Venetian Decree of 1474 and the British Statute of Monopolies of 1623 are the originators of the patent system (Salazar, 1998; Menell, 1999; and Morris, 2002). This has been incorporated into other countries' laws over time. Patents are granted in a specific territory and for a limited period of time, as per the TRIPS Agreement the minimum period is 20 years. Though the protection is territorial in nature, its disclosure is global and allows anyone, anywhere to learn from it.

2.2 Patent Information

Patent information comprises technical, legal, business-relevant and public policy-relevant information which can be used to stimulate further creativity and innovation. Moreover, the patent system not only transforms knowledge into intangible assets which can be traded, but also allows the legal use of this knowledge in territories where the patent has not been granted or when the patent has expired or been abandoned. Use of this information for further research and development activities has driven technology and innovation to its current frontiers through the exclusive rights granted under patent system and technological disclosure contained in the patent document.

Advantages of the patent documentation are the following:

- Worldwide over 60 million patents are free for use
- 80 per cent never published elsewhere
- No copyright
- Obligatory publication: no editor's review
- Patent family (Several languages)
- Standardized publication (uniform structure)
- Available in on-line databases (easily accessible)

Patent information is increasingly available via easily-accessible services that are delivered over the Internet as either free-of-charge or as commercial fee-paying services. The former services are provided mostly by national and regional patent offices. Some of the free of charge databases are:

- http://www.espacenet.com
- http://www.european-patent-office.org
- http://www.ep.dips.org
- http://www.uspto.go
- http://ipdl.wipo.int/en/

However, coverage and accessibility of data are available mostly for industrialized countries with much less content and much more difficult access in developing countries including Tanzania.

2.3. Exploiting Patent Information in Tanzania

According to a study carried out by COSTECH in 2010, Tanzanian researchers are not exploiting patent information. The study was carried out in seventy one (71) R&D and S&T institutions in Tanzania. Five hundred and fifty (550) questionnaires were sent to twenty six (26) institutions in Dar es Salaam and forty five (45) institutions outside Dar es Salaam. Three hundred and forty (340)) filled questionnaires were received. The analysis revealed the following: Only 5.3 per cent of the respondents indicated that they contact the patent documentation mostly and 6.3 per cent frequently, but 40.9 per cent indicated that they do not contact the patent documentation at all in their research planning (Figure 16.1).

This also shows that Tanzania researchers are not exploiting patent information. The reason may be due to lack of awareness of the existence of the patent documentation as a source of information. On the other sources of information used

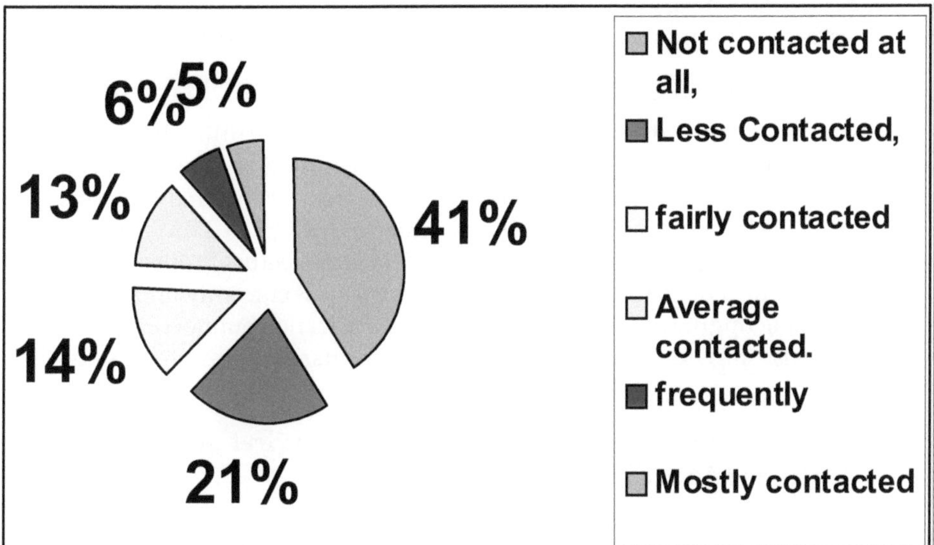

Figure 16.1: Percentage of Respondents using Patent Information in their Research Work Planning.

***Source*: COSTECH (2010): Policy Brief on Accessing Patented Knowledge for Innovation Research.**

during research, the results indicated that 19.2 per cent of researchers frequently use books, while 25.1 per cent use journals and 40.8 per cent use the internet.

WIPO, 2006 indicated that 80 per cent of technical information is available only in patent documentation. This suggests that Tanzanian researchers use or contact only 20 per cent of the technical information. This creates a possibility for the researchers to conduct a research of which the results are already in the patent documentation. This leads to ineffective utilization of the scarce resources available for research (IDRC, 2007).

Efforts made by COSTECH to create awareness among the researchers on the existence of patent documentation and how to search for patent information from the Internet did not bear fruits. Researchers did not use patent documentation database as a resource for information as shown by these results. Several factors were identified to have contributed to the inadequate use of patent documentation as a source of technical information. These include among others, the fact that researchers were not used to the patent information as a source of information during their research planning activities. This was new to them and they felt uncomfortable to use this source. Another factor is that in many R&D institutions access to the Internet was a limiting factor. In the institutions where there was Internet connection, it was very slow and sometimes difficult to down-load such documents. This issue of non-access to the Internet will soon be solved as the R&D institutions are going to be connected through COSTECH to the optic fiber network in Tanzania.

Furthermore, there is an urgent need for interventions to make the researchers use patent information for their research work. There is a need to conduct awareness creation seminars on the existence of the patent document databases and on how to search for patent information in universities and R&D institutions.

3. Initiatives to Foster Use of Patent Information in Tanzania

There have been some initiatives taken to foster the utilization of patent information in the country. The initial initiatives were through creation of awareness of the existence of patent databases and how to search for information. This was done during the IPR sensitization seminar conducted by COSTECH. More initiatives were taken including the establishment of Tanzania Intellectual Property Advisory Services and Information Centre (TIPASIC). This centre is currently undergoing the process of being upgraded to the Technology and Innovation Support Centre (TISC) which will also provide non-patent scientific information from well established journals.

3.1 Tanzania Intellectual Property Advisory Services and Information Centre (TIPASIC)

In recognition of the importance of intellectual property rights as a tool for socio-economic development and the difficulties in accessing patent information, the Business Registrations and Licensing Agent (BRELA) and Tanzania Commission for Science and Technology (COSTECH) in collaboration with the World Intellectual Property Organization (WIPO) established the Tanzania Intellectual Property Advisory Services and Information Centre (TIPASIC) to provide services for furtherance of intellectual property rights and technological development. This Centre was established in 2007.

The overall goal for the establishment of TIPASIC was to provide Intellectual Property Information (Patent documentation) and advisory services on issues related to IP and IPRs for the advancement of technological capacity and economic development of Tanzania. TIPASIC provided four major services which are: providing Patent Information to walk-in users; providing both technical and legal advices to clients on IP and IPRs; assisting clients on preparation of patent application documents; and creating awareness and sensitization on IP issues. Over the years TIPASIC has managed to make some achievements in attaining its goals, however there were also some challenges which faced the Centre.

3.1.1. Achievements

From its establishment, TIPASIC has managed to serve 1680 clients who visited the Center seeking advice and technical assistance. The clients included researchers from R&D institutions, innovators and students from secondary schools and universities among others. Also awareness creation was made through conducting sensitization seminars to R&D institutions, SMEs and students. Other means used to create awareness included participating in exhibitions and conferences as well as dissemination of IP awareness materials. These achievements are summarized in Table 16.1.

3.1.2. Challenges

The following are among the challenges faced by the Centre in accomplishing promotion of the utilization of the TIPASIC services:

- ☆ Low understanding of IP language among the clients. One has to teach the client issues of IP before providing him/her advise or service. This has led to taking of long time to serve one client,
- ☆ Inadequate expertise in IP issues, including competent patent agents to assist innovators in preparation of the patent application documents,
- ☆ Lack of fast Internet connectivity among the R&D institutions, which discourages researchers from developing the practise of searching patent documents.

3.2 Technology and Innovation Support Centre (TISC) of Tanzania

World Intellectual Property Organisation (WIPO) was given a mandate by its Member States to carry out a pilot project to establish Technology and Innovation Support Centers (TISCs) within the framework of its Development Agenda. The project intends to address Recommendation 8 of the Development Agenda of WIPO Member States, which calls on WIPO to *"[facilitate] the national offices of developing countries, especially LDCs, as well as their regional and sub regional intellectual property organizations to access specialized databases..."* Tanzania is among the few LDC which was selected to implement the pilot project. The project will cover two main groups of activities, namely (i) Access to specialized databases; and (ii) Capacity building. So, Technology

Table 16.1: TIPASIC Services Provided 2007-11

Category of Clients	*Service Offered*	*Number of Clients Served*
Walk-in users	General advise on IP&IPR issues	28
	Preparation of Patent applications	15
	Patent searches	52
	Advise on IP protection application procedures	88
	Advice on registration of Trade marks	2
	Students special projects on IP	85
	Legal advices on Intellectual Property Rights	11
	Others: patent registration fees, presentation in conferences and technology evaluation	49
IP awareness and sensitization seminars	Client tailored seminars	4
	Seminars supported by COSTECH	991
	IDRC project on Accessing technologies and Information Contained in Patent Documents to Enhance Innovative Research in Tanzania: The TRIPS Agreement Research Exemption	340
Establishment of Intellectual Property Management Office in R&D Institutions	Training of responsible staff (Institutions)	15
	Establishment of IPMO (Institutions)- NBRA, TEMDO, IHI and TATC	4
	TOTAL	1680

Source: TIPASIC Annual Reports (2009/2010 and 2010/2011).

and Innovation Support Centres (TISCs) will promote the use of two (2) WIPO programmes designed to facilitate access to knowledge for the LDCs namely: Access to Specialized Patent Information (ASPI) and Access to Research Development and Innovation (ARDI). ASPI programme provides access to more sophisticated search and analysis tools available in commercial patent databases, while ARDi programme provides access to scientific and technical journals. All these programmes are to be provided by WIPO at no cost. In addition, the World Intellectual Property Organization is committed to provide and organize training workshops and capacity building in innovation and creativity areas for the staff of TISCs.

BRELA, COSTECH in collaboration with WIPO is upgrading TIPASIC to TISC. The new Centre will expand the objectives and roles of the former TIPASIC whereby the Technology and Innovation Support Centre of Tanzania will not only provide information from patent sources but also the non-patent (scientific and technical) information will be available and easily linked through the Centre.

Conclusion and Recommendations

Conclusions

Tanzania has not yet embraced the Patent system. Researchers in universities and R&D institutions do not make effective use of the system. The utilization of the patent system especially its information function could make the Tanzanian researchers conduct research work which will solve the problems hindering economic growth with the little resources available.

Despite the few successes which TIPASIC achieved, it is still underutilized. We urge the scientific community, innovators and inventors, entrepreneurs, and the public at large to make use of this facility.The envisaged initiatives to foster utilization of knowledge by upgrading TIPASIC to TISC will contribute to the technological and economical development of Tanzania.

Recommendations

- ☆ Tanzanians should make use of the TISC project. As a Least Developing Country, it will receive the information for free whereby institutions in Tanzania will be saving up to $400,000 subscription costs.
- ☆ Encourage the use of patent information among researchers in universities, R&D institutions and other tertiary learning institutions to avoid re-inventing the wheel.
- ☆ R&D institutions and universities should be prepared to establish their TISCs, which will be linked to TISC of Tanzania at COSTECH.

References

1. African Regional Intellectual Property Organization (ARIPO) (1998). "Technological Information in Patents" ARIPO Patent Information 23/10/98.
2. Cullet, P. (2003). "Patents and medicines: the relationship between TRIPS and the human right to health" International Affairs Journal, 79(1), 139-160.
3. Drahos, P (2005). "Intellectual property rights in the knowledge economy" in Rooney, Handbook on the Knowledge Economy at http://cgkd.anu.edu.au/menus/publications.php#drahos visited on October 28, 2006.
4. Grawbowski, H.G. and Vernon, J.M. (2000). "Effective Patent Life in Pharmaceuticals" International Journal of Technology Management, 19 *(1/2)*, 98-120.
5. Gupta, G. and Rastogi, A. (2002). "Intellectual Property Rights: Theory and Indian Practice" Working Paper Series, Centre for Civil Society, New Delhi: Center for Civil Society at, http://ccsindia.org/ccsindia/policy/rule/articles/IPR_India.PDF, visited on November 8, 2005.
6. IDRC (2007). "Issues related to accessing patented knowledge for innovation" Background paper at www.idrc.ca/intellectual-property visited on 17 September 2007.

7. Menell, P. (1999). "1600 Intellectual Property: General Theories" at http://encyclo.findlaw.com/1600book.pdf, visited on November 8, 2005.

8. Morris, J., Mowatt, R., Reekie, W.D. and Tren, R. (2002). "Ideal Matter: Globalization and Intellectual Property Debate" Centre for New Europe Publication, ISBN 90-75724-23-3, p. 86.

9. Salazar, S. (1998). "The Intellectual Property and the Right to Health" Intellectual Property and Human Rights Panel Discussion November 9, 1998, Geneva-Switzerland.

Chapter 17

Intellectual Property (IP) Rights System in Turkey and Tübitak's IP Related Practises

*Murat BAYBALI**

Expert/Patent and Trademark Attorney,
The Scientific and Technological Research Council of Turkey,
Ankara, Tubitak

ABSTRACT

Starting in 13th-14th centuries with Akhism, followed by IP regulations in 1870s together with contemporary countries and signing multilateral agreements in mid 1990s today's legal framework for intellectual property rights in Turkey has been constituted.

Legal regulations related with Intellectual Property Rights go back to 1870s, when most European countries were also establishing similar regulations. First laws related with the Intellectual Property were not late to be enforced than the contemporary countries. Ottoman's trademark law was enacted in 1871 (Alamet-i Farika Nizamnamesi) and patent law was enacted in 1879 (Ihtira Beratý Kanunu). Today, Turkey is a party for almost all leading Agreements and Conventions including, Paris Convention, Berne Convention, Patent Cooperation Treaty (PCT), Protocol Relating to Madrid Agreement, European Patent Convention and Agreement Establishing World Trade Organization (WTO).

Intellectual property system is believed to be settled on four pillars, namely, legal framework, office for granting IP, specialized courts and attorneys. Turkey had all four pillars strengthened in the past two decades and acquired a well working Intellectual Property system.

* E-mail: murat.baybali@tubitak.gov.tr

The Scientific and Technological Research Council of Turkey (TÜBITAK) is the leading agency for management, funding and conduct of research in Turkey. It was established in 1963 with a mission to advance science and technology, conduct research and support Turkish researchers. The Council is an autonomous institution and is governed by a Scientific Board whose members are selected from prominent scholars from universities, industry and research institutions. More than 1,500 researchers work in 15 different research institutes of TÜBITAK where contract research as well as targeted and nation-wide research is conducted.

During the studies conducted in TUBITAK many kinds of Intellectual Property are arisen. TUBITAK Intellectual Property Rights Office is a branch of TUBITAK's Legal Department and deals with all kinds of Intellectual Properties and also conducts a part of Patent Application Promotion and Support Programme.

Keywords: *Intellectual property rights, IP in Turkey, TUBITAK, Patent Incentive Program.*

1. Introduction

1.1. Intellectual Property Rights

1.1.1. History of Intellectual Property Rights in the World [1]

One of the first known references to intellectual property protection dates from 500 B.C.E., when chefs in the Greek colony of Sybaris were granted year-long monopolies for creating particular culinary delights.

The basis of the first lasting patent institution of intellectual property protection is found in a 1474 statute of the Venetian Republic. This statute appeared 150 years before England's Statute of Monopolies; moreover, the system was sophisticated. The rights of inventors were recognized, an incentive mechanism was included, compensation for infringement was established, and a term limit on inventors' rights was imposed.

American institutions of intellectual property protection are based on the English system that began with the Statute of Monopolies (1624) and the Statute of Anne (1710). The Statute of Monopolies granted fourteen-year monopolies to authors and inventors and ended the practice of granting rights to "non-original/new" ideas or works already in the public domain. In contrast to patent institutions in Europe, literary works remained largely unprotected until the arrival of Gutenberg's printing press in the fifteenth century. Even then there were few true copyrights granted—most were grants, privileges, and monopolies.

Here are some of the first intellectual property legislations enacted in the stage of the history.

1474: Venetian Statute (FIRST PATENT LAW)

1624: England (Statute of Monopolies)

---

1. Moore, Adam, "Intellectual Property", The Stanford Encyclopedia of Philosophy (Summer 2011 Edition), Edward N. Zalta (ed.) http://plato.stanford.edu/archives/sum2011/entries/intellectual-property (accessed 09 July 2012)

1710: Statute of Anne (Copyright Act in England)

1790: USA (An Act to promote the progress of useful Arts)

1791: French Patent Law

1871: Alamet-i Farika Nizamnamesi (Ottoman Trademark Law)

1877: Patentgesetz (German Patent Act)

1879: Ihtira Beratý Kanunu (Ottoman Patent Law)

1883: Paris Convention for the Protection of Industrial Property (almost like the constitutional Law of IP)

1886: Berne Convention for the Protection of Literary and Artistic Works (almost like the constitutional Law of Copyrights)

1.1.2. History of Intellectual Property Rights in Turkey [2]

Turkey is one of the countries which enacted the very first regulations about Intellectual Property Rights together with the contemporary countries. First regulations were established in 13th-14th centuries, Ottoman Empire ages, under the name of "Akhism". This was different from the Guild concept of the Europe at the same era, Akhism, in fact, was relying on innovation, thus encouraging inventions. In Akhism, in order to establish an Akhi guild, an innovative product had to be introduced or an innovation in the technology must have been achieved. That innovation, just like the same in patents today, was rewarded with a monopoly right. The monopoly right granted for the Akhi guild was limited to a certain region and was granted with the provision that the Akhi guild had to train and educate new craftsmen.

Legal regulations related with Intellectual Property Rights goes back to 1870s, when most European countries were also establishing similar regulations. First laws related with the Intellectual Property were not late to be enforced than the contemporary countries. Ottoman's trademark law was enacted in 1871 (Alamet-i Farika Nizamnamesi) and patent law was in 1879 (Ihtira Beratý Kanunu).

In mid 1990s Turkey signed the Agreement Establishing World Trade Organization (WTO). Then Customs Union came into force between Turkey and the European Union. Today's legal framework for intellectual property rights had to be constituted at the time, as a consequence of Turkey's responsibilities arising from the agreements.

Today, Turkey is a party for almost all leading Agreements and Conventions including, Paris Convention, Berne Convention, Patent Cooperation Treaty (PCT), Protocol Relating to Madrid Agreement, European Patent Convention and Agreement Establishing World Trade Organization (WTO).

---

2. Turkish Patent Institute (TPI) website http://www.tpe.gov.tr/portal/default2.jsp?sayfa=602 (accessed 09 July 2012)

1.2. Types of Intellectual Property[3]

Intellectual Property Rights can be divided into two main branches, namely, "Copyright and Related Rights" and "Industrial Property Rights".

The areas mentioned as literary, artistic and scientific works belong to the "copyright" branch of intellectual property. The areas mentioned as performances of performing artists, phonograms and broadcasts are usually called "related rights," that is, rights related to copyright.

The areas mentioned as inventions, industrial designs, trademarks, service marks and commercial names and designations including indications of source and appellations of origin, constitute the "industrial property" branch of intellectual property. The area mentioned as protection against unfair competition may also be considered as belonging to that branch.

2. Legal Framework of Intellectual Property Rights in Turkey

Started in 13th-14th centuries with Akhism, followed by regulations in 1870s together with contemporary countries, Turkey was aware of intellectual property rights protection. As a consequence of international agreements signed in mid 1990s Turkey had to set down minimum standards for many forms of intellectual property (IP) regulation as applied to nationals of other WTO Members. In order to accomplish the task a series of Decree Laws were implemented. Also Turkey signed many other international agreements related with intellectual property rights and strengthened the protection of intellectual property in the country. The following list shows the main legal framework for intellectual property rights in Turkey:

2.1. National Legislation

- ☆ Copyright Law, No. 5846 on Intellectual and Artistic Works (1951) (revised in 1983, 1995, 2001, 2004, 2006, 2008)
- ☆ Patent Decree Law, No. 551 (1995)
- ☆ Trademarks Decree Law, No. 556 (1995)
- ☆ Industrial Design Decree Law, No. 554 (1995)
- ☆ Geographical Indications Decree Law, No. 555 (1995)
- ☆ Protection of Integrated Circuits Topographies Law, No. 5147 (2004)
- ☆ Amending Decree Laws No. 551, 556, 554 and 555 Law, No. 5194 (2004)
- ☆ Protection of the Plant Breeders' Rights Law, No. 5042 (2004)

2.2. International Agreements

- ☆ Paris Convention for the Protection of Industrial Property (1925)
- ☆ Berne Convention for Literary Arts (1971)
- ☆ Convention Establishing World Intellectual Property Organization (1976)

---

3 WIPO Intellectual Property Handbook: Policy, Law and Use, WIPO 2004, Second Edition, pp 3-4, ISBN 978-92-805-1291-5.

- ☆ Agreement Establishing World Trade Organization (WTO) (1995)
- ☆ Patent Cooperation Treaty (PCT) (1996)
- ☆ Nice Agreement Concerning the International Classification of Goods and Services for the Purposes of Registration of Marks (1996)
- ☆ Vienna Agreement Concerning International Classification of the Figurative Elements of Marks (1996)
- ☆ Strasbourg Agreement Concerning the International Patent Classification (IPC) (1996)
- ☆ Budapest Agreement of the International Registration of the Deposit of MicroOrganisms for the Purposes of Patent Procedure (1998)
- ☆ Locarno Agreement Establishing an International Classification for Industrial Designs (1998)
- ☆ Protocol Relating to Madrid Agreement (1999)
- ☆ European Patent Convention (EPC) (2000) → EPC 2000 (2007)
- ☆ Patent Law Treaty (PLT) (2000)
- ☆ The Hague Agreement Concerning the International Registration of Industrial Designs (Geneva Act) (2005)
- ☆ Trademark Law Treaty (TLT) (2005)
- ☆ Singapore Treaty on the Law of Trademarks (2006, not in force)

Legal entities dealing with copyrights or industrial property rights in Turkey are diversified.

The Ministry of Culture and Tourism is in charge of copyright protection. In Turkey, only musical works, cinematographic works and computer programmes are subjected to a mandatory recording and registration procedure at the Ministry of Culture and Tourism. Other types of intellectual and artistic works defined under the provisions of Copyright Law, No. 5846 might be subjected to an arbitrary recording and registration procedure at the Ministry.

Legal entities dealing with industrial property rights protection are further diversified. Leading institution for industrial property is Turkish Patent Institute (TPI). Patents, trademarks, industrial designs, integrated circuit designs and geographical indications are under the responsibility of Turkish Patent Institute. The only exception of industrial property which is not administered by the Turkish Patent Institute is plant breeders' rights. This is under the responsibility of Ministry of Food, Agriculture and Livestock.

Recently, a comprehensive draft law which was proposed for adoption by the Turkish parliament was prepared by the Turkish Patent Institute. This draft law aims to make changes in national legislation related with the industrial property rights, *i.e.* patents, trademarks, industrial designs, geographical indications, to strengthen their provisions, to bring them to a more practical level and to harmonize legal framework with other countries.

One of the major changes brought by the provisions of the draft law is the change in holder of the rights for the inventions of university staff.

Patent decree law, No. 551, states that inventions that are made by the employee in the course of his employment in a private enterprise or public authority while performing, by virtue of his obligations, the tasks assigned to him, or those that are based to a large extent on the experience and work of the said private enterprise or public authority are service inventions. On the other hand it is stated that inventions made by the teaching staff of universities in the course of their scientific studies at universities or schools of higher education, shall be free inventions. This concept is known in practice as professor's privilege or academic exemption.

The draft law, however, proposes to abolish the professor's privilege on patents from academic research. If the draft law is adopted by Turkish parliament, inventions made by the teaching staff of universities will also be service inventions and the holder of the rights for these inventions will be the universities.

3. Patent Protection in Turkey

There are 3 main routes in Turkey to have a patent protection.

Firstly, an applicant can either choose to file a patent application directly to Turkish Patent Institute or extend his earlier patent filing to Turkey using its priority right, for a national patent protection. This route is called the national route.

Secondly, an applicant may prefer to file a patent application before World Intellectual Property Organization (WIPO) or extend his earlier patent filing to WIPO using its priority right and have an international PCT filing. And after 30 months (+3 months extension is available in Turkey) in international phase he might like to extend the application into national phase for Turkey. This is called the international route.

And thirdly, an applicant may file a European patent application under the provisions of European Patent Convention before the European Patent Office (EPO) or extend his earlier patent filing to EPO using its priority right. All granting procedures would take place before the EPO and if a patent is granted the applicant has to validate the European Patent before Turkish Patent Institute, *i.e.* give the translation of the document within 3 months from the publication of the grant of the European Patent.

National patent applications coming from the national route and national phases of PCT applications coming from the international route are granted and protected under the provisions of patent decree law No. 551. For European patent applications all of the procedures are completed before the EPO from application to grant, opposition and appeal and once the patent is granted and the granted patent is validated in Turkey, enforcement of the patent is subjected to the provisions of patent decree law No. 551. If the European patent is revoked after the opposition and/or appeal procedures before the EPO, the patent is revoked as if it never existed in Turkey, *i.e.* the patent will directly be revoked without need for the invalidation procedures defined under the provisions of patent decree law No. 551 are fulfilled. The decision taken by EPO is directly applicable without looking at national legislation.

Patent decree law No. 551, states that inventions that are novel, go beyond the state of the art and are applicable in industry shall be protected by patents. The law defines 3 types of protection, namely, patent with substantive examination, patent without substantive examination and utility models.

The term of a patent granted with substantive examination shall be a non-renewable period of 20 years from the filing date of the application. In order to obtain a grant for a patent with substantive examination, search report and examination report(s) have to be established for the application and according to the reports the application has to meet the patentability criteria of novelty, inventive step and industrial applicability.

The term of a patent granted without substantive examination shall be a non-renewable period of 7 years from the filing date of the application. In order to get a grant for a patent without substantive examination, a search has to be conducted for the application. However, without assessing the patentability criteria, the patent can be directly granted if so requested by the applicant. Actually the system of granting without substantive examination was first intended for the applicant to delay the examination for 7 years in case they might not have enough funds for the rest of the procedures. That was a critical decision made by the law makers when the patent decree law No. 551 was drafted so as to make sure the applicants would not be discouraged by the high procedural fees. An applicant is allowed to delay the examination procedures for 7 years during the procedures. However once the statistics are analyzed it could be noticed that the main purpose of the system is misused and many patents were granted with negative search reports meaning patentability criteria had not been met in the application.

Where the request for substantive examination is not filed within seven years from the date of filing, the right to a patent shall lapse. Later substantive examination of a patent granted without substantive examination shall require the filing of a request to that effect. Such a request shall be filed by the patentee or by third parties within seven years from the filing date of the application. The substantive examination fee shall be paid by the party who filed the request for the examination. No request for substantive examination may be filed after the seven-year period has expired.

A utility model certificate is granted for a non-renewable term of 10 years from the filing date of the application. In order to get a grant for a utility model neither search nor examination report is required. The decision on merit for grant is made by Turkish Patent Institute officers. Also in utility model certificates inventive step criteria is not required. Therefore the officers check for novelty and industrial applicability. It has to be noted that the powers of the officers of the Turkish Patent Institute are not absolute since the applications are published for third party oppositions. The applicant may, within three months of being notified of the oppositions filed, submit a duly reasoned response to the said oppositions, or amend the claims if he sees fit or request the Institute to issue the certificate without taking the oppositions filed into consideration.

The search report shall be drawn up, in the light of the specification, the drawings if any and the claims by the Institute or by the search authority designated by the

Institute from among internationally recognized search authorities. Turkish Patent Institute conducts search and examination reports on particular IPC classes and for other IPC classes, which Turkish Patent Institute does not conduct a report, the applications are sent to internationally recognized search and examination authorities.

Once patents are granted by the Turkish Patent Institute for any of the above mentioned protection types, *i.e.* patent with substantive examination, patent without substantive examination or utility model, invalidation of the grant can only be achieved through the national courts.

The draft law proposed for adoption provides some changes in patent protection types. In the draft law, provisions for patents without substantive examination are revoked and search report is put as a requirement for utility models certificates. Another provision proposed by the draft law is opposition mechanism against the grant of a patent before the Turkish Patent Institute. According to decree law, No. 551, after grant of a patent by the Turkish Patent Institute, third parties can only ask for invalidation of that patent at the national courts.

4. Closer Look at the Trademark Protection in Turkey[4]

In Turkey, trademark protection is granted according to the provisions of the Decree-Law No.556 which pertains to the Protection of Trademarks. Trademarks are registered for a period of ten years from the date of filing of the application. Registration may be renewed for further periods of ten years.

Basically, there are two ways of applying for a trademark protection in Turkey, namely; direct application to Turkish Patent Institute and international applications through the Madrid System.

The Trademarks Department of the Turkish Patent Institute carries out an examination system, which consists of examination for absolute grounds for refusal and also ex-officio examination for prior rights. If no grounds for refusal are found in the first examination, the application will be published in the monthly Official Trademark Bulletin. Third persons may file oppositions within 3 months from publication in the Bulletin.

If there are no oppositions filed within the above mentioned time limit, the application will be registered in the Trademark Register and it will be published in the Official Trademark Gazette. If the application is refused totally or partially in the first examination, the applicant may lodge an appeal to the Institute within 2 months. In this case, the application should be re-examined regarding the appeal. If the appeal is found acceptable, the application will be published totally or partially in the Bulletin, this means that the application may be the subject of a further refusal following an opposition.

The Turkish Patent Institute, Trademarks Department has a separate division (oppositions and appeals division) for the examination of oppositions and appeals.

---

4 Turkish Patent Institute (TPI) website http://www.tpe.gov.tr/portal/default_en.jsp?sayfa=131 (accessed 11 July 2012).

Parties who are not satisfied with the decisions of this division can also appeal to the decisions before the Institute. "Re-examination and Evaluation Board" is the final decisive organ of the Institute; the decisions of the board are open to court actions within 2 months.

The second alternative for making a trademark application in Turkey is to use the Madrid System which is administered by World Intellectual Property Organization (WIPO). Madrid system is formed by two treaties complementing each other. These treaties are the Madrid Agreement and the Madrid Protocol. Turkey is a member of the Protocol only. Therefore, it accepts applications from the States which are party to the Protocol only or from the States which are party to both the Agreement and the Protocol. In both cases, the governing treaty for the international applications filed to Turkish Patent Institute is the Madrid Protocol.

5. A Strong Intellectual Property Rights System

It is accepted that a strong intellectual property system settles on four pillars. These are; legislation for granting and protecting the rights, qualified patent/ trademark attorneys to prepare the documents for grant, patent institute for granting the rights, and specialized courts for resolution of the intellectual property disputes.

Turkey has established all four pillars since mid-1990s and has kept strengthening them. Legislations are meeting requirements for granting and protecting intellectual property rights, yet a very comprehensive draft law has been proposed for adoption by the Turkish parliament which aims to strengthen the provisions, to bring them to a more practical level and to harmonize the legal framework with contemporary countries.

Patent and trademark attorneys are subjected to an examination carried out by the Turkish Patent Institute. Without passing the examination one cannot represent a client before the Turkish Patent Institute. Professional standards of the attorneys are desired to be upgraded legally and Patent and Trademark Attorneys Association and Patent and Trademark Attorneys Sector Assembly under Turkish Union of Chambers and Commodity Exchanges are conducting some studies in order to improve the standards for attorneys.

The Turkish Patent Institute was established with the objective of supporting the technological development in Turkey and of establishing and protecting of industrial property rights, as well as providing the public with the worldwide information on industrial property rights, thereby supporting the cultivation of a competitive environment and the development of research and development activities.

In 2003, Specialized Courts in the area of intellectual property rights is established in Turkey. The judicial resolution of the intellectual property disputes is performed by these competent specialized courts. Where no specialized court exists then Civil Court of First Instance and Criminal Court of First Instance are in charge. A drawback of the system is that no special establishment and judicial procedure act that regulates the establishment and jurisdiction of this specialized courts exists. Therefore, the general rules of the judicial procedure are being applied to the civil and criminal cases of intellectual property rights.

6. The Scientific and Technological Research Council of Turkey (TÜBITAK)

6.1. Introduction

The Scientific and Technological Research Council of Turkey (TÜBITAK) is the leading agency for management, funding and conduct of research in Turkey. It was established in 1963 with a mission to advance science and technology, conduct research and support Turkish researchers. The Council is an autonomous institution and is governed by a Scientific Board whose members are selected from prominent scholars from universities, industry and research institutions.

TÜBITAK is responsible for promoting, developing, organizing, conducting and coordinating research and development in line with national targets and priorities.

TÜBITAK acts as an advisory agency to the Turkish Government on science and research issues, and is the secretariat of the Supreme Council for Science and Technology (SCST), the highest S&T policy making body in Turkey.

Setting its vision as *'to be an innovative, guiding, participating and cooperating institution in the fields of science and technology, which serves for improvement of the life standards of our society and sustainable development of our country'*, TÜBITAK not only supports innovation, academic and industrial R&D studies but also in line with national priorities develops scientific and technological policies and manages R&D institutes, carrying on research, technology and development studies. Furthermore, TÜBITAK funds research projects carried out in universities and other public and private organizations, conducts research on strategic areas, develops support programs for public and private sectors, publishes scientific journals, popular science magazines and books, organizes science and society activities and supports undergraduate and graduate students through scholarships.

More than 1,500 researchers work in 15 different research institutes of TÜBITAK where contract research as well as targeted and nation-wide research is conducted.

6.2. Activities of TÜBITAK

Besides its administrative duties mentioned above, from many of TÜBITAK's activities intellectual property rights arise. These activities can be grouped as:

- ☆ **Conducting research**: R&D activities on strategic areas are conducted through its research institutes.
- ☆ **Funding research**: Funding research projects carried out in universities and other public and private organizations, developing support programmes for public and private sectors.
- ☆ **Promoting Science**: Publishing scientific journals, popular science magazines and books. Organizing science and society activities and supporting undergraduate and graduate students through scholarships.

6.3. TÜBITAK's IP Related Practices

Under the course of conducting and funding research mainly, patent rights arise. Holder of rights for the invention for which a patent protection is sought is determined by Article 21 of the Law, No. 278, Establishing TÜBITAK.

According to article 21, holder of the right is set in two paragraphs as given below;

> *Intellectual property rights that arise during the projects executed by TÜBITAK, meaning when research is conducted by TÜBITAK, holder of the right is TÜBITAK*
>
> and
>
> *Intellectual property rights that possibly will arise during the projects executed by others relying on a contract to which TÜBITAK is a party*, meaning intellectual property is arisen when TÜBITAK is funding a research, holder of the right will be arranged in the contract.

First paragraph actually states in accordance with the provisions of patent decree law, No. 551, defining employee inventions which are accepted as service inventions. Therefore inventions made by employees of TÜBITAK, *i.e.* service inventions, are evaluated; drafts for patent applications are prepared and all procedural steps during grant process are dealt by the group of patent and trademark attorneys working at Intellectual Property Rights branch of Legal Affairs Office in TÜBITAK.

Intellectual Property Rights branch of Legal Affairs Office is also responsible from all of the other types of intellectual property. These include trademarks, industrial designs, integrated circuits that may arise during researches either conducted by TÜBITAK itself or conducted in accordance with a contract.

Moreover another major source of intellectual property encountered in TÜBITAK arises from the work of promoting science. Publishing scientific journals, popular science magazines and books mean copyright issues to be assessed by the Intellectual Property Rights branch of Legal Affairs Office.

TÜBITAK also supports inventors of Turkish nationality under a program called Patent Application Promotion and Support Program. The purpose of Patent Application Promotion and Support Program is to increase the number of national and international patent applications of Turkey, to encourage people to make patent applications, and to increase awareness about registering intellectual and industrial property rights.

For national (TR), international (PCT) and regional (EP) applications TÜBITAK grants 3000 TL plus 450 TL for representatives. For later stage of international (PCT) or national applications (providing EP, US and JP applications have already been filed) which has chance to be granted as triadic patents, TÜBITAK supports the applicants up to 75,000 TL, the amount of which is decided by a panel composed of TÜBITAK and Turkish Patent Institute experts. Here, later stage means the rest of the procedures after a search report has already been established and the amount decided by the panel is transferred to applicant as credit. If the application turns into granted triadic patent the credit will be converted to a grant, if not the applicant has to pay the credited amount back.

6.4. Last Remarks

Today, Turkey is a country where intellectual property rights can be granted and protected on high standards with modern legislations, qualified registration offices, specialized courts and attorneys and everything. However none of these would serve for benefit if intellectual property is not managed well.

Management of intellectual property is not only managing registration and grant procedures of various types of intellectual property but much more than that.

Management starts with the first sparks of an idea, continue with registration and grant procedures where the spark becomes an intellectual property, further continues with commercializing and making profit and lasts with termination of the rights. From an idea to a granted right and then from commercializing to termination, a step-by-step approach in intellectual property management will be roughly discussed here after.

Creativity is the key for sparks of an idea and that could either come up unintentionally or with motivation. No matter how, once an idea comes up, first step to be taken is to identify existing intellectual property information related with that idea. In order to identify that, a search has to be made, results must be evaluated and a comparison has to be made between the information gathered and the idea. This will help to decide whether or not the idea is worth protecting. Management in this very first step is vital and must be handled professionally. In case of inventions this step corresponds to prior art search, in case of trademarks it is similarity search. Unless it is not managed well the consequence of failure will be loss of money and time. For inventions, this step benefits as to avoid duplication of R&D work, it might contribute to the idea with some new ideas found the information gathered and also shows information about what do the competitor companies do. This is very important for companies as it prevents falling behind the demands of the market and see where the market is shifting.

After a neat first step has been taken, now, management of the filing and procedures before the registration and grant offices comes as a second step to be taken carefully. At this step again professional assistance should be considered. Questions like; should an application for registration and/or grant be filed or should it stay as secret, if filing is preferred, when to file, where to file, how to file, are there any incentives, are there any funds, must be answered correctly in order to manage the step well. In case of patents, at this step a market analysis is required in order to determine whether to file a national application or an international application would serve better. Another important aspect is to determine scope of protection. Scope of specification and claims must be defined wisely. Using the information gathered in the first step, like the prior art search results, a draft specification and claims are prepared. Specification must give information about prior art and claims must be formulated, especially in two-part claims, so as to involve preamble and body parts where preamble discloses prior art and body discloses the invention. Managing the patent drafts are crucial as it constitutes the scope of protection.

Third step in management might involve commercializing aspects. After the second step, where a well managed application is filed, possibly but not necessarily after grant is obtained, now it is time to take the next step into commercializing. At this step it would be convenient to decide whether the granted right will be used by the holder of the right or will there be a contract for transferring or licensing the right. In order to decide on that, the intellectual property must be analyzed in following aspects:

for its strength; how strong is it against revocation or invalidity?,

for possible infringement issues; if the use of it will cause an infringement to any third party rights,

for its term; how long will it stay in force?,

for the commercial demand; is the product protected by IP widely sold in the market or is there an opportunity for it become widely sold in future?,

for prospective licensees or buyers; are there any companies that might be interested in cooperation?

for the competitors in the market; who will be your opponents?

Many more considerations may arise due to the nature of the intellectual property. All have to be managed well for this step to be taken wisely.

First step determines if we have an intellectual property or not, then second step, whether or not and how a protection to be obtained, third step for how to benefit from the intellectual property and now finally termination of intellectual property comes. Many types of intellectual property are maintained with considerable amounts of expenses. When the value of the intellectual property is decreased, expenses for keeping the IP alive become more than incomes made out of it. When such a scenario comes true, it is the best to withdraw the intellectual property without spending any more resources on it. This procedure is mainly related with industrial property as far as copyrights are not subject to annual fees or such expenses. Value of an intellectual property might fall due to many reasons some of which are improvements in the technology, introduction of newer and better equivalents of the products, later realization of some drawbacks of the products, decrease in the demand to the product, termination of license agreements, and so on. Therefore this step must also be managed well and meaningless expenses must be avoided.

Management of intellectual property from birth to death of an idea stands like a cycle where the last step is triggering the first step of the next cycle. That is, when one intellectual property starts losing its value, it is time to look for a new spark of an idea to restart from the beginning. In practice, it is recommended that new spark of an idea is looked for before the old one is actually terminated. In such a way the cycles will be overlapping in last and first steps therefore no standby between cycles happens.

6.4.1. Managing Tips for Inventions in Turkey

Among all types of intellectual property patents are the ones which require more expenses. Therefore it has to be managed correctly in order not to lose time and money.

As it is explained above, there are 3 routes to have a patent protection in Turkey. The market of interest determines which route has to be followed.

If the invention is valuable in one country or in only a few countries like Turkey and a few neighbors, then following the international route is pointless. International PCT applications have two phases, namely international phase and national phase. After completing the international phase before the international bureau of WIPO, applicants proceed to national phase where the application is extended to national IP offices. Grant of the patent is decided by national offices and further search and examination reports might be asked from the applicants. Fees for international phase plus the fees for national offices makes the process rather expensive. Instead of that, filing a national first filing to Turkey and extending it to other few countries in 12 months using the priority right would be the most efficient route.

On the contrary, if the market is global, filing an international application must be considered right away. PCT filing fees are not so cheap therefore if the applicant is not sure about the invention for its patentability, before filing a PCT application, a national application can be filed and a search report from the national office may be received. Mostly, national office fees for filing and search report are cheaper than international PCT filing and search report fees. As soon as a search report is established in national office the applicant has a concrete evidence for evaluating the invention and deciding whether or not to go for an international application. If search report is positive within 12 months from the first national filing the applicant will have a chance to extend the application into PCT international application using the priority right.

If an applicant files first in Turkey national office, then extends the application into PCT international application within 12 months using the priority right, Turkey may again be chosen in national phase of international PCT application. The term for PCT applications is 20 years from the filing date of the PCT application. Considering that the filing date of PCT application is one year later than the first filing (via priority right), once PCT application is extended into Turkish national phase, term of this patent gives the applicant another 20 years of protection. Note that, first application filed as priority in Turkey has already started protecting the invention from its application date. Then, the second patent protection coming through national phase PCT application comes into force with a term 1 year longer. By this method an applicant might prolong the term for protection of an invention to 21 year while actually, the term for a patent with substantive examination is 20 years in Turkey. This method is not only effective for Turkey but also other countries where the first filing is made.

Conclusion

Intellectual property rights protection is important not only in companies' development but also in the development of strong national economies.

Intellectual property rights help companies get known by the customers. Also, having monopoly rights give companies advantage over competitors and they receive recompense for their investments put in creating their intellectual property. Meanwhile, the competitors, in order to enter the market without infringing others' rights, have to add on the intellectual property that others protect, create new ideas as their own intellectual property and survive in the market.

Providing an infrastructure that motivates creating new ideas, allowing incentives to encourage this creation and rewarding the creation by protecting them as intellectual properties is crucial for strong economies to be developed. Unless that is provided, imitation takes over and creations made by others are copied, and that would lead to degradation in economy.

Turkey has established legislations for protecting and enforcing intellectual property rights in the country. Having all the aspects of a functioning intellectual property system has not only served well for increase in national investments in creating intellectual property but also Turkey has become a centre of attraction for foreign investments.

Patent Application Promotion and Support Program which is conducted by The Scientific and Technological Research Council of Turkey (TÜBITAK) led a considerable increase in patent filings both in national and international routes. The aim of the program is achieved by the increase in patent filings and also by the increase in awareness about registering intellectual property rights. After five years from the initiation of the program, at the end of 2011, roughly about 5500 patent applications are supported by the program.

A strong intellectual property system leads to economic growth and competitiveness. However the system must be used wisely by the companies and entrepreneurs with good intellectual property management skills. It has to be noted that failure in management of intellectual property ends up in loss of time and money.

References

1. Moore, Adam, "Intellectual Property", The Stanford Encyclopedia of Philosophy (Summer 2011 Edition), Edward N. Zalta (ed.),http://plato.stanford.edu/archives/sum2011/entries/intellectual-property (accessed 09 July 2012)
2. Republic of Turkey Ministry of Culture and Tourism - Go Turkey, Gateway to Turkey: The Official Travel and Holiday Guide © 2012http://www.goturkey.com/turkiye.php?lng=en&content=history (accessed 09 July 2012)
3. Republic of Turkey Ministry of Culture and Tourism - Go Turkey, Gateway to Turkey: The Official Travel and Holiday Guide © 2012http://www.goturkey.com/turkiye.php?lng=en&content=ceography (accessed 09 July 2012)
4. Turkish Patent Institute (TPI) websitehttp://www.tpe.gov.tr/portal/default2.jsp?sayfa=602 (accessed 09 July 2012)
5. Turkish Patent Institute (TPI) websitehttp://www.tpe.gov.tr/portal/default_en.jsp?sayfa=131 (accessed 11 July 2012)
6. WIPO Intellectual Property Handbook: Policy, Law and Use, WIPO 2004, Second Edition, pp 3-4, ISBN 978-92-805-1291-5

Chapter 18

Country Report: Analysis and Review of the Current Situation on Intellectual Property in Uganda

*Dwight Bigala**

Advocate of the High Court of Uganda,
P.O. Box 29937 Kampala, Uganda

ABSTRACT

This is a paper presented for the International Advanced Training Course on Contemporary Management Strategies in Intellectual Property Rights (IPR) relevant to NAM and Other Developing Countries which took place in Manesar (Haryana), India from the 16th to the 20th day of July 2012. In this paper, the author reviews the current law governing intellectual property in Uganda in light of the prevailing social and economic conditions and the various regional and international legal instruments which Uganda is bound to. In his analysis, the author points out areas for reform where necessary.

Keywords: *Copyrights, Patents, Trademarks, Geographical indications, Industrial designs, Trade secrets, Indigenous knowledge and folklore.*

1. Introduction

Intellectual Property (IP) refers to creations of the mind: inventions, literary and artistic works, and symbols, names, images, and designs used in commerce. IP is

---

* E-mail: dwightbigala@gmail.com

divided into two categories: Industrial property, which includes inventions (patents), trademarks, industrial designs, and geographic indications of source; and Copyright, which includes literary and artistic works such as novels, poems and plays, films, musical works, artistic works such as drawings, paintings, photographs and sculptures, and architectural designs.[1]

The main IP laws in Uganda for patents, trademarks and other forms of intellectual property in Uganda are: the Trademarks Act 2010, the Trade Secrets Protection Act 2009, the Copyright and Neighbouring Rights Act 2006, the Patents (Amendment) Act 2002, the Patents Act 1993, and the United Kingdom Designs (Protection) Act 1937.

In this paper, the author analyses and reviews the current situation of intellectual property in Uganda. He does so by focusing on copyrights, patents, trademarks, industrial designs, geographical indications, trade secrets, indigenous knowledge and folklore and the administrative aspect of intellectual property rights.

2. Copyright

Copyright in Uganda was until 31st May 2006 protected under the Copyright Act of 1964. In 2006, this law was amended in agreement with Ugandas' treaty requirements under the TRIPS Agreement of 1994. The subsequent revised version is The Copyright and Neighboring Rights Act 19 of 2006.

2.1. Eligibility

Under the current law, the nature of works eligible for protection is extensive encompassing "*...any other work in the field of literature, traditional folklore and knowledge, science and art, in whatever manner delivered, known or to be known in future.*"[2]; the exceptions being ideas, government laws and reports and also news from the media.[3] The benchmark for eligibility for protection is that the work must be original and published.[4] The protection is conferred for 50 years from the date of publication or 50 years from the date of death of the author. [5]

2.2. Consequence of Copyright

This protection gives the author exclusive economic rights[6] in respect to work which in its broadest application means '*...the right to do in relation to that work, any act known or to be known in future.*"[7] However, fair use of a protected work does not constitute infringement.[8] The infringement of the copyright entitles the owner to

---

1. World Intellectual Property Organization: http://www.wipo.int/about-ip/en. (accessed 5th November 2011)
2. S.5(j) of Act 19 of 2006
3. S.6 & 7 ibid
4. S.4 ibid
5. S.13 ibid
6. S.9 ibid
7. S.9(h) ibid
8. S.15 ibid

damages for the loss arising from the infringement, an injunction to restrain further infringement and an order of forfeiture issued by a court of law in respect to the thing used in connection with the offence.

2.3. Ownership of Copyright

Ordinarily, it is the actual creator of eligible work who is entitled to copyright protection. However, in cases where work is created during the course of employment, the economic right remains with the employer, whereas the moral right remains with the actual author.[9] The moral right is the right to claim authorship or performance.[10] Apart from moral rights, the current law also creates neighbouring rights, which were not provided for in the earlier law.[11] "Neighbouring rights" include rights of performing artistes in their performances, rights of producers and music publishers and rights of broadcasting companies in their programmes and others as is provided under Part IV of the Act.[12]

Where work is created by more than one person each of whom have an indistinguishable interest in the work, the co-authors are granted equal rights in respect to that work. [13]

2.4. International Rights

Uganda is a signatory to the Berne Convention. The Berne Convention held in 1886 in Berne, Switzerland. The treaty states that if copyright exists in one of these countries, then this copyright is valid in all member countries who are signatories of the Berne Convention.[14] Broadly speaking this convention makes provision for the nationals of all participating countries to enjoy in these countries the same protection as they would have at home. No formalities are required to benefit under the Berne Convention.

3. Patents

The relevant law applicable in regard to patents in Uganda is:

a) The Patents Act Cap. 216
b) The Patents Regulations Statutory Instrument 216-1
c) Patents Amendment Act 7/2002
d) The ARIPO Protocol
e) Patents Cooperation Treaty 1970
f) The Paris Convention.

---

9. S.8 & 9 ibid
10. S.2 ibid
11. Part IV ibid
12. S.2 ibid
13. S.11 ibid
14. See List of Berne Convention Signatories: http://www.copyrighthouse.co.uk/countries-berne-convention.htm (accessed 7th November 2011)

3.1. What is Patentable?

In the broadest sense, any technical invention in a product, machine, material or process is patentable. There are a number of specific exclusions, such as pure discoveries, scientific theories, business schemes, animal or plant varieties, medical or veterinary therapy or surgery.[15] Plant varieties although not covered under this law are set to be protected under the Plant Variety Protection Bill 2002 when enacted.[16]

In order for an invention to be protected, it must be new, involve an inventive step and must be industrially applicable.[17]

3.2. Procedure for Application

An application for the grant of a patent is lodged to the Registrar of patents by the applicant or his agent.[18] Certain particulars should accompany the application. These include: a request in Form 1, a description of the invention; claim defining the matter to be protected; relevant drawing; abstract containing technical information to be used to interpret the scope of the protection sought and relevant fee.[19]

The registrar thereafter carries out a search and a substantive examination of the application.[20] For purposes of the examination, the registrar may transmit the application, with all accompanying documents, to the ARIPO Office or any other statutorily designated recognized authority for a preliminary examination as to the patentability of the invention claimed.[21] Upon being satisfied by the applicant, the Registrar grants the patent, issues the relevant certificate, records the patent in the Register of Patents and publishes it in the Gazette[22]

Regional Protection for a patent can be secured through the ARIPO Office. The application is made through the local Office of the Registrar of Patents in Uganda.[23] The contents of the application are not different from those demanded for a local registration.[24] Upon receipt of the application, the ARIPO Secretariat examines whether the formal requirements have been complied with.[25] If these are in order, the Registrar General accords the application a filing date.[26] Thereafter the application is examined

---

15. S.7(2) of the Patents Act As Amended
16. The United Nations Convention on Biological Diversity, 1992 provides for the setting up of protection regimes for plant varieties
17. S.8 of the Patents Act ibid.
18. S.13 of the Patent Act
19. Reg.16 of the Patent Regulations
20. S.20 of the Patent Act
21. S.20(3) ibid
22. S.21 (1) & (2) of the Patent Act and Reg.29 of the Patent Regulations
23. S.2(1) of the ARIPO Protocol
24. Reg.5 ibid provides for the contents of the application.
25. S.3(2)(a) ibid
26. Reg.14 ibid

as to patentability.[27] If it is compliant, then a patent is granted and published under the ARIPO Journal.[28] The applicant is issued with the requisite certificate and ARIPO Secretariat duly notifies its member states of this patent.[29]

In regard to international protections, the Uganda Patent Office is a receiving office for PCT applications.[30] The ARIPO office transmits the application to the International Bureau of the World Intellectual Property in Geneva.[31] Upon receipt of the application, the Bureau conducts formality examinations and preliminary searches[32] and examination,[33] and provides a written opinion on patentability. It should be noted that the Bureau doesn't grant patents. It is the member states that grant patents during the national phase of PCT applications.

3.3. Duties of the Patent Owner

The patentee is required to: disclose the invention clearly and completely and also indicate the best method of its execution; work the patented invention within the prescribed time; pay the prescribed fees; pay the annual fee to maintain the application or grant.[34]

3.4. Rights of the Patent Owner

The owner of a patent is entitled to: the exclusive right to make, use, exercise, vend the invention and preclude any person from exploiting the patented invention without his/her authority; assign or transfer the application for a patent or patent[35]; institute infringement proceedings in court to secure damages[36], an injunction to prevent the infringement or continuing infringement, any other civil remedy;[37] a hearing prior to a Government directive to exploit the patent;[38] payment by the Government or other person for a Ministerial directed exploitation of his/her patented invention;[39] appeal to the High Court against the direction of the Minister[40] or decision

---

27. Reg.18 ibid
28. Reg.20 ibid
29. Reg.20(1)(e) ibid
30. S.3 ibid
31. Art. 12 of the Patents Cooperation Treaty
32. Art.15(1) ibid
33. Art.35 ibid.
34. Ss 24 & 32of the Patent Act
35. Ss 25, 33 & 34 ibid
36. S. 26(2) ibid
37. S.29(1)(a) ibid
38. S.29(1)(a) ibid
39. S.29(1)(b) ibid
40. S.29(2)(a) ibid

of the Registrar fixing the payment for the exploitation of the invention;[41] apply for the extension of the patent after the expiration of fifteen (15) years following the grants;[42] surrender; some or all the claims in respect of the patent subject to the consent of a licensee thereof;[43] *(Patents Act, S.35)* issue a licence to another person in respect of the patented invention.[44]

3.5. Limitation of the Rights of the Owner

The utilization of the patented invention by the patentee is restricted to industrial or commercial purposes[45] and the terms of the claims[46] The patentees' rights are not infringed by: acts in respect of articles which have been put on the market in Uganda by the patentee or with the patentees' express consent, acts done in pursuance of research; the use of a patented article on foreign aircrafts, land vehicles or vessels of other countries which temporarily or accidentally enter the borders of Uganda; acts done in good faith before the filing or determination of the priority date of the patent[47]. It should also be noted that in public interest, the government can without the authority of the patentee, direct that a patented invention be exploited by a government agent or other person.[48]

3.6. Maintenance and Duration of Patent

The patent expires at the end of 15 years from the date of grant of the application.[49] The patentee may request the registrar to extend the patent for a further period of 5 years i.e. the patent can last for a maximum of 20 years only.[50] The request for an extension should be made less than one month before the expiration of the patent and should be accompanied with the prescribed fee. In addition, the patentee should satisfy the registrar that the patented invention is being effectively used in Uganda on a reasonable scale at the date of the request or that there is a legitimate request for failing to work the patented invention.

In order to maintain the application or the patent, an annual fee should be paid in advance to the registrar starting with the first anniversary of the date of filing the application.[51] If the annual fee is not paid, the application is deemed to have been withdrawn or the patent lapses and the lapse of the patent is published by the

41. S.29(2)(b) ibid
42. S.31(2) ibid
43. S.35 ibid
44. S.37 ibid
45. S.28 ibid
46. S.27 ibid
47. S.28 ibid
48. S.30 ibid
49. S.31(1) ibid
50. S.31(2) ibid
51. S.32(1) ibid

registrar.[52] Thereafter, any interested person may apply to the registrar to restore the application upon payment of the prescribed fee and all annual fees due.[53] The decision of the registrar can be appealed to the High Court. [54]

3.7. Reform

An analysis of the existing law reveals the following issues:

3.7.1. Liability of Registrars and their Staff

The law does not protect officers working with the Patent registry from personal liability arising from bona fide acts done during the course of employment. It is recommended that; the law should provide for this so as to ensure that the concerned officers perform their duties effectively.

3.7.2. Patentable Subject Matter

The Patents Act provides for a limited form of patentable matter.[55] It should be noted that the ARIPO Protocol, the PCT and WTO Agreements which Uganda is a signatory to, provide for a much broader patentable matter. It is submitted that the current domestic law in Uganda should adopt this position a much broad position in light of our international commitments. For instance, the new law should provide for patenting life forms. The Doha Declaration on TRIPS Agreement and Public Health provides that LDC's could choose not to provide protection for pharmaceutical products until 2016. It is submitted that Uganda being an LDC should adopt this pragmatic position so as to ensure that the health needs of its population are catered for. This approach should be adopted together with parallel importing. For a country like Uganda, parallel importing would be cost effective way of improving access to crucial drugs in light of the restricted local capacity.

3.7.3. Publication of Application for a Patent

The current domestic law does not provide for publication of a patent application. It is submitted that this can lead to fraud and abuse of the process. It should be noted that publicizing the application promotes integrity in the whole process as considerable information can be obtained from the public. Therefore, it is recommended that there should be a stipulation in the domestic law providing for publication of an application either in the Gazette, a medium that is widely circulated or through an intellectual property journal.

3.7.4. Duration of the Patent

Under Art.33 of the TRIPS Agreement, the duration of a patent is for a period of twenty years from the date of filing. The Patents Act Cap. 216, provides for a period of fifteen years. This is insufficient and does not encourage innovation and technology

---

52. S.32(4) ibid
53. S.32(5) ibid
54. S.32(7) ibid
55. S.7(2)(b) of the Patents Act

transfer. Although the Act provides for an additional five years, this is conditional. Therefore it is recommended that the term should be extended to twenty years.

3.7.5. Compulsory Licensing

These are granted in 'public interest'. However, the Patents Act is silent on what amounts to public interest. The TRIPS Agreement permits such acquisition if it is in necessary to protect a nation's health, in case of an emergency or where an interested manufacturer has failed in his or her efforts to obtain the authorization on reasonable terms and conditions.[56] The requirements imposed by the TRIPS Agreement should be incorporated in the domestic law. In addition, in order to promote economic growth, licensing should be granted in this respect for purposes of producing predominantly for the local and regional market.

3.7.6. Contractual Licenses

An analysis of the provisions of under the Patents Act Cap. 216 reveals two inadequacies.

For starters, the law does not provide for the effect of a contractual license in the event that a patent is invalidated or revoked. In this respect, it is recommended that the law make provision for cases where consideration and royalties has been duly paid.

Secondly, the law is silent on whether a patent holder who grants a license to another person can still use the invention even when the license is still with the other party. It is recommended that the law should clearly permit a licensor to grant further licenses unless the initial license granted was exclusive.

3.7.7. Exceptions to the Exclusive Rights

It is recommended that the exceptions under the Patents Act, should be widened to cater for:

(*a*) experimental use of the patented invention,

(*b*) use of the patented invention for teaching,

(*c*) use of an invention with the aim of obtaining approval of the generic product before the expiry of the patent,

(*d*) use of patented pharmaceutical products to prepare individual prescriptions,

Inclusion of these exceptions would have a positive impact on the socio-economic, educational and health needs of the majority of Ugandans.

3.7.8. Technovations

The current domestic law does not provide for Technovations. This is a solution to a precise problem in the field of technology proposed by an employee of a business

56. Article 31 of the TRIPS Agreement. The constitution of Uganda (Art 26 (2)) permits compulsory acquisition of property if it is necessary for public use or in the interest of defence, public safety, public order, public morality or public health.

in Uganda for use by that business, which on the date of the proposal, has not been used or actively proposed for use by that business. Under common law, in the absence of a clear contract, such Technovations are deemed to have been created in the course of employment, and thus belong to the employer. It is recommended that the law should clearly cater for Technovations covering matters to do with remuneration, use and protection.

3.7.9. Infringement

The provisions in this respect under the domestic law are inadequate. The TRIPS Agreement provides specific and ample provisions for enforcement of its rules or standards some of which are relevant to the prevailing conditions in Uganda. It does so by specifying a number of orders which the national courts of member states should be able to issue. For instance, a court order to preserve evidence of alleged intellectual property infringement, a specific injunction preventing an infringement from occurring through barring imported goods into the channel of commerce. In addition, once infringement has been established, a court should be able to order for the destruction of the infringing goods at the expense of the infringer. This last provision is critical in Uganda where the relevant authorities (*i.e.* the Tax Authority[57] and the Standards Body[58]) are finding it a burden bearing the cost of the destruction of counterfeit goods. Therefore, it is recommended that the law should domesticate these provisions as it would go a step further in strengthening the intellectual property regime in Uganda.

4. Trademarks

This relevant law applicable in regard to trademarks in Uganda is:

(*a*) The Trademarks Act No. 17/2010

(*b*) The Trademark Regulations Statutory Instrument 217-1

(*c*) The Trade Marks (Amendment) Rules Statutory Instrument 17-2005

(*d*) The Trademarks (Costs) Rules Statutory Instrument 217-2

(*e*) The TRIPS Agreement of 1994

(*f*) Banjul Protocol on Marks within the Framework of the African Regional Industrial Property Organization (ARIPO)

(*g*) The Paris Convention

4.1. Registration of Marks

The two main categories of registrable marks are invented words and dictionary words which bear no direct reference to the character or quality of the goods concerned.[59] Nevertheless, if a mark fails for one reason or another to meet the aforesaid rules but can actually be shown to be distinct, then it may be possible to obtain

---

57. Uganda Revenue Authority

58. Uganda National Bureau of Standards

59. S.4(1) of Act 2010

registration.[60] To cope with such borderline cases, or those whose evidence is not yet conclusive, the Register has been divided into Parts A and B,[61] the latter being for the category of doubtful marks. In practice, the distinction between the two parts is not great; but the reasoning at the root of it is important, namely the concept that marks must be, or be capable of becoming, distinctive, so as to identify the owner.[62]

It should be noted that the Trademarks Act 2010, allows for the registration of marks which though owned by different persons are similar to each where there is honest and concurrent use.[63] This takes into account the nature and length of use, the geographical area of trade, and the honesty of the adoption and subsequent use of the mark. A long period of concurrent use (at least five years) may help to overcome an opposition, and allow the two marks to coexist. However, a finding of honest concurrent use depends on a number of factors, including the likelihood of consumer confusion. Cases in which both parties are granted registration with, for example, a delimited geographical area of use for each company's mark, seem therefore to be an exception rather than the rule.[64]

This is a significant departure from the earlier law, *i.e.* the Trademarks Act Cap. 217, and in practice is likely to lead to intense debate, especially where there is confusion or a likelihood of confusion. Similarly, the Act provides that the bonafide use by a person of his own name or the name of his/her place of business or predecessors in business.[65] Whereas bonafide use of a person's name is acknowledged and protected under common law, this statutory recognition is critical.

Another prominent reform introduced by the new law is the provision for registration of service marks[66] and certification marks.[67] In regard to certification marks, it states that they will only apply to goods and not services.

4.2. The Application Process[68]

Having chosen the mark, the applicant has to decide which classes of goods or services it should cover. There need be no confusion or conflict in the market place when the same mark is used by different traders, provided the goods or services are sufficiently dissimilar. Trademarks are registered in one or more of 45 classes.[69] There are 34 classes of goods and 11 for services. These classes group products that are

---

60. S.4(2) ibid
61. S.7 ibid
62. S.10 ibid
63. S.27 ibid
64. WIPO, IP and Business: Trademark Coexistence, http://www.wipo.int/wipo_magazine/en/2006/06/article_0007.html (accessed 31-07-2013)
65. S.24 ibid
66. S.8 ibid
67. S.13 ibid.
68. This is Provided for under Part II of the Act and the attendant Regulations
69. S.8 Trade Mark Act.

deemed to be similar in function, and are identified by their number. Usually, a product or services will fall into a single class for instance class 25 for clothing or class 43 for restaurants. In certain cases however, applications in multiple classes are required to protect a single trade mark. An example of this is where a clothing brand wishes to open a retail outlet (under the same name) in which case two registrations are required in class 25 (clothing) and in class 35 (retail services). A separate application must be filed in each class in which protection is desired. Classification can be difficult if the mark is to be applied to a new product (usually the subject of a patent application) and in these cases it is also often advisable to protect the mark in more than one class to ensure that you are adequately protected.

When the mark and the required classes have been decided, a separate application must be made for each class. A form is filed (Form TM2) on which the mark is shown and the particular goods to be covered in the classes are listed, and a fee is paid. Subsequently, the registrar issues a report setting out the official view as to whether or not the mark is registrable. He will have searched existing registrations and applications in the relevant classes to find if there is any conflict with the proposed mark. In the course of these exchanges, it is common for the mark to be altered slightly, and/or the list of goods to be changed or limited. Sometimes a change may be negotiated from Part A to Part B of the Register.[70] This is because Part A requires a mark to be distinction from goods or services with which the owner of the trademark is or may be connected, in the course of trade, from goods or services in the case of which no connection subsists.[71] Part B on the other hand requires a mark to be capable, in relation to the goods or services in respect of which it is registered or proposed to be registered, of distinguishing goods or services with which the owner of the trademark is or may be connected in the course of trade from goods in the case where no connection subsists, generally.[72]

Once the Registry is satisfied, the details of the accepted applications are published in the Gazette,[73] so that the public, in practice other rival companies, may have the chance to object to the eventual registration of the mark. If no opposition is raised within 60 days from the date of advertisement, the mark is officially registered[74] and the applicant is issued with a certificate.[75]

It should be noted that the procedure for registration of a trademark under the new law is not so different from the old law save for two key reforms in the application process:

---

70. S.7(3) ibid

71. S.9 ibid

72. S.10 ibid

73. Rule 42 of SI 217-1

74. Rule 60 ibid

75. S.16(2) of the Trademarks Act 2010

(*a*) The requirement that an intending applicant for registration of a trademark should first carry out a search so as to determine whether or not the trademark exists in the registry.[76]

(*b*) Secondly the option for intending applicants to seek preliminary advice from the registrar in regard to distinctiveness.[77]

4.3. Foreign Applications

The Madrid system[78] is the primary international system for facilitating the registration of trademarks in multiple jurisdictions around the world. It is administered by the International Bureau of WIPO located in Geneva, Switzerland. Its legal basis is the *Madrid Agreement Concerning the International Registration of Marks*, which was concluded in 1891, and entered into force in 1892, and the *Protocol Relating to the Madrid Agreement*, which came into operation on 1 April 1996.

Any State which is a party to the Paris Convention for the Protection of Industrial Property may become a party to the Agreement or the Protocol or both.[79] It's because of this reason that Uganda can utilize this system.

Under this system, a trademark owner is offered the possibility of having his trademark protected in several countries by simply filing one application directly with his own national or regional trademark office. An international mark so registered is equivalent to an application or a registration of the same mark effected directly in each of the countries designated by the applicant. This is a priority system which allows a period of six months for filing in other countries, while claiming priority from the first filing date. If the trademark office of a designated country does not refuse protection within a specified period, the protection of the mark is the same as if it had been registered by that Office. The Madrid system also simplifies greatly the subsequent management of the mark, since it is possible to record subsequent changes or to renew the registration through a single procedural step.[80]

Prior use or publication of a mark is not a bar to registration and in Uganda, the fact of using a mark generally gives the owner the right to continue using it even if another trader applies to register the same mark. However, in certain countries[81] it is necessary to register a mark as soon as trade with it is envisaged either because all marks in use must be registered, or because rights go to the first to register and a mere user is left unprotected.

---

76. S.5 ibid

77. S.6 ibid

78. Officially the Madrid system for the international registration of marks

79. Article 14 of the Madrid Union

80. WIPO: The Madrid International Trademark System, http://www.wipo.int/madrid/en/general/ (accessed 31-07-2013)

81. In countries which have a legal system based on common law, "prior use" is generally sufficient for claiming rights over a given trademark in case of dispute. In civil law countries, however, this is usually not the case.

4.4. Renewal of Rights

Under the law in Uganda, the registration of a trademark shall be for a period of seven years and shall be renewable every ten years upon payment of a prescribed fee.[82] These periods are longer than for patents because trademarks are inherently much longer term.

4.5. Challenges to Registration

Sometimes, there are reasons for removing marks from the Register, for example they may be wrongly registered. An application for removal must be made to the Registrar or the court. It should be noted that if the application is made by a foreigner, i.e. a non-resident or a person not carrying on business in Uganda, the registrar has powers to make an order for security of costs.[83]

One major reason for removing a mark from the Register is that it is not being used by its owner, and is unjustifiably blocking others from using it. If it can be shown that for 3 consecutive years a mark has not been used, then it may be removed.[84] The rule for traders can be expressed in the formula: *if you use a mark, register it; if you register a mark, use it.*

The Act also allows marks to removed on proof of prior registration in country with reciprocal arrangements with Uganda.[85] This is in line with the principle of national treatment under the Paris Convention. In addition, a mark can be challenged if it can be shown to be no longer distinctive. This is a danger chiefly for the owners of very well known and recognized trademarks, which can become so freely used that they cease to denote a particular owner's goods, and become a description of a particular product. The owners of registered trademarks Colgate and Blueband constantly face this challenge because the public especially those in rural settings in Uganda, tend to use the names generically for all toothpaste and all Margarines respectively.

4.6. Registered Users

A mark can also lose its distinctiveness if it is used persistently by someone other than the owner. This is an additional reason why an infringer must be stopped. On the other hand, an owner may want to give permission for another person or institution *e.g.* a subsidiary company, or a licensed manufacturer, to use the mark. There is therefore a procedure for registering someone else as a user, subject to certain conditions which are laid down and which will be scrutinized by the registrar.[86]

---

82. S.21(1) of the Trademarks Act 2010. Under the repealed Trademarks Act Cap 217, it was 14 years.
83. S.65 of Trademarks Act 2010
84. S.46 ibid
85. S.45 ibid
86. S.31, 32 & 33 ibid

4.7. Assignment or Transfer of Trade Marks

The Act permits this, subject to defined conditions. However in practice this can be costly, particularly if there are many marks to transfer, some of which have been registered abroad. Nevertheless, it is advisable to register any change of ownership, since otherwise continuing use of the mark by someone who was not the registered owner would mean that after 3 years, there is likelihood that the mark could be cancelled.[87]

4.8. New Offences

The Trademarks Act 2010 introduces new offences which were lacking in the repealed law. These include:[88] falsely applying a registered trademark, falsifying or unlawfully removing a registered trademark, selling goods with false marks, prohibition of import and export of registered trademarks and offences by all legal persons including companies. Intention (*animus*) is a critical component of these offences. The Act proposes a maximum monetary fine of 48 currency points or UGX 960,000 (Approximately US $ 350) in respect to these offences or a 2 year prison sentence or both. It is submitted that these penal provisions are not deterrent enough. Most cases of counterfeit involve products in bulk e.g. medicines, which have adverse social and economic implications in Uganda and East Africa. It is recommended that a maximum figure of US $ 100,000 is a more realistic deterrent.

4.9. Appointment of Inspectors

The Act provides for the appointment of trademark inspectors. It should be noted that the appointment of inspectors is also provided for under the Copyright and Neighbouring Rights Act. The Uganda Registration Services Bureau in charge of appointing who are given powers of entry, seizure, inspection, and detention.[89] Currently, Trademark inspectors are yet to be appointed. On October 19th, 2010, the government of Uganda passed out copyright inspectors, four years after the relevant law *i.e.* the Copyright and Neighbouring Rights Act commenced. In fairness, in enforcing the Act, they have registered some success. In a copy of its bulletin' *My Copyright*, The Uganda Performing Rights Society reported that between December 2010 and February 2011, a minimum of 100 former illegal distributors and unauthorized mechanical rights uploaders have legalized their operations. Nevertheless, it is submitted that trademark inspectors are bound to find their work more cumbersome than copyright inspectors given the fact that a lot of evidence is needed to prove trademark infringement *e.g.* sales figures of several years, advertising expenditure, declarations from customers etc.

5. Industrial Designs

Industrial designs are primarily protected under the Copyright and Neighboring Rights Act of 2006. These are drawings which any company uses for the production

---

87. S.46 ibid.

88. S.71-80 ibid

89. S.82 ibid

of its manufactured articles. The position of the law is, briefly, that copyright does exist for industrial designs, working drawings etc. It provides protection against copying, including any reproduction of those drawings as a three-dimensional product. The original designer is protected even when his drawings themselves have not been seen by the copyist and the new product can only have been copied from an article made from the copyrighted drawings. Consequently, making what is locally colloquially termed a 'Chinese' copy is an infringement of the copyright of the first manufacturer.

Broadly speaking, the assumption is made that any product which has been made in infringement of copyright actually belongs to the copyright owner. Sale of this product by the infringer is treated as depriving the copyright owner of the full value of the product and damages are awarded accordingly. Any direct copying of the product of a competitor therefore is an extremely foolhardy activity, since it could result in an award of damages sufficient to cripple a business or drive it into bankruptcy.

From the point of view of a producer of new products of original design, industrial design presents a weapon of great force. The producer does not have to file an application; all he need do is ensure that the original drawings of all products are dated and kept, and that the ownership of the copyright is vested in the business by means of a proper agreement with the author.

6. Geographical Indications

Uganda currently does not have a specific law governing geographical indications. Nevertheless by virtue of being signatory to the WTO TRIPS Agreement, the provisions of that Treaty on Geographical indications are applicable in Uganda. Technically, however, those provisions require domestication into Ugandan law by appropriate legislation. An attempt in this direction is evident from the Geographical Indications Bill 2008 which awaits approval by Parliament of Uganda. The object of the law is to provide inter alia for: the registration and protection of geographical indications; their term of protection; the prohibited use of geographical indications and remedies for their infringement and the appointment of a registrar.

7. Trade Secrets

Article 39 of the TRIPS Treaty, provides for the protection of undisclosed information under the Paris Convention, 1967 including secret information; information which has commercial value because it is secret; and information subjected to reasonable steps by the person lawfully in control of it to keep it secret.

On the 12th of June 2009, the above provision was incorporated in the domestic law in Uganda with the commencement of the Trade Secret Protection Act 2009. This Act provides for the protection of undisclosed information in commercial transactions. In order for information to be protected under this law, it must be a secret, have commercial value because it is a secret, and have been subjected to reasonable steps by the person lawfully in control of it to keep it a secret. [90] This right however is not exclusive and is subject to other rights in intellectual property.[91]

7.1. Improper and Proper Disclosure

The law prohibits improper acquisition of undisclosed information through commercial espionage, physical entry, fraudulent misrepresentation, breach of contract or confidence, breach of privacy, unlawful acquisition directly or through a third party.[92] However, it is not unlawful, if the trade secret is arrived at by independent development or reverse engineering, [93]or got from:[94] public sources or from circles that normally deals with that information, inspection or analysis of a commercially available product embodying the undisclosed information, independent invention or discovery; or by way of gift, purchase of inheritance or without knowing it to be confidential information.

7.2. Rights of the Owner of a Trade Secret

The law permits the assignment, transfer or license of trade secrets, although the contract has to be written down.[95] The owner of a trade secret which has been unlawfully disclosed various remedies such as a court injunction, specific and exemplary damages, and account for profits and an adjustment order regulating future exploitation of the trade secret by the offender.[96] Nevertheless, such judicial proceedings are time barred if brought after 2 years from the discovery of the disclosure of information.[97]

It should also be noted that a person who discloses, acquires or uses a trade secret in good faith, can bring a court action for declaration of rights, which may essentially leads the court to make a just order in light of the prevailing circumstances.[98]

8. Folklore and Indigenous Knowledege

A Bill on Folklore and Indigenous Knowledge has been drafted by the Uganda Law Reform Commission. The object of the Bill is to protect the wealth of knowledge that is unwritten but well preserved by individuals or local communities in Uganda. The Bill aims at recognizing the innovations and knowledge of traditional and local people as their intellectual property (Atwine 2003).

---

90. S.2 & 4 of the Trade Secrets Act 2009
91. S.8 ibid
92. S.6 ibid
93. S.5 ibid
94. S.7 ibid
95. S.9 & 10 ibid
96. S.12-17 ibid
97. S.21 ibid
98. S.18 ibid

9. Administration

The Intellectual Property Office in Uganda is the Registrar Generals Department. This is under the Ministry of Justice and Constitutional Affairs. The office is statutorily created under the Uganda Registration Services Bureau Act Cap. 210. The office handles matters to do with registration of copyrights, trademarks and patents and their assignment and transmission, registration of collecting societies, and advising the government on matters to do with intellectual property rights.

Conclusion

Uganda's Intellectual Property Legal system has existed since the mid 20th Century; however as noted in the review above, it was not until 2001, that the Government of Uganda embarked on revising and enacting a number of intellectual property laws which complied with the international standards to which Uganda had committed itself to under the various intellectual property treaties. This legislative reform has set Uganda apart from many countries, and currently it has one of the most robust and internationally up to date intellectual property legal system.

It is because of this strong legal system that Uganda is one of only three countries in the world (and the only country in Africa) selected by WIPO to promote economic and social development through the use of intellectual property and the branding of products with historical, cultural and economic relevance. In Uganda, the project has at its forefront the promotion of key agricultural products which provide income to the local communities; cotton, vanilla and sesame, on the international market through the use of branding and IP tools. Intellectual Property is thus making a positive difference in Uganda.

References

A. Articles

1. Atwine. J (2003) "Review of the Current Situation Regarding Intellectual Property Policy: Issues, Opportunities and Challenges", Uganda *Living Law Journal, Volume 1 No.2, 192*
2. David Bakibinga (2006), "Intellectual Property Rights in Uganda: Reform and Institutional Management Policy Formulation", Paper delivered at the Network of Academies of Sciences in Organisation of Islamic Countries (NASIC), International Seminar on "Intellectual property and Innovation: Value Creation in the Knowledge Economy" held in Islamabad, Pakistan, 12-14 December 2006.

B. Statutes[99]

1. The 1995 Constitution of the Republic of Uganda As Amended.
2. The Copyright and Neighboring Rights Act 19 of 2006.
3. The Uganda Registration Services Bureau Act Cap.210.

---

99. Laws of Uganda 2000 Edition

4. Trade Secret Protection Act 2009.
5. The Patents Act Cap. 216.
6. Patents Amendment Act 7/2002.
7. The Trademarks Act No. 17/2010.

C. Statutory Instruments

1. The Trademark Regulations Statutory Instrument 217-1.
2. The Trademarks (Amendment) Rules Statutory Instrument 17-2005.
3. The Trademarks (Costs) Rules Statutory Instrument 217-2.
4. The Patents Regulations Statutory Instrument 216-1.

D. Treaties

1. The Protocol on Patent and Industrial Designs within the Framework of the African Regional Industrial Property Organization (ARIPO) concluded on December 10th, 1982, at Harare.
2. Paris Convention for the Protection of Industrial Property signed on 3rd March, 1883, as last revised
3. Patents Cooperation Treaty 1970.
4. World Trade Organisation (WTO) Agreement on Trade Related Aspects of Intellectual Property Rights (TRIPS) of 1994.

Chapter 19

Challenges faced by Developing Countries in Africa in taking Full Advantage of IPR's for Development: The Zimbabwean Case

R. Karimanzira[1], R. Mlambo[2] and Ngoni Dupwa**[3]*

[1]Director Commercialisation of Research Development and Innovation Ministry of Science, Technology and Innovation, Harare, Zimbabwe
[2]IP Expert and Consultant, Intellectual Property Business Solutions, Zimbabwe
[3]Science and Technology Officer, Ministry of Science and Technology Development, , Zimbabwe

ABSTRACT

Developing countries face many challenges as they try to strengthen Intellectual Property (IP) regimes for socio-economic development. Africa, in general, and Zimbabwe- in particular also encounter equal challenges in tapping into the IPR regime. This paper discusses the current challenges faced by Zimbabwean researchers, innovators and inventors in R&D facilities in both public and private sector institutions towards realising full and effective implementation of the provisions contained in the Second Science, Technology and Innovation Policy of Zimbabwe launched in June 2012 – for the benefit of socio-economic development.

E-mail: *rungano.pu@gmail.com; **ngdupwa@gmail.com

IP is increasingly being used as an economic asset in developed countries and yet developing countries, especially those in Africa still lag behind in the conversion of IPRs into economic assets.

Other major challenges include low level of general IP awareness and appreciation, absence of IP institutional infrastructure such as technology transfer offices and Technology and Innovation Support Centres (TISC); Technology Hubs; limited (if any) qualified IP skilled personnel (technology managers, patent examiners, attorneys, IP auditors, etc.), financing of research in STI whose results that can be commercialized (a basis for new business ventures) and whose patents are locally registered, policy co-ordination and implementation. In addition, instruments to measure the effectiveness of financing of R&D as a ratio of GDP growth (Gross Expenditure on Research and Development (GERD/GDP) are critical knowledge based economic growth measurement tools. Another challenge is the lack of an IP protecting culture by local researchers and innovators. According to C Cannaby (2009) developing country research institutions to a large extent do not patent their own research results, in their own countries or in foreign jurisdictions. However, in many cases, their research results are merged with research from their sponsors, on whom they are dependent for funding because of express prohibitions on patenting in grant documents and/or because of inadequate budgetary support for tertiary education and scientific research. In Zimbabwe, IP remains largely in the legal domain with internal drivers being the Ministry of Justice and Legal Affairs who at times lack the pre-requisite scientific knowledge, appreciation, understanding and drivers in R&D institutions – in the scientific aspects of IPR. This has resulted in inadequate development of relevant and supportive IP legislation and the granting of patents which are contradictory to the interests of national priorities such as responding to the pro-poor national agenda in all sectors.

1. Introduction

1.1. Intellectual Property and Development

Intellectual property and development has been the subject of various studies and debates especially in developing economies, but these studies have been conducted mainly by researchers in developed countries with little relevant experience and knowledge of the dynamics in each of these economies. Each developing country is unique in its own way and the generalisations of IP and development can not apply to all developing countries. One peculiarity of the studies is that some data is obtained from secondary or even tertiary sources and at times is out of date. There has not been much in terms of actual data collection and the type of data collected as studies of developed countries are applied to those in developing countries. This has resulted in the impression that there is not much in terms of IP and yet this is not the case, what is actually lacking is the proper management of IP especially in terms of gaining economic leverage out it, at individual, firm and national level.

The importance of turning IP into an economic asset in developing countries has never been more important than it is right now, with traditional knowledge, biodiversity and geographical indications gaining popularity. This coupled by the fact that developing countries are custodians of most of the valuable traditional knowledge and 90 per cent of biodiversity being in developing countries. Developed countries have taken advantage of this situation with high levels of bio-piracy taking place and have been taking place for a long time now. These bio-pirates even go a step further to register patents and trademarks out of stolen indigenous knowledge, for example registering patents from traditional medicine they found in developing countries and resale the drugs at higher prices to those same countries. Developed countries have been taking advantage of the low levels of awareness and lack of proper IP management systems and gaining economically out of the intellect of nationals of developing countries.

IP management has now got a critical role to play in harnessing IP in developing countries. Challenges that have been faced by developing countries now need to be addressed for the socio-economic development of the countries.

1.2. Challenges Faced by Developing Countries in Harnessing Benefits from IPR's

According to Deere (2009) three core factors make a difference to the kinds of IP reforms governments pursue: (i) the degree of public engagement; (ii) the internal capacity of governments on IP matters; and (iii) the degree of government coordination. These variables affect the way in which IPR's are managed and also the capacity to manage them. Also key are international pressures to which developing countries are subjected to, which may be in the form of international, bilateral and regional treaties and agreements or by special interest groups which have influence in these countries.

1.3. Public Engagement

The degree of public engagement on IP decision-making affects the pace and nature of national IP reforms. Across the developing world, the degree of debate in national legislatures in IP decision-making processes varies significantly. The technical capacity of the governments greatly influence legislation, this is largely so where the IP is under the Ministry of Justice where lawyers are the main custodians of IP law with very little if any participation of Scientists, technologists, innovators and researchers resulting in poor legislation which is not reflective of the technical nature of IP law especially patent law. The process of parliamentary review of legislation is also very weak and the lack of IP awareness and technology related issues by legislators in most developing countries Interest group politics can also play a role in the development of IP legislation. These civil society actors vary and include associations of academics, consumer organizations, scientists, inventors, creators, musicians, authors, and IP attorneys. Interest groups have emerged in response to specific challenges, such as improved access to essential medicines and the misappropriation of indigenous knowledge for examples include India, Brazil, Philippines and action in South Africa which led to the DOHA declaration on the TRIP's agreement.

1.4. Government Capacity

The capacity of national governments is critical to the drafting and implementation of IP legislation. In addition to the technical capacity described above, the strength and efficiency of government institutions, and the relative autonomy of IP offices are also critical. Common to developing countries are low capacity in institutions, lack of technical expertise, poor funding, political and economic instability just to mention a few. Governments in most developing countries delegate responsibility of IP issues to Ministries of Justice and legal practitioners trained in general law or at times specialised in IP but with no technical expertise or broader appreciation of public policy goals.

Making a further consequence of this delegation to IP offices is that IP decision-making is often driven more by concerns for compliance with international law rather than the challenge of tailoring implementation to national development needs.

IP offices have responsibility for drafting national laws, administering laws, disputes, coordinating public outreach regarding the internal national IP system, and participating in international norm-setting negotiations, as well as securing technical assistance and capacity building from international donors. Further in some countries especially in Africa the situation is worsened by the lack of IP professionals, such as IP attorneys, IP auditors and valuators etc.

1.5. Government Co-ordination

Co-ordination within government is another key aspect which influences the implementation and development of IP legislation in developing countries. This includes coordination between the internal and external faces of governments in respect of relationships with foreign donors and international organizations at the regional and multilateral level. There is low co-ordination amongst government ministries, departments. In some countries there is low appreciation of the role of IP for the development of relevant sectors. The Ministries of Justice are responsible for all relations with IP organisations and issues for example WIPO. Even with regional blocks such as the African Regional Intellectual property organisation there is still low capacity in terms of IP professionals such as Patent examiners. In Zimbabwe were ARIPO is based there is no substantive examination of patent documents at the National IP office. It is worth acknowledging though that the WIPO-ARIPO sponsored Masters in Intellectual Property has gone a long way in alleviating the shortage of IP professionals both within and outside the legal domain. The programme is also helping in raising IP awareness and stimulating interest and debate on the role of IP in economic development.

1.6. International Pressures on Developing Countries

For many developing countries, foreign policy imperatives spur them to pursue bilateral trade agreements, despite potential economic or social costs, because the existence of such agreements is considered a valuable symbol of cooperation and consolidates relationships with valuable political allies. Because developing countries are very much in need of trade and other benefits, such as development assistance, they are vulnerable to developed countries' efforts to make assistance contingent on agreeing to strengthened IP protection, including TRIPS-plus IP standards and enforcement. Multinational corporations with strong interests in higher IP protection in developing countries also undertake a variety of activities to pressure developing countries, including lobbying national officials, legal challenges in national courts, and calling on their own developed country governments to pressure developing countries.

The possession of key IP skills has led to the different negotiation capacity of different developing countries. The most technically competent governments, such as Chile, have negotiated marginally better deals for themselves than those with less capacity, such as Morocco when dealing with the United States.

External Drivers

The debate concerning the economic implications of intellectual property rights (IPRs) has gained considerable attention over the past two decades in the context of the World Trade Organization's (WTO) Agreement on Trade-Related Aspects of Intellectual Property Rights (TRIPS), and the subsequent increase of regional and bilateral free trade agreements in the TRIPS-plus era. TRIPS aims to narrow the gaps in the way that IPRs are protected around the world, and to bring them under common international rules. It establishes minimum levels of protection that each WTO Member State must provide. The following rapid proliferation of regional and bilateral free trade agreements include elements of IPRs building on and raising minimum standards defined by TRIPS. These agreements indeed integrate TRIPS-plus norms, including undertakings by developing countries not to use specific TRIPS flexibilities. Developing countries are under increasing pressure to strengthen their national intellectual property (IP) regimes, in order to harmonise them with those of developed countries.

2. Challenges and Opprotunities for Zimbabwe

The Zimbabwean economy has been experiencing serious challenges over the last decade with unemployment and hyperinflation reaching unprecedented levels and extensive economic and political turmoil. In September 2008, the ruling party and the two main opposition parties signed a Global Political Agreement (GPA) whose intention, amongst other things, was the "Restoration of Economic Stability and Growth"1. The GPA led to the formation in February 2009 of a Government of National Unity (GNU), a coalition government involving the three parties to the GPA. Following the formation of this new Government, the Zimbabwean economy abandoned its national currency, the Zimbabwean Dollar, in favour of a foreign multicurrency system. Although this led to a degree of stabilization of the economy, it is still in desperate need of a very large injection of liquidity to kick start all sectors, especially manufacturing, whose base was seriously eroded during the years of economic turmoil.

2.1. IP Legislation in Zimbabwe

IP legislation in Zimbabwe includes Patents amendement Act of 2002, Trade Marks Act Chapter 26:04, Industrial Designs Act Chapter 26:02, Geographical Indications Chapter26:08, and copyright and neighbouring rights Chapter 26:05. Other laws with a bearing on IP are Plant Breeders Rights Act Chapter 18:16, Seeds Act Chapter 27:08, Public Health Act Chapter 15:05, Intergrated circuit layout-designs Act, The armorial bearings, names, uniforms and badges Act.

2.2. Implementation of TRIPS in Zimbabwe

Zimbabwe's legislation has developed in line with International law particularly the TRIPS Agreement. In order to comply with this agreement Zimbabwean IP legislation has been amended several times. These amendments have not reflected the developmental goals of the agreement as contained in the TRIPS flexibilities. Some of the weaknesses in relation to the implementation of the TRIPS flexibilities are described below.

2.3. Bolar Provision

The research and experimental use exception is aimed at ensuring that scientific research aimed at generating new knowledge is fostered and is not impeded by patents. It is a longstanding exception which is justified on the basis that one of the main aims of patent laws is to facilitate the dissemination of knowledge, promote innovation and thereby facilitate the advancement of science. The exception is useful in fostering pharmaceutical technological progress by exempting experimentation acts for purposes such as inventing around the initial invention, improving on the invention or for the purposes of evaluating the invention and determining if it works (Correa 2000).

The early working exception, on the other hand, relates to a situation where a potential competitor uses an invention without the authorization of the patent holder to undertake acts necessary for obtaining regulatory approval and registration of a generic product before the expiry of the patent term. The exception is intended to ensure that generic versions of the product are available on the market immediately or within a reasonable time of the expiry of the patent (Lettington and Musungu 2000).The Bolar provision in the Patent Amendments Act, 2002 includes an unnecessary time limit.

Section 7 of the Patent Amendment Act, 2002, states that:

"The principal Act is amended by the insertion after section 24 of the following sections

24B Test batches of patented products

(1) *Test batches of a patented product may be produced without the consent of the patentee six months before the expiry of the patent: provided that the test batches shall not be put on the market before the expiry date of the patent.*

(2) *Where test batches of a patented product have been produced in terms of subsection (1) the patent term of the original product shall not be extended".*

The inclusion of a time limit to the Bolar exception in the Zimbabwean patent act is reflective of the lack of technical expertise and consultation as it has serious implications for example the generic drug development and approval process which can take years. Those involved in the R&D of generic drug products still protected by patent in Zimbabwe are infringing patent rights of others if they are carrying out these activities prior to the six months stated in the legislation which, to all intents and purposes, should be happening for those local generic companies which have a strategic perspective.

The Zimbabwe Patent Act as amended does not make provision for the use of patented inventions for research and experimental use, to generate new knowledge, to "invent around", improve on the protected invention, evaluate an invention in order to request a licence, or for other legitimate purposes, such as to test whether the invention works and the patent granted is valid. This is very disturbing because research and experimentation allows for use of patent information for development and with this kind of law the purpose of the IP system for economic development is suppressed.

2.4. Parallel Importation

Parallel importation refers to a situation where a third party, without the authorization of the patent holder, imports a foreign manufactured product put on the market abroad by the patent holder, his licensee or in another legitimate manner in competition with imports or locally manufactured products by the patent holder or his licensee (Lettington and Musungu 2000).

It is important to note that the Medicines and Allied Substances Control (Import and Export of Medicines) Regulations, 2008, limit the interpretation of parallel importation according to TRIPS and state that:

"No person shall import into or export from Zimbabwe any registered medicine, for the purpose of wholesale dealing, unless he is duly appointed as an authorized importer or exporter by the principal in respect of that medicine.

These regulatory provisions have been made necessary by the need to control the influx of registered, unregistered and counterfeit medicines into the country. From a regulatory point of view, medicines are registered by source of the manufacturing country and this makes it difficult to parallel import from an import source of choice, which might not necessarily be the registered source. This runs contrary to public health policy initiatives. There is thus a need to find a solution to this conflict in the overall interests of public health.

2.5. Data Protection

Zimbabwean law does not provide for data exclusivity, that is the granting of exclusive rights to innovator companies to prevent subsequent applicants from using data submitted for the registration of new molecule entities. Article 39.3 of TRIPS is being interpreted by multinational corporations and some developed countries, particularly the USA, to mean that WTO member states are required to grant data exclusivity for a specified period of time (Chaudhuri 2005).

Data exclusivity provisions have implications for generic entry and hence for competition and prices. They imply that a regulatory authority cannot make use of innovator submitted data on safety and other relevant clinical data for marketing approval purposes for a generic submission during this period of exclusivity. Thus Zimbabwe has been able to use an important TRIPS flexibility with positive implications for generic competition and prices. However, due to the flawed Bolar exception, if the drug substance is patented at the same time, a generic competitor cannot use it until six months before patent expiry, thus limiting the flexibility on test data (UNIDO 2011).

2.6. Policy Developments

The Zimbabwean government has come up with new dynamic policies that are responsive to the current challenges and gaps. These include the new trade and industry policy (IDP) 2012, the traditional medicines policy and the STI policy.

The IDP has put out strategies that will help in increasing innovation and development in industry. The policy articulates the need to develop R&D, partake in technology transfer, finance industry through the formation of a Bank for industry, establishment of a council for technology upgrades and most importantly increasing the GDP for R&D to 2 per cent. This will provide a platform through which the local manufacturing sector will increase innovative activities. This however may not be successful if IPR awareness and IPR management as this is the vehicle through which innovations including R&D results can be used in industry *i.e.* through technology transfer and commercialisation.

The Council for technology upgrades is a good initiative for technology transfer but technology upgrades can also relate to patented technology and know-how protected by IPR regimes. In order for such an initiative to be successful there is need to integrate and co-ordinate it with other relevant institutions and policy. This can be done through institutions such as Technology and Innovation Support Centre's (TISC) that are being initiated by WIPO.This will help alleviate problems of duplication of efforts and co-ordinated resources and efforts with other relevant government departments with an interest in technology upgrades such as the MSTD etc. Traditional knowledge is critical to developing countries especially in the form of traditional medicine as 90 per cent of biodiversity is in developing countries. Exploitation of this form of IPR is crucial to developing countries. New protection regimes have emerged in the form of the ARIPO Swakopmund Protocol and the IGC texts that are still under debate, the Access and Benefit Sharing systems contained in the Convention on Biological Diversity (CBD) and its Nagoya Protocol.

The Access and Benefit Sharing regimes are a noble gesture as they try to compensate for biopiracy but a lot needs to be done by developing countries themselves in terms of building scientific capacity in order to exploit the resources.

In Zimbabwe the infrastructure for research into these resources such as traditional medicine are inadequate for full exploitation. Research efforts into traditional medicines are scattered across different departments and institutions facilities and equipment are also outdated in public research institutes. This is seen by the lack of specialised programmes in universities for traditional medicine and related studies. Where these are found they form a small portion of studies by pharmacy and medical students. The traditional medicine policy is thus crucial for the development of the scientific capacity required for development of this IP and ensure that not only are the knowledge holders compensated for but also the country as a whole benefits leading to reduced costs of drugs and contributing positively to the national health delivery system.

The Zimbabwe traditional Medicine policy is a policy in which IPR's, R&D And technology transfer are critical for successful implementation. Developed in 2007 the policy is yet to be implemented. The policy among its objectives intends to promote

Table 19.1: PRIMARY GOAL 2: Learn and utilize emergent technologies to accelerate development.

	Goal	*Activity*	*Indicators*
2.1	**Strengthen medical biotechnology research**	Collaborate with Ministries of Agriculture and Health to identify human as well as plant and animal diseases that need to be prioritised for biotech research.	☆ Number of research projects on disease identification, prevention, treatment and eradication funded under ICF; ☆ Number of new tools and methodologies of disease identification, prevention, treatment and eradication; ☆ Patent applications and grants issued to Zimbabwean researchers relating to disease identification, prevention, treatment and eradication.
2.2	**Exploit the biodiversity in the environment through biotechnology such as herbal products, fermentation processes and bio-leaching**	1. Engage the Medical Research Council of Zimbabwe and other relevant research institutions to identify potential herbal products for research. 2. Protect such herbal products using intellectual property. 3. Optimize collaborative success by building up IP assets and avoiding unprotected exposure of national biodiversity resources. 4. Engage in licensing and development collaboration agreements that recognize and protect the value of IP based on national biodiversity.	A list of potential products from exploitation of biodiversity through biotechnology; ☆ Number of institutions or entities engaged in the exploitation of biodiversity through biotechnology.
2.3	**Develop a database on IKS with a view to identifying aspects that can be exploited using modern S&T (*e.g.* synthetic biology) for national benefit.**	Facilitate patenting of useful outcomes/ products from the above research to protect such knowledge from being easily accessible and exploitable by external parties without reaching agreed; fair and equitable benefit sharing protocol. In collaboration with traditional leadership nationwide, develop enforceable legal frameworks to guard against misappropriation of national IP assets from IKS.	☆ IKS resource leads and related products that are patented; ☆ IP assets registered for commercial use; ☆ Revenue generated from commercialization of IP assets from IKS

Contd...

Table 19.1: PRIMARY GOAL 3: Commercialisation of Research Results

	Goal	*Activity*	*Indicators*
3.1	**Identify and document national and global research results and technologies that can enhance value addition to national resources.**	Guided by the national priorities in R&D, identify available intellectual property including patents, copyright works and know how (IP) (be it available gratis because it is not protected in Zimbabwe or in relevant export markets, or because it can be licensed from IP owners into Zimbabwe parties, and that can be adapted or adopted to; local situation for national benefit. Work with Zimbabwe technology managers to identify such available IP and negotiate contracts, as needed. Train and install Zimbabwe technology managers with capacities to perform "Key Practical IP Skills" critical to research commercialization, including IP identification and opportunity assessments, patent application drafting, technology contract negotiation, and technology marketing/branding.	As instruments for evaluating the policy implementation, the following should be computed: ☆ Data on growth in indigenous IP assets (especially patents filed nationally and foreign export markets). Identification of available foreign IP assets and IP licensing opportunities that can be improved and used as a base for indigenous IP asset development and/or adapted to local situation for national benefit; ☆ Training of technology managers with the capacity to improve Key Practical IP Skills; ☆ Deployment of a select cadre of technology managers in a Technology Management Hub available to a network of Zimbabwe research institutions and related Zimbabwe technology enterprises
3.2	**Strengthen national Intellectual Property Rights regime.** The proposed activities aimed at implementing this Policy will require regular consultations with key players in the Ministry of Legal and Parliamentary Affairs to ensure consistency with provisions of regional and global agreements on trade and technology transfers entered into by Government contained in the World Trade Organization including programmes of the Regional Intellectual Property Organization (ARIPO).	1. Train Zimbabwe technology managers with educational background in scientific disciplines in Zimbabwe's technology focus areas (*e.g.* ICT, health, renewable energy, environmental technologies and agriculture) 2. Patent research in foreign patent regimes; 3. Opportunities in identification and patent drafting for indigenous research and development 4. Identify any aspects of the current national IP laws and treaties that require review in order to promote Zimbabwe's national interests. In particular, study and implement national laws clarifying ownership of IP arising from R&D from Zimbabwe's S&T research institutions	As instruments for evaluating the policy implementation, the following will be needed: ☆ Data on patent filing and grant by Zimbabwean research institutions, businesses and individual inventors in Zimbabwe and in key anticipated export jurisdictions (where Zimbabwe will make, use or sell technology products or services or with whom Zimbabwe entities will conduct development and manufacturing collaborations). This data should be collected on an annual basis and according to the Zimbabwe focus areas; ☆ Number of Zimbabwe personnel trained in Critical IP Skills, as defined above, as well as number of such persons who are actively engaged in providing such skills to Zimbabwe research institutions and enterprises

Contd...

Table 19.1–*Contd...*

	Goal	*Activity*	*Indicators*
		Develop an incentives programme to encourage, facilitate and reward filling of patent applications and successful prosecution of such applications from Zimbabwean Research Institutions and technology enterprises	
3.3	**Forge linkages between tertiary institutions and industry dedicated to harnessing research results for commercialization**	Develop a set of formal technology transfer contracts that implement national policies on IP asset development and research commercialization approaches.	☆ Number of industry based research challenges identified and effectively addressed; ☆ Number of suitably qualified researchers and technology managers capable of addressing the technical challenges faced by industry.

Source: Zimbabwe 2nd Science, Technology and Innovation Policy Implementation Plan 2012.

research and local production of traditional medicines and to promote the protection of intellectual property rights (IPR's) of traditional medicine and indigenous knowledge. If successful this policy will result in the stimulation of activity and development in the pharmaceutical manufacturing industry.

3. IPR Strategies in 2nd National STI Policy (June 2012)

The second STI policy launched in June 2012, seeks to bring STI to the forefront of socio-economic development in Zimbabwe. Developed through a rigorous consultative process including a S&T status review with inputs from the Academy of sciences and other S&T implementing institutions, the policy recognises the important role of IPR's in technology development. These aspects of IPR as outlined in the implementation plan are outlined in Table 19.1.

In this highly competitive environment where technology development is happening at an ever increasing pace, it is critical that developing countries, especially Africa and Zimbabwe do not remain far behind. Whereas the colonial era had its own political ills, however, in the area of R&D infrastructure particularly that for agriculture and mining, the regime should be commended for their foresight. However, in post-colonial era, the tendency of researchers to abandon such infrastructure and seek greener pastures in the diaspora where they were simply contributing either to research in their laboratories whose outcomes they had very little control over. It is for that reason that there was dearth in R&D, publications and innovation in Africa. In Zimbabwe, evidence is in the short season seed varieties that were developed to respond to recurrent droughts of the 1970s and other mining and mining processes that were central to the successes in the early years of independence. In this discussion it can therefore be inferred that, over the years, there was ever decreasing efforts to build on the IP assets from nationally conducted research. As such, the role of IPR as a source of economic wealth faded from the scope of policy makers even at the highest levels of government. It is therefore for this reason that the new Science and Technology Policy is designed to ensure that STI through the IP assets from R&D activities form the basis for a more robust socio-economic recovery of the nation.

Conclusion

The 3 policies interact in a number of ways but mainly through the need to increase R&D, innovation and partake in technology transfer and intellectual property. IP management, skills development, and proper co-ordination are also needed if these policies are to be successful. This also offers an opportunity for co-ordinated projects which can be funded. For example the Global Strategy on Public Health Innovation and Intellectual Property. This strategy aims to promote new thinking on innovation and access to medicines, as well as, based on the recommendations of the Commision on Public Health Innovation and Intellectual Property (CIPIH) report, provide a medium-term framework for securing an enhanced and sustainable basis for needs driven essential health research and development relevant to diseases which disproportionately affect developing countries, proposing clear objectives and priorities for R&D, and estimating funding needs in this area. It has principles on the promotion of technological innovation and the transfer of technology supported by intellectual property rights. The strengthening of the innovative capacity of developing countries is essential to respond to the needs of public health including stimulation of R&D in traditional medicine.

If the policies are co-ordinated all 3 ministries (Ministry of Science and Technology Development, Ministry of Health and Chlid Welfare and the Ministry of Industry and international Trade), the IP office could benefit from a project which engages R&D in traditional medicine with the transfer of technology and commercialisation of the R&D results to the pharmaceutical manufacturing industry. This type of co-ordinated approach will result in a successful project in which each ministry has a responsibility which helps them achieve the goal of their policy *i.e.* the R&D is the mandate of MSTD, traditional medicine is that of the MoHCW whilst manufacturing industry is that of the Ministry of Industry.

With the recognition of the role of IPR's in the implementation of these policies these stakeholders must now review IP legislation in Zimbabwe and make recommendations for amendements. They should also now participate in the drafting of the national IP policy which is in progress with assistance from WIPO and ARIPO.

Abbreviations

MSTD: Ministry of Science and Technology Development
MoHCW: Ministry of health and child welfare
ARIPO: African regional Intellectual Property Office
WIPO: World Intellectual Property Organisation
CIPH: Commission on Public health, Innovation and intellectual Property
STI: Science, Technology and Innovation
R&D: Research and Development
IPR: Intellectual Property Rights

References

1. Cannaby (2009). Access to climate change technology by developing countries, A Practical Strategy http//www.ictsd.org/i/news/bioresreview/64053/ (Accessed on 2 April 2012).
2. Lettington (2004). Willingness and Ability to use TRIPS Flexibilities by developing countries, Kenya case Studywww.who.int/hiv/amds/countries/ken_UseTRIPs FlexibilitiesDFID.pdf.
3. Musungu, *et al.* (2004). Utilizing trips flexibilities for public health protection through south-south regional frameworks, South Center. Http//www.who.int/ medicinedocs/pdf/s4968e/s4968e.pdf (Accessed 7May 2012).
4. Correa, C. (2000). Integrating Public Health Concerns into Patent Legislation in Developing Countries, South Centre, Geneva.
5. Lettington, R. and Musungu, S. (2000). "In Defence of Kenya's Health: Proposed Amendments to the Industrial Property Bill 2000", Kenya Coalition for Access to Essential Medicines, Nairobi.

6. UNIDO (2011). Pharmaceutical Sector Profile: Zimbabwe Global UNIDO Project: Strengthening the local production of essential generic drugs in least developed and developing countrieshttp//www.unido.org/./Zimbabwe_Pharma per cent 20Sector per cent 20Profile_032011 (Accessed 5 Jan 2012).
7. Carolyn Deere (2009). The politics of intellectual property Reform in developing countries, The relevance of the World intellectual property organizationhttp//www.papers.ssrn.com/sol3/papers.cfm?abstract_id=1412673 (Accessed 3 May 2012).
8. W. Lesser (2001). The effects of trips-mandated intellectual property rights on economic activities in developing countries, Cornell university.http//www.wipo.int/about-ip/en/studies/pdf/ssa_lesser_trips.pdf (Accessed 5 May 2012).
9. Zimbabwe 2nd Science,Technology and Innovation Policy of Zimbabwe – 2012.
10. Zimbabwe 2nd Science, Technology and Innovation Policy Implementation Plan – 2012.
11. Zimbabwe Industrial Development Policy 2012.
12. Zimbabwe Traditional Medicine Policy 2007.

Chapter 20

Intellectual Property and Technological Capability in Agro Biotechnology: Policy Option before India

*Bijaya Kumar Sahu**[1]

Scientific Officer (IPR),
Intellectual Property Consultancy and Management Division,
National Research Development Corporation (NRDC),
New Delhi, India

1. Introduction

A nation's future and its ability to compete in the global market depend to a great extent on how it generates new ideas and technological innovation, where Intellectual Property (IP) creation and protection are playing vital role in global knowledge based economy. IP is no longer as a self-contained domain. It is an integral part of the socio-economic development of industrial economies, where Intellectual Property Rights (IPRs) are part of the institutional infrastructure that encourages private investments in formal research and development (R&D) and other inventive. In contrast, most developing countries have been trying relied on IPRs protection as a major mechanism to foster innovation. Countries like China, USA, Japan and Korea have enhanced their respective IP systems through intense capacity building with a view to achieving

* E-mail: bksahu@nrdc.in

1 The views expressed in the Paper are of the author only and not necessarily of the Organization he works for.

greater technological innovation. It has become imperative for India to scale up efforts to build a world class IPRs infrastructure and ensure that IPRs are used in the best national interest for more extensive innovative research, technology transfer, wealth creation and overall benefit of country.

IP has become a much more affluent field of endeavor as it moved from isolationism in the world of policy to a position of management. From a one-dimensional technical specialization, IP has become a multidimensional complex of policies. The role of IPRs in the technological capabilities of India in agriculture biotechnology sector is in a nescient stage particularly in crop biotechnology and there is yet to be linking with IP protection s and technological development in this sector. The performance of the IPRs system of the country and its interaction with national innovation system with some degrees of success has been discussed. It is believed that India's experience of the role of IPRs protection has not only invaluable contribution for its own future economic and industrial development, but it may also have some policy implications and lessons for other developing countries with similar and common characteristics.

The IP system is one of the cornerstones of modern economic policy at the national level and a catalyst for development. It will increasingly become an important tool for sustainable development, in the knowledge-based society. The focus of this paper is primarily on IPRs issues in agricultural biotechnology because agriculture is overwhelmingly important for the economies and livelihoods of developing countries particularly India, where more than 1.1 billion peoples' lives. It is also a sector in which modern biotechnology has already made a substantial impact and where supporters of biotechnology point to significant future benefits. IPRs were designed to encourage innovation, creativity and knowledge dissemination in a commercial, industrial context (Gerster 2001). Their use is widespread in developed countries and heavily supported by economists and those within knowledge intensive industries that argue IPRs are an engine for research and development (R&D), particularly for sectors with high research costs, such as the biotechnology sector (Dodds *et al.*, 2001).

2. IPRs and Technological Capabilities

Firstly, some of the main relevant literature of the role of IPRs in technological development has been discussed in below. The performance of the IPRs system of the country and its interaction with national agri-biotech innovation system with some degrees of success has been discussed. Finally, some suggestions and policy implication regarding the improvement and promotion of IPRs system in India will be discussed. It is believed that India's experience of the role of IPR has not only invaluable contribution for its own future economic and industrial development.

This paper will not only focus on different form of IPRs of TRIPs regimes *vis a vis* the development of Indian agriculture biotechnology and genetic resources, but also focus on the development of Indian agriculture biotechnology sector with its high technological activity. It is believed that, the impact of TRIPs will vary according to each country's economic and technological development. India, which is endowed with a large intellectual infrastructure, can gain in the long term by stronger IPR protection. The IP system is one of the cornerstones of modern economic policy at the national level and a catalyst for development. It will increasingly become an important tool for sustainable development in the knowledge-based society of this millennium. There has been a lot of issues and debate on the role of IP protection especially the patent system in fostering innovation, technological capabilities and industrial development. The Intellectual Property Protection (IPP) is expected to encourage innovation by rewarding the inventor. Strong IPP regime may also inhibit diffusion of knowledge and even technology development to the technology followers' country.

2.1. Technological Capabilities

Technological capabilities have always been a fundamental component of economic growth and welfare. Technological capabilities can also vary between sectors. In the industrial sector, the elements of technology capability - production engineering, manufacture of capital goods, and research and development, etc. - are different from those essential for the services sector. Technological capabilities may exist in both large and small industrial sectors. In general, technology capabilities in developing countries, whether considered in macro terms or in terms of elements, would depend on such factors as: adequate number and quality of human resources with practical experience, skills, and aptitude; useful technological information on sources and conditions of technology transfer; institutions for education and training, for research and development, and for engineering design and consultancy; favourable natural environment and factor endowments, attitudes and customs, etc. Technological Capability may be defined as the ability to make use of knowledge to acquire, assimilate, adapt, and change existing technologies and develop new products and processes or the process of accumulating the capability to innovate. The concepts "technological capability" and "absorptive capacity" both refer to the ability to develop and exploit knowledge commercially, what in recent literature is often seen as reflecting the "innovation system" of a country. As for "innovation capability" (to use the term suggested by Kim 1997) research and development (R&D) expenditures measure some (but not all) resources that are used for developing new products or processes while patents count (patentable) inventions.

The legal system in the IPR protection is very sensitive and complex in case of biotechnology in and agricultural biotechnology in particular because of technical, ethical and legal issues involved. The Indian Patent Act 1970 as amended by the by Patent (Amendment) Act 2002, Patent Rule 2003, Patents (Amendment) Rule 2005 and Patents (Amendment) Rule 2006 defines patentable invention as: a new product or process involving an inventive step and capable of industrial application. Presently Indian agri biotech industry has great challenges of the emerging Trade Related Aspects of Intellectual Property Rights (TRIPS) compliant patent system. Where Article 27.3(b) of TRIPS excludes biological processes for the production of plants or animals as a patentable subject matter, but patents can be granted to the microorganisms, non-biological, and microbiological processes used in the production of plants and animals. This covers even the gene sequences, which may be for a particular character, or a promoter or genetic markers or similar ones. With the increase of transgenic research both in public and private research organizations, the issues of royalty payments, material transfer agreements (MTA), and legal obligations and bindings are to be understood too. In the case of biotechnology innovations, it is difficult to say whether the new life form in the form of gene, DNA, cell, etc. is a scientific discovery or a technological invention. Discovery is merely making available what already exists in nature. A substance freely occurring in nature, if merely found or discovered, is not patentable. However, if the substance found in nature has first to be isolated from its surroundings, and a process for obtaining it is developed, that process is considered an invention and hence is patentable.

The consideration of industrial application is yet another obstacle for securing patents for inventions in biotechnology. However, in India there are several ethical issues too related to patenting of life forms, the most important being extent of private ownership that could be extended to life forms. Under Article 27 (3)(b) of TRIPs agreement allows members to exclude from patent protection, plants and animals other than micro-organisms; and biological processes for the production of plants or animals other than microbiological processes. TRIPs provide option to member states protecting new plant variety by means of patent or sui generis system or both. India opted for *sui generis* protection and legislated *"Plant Varieties Protection and Farmers Right Act-2000"* that enables the farmer to save, use, sow, re-sow, exchange, or share the seeds of protected variety, besides offering protection on farmers' variety, extant variety and essentially derived variety. The Plant Variety and Farmer Right Authority (PPV&FRA) has been playing important role in establishment of an effective system for protection of plant varieties, the rights of farmers and plant breeders and to encourage the development of new varieties of plants it has been considered necessary to recognize and protect the rights of the farmers. Whereas plant variety protection could boost research in the area of plant biotechnology by both public and private bodies, it could also result in higher prices for seeds, thus naturally excluding the small and marginal farmers from accessing such new technologies.

3. National Biotechnology Innovation System

Government of India has played a major role in the formation of innovation system in India. The potential for biotechnology development is strongly influenced by the size and strength of the national economy, the structure of existing industry and the intensity of R&D (Arora, 2007). The national approaches and initiatives to promote the growth of biotechnology and its innovative performance could be depicted with the help of various S&T indicators. A comparison of India with other developed and developing countries in the development of biotechnology is also reflected.

From the above, it is well understood that the role of the government in driving the Indian innovation system is very much high, where private institutions are not playing active role. Government of India has already set up national agriculture innovation project, new IPR management infrastructure to enable the smooth transfer of agriculture technology for benefit sharing with all stakeholders. But, there is an urgent need to boost the investments in R&D with strong participation from the private sector to catch up and to realise the target set in the Science and Technology Policy (STP) 2003.

Table 20.1: Indicators of Expenditure and Sources of Funds on R&D for Select Countries

Sl.No.	*Country*	*Per Capita R&D (in Us $)*	*R&D Exp. as % GDP*	*Source of R&D Funds (per cent)*		
				Industry	*Government*	*Other*
1.	Germany	613.94	2.64	67	30	3
2.	China	12.15	1.23	66	27	7
3.	**India**	**3.53**	**0.80**	**20**	**80**	**0**
4.	Italy	220.76	1.11	43	51	6
5.	Japan	976.58	3.11	75	18	7
6.	Korea, Rep.	288.50	2.91	75	23	2
7.	Russian Fed.	29.91	1.24	31	61	8
8.	United Kingdom	436.40	1.88	44	31	25
9.	United States	962.15	2.67	64	31	5

Source: Arora P, 2007.

Note: China excludes Hong Kong, Other- includes International sources etc.

R&D and GDP figures for the various countries are for the period 2000-02.

Table 20. 2: Trends in Biotechnology Patents in India (2002-11)

Year	*Application #*	*Granted*
2002-03	46	NA
2003-04	23	NA
2004-05	1214	71
2005-06	1525	51
2006-07	2774	89
2007-08	1950	341
2008-09	1844	117
2009-10	1303	449
2010-11	1497	165

Note: #: Excluding PCT National Phase.

Source: Annual Report, Indian Patent Office.

The growing IP protection, emerging domestic market and forecasted revenue in biotechnology sector (Table 20.2, Figures 20.1 and 20.2) is significantly growing up. The globally harmonized IPR regime in India is believe to be best guarantor of protection of indigenous and traditional knowledge systems as well as new inventions in modern agricultural biotechnology. India's both public and private research institutes need to take up many organizational IP capacity building approach and management challenges, which include the establishment of an IP management and

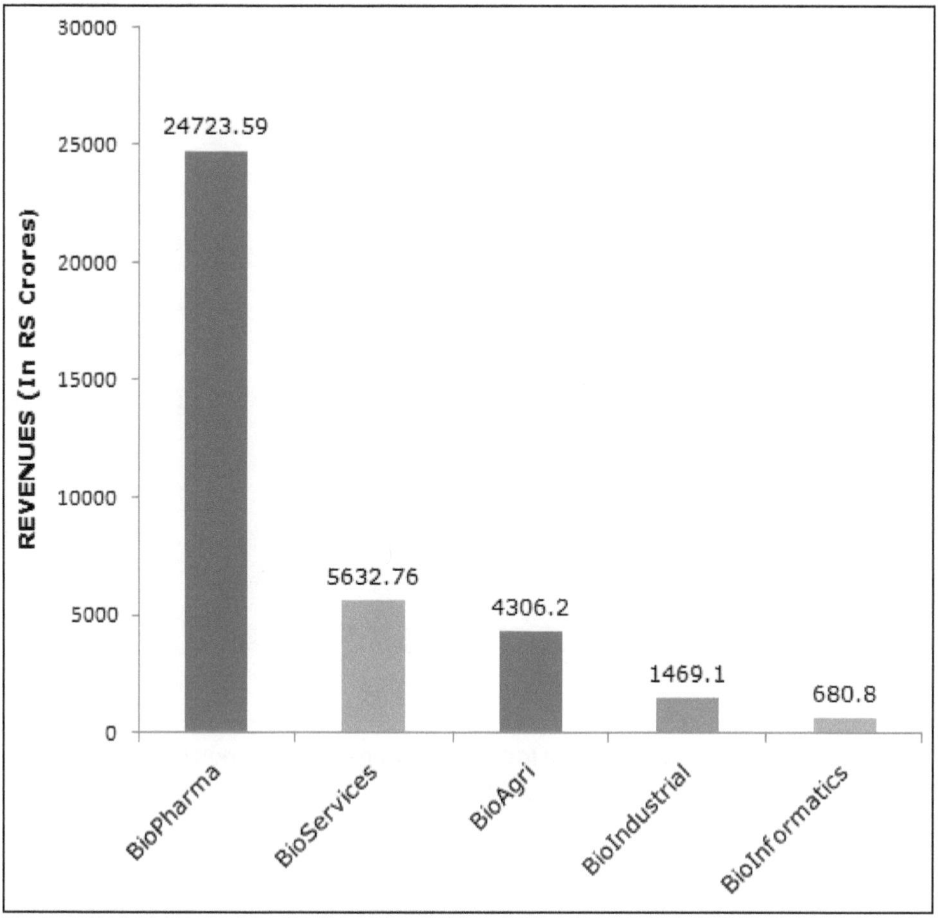

Figure 20.1: Forecasts for Sector Specific Biotechnogy 2015.
***Source*: NISTADS, 2008.**

technology transfer office, developing negotiation skills and honoring IPR legislation and agreements, and meeting the financial burden of maintaining an IPR system. It is well-known that India's economic progress in the last decade evident the booming of knowledge intensive sectors be it information technology, biotechnology and pharmaceuticals among many more skill intensive service sectors. The stronger patent regime raises strong hopes that it will stimulate creative and innovative technological capability in India's knowledge based industries. By stimulating broad based expansion in R&D in agro-biotechnology through low end human capital and technological capability building, India could bring on board more than 300 million poor who have been secured food security through its emergence as a major economic player in the world economy.

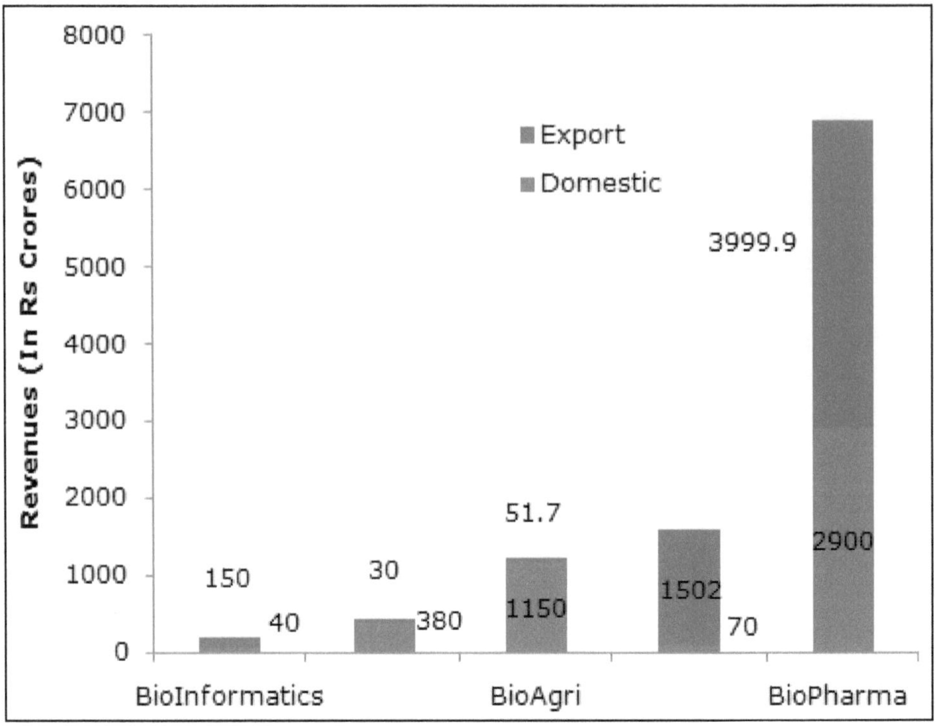

Figure 20.2: Biotech Industries (Domestic Vs Export).
Source: NISTADS, 2008.

References

1. Arora, Praveen (2007). Biotechnology Innovation System in India: Role of Government in the 5th Globelic International Conference, Sartov, Russia 20-23, September 2007.
2. Correa, Carlos (2007). "Intellectual Property and Competition Law: Exploration of Some Issues of Relevance to Developing Countries, ICTSD IPRs and Sustainable Development Programme Issue Paper No. 21, International Centre for Trade and Sustainable Development, Geneva, Switzerland.
3. Correa, Carlos (2005). "Can the TRIPS Agreement foster technology transfer to developing countries? in "International Public Goods and Transfer of Technology: Under a Globalized Intellectual Property Regime", edited by Keith E. Maskus and Jerome H. Reichman, Cambridge.
4. Correa, Carlos, (2000). "Intellectual Property Rights, the WTO and Developing Countries", Third World Network, Penang.
5. Correa, Carlos, (1998). Implementing the TRIPS Agreement: General context and implications for developing countries, Third World Network, Penang.
6. Correa, Carlos, (1997). "Technology transfer and sustainable development after the Uruguay Round", Third World Network, Penang.

7. Daniele Archibugi and Alberto Coco (2002). A New Indicator of Technological Capabilities for Developed and Developing Countries (ArCo), Preliminary Draft 11 June 2002, Italian National Research Council, Italy, p. 1.

8. Dodds, J.H.; Ortiz, R.; Crouch, J.H.; Mahalasksmi, V. and Sharma, K.K. (2001). Biotechnology, the Gene Revolution, and Proprietary Technology in Agriculture. A Strategic Note for the World Bank.*bio* Developments-International Institute Inc., Ithaka New York, USA.

9. Gerster, Richard, (2001). "Patents and Development: Lessons Learnt from the Economic History of Switzerland", Third World Network.

10. Gurry F. (2007). Forward in intellectual property management in Health and Agriculture Innovations: A hand book of Best Practices (Eds A Krattiger, RT Mahony, L. Nelson, *et al*), MIHR, Oxford UK and PIPRA, Davis, California, USA.

11. Farhana Yamin (2003). *"IPRs, biotechnology and food security"* IDS Working Paper 203, Institute of Development Studies, Sussex BN1 9RE, September, p. 1.

12. Kim, Linsu and Nelson, Richard R eds. 2000, "Technology, Learning and Innovation", Cambridge University Press.

13. Mashelkar, R. A., (2002). Intellectual property rights and the third world, Journal of Intellectual. Property Rights, 7: 308-323.

14. Science and Development Network Please see http://www.scidev.net/en/science-and-innovation-policy/definitions/technology-transfer-2/t/

15. Jan Fagerberg and Martin Srholec (2007). The role of *"capabilities" in development: Why some countries manage to catch up while others stay poor"*, Centre for Technology, Innovation and Culture, University of Oslo, DIME Working paper 2007.08 in the series on "Dynamics of Knowledge Accumulation, Competitiveness, Regional Cohesion and Economic Policies", Oslo, pp 13. For more http://www.dime eu.org/files/active/0/WP2007_8Fagerberg.pdf

16. DST (2013). Science and Technology Policy 2013, Govt of India, New Delhi Please see www. dst.gov.in

17. Kumar. A. (2008). Biogeneric manufacturing in India, in Advances in Biopharmaceutical Technology in India, Ed. E.S. Langer, Bioplan Associates, Rockville, USA, pp. 203-235.

18. Kumar N (1998). India, Paris convention and TRIPs, Economics and Political Weekly, September.

19. Lall Sanjay (1992). Technological capabilities and Industrialisation world development, 20: 165-86.

20. Mani, Sunil (1990). Biotechnology Research in India, Economic and Political Weekly, Aug. 25.

21. Protection of Plant Varieties and Farmer Rights Autherity, Govt of India, please visit http://www.plantauthority.gov.in/pdf/G_Brochure_English.pdf.

22. UNU (1994). "The uncertain quest: science, technology, and development', Edited by Jean-Jacques Salomon, Francisco R. Sagasti, and Céline Sachs-Jeantet, Tokyo, Part 2, Chapter 8.
23. Visalakshi, S., Mehrotra, N.N., Tandon, P. (1993). Evaluatrion of Technology Transfer in India : A case study of healthcare related biotechonology, International Journal of Technology Management, Special Issue, pp. 129-141.
24. Visalakshi, S. (2008). *Biotechnology,* India Science and Technology , NISTADS, India.

Chapter 21

Repurposing Strategies: Churning Out Research

*Sripathi Rao Kulkarni**

Scientist, Division of S&T Management,
CSIR-Central Drug Research Institute,
Lucknow – 226031, Uttar Pradesh, India

ABSTRACT

Innovations relating to the pharmaceutical sector normally see the churning out of ideas, reduction to practice and ultimately taking to the market place. This may be termed as 'purposing' that has a specific objective and efforts to realizing the same by way of a product or a process showing presence in the market for certain time. Then, the downfall is observed sending signals for the need for same entities to be tried and tested for different purposes towards extension of the shelf-life of the invention, in other words 're-purposing'.

This may overlap with 'ever-greening' however, incremental improvements are considered as a boon for the researchers to extend the life of innovation. Repurposing has been successfully done by the academia and to some extent by the generic players in the Pharmaceutical sector. Though many countries recognize this concept as such or by way of second medical use, that gives space to the inventor, there are certain countries that discourage it. India has shown its stand through the decision on the Novartis case. However, the administrative constraints have to be looked at.

Keywords: *Invention, Innovation, Repurposing, Ever-greening.*

---

* E-mail: sripathi_kulkarni@cdri.res.in, sripathi.kulkarni@gmail.com

1. Introduction

Presumably, everyone agrees that 'Invention is made only once, rest that can happen is discovery'. If the existence of key players in bringing out life-saving drugs is taken into consideration, innovator companies spend hugely on innovations without the guarantee of returns. In case the endeavors click then the life saving drug is priced out of reach of a common man. Such are the pricing patterns by the innovator companies. Thanks to the efforts of certain organizations fighting against such monopolistic approaches and pressing upon the Government to adopt newer policies to encourage the generic players, placing the medicines at affordable prices and bringing the drugs accessible for better health of the society. Not to forget, innovator company invests a lot to bring the potential drug into the market, however, there must be a cap on the pricing scenario. There is another angle of threat to the innovator companies' products that go about with a little bit of modifications and re-release of the known drug for entirely different and unknown activity. If one is considered 'purposing' the other may be termed as 're-purposing' and the latter is the most worked and used alternative for benefit of the society.

2. Background

2.1. Access to Medicines

Late 1990s; the price of first line patented AIDS medicines wasafter discount–US$10,439/patient/year. Millions died, particularly in Africa, as prices were high. Patents on medicines are a key to make medicines affordable (Médecins Sans Frontières briefing note, 30 September 2011).

Generic competition brought prices down making treatment possible. 84 per cent of the antiretrovirals to HIV/AIDS patients worldwide come from Indian generic companies and are used to treat over 80 per cent of the people in more than 30 countries. There was a pressure from the organizations fighting for accessibility of medicines in support for India to be allowed to remain the 'pharmacy' of the developing world. (The Controversy of Section 3(D) of The Indian Patent Act)

3. Repurposing Approach

This approach was successfully managed by academia and to some extent by generic pharma companies. The issue involving Thalidomide was considered a landmark which, was originally used to prevent morning sickness in pregnant women and later found to cause tragic birth defects. New interest in thalidomide was sparked when scientists discovered that the drug had potent anti-angiogenic and immunomodulatory activities. Thalomid is now approved by the Federal Drug Administration for treatment of leprosy (Melissa Hunter-Ensor *et al.*, 2010).

AZT also known as Zidovudine, was originally developed as a treatment for cancer, but was shown to lack efficacy against neoplastic cells. The discovery that AZT was effective as a treatment for patients with HIV/AIDS transformed the failed chemotherapeutic into an anti-retroviral blockbuster (Melissa Hunter-Ensor *et al.*, 2010).

Examples of approved drug molecules identified using low-throughput screening methods as having effects against diseases other than the original target[a]

Molecule	Original use	New use	Method of discovery
Aprepitant	Nausea: NK-1 receptor antagonist	Drug-resistant HIV-1 infection: downregulates CCR5 in macrophages Cryptosporidiosis in immunosuppressed hosts	Initial hypothesis tested with another NK-1 receptor antagonist *in vitro* Tested *in vivo* in immunosuppressed mice infected with *Cryptosporidium parvum*; decreased substance P levels
Amiodarone	Class III anti-arrhythmic	Chagas disease: blocks ergosterol biosynthesis	Literature search
Glybenclamide	Antidiabetic	Antithrombotic activity in mouse models IC_{50} 9.6 μM	Common pharmacophore with an experimental TP receptor antagonist SQ29,548
Tamoxifen	Antiestrogen	Anti-protozoal: *Leishmania amazonensis* IC_{50} 11.1–16.4 μM	Focused screening to test hypothesis and *in vivo* mice studies
Trimetrexate	Antifolate used in *Pneumocystis carinii* infection in patients with AIDS	Inhibitor of *Trypanosoma cruzi* DHFR IC_{50} 6.6 nM	Enzyme activity and antiparasite activity assays for one compound
Riluzole	Amyotrophic lateral sclerosis: inhibits glutamate release and reuptake	Currently in clinical trials for treating melanoma, but might have activity against other cancers	Treatment of GRM1-positive human melanoma cells reduced levels of released glutamate, suppressed melanoma cell growth and also suppressed tumor growth in xenograft model; induced cell cycle arrest, leading to apoptosis
Sertraline	Antidepressant (selective serotonin reuptake inhibitor)	Neuroprotective, prolongs survival, improves motor performance and ameliorates brain atrophy in the R6/2 HD model	Previously shown that another SSRI was neuroprotective

Source: Sean Ekins *et al.*. Drug Discovery Today, Volume 16, Issues 7–8, April 2011.

Examples of approved drug molecules identified using HTS or *in silico* screening methods as having effects against diseases other than original target[a]

Molecule	Original use	New use	Method of discovery
Itraconazole	Antifungal: lanosterol 14α-demethylase inhibitor	Inhibition of angiogenesis by inhibiting human lanosterol 14α-demethylase; IC_{50} 160 nM	*In vitro* HUVEC proliferation screen against FDA-approved drugs (JHCCL)
Astemizole	Non-sedating antihistamine (removed from US market by FDA in 1999)	Antimalarial IC_{50} 227 nM against *Plasmodium falciparum* 3D7	*In vitro* screen for *P. falciparum* growth of 1937 FDA-approved drugs (JHCCL)
Mycophenolic acid	Immunosuppressive drug: inhibits guanine nucleotide biosynthesis	Inhibition of angiogenesis by targeting type 1 inosine monophosphate dehydrogenase; IC_{50} 99.2 nM	*In vitro* HUVEC proliferation screen of 2450 FDA- and foreign-approved drugs (JHCCL)
Entacapone and tolcapone	Parkinson's Disease: catechol-*O*-methyltransferase inhibitors	Antitubercular: entacapone inhibits InhA; IC_{50} 80 μM	Used a chemical systems biology approach
Nitazoxanide	Infections caused by *Giardia* and *Cryptosporidium* spp.	Antitubercular: multiple potential targets	Screens against replicating and non-replicating Mtb
(±)-2-amino-3-phosphonopropionic acid	Human metabolite, mGluR agonist	Antimalarial: inhibits HSP-90; IC_{50} 0.06 μM against *P. falciparum* 3D7	HTS screening of 4000 compounds
Acrisorcin	Antifungal	Antimalarial: inhibits HSP-90; IC_{50} 0.05 μM against *P. falciparum* 3D7	HTS screening of 4000 compounds
Harmine	Anticancer	Antimalarial: inhibits HSP-90; IC_{50} 0.05 μM against *P. falciparum* 3D7	HTS screening of 4000 compounds
Acetophenazine, fluphenazine and periciazine	Antipsychotics-D2 and 5-HT_2 inhibitors	Human androgen receptor antagonists acetophenazine (K_i 0.8 μM), fluphenazine(K_i 0.8 μM), periciazine (K_i 3.0 μM)	Docking of known drugs into androgen receptor followed by *in vitro* screening

Source: Sean Ekins *et al.*. Drug Discovery Today, Volume 16, Issues 7–8, April 2011.

There are many instances where repositioning of FDA approved drugs has been considered and have reportedly proved to be showing positive effects on the activities other than those they are initially meant for.

On the global context, especially when IP laws are territorial in nature, each country responds to the current aspect of re-positioning in its own way, justifying its stand on the compliance towards WTO-TRIPS. United States of America, for instance encourages the new use of a known compound provided certain unexpected results are established whereas, Europe looks in a little different was limiting it to a purpose on claimed product. India, views it as a non-patentable subject matter. The stand taken by India, specifically by way of Section 3(d) of the Indian Patents Act has invited controversies from many corners.

4. Section 3(d)

The ACT reads, as follows:

The mere discovery of a new form of a known substance which does not result in the enhancement of the known efficacy of that substance or the mere discovery of any new property or new use for a known substance or of the mere use of a known process, machine or apparatus unless such known process results in a new product or employs at least one new reactant.

Explanation: For the purposes of this clause, salts, esters, ethers, polymorphs, metabolites, pure form, particle size, isomers, mixtures of isomers, complexes, combinations and others derivatives of known substance shall be considered to be the same substance, unless they differ significantly in properties with regard to efficacy(The Patents Act 1970; http://ipindia.nic.in/ipr/patent/patents.htm).

The Section 3(d) has been the bone of contention for many IP related entities; firstly the interpretation of the clause was different by different people, for their own benefit and secondly, the need for this point to be included under the Section 3 itself was a point of conflict.

4.1. WTO-TRIPS and Section 3(d)

India became a member of WTO-TRIPS on 01.01.1995, had a challenge to introduce Pharmaceutical products patenting to be TRIPS compliant. The year 2002 amendment on Term of Patent, Reverse of burden of proof etc. and the year 2005 amendment on granting patents in chemicals, food, drugs and agrochemicals.

4.2. Glivec - Legal challenge

The case can be traced to 1997 when a patent application was filed by Novartis AG for the beta-crystalline of imatinibmesylate (brand name Gleeve/Glivec) which was a slightly different version of their 1993 patent, a vital anti-leukaemia drug, filed in the Chennai (Madras) Patent Office.The claim was to invent the beta crystalline salt from the free base of imatinib. In 2003, Glivec was granted EMR in the Indian market. Novartis obtained orders preventing some of the generic manufacturers from producing the generic equivalents of Glivec in India. Soon, Novartis was selling Gleevec at USD 2666 per patient per year. Generic companies had been selling their generic versions at USD 177 to 266 per patient per month. (Glivec: Rs. 1,20,000 versus Generic version: Rs. 8000).

According to Novartis, Imatinib, could not be administered to patients and represented only the 1st step in the process to develop Glivec as a viable treatment for cancer.Novartis claims to developed the mesylate salt of imatinib and then the beta crystal form of imatinibmesylate to make it suitable for patients to take in a pill form that would deliver consistent, safe and effective levels of medicine.The process, which took years, was more than just an incremental improvement – it was a breakthrough — and certainly cannot be interpreted as "ever-greening."(Glivec Patent Case in India: Fact Vs. Fiction, 2011)

In 2006, the Indian Patent Office ruled that Novartis did not deserve a patent for Imatinibmesylate, a salt form of a lifesaving cancer drug, on the grounds that the application claimed a new form.

In this case Novartis challenged the part of India's patent law – Section 3(d) – which read with other provisions of the patent law and the Madras High Court decision says that a new form of a known drug can only be patented if it is not obvious and shows significantly improved therapeutic efficacy over the known substance. In 2007, the Madras High Court dismissed the writ petition filed by Novartis challenging the constitutionality of Section 3(d) of Indian Patent Act.

With respect to Section 3(d) of the Indian Patent Law, Novartis claims as: unconstitutional law, and violated TRIPS. The Court affirmed that Section 3(d) of the Indian Patent Act was not unconstitutional. Violation of TRIPS is a matter to be decided by an appeal made to TRIPS forum. A win for Novartis would have made it harder for Indian companies to produce generic versions.

ERLOCIP-Legal Challenge

Cipla wanted to sell 'Erlocip' (pancreatic cancer), Roche sued Cipla for infringement, Ciplaquestionedvalidity aspect.

What the Court saw was:

that Erlotinib is not a derivative of Gefatinib.

Even if it is assumed as a derivative, it passes the section 3(d) test, as it demonstrates enhanced "efficacy".

Conclusion

Re-purposing is a quick way to churn out R&D endeavours. A specific reference to Section 3(d) of Indian Patents Act, tries to prevent the so-called concept of ever-greening with a recommendation that only those derivatives that show enhanced therapeutic efficacy are patentable but not anything that shows incremental improvement over a known substance. However, the research and development endeavors towards re-purposing' have proven to be minting monies and churning out the economies at large.

Acknowledgement

The author is thankful to CSIR-CDRI, Dr. Sabyasachi Sanyal, Scientist, CSIR-CDRI for providing tables having the information on examples of Approved drugs (Sean Ekins *et al.*).

CSIR-CDRI Communication No.: 173/2013/SRK

References

1. The Controversy of Section 3(D) of The Indian Patent Act; (http://www.legalserviceindia.com/article/l400-Controversy-of-Section-3(D)-of-The-Indian-Patent-Act.html)
2. WHAT NOVARTIS SAYS...AND WHY IT'S WRONG; Médecins Sans Frontières briefing note, 30 September 2011. (http://www.doctorswithoutborders.org/publications/article.cfm?id=5770&cat=briefing-documents).
3. *Melissa Hunter-Ensor et al.* Exploiting Newly Discovered Indications of Known Therapeutics, 2010.
4. http://ipindia.nic.in/ipr/patent/patents.htm.
5. Glivec Patent Case in India: FACT vs. FICTION(http://www.novartis.com/downloads/newsroom/glivec-information-center/Fact_vs_fiction_of_Glivec_India_Case.pdf., 2012-11-25)
6. *In silico* repositioning of approved drugs for rare and neglected diseases, Drug Discovery Today, Volume 16, Issues 7–8, April 2011, Sean Ekins, Antony J. Williams, Matthew D. Krasowski, Joel S. Freundlich.

Chapter 22

Protection of Plant Varieties, Farmers' Rights and Benefit Sharing

*H.S. Chawla**

Professor and Head,
Genetics and Plant Breeding Department,
Nodal Officer Intellectual Property Management Centre
G.B. Pant University of Agriculture and Technology, Pantnagar, India

ABSTRACT

The gene rich developing countries want global action on conservation, sustainable use of biodiversity, sharing of benefits from the use of bioresources and to prevent biopiracy of genetic resources. Various international treaties and agreements WTO- Trade related Aspects of intellectual property Rights (TRIPS), the Convention on Biodiversity (CBD), ITPGRFA (Seed Treaty) have been addressing to the issue of plant genetic resources and access and benefit sharing. The TRIPS is one of the agreements influencing access to genetic resources and its monopolization. The expansion of scope of intellectual property protection to include plant varieties and the ensuing monopoly on genetic resources has raised concerns as it affects traditional rights of farmers. The International Union for the protection of new varieties of Plants (UPOV) is one of the most accepted *sui-generis* system for the protection of new varieties of plants and recognition of plant breeders rights. The International treaty on Plant genetic resources for food and Agriculture (ITPGRFA) provides an international recognition of farmers' rights. In response to TRIPS agreement provisions, India enacted different laws and even amended existing laws for protection of genetic resources. India enacted Protection of Plant Varieties and Farmers' Rights Act, 2001 to protect plant varieties that are new and also traditional farmers' varieties, which the farmers are conserving and

* E-mail: chawlahs15@gmail.com; chawlahs_pantnagar@rediffmail.com

maintaining over the years. Indian PPV&FR Act is unique in the sense that it provides so many rights to farmers which are not even available with UPOV and ITPGRFA. The present study aims to review the historical aspects of plant breeders rights and to analyse the farmers' rights development in Asian countries on the basis of membership to WTO, UPOV and ITPGRFA vis-a-vis PPV&FR Act of India. Pantnagar University of India has enabled farmers to register traditional farmers' varieties under PPV&FR Act of India with ownership rights and now getting benefits under the law which is a unique thing in the world. By registering farmers' varieties in India it has shown the world that biopiracy can be prevented under the IPR regime.

Keywords: *IPR, Farmers' varieties, TRIPS, PPV&FR Act, Farmers' rights, Benefit sharing, UPOV Acts, ITPGRFRA.*

1. Introduction

The process of globalization has posed major challenges to developing countries of the world in context of emerging regime of intellectual property protection. The first step in this direction has been the formalization of the Agreement on TRIPS (Trade Related Aspects of Intellectual Property Rights) under the aegis of the World Trade Organization (WTO). The TRIPS agreement is designed to "promote effective and adequate protection of intellectual property rights" and to "reduce distortions and impediments to international trade" resulting from the enforcement of IPRs. The agreement covers a broad range of intellectual property rights, including patents, copyright, trademarks, geographical indications, trade secrets, designs and integrated circuits. It requires Members to grant IPRs to the nationals of other Members on the same terms as they do their own nationals ("national treatment"- Article 3), and to extend the same favourable terms they grant to the national of any Member to the nationals of every other Member ("most favoured nation"-Article 4).

The TRIPS Agreement includes a number of forms of IPR with implications for biodiversity conservation and for plant variety protection. The interest of gene rich developing countries is best served by global action aimed at conservation, protection of plant genetic resources by IP laws, sustainable use of biodiversity, sharing of benefits from the use of bioresources and to prevent biopiracy of genetic resources. However, it is necessary to analyse what the genetic resources rich countries are doing to protect their plant genetic resources and giving benefits to the farming community. Farmers are an important part of the economic, social and political fabric of the society in genetic resources rich developing countries. Their role in agro-biodiversity conservation and innovation is acknowledged worldwide since the revised agreed interpretation (FAO Conference Resolution 5/80) under the International Undertaking on Plant Genetic Resources. This paper aims at reviewing the system of IPR protection for plants by elucidating the various sections of Indian Protection of Plant Varieties and Farmers' Rights (PPV&FR) Act, 2001 and comparing the rights available to farmers under different national legislations in Asian countries, including India vis-à-vis *sui-generis* intellectual property protection in agriculture.

2. Historical Perspective

The Paris Convention of 1883 is the first multilateral agreement for harmonizing intellectual property laws. It extended protection to industrial property, which was recognized to also apply to agricultural and extractive industries and to all manufactured or natural products. The next 50 years witnessed various attempts by different countries in Europe to extend the intellectual property protection to the field of agriculture. These involved the recognition to the seeds and seedlings, introduction of a Register for Newly Bred Plants, and setting up of a seed association as well as a Seed Control Committee (Dhar, 2010). However, the first attempt to recognize the intellectual property right of plant breeder was the enactment of the Plant Patents Act by USA in 1930. This Act aimed at protecting asexually propagated plants by patents. Later, USA extended plant variety protection by enacting the 1970 Plant Variety Protection Act. It provided protection to sexual reproduction in plants, including seed germination. The protection has two major exemptions, namely seed saving by farmers and use for research purposes. However, this enactment also fueled debate regarding the type of IPR protection to be extended to the agriculture. Two divergent views emerged; one was to extend patent protection to plants while the other was to extend the *sui-generis* protection, recognizing plant breeder's right.

In Strasbourg, a group of European countries adopted the Convention on the Unification of Certain Points of Substantive Law on Patents, which prescribed plant or animal varieties or essentially biological processes for the production of plants and animals as exception to patentable subject matter. Thus, Parties were not bound to provide for the grant of patents in respect of plant varieties or animal varieties or essentially biological processes for the production of plants and animals.

A General Agreement on Tariffs and Trade (GATT) was established in 1947 (came into force on 1 January 1948) to deal with post-world war scenario concerning multilateral trade issues, particularly with a view to serve as means of stimulating world trade in goods, remove/minimize impediments to trade among member countries, and to create a level playing field. In Uruguay the 8th round of such GATT negotiations started in 1986 but it was concluded on April 15, 1994 at Marrakesh, Morocco with the signing of an accord by 124 countries that led to the formation of World Trade Organization (WTO) on 1st January 1995. This round was significant because agriculture was included as a tradable commodity and agreement on TRIPS was achieved (Chawla, 2007).

The extension of intellectual property protection to agriculture also raised a few concerns. One such concern is that farmers in developing countries have traditionally enjoyed the right to save, share, exchange and sell the farm produce as well as seeds. The monopoly extended to plant breeders by granting intellectual property right on plant varieties may take away the traditional rights of farmers.

Further, monopoly in agricultural products could also raise the prices of such commodities. On the other hand, contribution of farmers in the conservation and preservation of varieties was considered important for further plant breeding. To address this, two options were considered relevant; first protect the interests or the privilege of farmers to save repeatedly and use for sowing their farm saved seed of protected varieties as an exception to the plant breeder's right, and secondly protect the right of farmers in terms of getting equitable share of benefits derived from the use of plant genetic resources conserved and preserved by them. The first approach is reflected in the UPOV Act, the European Nations' effort towards securing the plant breeders' right, while the second approach is reflected in the FAO International Undertaking on Plant Genetic Resources, which was renegotiated and adopted as the International Treaty on Plant Genetic Resources for Food and Agriculture (ITPGRFA).

In 1961, Five European countries agreed to provide *sui-generis* IPR protection to plant varieties and formed the Union for the Protection of New Varieties of Plants (UPOV). UPOV provided for the rights of plant breeders, and prohibited from extending two or more types of protection to a particular plant species. Article 5 of UPOV 1961 provides for the protection of the interests of the farmers with respect to rights of plant breeders. The act of farmers to save a part of their farm produce as seeds for the next crop season and to exchange seeds with other farmers were not considered as a part of "commercial marketing" under Article 5(1). Therefore, such acts were kept out of the scope of plant breeder's right as farmers' privilege. However, the farmers' rights as such were not recognized under the UPOV Act. The UPOV underwent three amendments in 1972, 1978 and in 1991. The 1978 Act came into force in 1981 and the 1991 Act in April 1998. There are at present two main Acts of 1978 and 1991 under which the parties to the convention have joined (UPOV, 2012).

The 1978 amendment of UPOV left the provision of farmers' privilege unaltered. However, it provided for restricting the plant breeders' right on the ground of public interest to prevent the adverse effect of the monopoly. This provision indirectly addressed the right of farmer to the adequate availability of the seeds. This aspect is also present in the UPOV 1991.The third amendment of UPOV, in 1991, made the farmers' privilege optional to the member countries. This provision allows farmers to use the product of the harvest of the protected variety, which they may obtain by planting on their own holdings, for further propagating purposes. However, the Convention requires that the farmers' privilege be regulated "within the reasonable limits and subject to the safeguarding of the legitimate interests of the breeder" (Singh *et al.*, 2011).

The concept of Farmers' Rights came up in 1980s as a response to the increased demand for plant breeders' rights, to draw attention to the unremunerated innovations of farmers. The first mention of farmers' rights was made in the First Meeting of the Working Group of the FAO Commission on Plant Genetic Resources, 1986, in context of the International Undertaking on Plant Genetic Resources (IUPGR). The concept of farmers' rights was based on the fact that the farmers have been engaged in the informal breeding process besides conserving and preserving biological and genetic resources for time immemorial. Hence, they deserved to be recognized and rewarded like the contribution of breeders in development of the new varieties and rewarded through plant breeders' right.

The Twenty-fifth Session of the FAO Conference of 1989 was a landmark in the history of recognition of farmers' rights. FAO Conference Resolution 4/89 first introduced the concept of farmers' rights into the IUPGR as one of its revised Agreed Interpretation. Further the farmers' rights were defined in the resolution 5/89. The IUPGR had observed that generations of farmers have conserved, improved and made available plant genetic resources, however, the contribution of these farmers were not sufficiently recognized or rewarded. The farmers should benefit fully from the improved and increased use of the genetic resources that they have preserved. It was in the light of these facts that the FAO Conference endorsed the concept of farmers' right, and defined these as right arising from the past, present and future contributions of farmers in conserving, improving, and making available plant genetic resources, particularly those in the centers of origin/diversity. These rights are vested in the International Community, as trustee for present and future generations of farmers, for the purpose of ensuring full benefits to farmers, and supporting the continuation of their contributions, as well as the attainment of the overall purposes of IUPGR.

IUPGR that had been advocating free exchange of plant genetic resources (PGR) for research use, being the heritage of mankind, released a revised agreed interpretation in 1991 that such free access will be subject to the sovereign rights of nations over their PGRs. This is directly relevant to both the CBD and the TRIPS Agreement.

The twenty-seventh session of the FAO Conference recognized the need to further the process of renegotiations for the two unresolved issues of the Nairobi Final Act, including the realization of farmers' rights, within the framework of IUPGR, and requested the Director-General to provide a forum for such negotiations among governments (Resolution 7/93). These negotiations culminated in the adoption of the ITPGRFA (also known as Seed Treaty), through Resolution 3/2001, by the FAO Conference in November 2001 (FAO, 2010). The Treaty recognized the enormous contribution that the local and indigenous communities and farmers have made and will continue the efforts on conservation and development of plant genetic resources (Article 9.1). It recognized following rights as main components of the farmers' right, (i) Right to save, use, exchange and sell farm-saved seed and other propagating material (Article 9.3), (ii) Right to fair and equitable sharing of the benefits arising from the use of plant genetic resources for food and agriculture, (iii) Right to participate in national decision-making process about plant genetic resources [entrusting national governments with the responsibility for implementing these rights in accordance with their needs and priorities subject to national legislation (Article 9.2)], and (iv) Protection of traditional knowledge. Thus, a full-fledged concept of farmers' rights came to an existence at the international forum.

In 1992, the Convention on Biological Diversity (CBD) was adopted. CBD was signed at the Earth Summit in Rio de Janeiro in 1992 with respect to biological resources. It deals with the sovereign rights of the nations over their genetic resources. CBD came into force in December 1993. CBD defines 'genetic resources' as 'genetic material of actual or potential value. 'Genetic material' is any material of plant, animal, microbial or other origin containing functional units of heredity. Documentation of a genetic resource can also cover its parts or components, such as organs, cells, cell organelles, genes, etc. This is the first legal mechanism which has very categorically highlighted that plant genetic resources are not to be the heritage of humankind, but are the properties of the countries and hence these are tradable commodities. However, this stand is in conflict with patenting of live forms such as plant varieties especially traditional farmers' varieties. It recognized the sovereign rights of the nation on their biological resources. The Article 8(j) of the convention also recognized the contribution of communities and indigenous local people in the conservation and preservation of biological resources. It also recognized the rights of community and indigenous people to have a fair and equitable share in the benefits arising out of utilization of such knowledge. Later, this benefit sharing was seen as the important component of the realization of farmers' right (CBD, 2012).

With the establishment of WTO in 1995, the TRIPS Agreement provided that intellectual property should be protected in the agriculture either by patents or by an effective *sui-generis* protection or both (Article 27.3b). This implied extension of some kind of protection to agriculture by all the developed as well as developing WTO member nations. Also, the provision for extending the *sui-generis* protection provided the legitimacy to protect the farmers' rights and balance the rights of the breeder and the farmer. It also provided to extend or limit the extent of farmers' right as per the need of the concerned nation.

It is in this context that "farmers' rights" gained importance. Various nations have passed their *sui-generis* plant variety protection legislations in order to comply with the TRIPS Agreement. Few countries have used their *sui-generis* PVP system to extend the farmers' rights. However, farmers' rights, thus extended, are not uniform. Countries have adopted the sui generis models as per their needs.

The IU, like the CBD, sits in an uneasy relationship with TRIPS Agreement. This is the case in relation to both access to resources as well as the sharing of benefits resulting from commercialization. Firstly, the TRIPS Agreement does not prohibit Members from granting patents over plant genetic resources. Patent give the patent holder exclusive rights over the resource for the duration of the patent, which they are likely to exercise by withholding access to the resources. If a patent is granted over resources that are covered by the IU, the resources may become unavailable to Members of the IU who wish to access through the system of multilateral access. The system of facilitated access is an essential feature of the IU. To respond to this problem, the current draft of the IU includes bracketed text representing two options. The first option prohibits recipients of material from the multilateral system from claiming IPRs that would limit facilitated access to the resource. The second option simply prohibits the recipients from claiming IPRs over material received via the system of facilitated access. Secondly, there is no mechanism in TRIPS to ensure benefits derived from patent protection over genetic resources relating to food and agriculture are collected and distributed fairly and equitably.

3. India Initiatives: Domestic Scenario

India has enacted three new laws which will help in the protection of genetic resources, traditional knowledge, and traditional plant varieties for giving rights to farmers and benefit sharing. These are: Geographical Indications of Goods (Registration and Protection) Act, 1999, the Protection of Plant Varieties and Farmers'

Rights Act, 2001 and the Biological Diversity Act, 2002 and made appropriate provisions and amendments in the Patents Act, 1970.

3.1. The Patents Act, 1970

Patents Act, 1970 has been comprehensively amended in 2002 and 2005. These amendments, *inter-alia*, provide for protection of traditional knowledge and bio-resources (Anonymous, 2011). The provisions in this regard are reproduced below:

3.1.1. Traditional Knowledge Non-Patentable

Section 3(p) provides that an invention which, in effect, is traditional knowledge or which is an aggregation or duplication of known properties of traditionally known component or components is not patentable.

3.1.2. Opposition and Revocation

In order to further protect the traditional knowledge from being patented, provisions have been incorporated in said law to include anticipation of invention by available local knowledge, including oral knowledge, as one of the grounds for opposition as also for revocation of patent. These are contained in Sections 25 and 64 of the Patents Act.

3.1.3. Mandatory Disclosure of Source and Geographical Origin of the Biological Material

Section 10 of the Patents Act provides that while applying for patents in India, disclosure of source and geographical origin of the biological material used in the invention is mandatory. Non-fulfillment of this requirement is a ground for opposition (Section 25) and revocation of patent, if granted (Section 64).

4. Geographical Indications of Goods (Registration and Protection) Act, 1999

The Geographical Indications of Goods (Registration and Protection) Act, 1999 seeks to protect the goods (agricultural, manufactured or processed) under geographical indications. The protection under the Act is available only to the geographical indication registered under the Act and to the authorized users. The Act permits any association of persons or producers or any organization or authority established by law representing the interest of the producers of goods to register a geographical indication. The holders of the traditional knowledge in goods so produced and sold using geographical indication can register and protect their traditional knowledge under this law. Some of the traditional agricultural resources as goods registered under the GI Act are: Darjeeling tea, Kangra tea, Coorg orange, Mysore betel leaf, Nanjangud banana, Palakkadan matta rice, Malabar pepper, Allahabad surkha, Tellicherry pepper, Mysore jasmine, Udupi jasmine, Hadagali jasmine, Alleppey green cardamom, Coorg green cardamom, Navara rice (Anonymous, 2009).

5. Biological Diversity Act, 2002

The key development in India concerning biodiversity is the enactment of legislation on The Biological Diversity Act, 2002. A National Biodiversity Authority has been created under the Ministry of Environment and Forests, with its headquarters at Chennai. The basic principle being, that no foreigner or foreign organization, could take away any biological resources for research or commercial use without permission of the country of origin. It has the clear mandate to control the biodiversity and no person shall without the prior approval of authority transfer the results of any research relating to any biological resources occurring in or obtained from India for monetary consideration or otherwise to any person who is not a citizen of India or body corporate which is not registered in India [Sec. 7]. The legislation ensures that benefits between conservers of the resources and users are equitably shared (BDA, 2002).

The Biological Diversity Act (BDA), 2002 also requires that permission of National Biodiversity Authority is a prerequisite for seeking patent/IPR on any Indian bioresource accessed by foreigners. This is in conformity with CBD, which recognizes that States have sovereign rights over their own biological resources and that the authority to determine access to genetic resources rests with the national governments and is subject to national legislation. The CBD also establishes the principle of fair and equitable sharing of benefits derived from the use of genetic resources and requires specific measures to be formulated at the national level to facilitate benefit sharing. In India, such benefit sharing is provided for in Sections 26 and 41 of the PPV&FR Act, 2001 and Section 21 of the Biological Diversity Act, 2002.

The BDA Act subject to Section 21 and Rule 20 of the Biodiversity Rules, insists on including appropriate benefit sharing provisions in the access agreement and mutually agreed terms related to access and transfer of biological resources or knowledge occurring in or obtained from India for commercial use, bio-survey, bio-utilization or any other monetary purposes. The Authority shall develop guidelines and shall notify the specific details of benefit sharing formula in an official gazette on a case-to-case basis. The suggested benefit sharing measures may include 'monetary benefits' such as royalty, joint ventures, technology transfer, product development, and 'non-monetary benefits' such as education and awareness raising activities, institutional capacity building, venture capital fund, etc.

6. Protection of Plant Varieties and Farmers' Rights Act, 2001

India is signatory to WTO agreements and it has to abide by the TRIPS regulations. As per article 27.3(b) of the TRIPS which demand that member countries should protect their plant varieties either by patent, or an effective system of *sui generis* protection, or a combination of these two. In this context India chose a *sui generis* system for protection of plant varieties. An Act named as PPV&FR Act 2001 has been passed and Rules have been framed. PPV&FR Authority has been constituted with its Head Office located at Delhi. The PPV&FR Act is TRIPS compliant and compatible with UPOV system of plant variety protection except for the question of granting farmers' rights.

The PPV&FR Act 2001 provides protection to following types of plant varieties (Anonymous, 2007):

6.1. Newly Bred Varieties; Extant varieties

The varieties which were released under Indian Seeds Act, 1966 and have not completed 15 years as on the date of application for their protection; Farmers' varieties – The varieties which have been traditionally cultivated, including landraces and their wild relatives which are in common knowledge, as well as those evolved by farmers; Essentially derived varieties; Transgenic varieties.

To qualify for registration under the Act, a new variety has to conform to the criteria of novelty, distinctiveness, uniformity and stability (NDUS). Besides, a denomination has to be given for the registration of variety. Denomination refers to the label or title of the variety. It is the denomination that is registered. For extant and farmers' varieties only DUS features will be considered. The novelty feature will not be taken because these varieties are in public domain and are not new.

Table 22.1: WTO Member Asian Countries as per their Membership in UPOV and ITPGRFA

WTO Members		*ITPGRFA*	
		Member	*Non-Member*
UPOV	Member	(Group D)	(Group C)
		Jordan	China
		Republic of Korea	Israel
		Kyrgyzstan	Japan
		Oman	Singapore
			Turkey
			Vietnam
	Non-Member	(Group B)	(Group A)
		Armenia	Bahrain
		Bangladesh	Brunei Darussalam
		Cambodia	Hong Kong, China
		India	Kuwait
		Indonesia	Macao, China
		Malaysia	Mongolia
		Maldives	Sri Lanka
		Myanmar	Chinese Taipei
		Nepal	
		Pakistan	
		Philippines	
		Qatar	
		Saudi Arabia	
		Thailand	
		United Arab Emirates	

6.2. Position of Farmers' Rights in Asian Nations

Although UPOV was established and revised to give intellectual property rights to breeders, it also acknowledged to some extent the privileges of farmers. However, these privileges were diluted and made optional in later amendments. Given this scenario, it is notable that only a few Asian countries became party to the UPOV convention. Some countries, who are not members of UPOV, have treated UPOV as a guiding legislation in matters of plant variety protection and the grant of plant breeders rights. Since most of the Asian countries are WTO members, they were required to comply with the minimum standards as laid down in the provisions of TRIPS. The *sui-generis* provision of the TRIPS has been used by interested countries to recognize farmers' rights. Further, members of the ITPGRFA treaty have also recognized farmers' rights.

The status of farmers' rights has been considered in the Asian countries which are members of WTO and further classified into four groups based on their membership of UPOV and/or ITPGRFA as shown in Table 22.1, which has been adapted from Singh *et al.* (2011).

Out of the four groups of WTO member Asian countries (Table 22.1), only some of the group B countries who are members of ITPGRFA but not the UPOV members, have opted for a *sui-generis* system, which provides for the farmers' rights.

In Group A countries, which have not joined both UPOV and ITPGRFA, only Sri Lanka has drafted a plant breeders rights legislation, known as Protection of New Plant Varieties (Breeder's Rights)-2001, which follows the model of UPOV 1991 and does not recognize the farmers' rights.

Table 22.2: Legislations in the Asian Countries to Protect Farmers' Rights

	Countries	*Legislations dealing with Farmers' Rights*	*Status*
Act	India	The Protection of Plant Varieties and Farmers' Rights Act, 2001	In force
	Indonesia	Law on Plant Variety Protection, 2000	In force
	Thailand	Plant Varieties Protection Act, 1999	In force
	Malaysia	Protection of New Plant Varieties Act, 2004	Adopted
	Philippines	Magna Carta of Small Farmers, 1992	Adopted
		The Indigenous Peoples Rights Act, 1997	In force
Draft		Plant Varieties Act, 2002	Draft
		Community Intellectual Rights Protection Act, 2001	Draft
	Pakistan	Legislation on access to biological resources and community rights, 2004	Draft
		Plant Breeders' Rights Ordinance, 2000	
	Bangladesh	Biodiversity and Community Knowledge Protection Act, 1998	Draft
		Plant Varieties Act,1998	Draft
Policy	Nepal	Nepal Biodiversity Strategy, 2002	Policy document

In Group B countries, which are members of ITPGRFA but not UPOV, India, Thailand, Indonesia, Malaysia and Philippines have enacted their legislations with respect to farmers' rights (Table 22.2). Bangladesh and Pakistan have prepared their draft legislation while Nepal has prepared a policy document, which discusses the farmers' right. Other countries in the group (Table 22.2) do not have any legislation with respect to farmers' rights or plant variety protection.

7. Provisions Related to Farmers Rights vis-a-vis Indian PPV&FR Act: A Comparative Analysis of Group B Countries

India has enacted PPV&FR Act in compliance to the TRIPS requirement. The Act deals with plant variety protection as well as the farmers' rights. Indian law follows a holistic approach. The *sui-generis* system adopted by India is unique in the world in the sense that it has taken farmers' rights concept a step forward and genuinely addresses the concerns of farmers as breeders, innovators, conservers, etc. It has tried to incorporate the features of UPOV and ITPGRFA along with certain distinctive features of its own as per requirement of farmers. PPV&FR Act of India recognizes various rights of farmers as per Section 39 (Table 22.3). In the context of Indian legislation, other Asian countries' legislations with respect to farmers' rights have been compared.

Table 22.3: Rights Provided to Farmers in PPV&FR Act, 2001 of India

Type of Rights	*Description of rights*	*Available in ITPGRFA or UPOV*
Farmers' right	1. Rights to seeds	ITPGRFA, UPOV
	2. Right to register varieties	UPOV
	3. Right to reward and recognition as conserver	ITPGRFA
	4. Right to Information about expected performance and compensation for under-performance	–
Other rights	5. Right to Benefit Sharing	ITPGRFA
	6. Right to compensation for undisclosed use of traditional varieties	ITPGRFA
	7. Right to adequate availability of registered material	UPOV
	8. Right to free services	–
	9. Protection from innocent infringement of breeders' rights.	–

8. Definition of Farmer

Farmer in Indian PPV&FR Act (Section 2k) and in Malaysian PNPV Act (Section 2) has been defined as: any person who cultivates crops by cultivating the land himself; or cultivates crops by directly supervising the cultivation or land through any other person; or conserves and preserves, severally or jointly, with any other person any wild species or traditional varieties or adds value to such wild species or traditional varieties through selection and identification of their useful properties. The Philippines Plant Variety Act does not define farmer. However, Community

Intellectual Rights Protection Act, 2001 of Philippines defines farmers as all engaged in the cultivation of crops living within the territory of the Philippines [Section 3(f)]. Nevertheless, Conservation or preservation of any wild species or traditional variety is the distinctive feature of the definition of the farmer in Indian and Malaysian Plant Variety Act. It is not so well defined in other Asian countries legislations. However, the Community Intellectual Rights Protection Act of Philippines does define farmer innovator as an individual who has provided parent strains or the local community which has helped to conserve and develop the genetic stocks or the residents of a plant genetic resource area from which new variety has developed.

Both Malaysian and Philippine Acts use and identify small farmer, a feature absent in the Indian legislation, in the context of the limitations imposed upon the rights of the breeder. Section 2A of the Malaysian New Plant Varieties Act defines small farmer[1] in terms of size of holdings while the Philippines Plant Variety Protection Act of 2002 does not define it. However, Magna Carta of Small Farmers, another Philippine Act, defines small farmer in terms of income (Anonymous, 2012).

The term "Farmers' rights" *per se* is used only in the Indian legislation, ITPGRFA and Bangladesh draft. No other Asian countries' Act uses the term farmers' rights. There are subtle differences in the type of rights provided in the various legislations in the countries which are enumerated below.

9. Right to Farm Saved Seeds

Right to seeds is the traditional right of the farmers to save, use, exchange and sell farm-saved seed and other propagating material. UPOV 1978 Act has included this as farmers' privilege while UPOV 1991 Act has made it an optional exception. This privilege has been recognized as fundamental to the realization of farmers' rights by ITPGRFA as described in its preamble

Indian legislation protects the farmers' right to save, use, sow, re-sow, exchange, share or sell his farm produce including seed of a protected variety (Section 39). The right is available to all farmers irrespective of the size of their holdings. However, it prohibits the farmer to sell the branded seed of protected variety (Anonymous, 2007).

The Malaysian, Thailand, Philippines and Indonesian Acts do not recognize right to farm saved seeds under farmers' rights as such but provide it as an exception to the breeder's right. The exceptions are limited to small farmers only in the Indonesian, Malaysian and Philippines Acts. The small farmers in Malaysia can propagate by using the harvested seed material of the protected variety planted on their own holdings, and the amount to be sold must not be more than what is required in one's own holding (Malaysia PV Act, 2004). In Philippines, the provision of farmers' privilege in Section 43 of its PVP Act, allows a small farmer to exchange and sell seeds among and between other small farmers only (Philippines PVP Act, 2002). The Indonesian Act provides that if part of the harvested crop of a protected variety is used for non-commercial purposes it does not contravene the PVP rights [Article 10(1)]. The non-commercial purpose is further explained as the individual activities particularly those of small farmers for their own needs and this does not include activities to meet the needs of larger community.

Section 33(4) of PVP Act, 1999 of Thailand recognizes the right of farmer to cultivate and propagate the protected new plant variety from the propagating material made by himself, and it restricts the quantity to be used to three times of the quantity obtained (Thailand PVP Act, 1999). It also recognizes the right to sale or distribution by any means, for non-commercial purpose [Section 33(5) read with 33(6)].

10. Right to Register Varieties

Right to register varieties for the grant of intellectual property right has not been recognized as farmers' right by both UPOV and ITPGRFA. However, the Indian Act provides for right to register a variety bred, evolved or conserved by farmers, whether new or extant, as its breeder (Anonymous, 2007).

The Malaysian, Thailand and Philippines Acts do not define the term farmers' variety but these legislations recognize the right of farmer to register a new variety at par with the breeder. The definition of breeder in the Indonesian and Philippines Acts do not preclude the farmers to claim breeder's rights. Therefore, if new varieties developed by farmers comply with the distinctiveness, uniformity, stability and novelty (DUSN) criteria, farmers are entitled to a PVP title.

In Thai Act, farmers, as a group, cooperative or community, have the right to register the local domestic plant variety, which may exist only in a particular locality. Nevertheless, any *sui juris* person can also register a local plant variety if he has conserved and developed it exclusively (Thailand PVP Act, 1999).

Philippines Act, on the other hand, provides for a framework for community registration of locally bred varieties. Farming communities and bonafide farmers' organizations can establish their respective local registry system to register or build an inventory of locally bred varieties (Philippines PVP Act, 2002).

11. Right to Reward and Recognition

Right to reward and recognition to farmers is based on the fact that their generations have conserved, improved and made available plant genetic resources, and this contribution has not been sufficiently recognized or rewarded. ITPGRFA has recognized such a contribution but not identified it as a component of farmers' right under Article 9. Rather, Articles 13 and 18 of the Seed treaty provides for support to farmers who conserve plant genetic resources (FAO, 2010).

In India, Section 39(1)(iii) of the PPV&FR Act also provides for recognition and reward based on the contribution of farmers to conserve and preserve the genetic resources of land races and wild relatives, which have formed the basis for the development of registrable varieties. The reward is to be given from gene fund. In 2007, the PPV&FR Authority started the Plant Genome Savior Community Recognition for this purpose. However, such a provision does not exist in any other Asian country.

12. Right to Information about Expected Performance and Compensation for Under-performance Thereof

The Indian Act provides for farmers to be informed about the expected performance of the registered variety. The right is further extended by the right to compensation, if the registered variety does not perform up to the promised level. The farmers' right to compensation on non-performance of the variety seeds up to the expectation promised by the breeder is unique, and specific to India[2]. No other Asian country provides for such right. ITPGRFA and UPOV also do not identify it as farmers' right.

12.1. Right to Benefit Sharing

Right to benefit sharing is recognized as one of the farmers' rights under Article 9 of ITPGRFA (FAO, 2010). Section 26 of the PPV&FR Act of India recognizes the right of benefit sharing with the breeder of initial variety where a breeder may include a farmer.

Thailand Act provides for the person who is involved in conserving or developing local domestic plant variety a "right to profit sharing". It also provides for the percentage of profits to be allocated to these groups.

The Philippines PVP Act is silent regarding benefit sharing. Nevertheless, the Magna Carta for Small Farmers, Section 2 affirms the government policy for equitable distribution of benefits and opportunities realized through empowerment of small farmers (Anonymous, 2012). Further, Section 1 of the Guidelines for Bioprospecting Activities in the Philippines Series of 2005 also declares that the state is to ensure the fair and equitable sharing with the resources providers of the benefits derived from the utilization of biological resources. Moreover, Section 5 of the Community Intellectual Rights Protection Act of Philippines provides that a community, as a general owner of any form or product of traditional knowledge, is entitled to collect a justifiable percentage from all profits derived from the commercial use of their knowledge, for a period of ten years starting from the date of registration. No other Asian country provides for such right to benefit sharing.

12.2. Right to Compensation for Undisclosed use of Traditional Varieties

Article 9.2 (a) of the ITPGRFA identifies protection of traditional knowledge relevant to plant genetic resources for food and agriculture as one of the farmers' rights (FAO, 2010). Section 41 of PPV&FR Act of India provides for the right of farmers as a community to claim for compensation even if the breeder has not disclosed the source of varieties. Any NGO, individual or government institution may file a claim for compensation on behalf of the local community. This compensation will be granted from Gene fund. This right is unique to India (Anonymous, 2007).

12.3. Right to Adequate Availability of Registered Material

Compulsory licensing is a provision, which provides for the grant of license on the ground of public interest or non-adequate availability of the product for a certain period, to be used as a means to ensure the availability of the protected material. It may be arguably seen as a right of farmer to have adequate availability of protected variety at reasonable price. Both UPOV 1978 and 1991 Acts, provides for restricting the plant breeders right on ground of public interest. Compulsory licensing has been used by UPOV member countries as a means to restrict the breeders' right. However, ITPGRFA does not recognize it as a component of farmers' rights.

Section 8(2) and 51(1)(ii) of PPV&FR Act provides for the provision of compulsory licensing if the registered variety is not adequately available (Anonymous, 2007). Similarly, Section 36 of the Malaysian Act provides for ensuring availability of the protected material (*i.e.* needs of the farming community for the propagating material of the registered plant variety are met) by granting compulsory license (Malaysian PV Act, 2004). Article 46 of Law on PVP of Indonesia provides for the compulsory licensing on the ground of public interest. In Philippines Act, compulsory license can be sought in public interest and for reasonable requirement of the public. However, compulsory licensing can be opted for after 2 years while in other countries such as Indonesia, India or Malaysia it can be applied for only after the expiry of three years. Grant of compulsory licensing is an executive action in India, Malaysia and Philippines while in Indonesia it is judicial action. Provision for compulsory licensing does not exist in any other Group B countries.

12.4. Right to Free Legal Services

Indian PPV&FR Act in Section 44 has exempted farmers from paying any fees with respect to any proceeding before the Authority or Registrar or the Tribunal or the High Court (Anonymous, 2007). They also need not pay fees for registration of farmers' variety, DUS testing, etc. This provision is exclusive to India. However, Philippines Act provides for the free distribution of Plant Variety Gazette to small farmers groups, but does not provide any exemption from fees to the farmers. Right to free services has not been identified as a farmers' right by any other Asian country or ITPGRFA.

12.5. Right to Protection from Legal Infringement

Section 42 of Indian PPV&FR Act protects innocent infringement of the rights created under this Act by the farmer if the farmer was not aware of existence of such right at the time of infringement. Therefore, no relief or cognizance of any offence under the Act can be taken as the act is not considered as infringement.

Thailand protects any act committed in good faith relating to a protected new plant variety under section 47(2) of the PVP Act, 1999. The Section 33(3) of the Thailand Act has recognized such acts as an exception to the rights of the right holder of the new plant variety. It also protects any act done for non-commercial purpose from the legal infringement.

Malaysian Act provides for certain limitation on the breeders right under Section 31. It protects any act done privately on a non-commercial basis or any act done for an experimental purpose from being an infringing act. It, however, does not mention act done in good faith as an exception to the rights of the breeders.

13. Emerging Scenario in certain Asian Nations

Nepal recognizes in its Biodiversity Strategy that Intellectual Property Rights and Farmers' Rights are the two important aspects, which have not been touched by the Nepal legislation. It declares its policy to ensure the IPRs of farmers and local communities through appropriate strategies and legislation. Farmers' rights in Nepal will focus on rights arising from past, present and future contributions by the farming community in conserving, improving and making available plant genetic resources, particularly those originating in Nepal (Anonymous, 2012a).

Pakistan has passed Plant Breeders' Rights Ordinance, 2000. As per this ordinance, the farmer has been recognized as a breeder and is entitled to register new varieties. Farmers' right to save, use, exchange, share or sell his farm produce of protected variety has been protected in Section 31 but not seed. Section 30 of the ordinance provides for compulsory licensing also. The ordinance is silent about benefit sharing though draft legislation on access to biological resources and community rights seeks to provide for the benefit sharing. Farmers' right in benefit sharing as such has not been recognized but as a community right farmers are entitled to 10 per cent of the benefit obtained from any commercial use of biological resources (Anonymous, 2012b).

Farmers' right in Bangladesh draft does not include right to seed but provides for the right to collect, conserve, propagate and use the propagation material of any protected variety if it is for personal and non-commercial use. Exchange of propagating material for any monetary and financial gains is strictly prohibited. Farmer has not been explicitly recognized as a breeder and provision for the protection of farmers' variety is missing. Article 3 of the Act recognizes the farmer's right as innovator and rewards have been proposed in the draft provision (Anonymous, 2012c). The Right to Information in the Bangladesh draft guarantees access to biological and genetic resources, information regarding the new varieties and their holders, application and examination of the registration procedures and decision thereof. Moreover, Bangladesh draft aims to provide for protection if the infringing act has been done in the honest faith or for non-commercial purpose. It also provides other farmers' right *viz.* right to appoint an advisor, receive exemption of tax, and participate in research with the National Agricultural Research System, etc.

13.1. Group C Countries

Among the group C countries, which are members of UPOV as well as WTO, China is governed by UPOV 1978 Act while all the other Asian members of UPOV have joined under UPOV 1991 Act. Thus, China enjoys a greater liberty to provide farmers privilege in comparison to the others. All the other Asian countries in Group C have provided for plant breeders rights and have recognized only the right of farmer to save and use the seed in his own holding as a privilege of the farmer. These countries do not recognize the right of farmer to the seed as well as other rights such as benefit sharing, recognition of farmers' contribution in conservation and preservation and right to protection of traditional knowledge relevant to plant genetic resources for food and agriculture, etc.

13.2. Group D Countries

The provisions of ITPGRFA guide the status of farmers' rights in group D countries, which are members of WTO, UPOV as well as ITPGRFA. The farmers in these countries can enjoy the rights such as benefit sharing, and recognition of their contribution in conservation and preservation of plant genetic resource. These countries do not recognize right to seed but have an option to recognize farmers' privilege to seeds.

14. Registration of Farmers' Varieties in India: Uniqueness

Developing countries are endowed with rich genetic resources while developed countries are very poor in genetic resources. International agreements and treaties like CBD and Seed Treaty concerned more about conservation of genetic resources and access and benefit sharing but does not adequately describe how to stop misappropriation of genetic resources conserved by the farmers without giving benefit to conservers of resources. There has been large number of cases where traditional knowledge of genetic resources has been misappropriated. Question arises as how to stop this? The PPV&FR Act emphasizes and recognizes the contributions made by the farming community by specifically putting in the Act itself that varieties of farmers' origin will also be protected by registration. Had India followed patenting system for protection of plant varieties, then extant and farmers' varieties could not be protected? Because these traditional farmers' varieties are no more novel, they are in public domain. Not only has PPV&FR Act recognized the contribution of farmers as conservers but also as breeders.

15. Norms for Registration

The criteria of DUS are to be adopted for registration of a variety including farmer variety which may marginally vary from those specified for new varieties. It may also vary between species and also depending on whether the candidate is a variety or hybrid. In general, the selection criteria followed by farmers have been yield stability and tolerance to various risk factors but good attributes related to storage, cooking and taste. The farmer varieties are generally niche specific and these are not released and notified by Central Variety Release Committee (CVRC) or State Varietal Release Committee (SVRC). The farmer variety is not expected to be as uniform as the new variety developed by accomplished breeder. In view of this PPVFRA has relaxed the uniformity standards for farmer variety as compared to new variety (Anonymous, 2009a). PPV&FRA has started the process of registration of varieties from May 2007. The registration of varieties is now open for more than 60 crop species including cereals, pulses, oilseeds, vegetables and fruits, medicinal and aromatic, commercial and horticultural crops.

An application for registration can be made by any person claiming to be the breeder of the variety, successor of the breeder, assignee, any farmer or group of community of farmers, any person authorized for the above mentioned categories or any University or publicly funded agricultural institution claiming to be the breeder of the variety. However, to be considered as a farmer variety, the applicant can be any farmer or group of farmers or community of farmers. Then, this farmer variety application has to be endorsed by any one of officers *viz.* District Agricultural Officer, District Tribal Development Officer, Director Research of the concerned state Agricultural University, Chairperson/Secretary of the concerned Panchayat Biodiversity Management Committee. A farmer variety application can be filed only if the farmers are made aware of the PPV&FR Act, their rights and benefits of registration. Awareness programs for officers involved in agriculture and biodiversity management also need to be addressed.

The issue of maintenance of such farmer variety is a major thing to be done. As per the Act, once certificate of registration is granted, the concerned plant breeder has to do the maintenance breeding of material and produce true to type seeds during the period of validity of granted certificate. In case of farmer variety, the farmer is a breeder and technically the farmer breeder has to maintain that variety. However, this seems to be implausible and farmer applicant may not be able to maintain the variety as per the standards and rules laid out in the Act. If the applicant of a farmer variety is a group or community of farmers then it becomes all the more difficult who in the community or group of farmers will maintain the variety. Also the viewpoint of farmer for maintaining a variety is different as maintained by scientist/accomplished breeder as per the Act. Thus SAU's/ICAR institutes have to come forward for maintenance breeding of farmers varieties on behalf of the farmer(s) or community of farmers. G.B. Pant University of Agriculture and Technology, Pantnagar, India took a bold decision for maintaining seeds of all such farmers' varieties on behalf of the farmer(s) for which applications have been filed.

16. Status of Farmers' Varieties Registration

Intellectual Property Management Centre of G.B. Pant University of Agric. and Tech., Pantnagar has taken the lead in India by filing large number of applications of farmers' varieties in different crops namely rice, sorghum, French bean and maize on behalf of the farmers and for the benefit of farmers. After following guidelines, the PPV&FR Authority has registered three farmers' varieties of rice namely Tilakchandan, Hansraj and Indrasan. These are the first three farmers' varieties which have been registered in India by PPVFRA (Anonymous, 2010). Different models of registration of farmers varieties have been implemented such as an individual farmer who developed a variety, for group of farmers category applications were filed on behalf of registered group societies and from elected panchayats which were notified by Government of India so as to give the benefits to whole society, and also on behalf of traditional tribal communities. Different models of registration have been proposed because of diversity of Indian population and different types of norms in various communities so that benefits of conservation of genetic resources are distributed to genuine persons/community.

Registration of farmers' varieties by Govt. of India has shown to the whole world that even in the new regime of globalization how our traditional genetic resources can be protected under the overall system of TRIPS regulations.

17. Benefit Sharing

CBD dealt with the sovereign rights of the nations over their genetic resources. This CBD which has come into force in December 1993 as the first legal mechanism has very categorically highlighted that plant genetic resources are not to be the heritage of humankind, but are the properties of the countries and hence these are tradable commodities. Some of the controversial issues of *ex situ* collections held prior to CBD, and realization of farmers' rights were amicably resolved with the signing of the ITPGRFA which was enforced on 29 June 2004. A multilateral system of access and benefit sharing shall be established under the treaty.

The key development in India concerning biodiversity is the enactment of legislation on The Biological Diversity Act, 2002 for which the rules have also been framed (BDA, 2002). There are very few examples or models of benefit sharing arising out of the use of genetic resources from the holders of TK and TM. India has the distinction of being the first in the world in experimenting a benefit-sharing model that implemented Article 8(j) of Biological Diversity Act in letter and spirit. Example relates to medicine development which, is based on the active ingredient of *Trichopus zeylanicus* plant. Scientists at Tropical Botanic Garden and Research Institute (TBGRI), Thiruvananthapuram, Kerala, India isolated the active ingredients of the plant and incorporated these ingredients into a product, which they christened 'Jeevani' on the basis of knowledge of Kani tribals. TBGRI, which is the sole patent holder, struck an agreement with the tribal community to share a license fee and 2 per cent of net profits. This marks perhaps for the first time that compensation in the form of cash benefits has gone directly to the Kani tribals, traditional knowledge holders. Besides, there are examples of Africa San tribesmen, whose knowledge of Hoodia cactus (*Hoodia gordonii*) resulted in the isolation of appetite suppressing element (P57) by South African Council of Scientific and Industrial Research, which they patented. After negotiations a landmark agreement was reached in March 2002 by which the San people will receive a share of any future royalties.

PPV&FR Act of India recognizes the right of benefit sharing under Section 26 with the breeder of initial variety where a breeder may include a farmer. Under this section authority shall publish contents of the certificate of registration of a variety and invite claims of benefit sharing.

Grant of patents on non-original innovations, which are based on what is already a part of the traditional knowledge in developing world, has been causing a great concern in these countries. India has taken a positive view on IPR regime that patents should not be granted wrongly on traditional knowledge, traditional medicine or on genetic resources. India has developed Traditional Knowledge Digital Library (TKDL) and digitalized formulations written in ayurveda, sidha, unani, amchi, etc. in different languages of the world (English, German, French, Japanese, Spanish). This TKDL library is shared under MoU with different Patent Offices of the world for search of patent novelty only.

China, Brazil, India and several other world's most biodiverse countries have formed an alliance to fight biopiracy and are pressing for rules protecting their people's rights to genetic resources found on their land. This alliance was formed in Cancun, Mexico and formally known as the Group of Allied Mega-Biodiverse nations. The declaration was also signed by representatives of Indonesia, Costa Rica, Colombia, Equador, Kenya, Peru, Venezuela, Mexico and South Africa. The alliance wanted that the new rules should include among other things, certifying the legal possession of biological material and informed consent and mutually agreeable terms for transferring it. Thus the countries of this region which are rich in biodiversity should come together and develop effective benefit sharing mechanisms in such a way that benefits must reach the conservers of biodiversity and holders of traditional knowledge.

Conclusions

Sui generis protection to the intellectual property in agriculture has helped the nations to incorporate plant breeder's rights as well as provide for farmers' rights. However, the understanding of farmers' rights is diffuse and lacks any strict definition. The ITPGRFA has attempted to provide a uniform concept but the components of the farmers' rights vary from country to country as countries have freedom to choose ways and means as per their priorities and resources. Farmers' rights are mainly adopted as collective rights of farming populations and not of individual farmers. The emphasis is on the traditional crop varieties, wild races or land races. Almost all Asian nations have considered the farmers' right to seed as a farmer right barring the countries which are members of UPOV who have recognized the saving and exchange as an exception in form of farmers' privilege. These countries obviously provide for plant variety protection to recognize the plant breeder's rights, but the legislations recognizing the rights of farmers are lacking. India has used the sui-*generis* protection tool to balance the plant breeder's rights and the farmers' rights with wide scope. However, very few Asian countries have used it to protect farmers' right where it has been mainly used to protect the plant breeder's right. The "*sui-generis*" protection as provided in WTO clearly allows the member countries to adopt a legislation, which fulfills their need while protecting their interests. It is, nevertheless, up to the countries to decide as to how to identify and address the merits and/or inadequacies and deficiencies of the present day intellectual property rights system. India has protected the traditional farmer varieties and suitable mechanisms of benefit sharing are being evolved to prevent biopiracy of genetic resources.

References

1. Anonymous, 2007. The Protection of Plant Varieties and Farmers' Rights Act, 2001 and Rules, Universal Law Publishing Co., Delhi.
2. Anonymous, 2009. Geographical Indications Journal, No. 30.
3. Anonymous, 2009a. Plant Variety Journal of India, 3(9).
4. Anonymous, 2010. Plant Variety Journal of India, 4(2).
5. Anonymous, 2011. The Patents Act, 1970 along with The Patent Rules, Universal Law Publishing Co., Delhi, 2011.
6. Anonymous, 2012. Magna Carta of small farmers. http://www.chanrobles.com/republicactno7607.htm.
7. Anonymous, 2012a. Nepal Biodiversity Strategy available at http://www.ansab.org/UserFiles/Nepal per cent 20Biodiversity per cent 20Strategy per cent 202002.pdf.
8. Anonymous, 2012b. http://www.grain.org/brl_files/pakistan-pbr-2000.doc.
9. Anonymous, 2012c. Draft Plant Varieties Act of Bangladesh available at http://www.grain.org/brl_files/bangladesh-pvp-1998-en.pdf.
10. BDA, 2002. The Biological Diversity Act, 2002 and Biological Diversity Rules, National Biodiversity Authority, India, p. 57.

11. CBD, 2012. http://www.cbd.int/convention/articles.shtml?a=cbd-08.
12. Chawla, H. S., 2007. Managing intellectual property rights for better transfer and commercialization of agricultural technologies. J Intellectual Prop Rights, 12, pp. 330–340.
13. Dhar, B., 2010. Sui Generis Systems for Plant Variety Protection available at http://homepages.3-c.coop/tansey/pdfs/sg-col1.pdf.
14. FAO, 2010, http://www.fao.org/Legal/treaties/033s-e.htm.
15. Malaysia PV Act, 2004. http://pvpbkkt.doa.gov.my.
16. Thailand PVP Act, 1999. http://www.grain.org/brl_files/thailandpvp-1999-en.pdf.
17. Singh, A. P., Padmavati M. and Chawla, H. S., 2011. *Sui generis* IPR laws *vis-a-vis* farmers' rights in Asia and their implications under WTO. J Intellec Prop Rights, 16 (2), pp 107-116.
18. UPOV,2012. http://www.upov.int/en/publications/conventions/1961/w_up611_.htm#_5.

Chapter 23

Worldwide Pharmaceuticals Compulsory Licensing: An Indian Perspective

Nitin Shukla and Vinita Panchanadikar*

Scientist, National Innovations, National Chemical Laboratory, Pune, India

ABSTRACT

Compulsory License is a license given by Government without the consent of the patentee in case of a national emergency but only after negotiations for granting a voluntary license have failed. Compulsory licenses are especially important with regard to pharmaceutical patents in developing and least developed countries. This results in lowered costs of the drugs and better availability. This is a provision under TRIPS and Doha declaration. Provisions of granting a compulsory license exists in the Patent laws of various countries like Canada, France, UK, USA, Australia, Zimbabwe, Ghana, Brazil, Malaysia, Thailand and India. Recently India has granted its first compulsory license ever in March 2012. To obtain the compulsory license, section 84 of Indian patents Act was invoked and the issues for decision were 1. Unavailability of the drug at affordable price,2. Unavailability of the drug in sufficient quantity, 3. Drug not manufactured in Indian Territory. The result of the grant of compulsory license was that the price of the drug was made available at a fraction (INR 8800 instead of earlier 280,000).

This issuance has put India under a scanner, across world wherein the IP regime is being watched closely. However there needs to be a balance between the rights, incentives to a patentee and public interest in general so that major pharma players are not deterred in coming to India in particular and pro compulsory license countries in general.

Keywords: *Compulsory, License, TRIPS, Pharmaceutical.*

---

* E-mail: ns.tewari@ncl.res.in

1. Introduction

TRIPS provides the member countries provision for granting a compulsory license by the government in cases of national emergency provided the first level negotiations for a voluntary license with the patentee have failed. Provisions of compulsory license are available for both patents as well copyright are frequently used for patents and particularly pharma patents, given their impact of society. This involuntary license results in easy accessibility of drugs at lower costs. Several countries have provisions for granting a compulsory license utilizing which South Africa, Thailand, Taiwan have granted compulsory licenses earlier. Most recently India has granted its first compulsory license to Natco for Bayer's anticancer drug Nexavar. In this article we discuss the background for grant of compulsory license in India, the issues therein and its after-effects in national and international context.

2. What is Compulsory License?

"Compulsory license" as the name suggests is a license to a protected intellectual property (IP), which is compulsorily taken by Government under particular circumstances without the consent of the owner. It's also known as 'use without authorization of the rights holder'as per WTO fact sheet, 2003 Generally compulsory license is considered in respect of patents alone but compulsory license are granted in respect copyright as well, however we would discuss only patents in this article.

Various jurisdictions across the world have different rules and regulations for granting a compulsory license however the underlying basis for the same is the Agreement on Trade Related Aspects of Intellectual Property Rights (TRIPS).

3. History of Compulsory License

As is well known, TRIPS is an international agreement administered by the World Trade Organization that sets down minimum standards for many forms of intellectual property regulation as applied to nationals of other WTO Members. It outlines some basic rules for IP protection and enforcement, which sets all member countries at a minimum level of uniformity. This uniformity helps to foster science and technology development across borders and making available the best outputs of science accessible to people worldwide. Provisions of granting a compulsory license exists in the Patent laws of various countries like Canada, France, UK, USA, Australia, Zimbabwe, Ghana, Brazil, Malaysia, Thailand and India. Several compulsory licenses have been granted till now worldwide and reviewed by Love James Packard, 2001.

The use of compulsory license in extreme urgent health conditions was sparked off from South Africa where AIDS cases were increasing exponentially, one in every 10 people were suffering from AIDS. As observed by Love, 2007, South African government attributed the shortage of drug and the high prices to the pricing strategies adopted by multinational pharmaceutical companies who held patents in South Africa on most antiretroviral drugs. They wanted to reserve the right "to purchase form the section that suits their purse".

To find a permanent solution to the resistance by the Multi-National Companies and South African pharma companies, South African government inserted Section

15C into the South African Medicines and Related Substances Control Act in 1997. As mentioned by Attaran, 2001, the primary purpose of this amendment was to enable South Africa to benefit from lower prices abroad for the same drugs.

Further, Cronin, 2008 reported that Taiwan in 2004 allowed a compulsory license to Taiwan based optical disc storage company Gigastorage to use the patented technology of Dutch giant Phillips however it was later called–off.

Taiwan has also become the first country to issue a compulsory license for the generic production of Tamiflu, the only drug currently available for the treatment of avian flu, in order to ensure that the country has sufficient quantities of the medicine in the event of a pandemic (Katherin, 2005).

In 2007 Government of Bangladesh planned to grant a compulsory license for anti-HIV drugs but it received letters from European Union trade commissioner Peter Mandelson and U.S. Ambassador to Thailand, Ralph Boyce saying it would have to "deal with the patent holders" in case they wanted to access the patented medicines by way of compulsory license, which was obviously not in Pharma giants interest. Finally Bangladesh government relented and did not grant any compulsory license probably with a fear to "deal with the patent holders" (Worldcrunch, 2012).

Between November 2006 and January 2007, Thailand issued compulsory licenses for two AIDS drugs (Efavirnz and the combination of Lopinavir+Ritonavir) and one antihypertension drug (Clopidegrel) (Keionline, 2007).

According to TRIPS compulsory licensing or government use of a product without the authorization of the owner can be obtained only under certain conditions. These include (WTO, fact sheet, 2003).

- ✰ Having first sought voluntary licensing from the patent holder and been unsuccessful.
- ✰ There is a 'national emergency', 'other circumstances of extreme urgency' or 'public non-commercial use'.

Compulsory licenses are generally given for public welfare or non working of granted patents but China and Japan also grant compulsory license for improvements on the existing patents.

One would appreciate that access or non-access to working of pharmaceutical patents has far pronounced effects than say an electronic or business method patent without undermining importance of either. Hence to balance the use, access of pharmaceutical drugs and development of new drugs there needs to be a balance between patent rights and compulsory licenses granted. Initially the US regarded compulsory licenses as a threat to innovator drugs and incentives to the manufactures. But after the 2001 anthrax threat it also agreed to grant compulsory license for Ciprofloxacin, the drug to combat the likely infection (Cptech, 2001).

It was probably then everybody realized that when a super power like the US can have something like a national emergency in terms of public health what will be the fate of developing or least developed countries where even basic infrastructure to utilize the granted compulsory license are limited.

Therefore to address "gravity of the public health problems afflicting many developing and least developed countries, especially those resulting from HIV/AIDS, tuberculosis, malaria and other epidemics" on November 14, 2001, Doha declaration on the TRIPS Agreement and Public Health was adopted by WTO ministerial Conference. "Doha" is the place where the declaration was executed. The Doha Declaration affirms that "the TRIPS Agreement does not and should not prevent Members from taking measures to protect public health". The Doha Declaration refers to several aspects of TRIPS, including the right to grant compulsory licenses and the freedom to determine the grounds upon which licenses are granted; the right to determine what constitutes a national emergency and circumstances of extreme urgency, and the freedom to establish the regime of exhaustion of intellectual property rights (World Trade organization, Declaration, 2001).

4. Indian Scenario

In a recent landmark case in March 2012 India granted its first compulsory license to Natco a generic company, for Bayer's patented drug Nexavar a kidney/ liver cancer drug that goes by the generic name of Sorafenib Tosylate. The patented drug which was available at INR 2, 80,000 per month was made available by Natco at INR 8,800. Natco would be paying 6 per cent of the net sales as the royalty to Bayers.

Earlier also there have been applications for compulsory license like Cipla applying for Merck's patented anti-HIV drugs on the basis of section 84 of the Indian Patents Act (Money Control, 2011).

However Natco successfully put up its case against in terms of invoking every fine details of section 84 of the Indian Patents Act which reads as:

> "(1) *At any time after the expiration of three years from the date of the 1[grant] of a patent, any person interested may make an application to the Controller for grant of compulsory license on patent on any of the following grounds, namely:–(a) that the reasonable requirements of the public with respect to the patented invention have not been satisfied, or (b) that the patented invention is not available to the public at a reasonably affordable price, or (c) that the patented invention is not worked in the territory of India."*

Mr. P.H. Kurain, the Controller of patents finalized that the three main issues to be dealt were sections 84(1)(a,b and c) of the Indian Patents Act *i.e.* whether:

- *that the reasonable requirements of the public with respect to the patented invention have not been satisfied* for which Natco clearly demonstrated that the considering the requirement of ~16,000 bottles for liver cancer and 7,120 for renal cancer the supply was "nil" in 2008 and ~200 bottles in 2009. Records of 2010 supply were not available. This means less than 1 per cent (~0.85 per cent) according to Natco (and 2 per cent as per Bayer's admission) of the population had access to the medicine.
- *patented invention is not available to the public at a reasonably affordable price.* Natco argued strongly that the life saving drug like Nexavar priced at INR 2,80,000 in India cannot be called "reasonably" priced by any stretch of imagination.

- ☆ *the patented invention is not worked in the territory of India.* The drug was not manufactured in India but imported which according to Controller did not amount to working in the territory of India.

These were the issues framed to come up with a decision for granting a compulsory license or not. However key points of this Decision, apart from basic yes or no for compulsory license, are specific points raised (discussed further) which may prove to be guideline in future for such cases.

The first noticeable point was the method to price a drug in developing country like India. Is it rational to price a drug in India at par with the West while the GDP is low and prevalence of disease high when compared to the West?

To simplify the matter and answer the issue of what is the "reasonably affordable price" the Applicant's (NATCO) submission on pages 24-25 have referred to

1. Shanti Mendis *et al.* "The availability and affordability of selected essential medicines for chronic diseases in six-low and middle income countries", Bulletin of The World Health Organization, April 2007, 85(4),
2. Laurens M Niens *et al.*, "Quantifying the Impoverishing Effects if Purchasing Medicines: A cross-country comparison of the affordability of medicines in the developing world", PLOS Medicine, August 2012, Vol. 7, Issue 8.

Also reviewed was affidavit by Mr. James Packard Love, Director, Knowledge Ecology International and an invited IP expert in meetings and consultations organized by World Intellectual Property Organization, World Health Organization, World Trade Organization, United Nations Development Program United Nations Conference on Trade and Development. He has served as principal consultant to evaluate a complaint that the prices of AIDS medicines were excessive. According to Mr. Love's submission World Bank estimate Indian Gross National Income per capita for 2012 is \$1330 ~INR 60,455.

All three yardsticks happen to be independent, internationally recognized but according to none of them the cost fixing is reasonable. Learned Controller rebuts Bayers argument about "reasonable price" both for patentee and public saying "reasonable" is "predominantly with reference to public" (page 36 line 4 of the Decision). For deciding on the reasonable price, Learned Controller suggested "differential pricing" for different classes and sections of public in India which was also acceptable to the Patentee.

The decision further throws light on what is called cycle of drug and interests of Patentee. Generally, high prices of drugs are justified saying that the potential drugs have huge investments in terms of money and human resources so while the price of the drug is being notched "reasonable gain or profit to the Patentee" should also be considered. The marketed product should be paying "not only for its own R&D but also for the cost of underlying failed R&D" page 28 lines 9-11 of the Decision. However does this mean that the pharma companies should not be considering the tax rebates etc given to them by Governments like in this case where Nexavar is regarded as "orphan drugs in EU and US"? Should this tax credit and consequent lowering of costs for companies percolate down for benefit of developing and least developing countries?

Another take-away from the proceedings of the case and the final decision is that according to Indian Patent Law there is a clear difference between local working to produce drugs and importation of the same. Both cannot be mistaken as one. This is also in sync with the spirit of the patent laws worldwide and TRIPS "to foster technology advancement". Does importation in any way cause advancement of technology in the jurisdiction where a product is patent protected? The answer is a clear "no". The reason behind not manufacturing the drug in India in spite of having full manufacturing capability in India leaves much to be thought about.

One more very pertinent point coming out of this decision was the importance of Form-27 or commercial working statement in Indian Patent Office. It cuts a sorry figure, but is a well- known fact among patent professionals, how casual Patentees have been about Form-27. The importance of Form-27 has been emphasized in the pro patent fraternity wherein the information provided was used against the patentee finally leading to grant of compulsory license.

5. After Effects

The immediate and positive effect of the grant of compulsory license to Natco was that its shares had gained 12.76 per cent on BSE since 12 March 2012, while the benchmark Sensex index had declined 1.76 per cent in the same period. In the year ended 31 March, Natco Pharma sales grew 15 per cent to Rs. 555.58 crore, of which the oncology segment contributed about 60 per cent. It earned a net profit of Rs. 58.47 crore, an increase of 12.29 per cent over the previous year.

Singh, 2012 report that having won a landmark decision, Natco Pharma is said to be collecting data to identify other life saving drugs where they can apply for compulsory licensing.

Experts such as Shamnad Basheer, a professor of intellectual property (IP) law at the Kolkata-based National University of Juridical Sciences (NUJS), say the company may be eyeing compulsory licences for drugs such as Pfizer Inc.'s anti-HIV/AIDS treatment Selzentry and anti-cancer therapy Sutent, and Roche Holding AG's Tarceva, another anti-cancer drug (Pilla, 2012).

Swiss-based Roche Holding AG and local drug maker Cipla Ltd have decided to sharply cut prices for five of their high-cost oncology brands after the Indian patent office made its first compulsory license order (Unnikrishnan, 2012).

Course of such moves by Natco pharma and other generic manufacturers will depend much on fate of the Bayer's appeal against the compulsory license (hearing slated on September 3, 2012) as this is supposed to stir the judiciary as well as policies of Indian government in long run.

India is likely to face economic sanctions or some modifications of the ones after nuclear tests in Pokharan. One such move seen as a non-tariff barrier is the European Commission directive to make it mandatory from July 2013 for all active pharmaceutical ingredients exported from India to be certified by the country's s drug controller for EU equivalence certificate. There are concerns that India does not have the manpower or resources to comply with this norm which may affect exports to the region worth about $2 billion. According to the Pharmaceuticals Export Promotion Council of India (Pharmexcil) lobby group, the country's drug exports to the European Union (EU) were worth $1.93 billion (around Rs. 10,769 crore) in 2010-11. If India fails to get an EU equivalence certificate by 2 July 2013, when the rule is set to go into effect, 30 per cent of this could be affected, the lobby group said (Krishnan Vidya, 2012)· This may have serious implications in the Indian pharma companies which are already lobbying against the EU move.

According to 2012 special US 301 list China, India and Thailand are on "priority watch list". It is to be noted The 2012 Special 301 review process examined IPR protection and enforcement in 77 trading partners. Report says that "The United States will closely monitor developments concerning compulsory licensing of patents in India following the broad interpretation of Indian law in a recent decision by the Controller General of Patents, while also bearing in mind the Doha Declaration on TRIPS and Public Health found in the Intellectual Property and Health Policy section of this Report"(USTR, 2012).

It is to be recalled that South Africa was also put on the Special 301 "watch list"32 both in 1998 and 1999 upon a determination by the U.S. Trade Representative (USTR) that South Africa lacked adequate intellectual property protection to an extent that merited bilateral attention (USTR, 1999).

Another after effect of the grant of compulsory license and a welcome move is that the Swiss healthcare major Roche Holding AG released the news of its collaboration with an Indian pharmaceutical company to repackage and sell its cancer drugs at a low and affordable cost.

Following the grant of Compulsory license in India was amendment of Chinese IP laws to allow its drug makers to make copies of patented drugs from May 1, 2012 accessible at link.reuters.com/tu68s. Tan, 2012 observe that the Chinese generic pharma companies are getting ready for producing Gilead's tenofovir the HIV-AIDS drug. The interesting thing to note here is that Gilead shared it patent pools with generics in many countries but not China, as a result China had to pay higher prices for the drug. The table turned with the amendment of Chinese IP laws after which Gilead offered certain concessions and gave them donations as well.

It has been also been observed that the China's generic manufacturers have been producing the active pharmaceutical ingredient and exporting to foreign Pharma companies which in turn sell the final patented drugs in China at a higher price which is unaffordable to general Chinese population. The approach of the major pharma players towards India and China is not at all welcoming. Given these consequences and stand of compulsory licensing in today's patent scenario it seems as if compulsory license has become a stick to demand a better and considerate treatment to the developing world and more respect for national laws. Matthew, 2012 report that China also faces the consequences of EU directive starting from July 2013, China and India being lead exporters of generics. The pharma companies can definitely not ignore them and particularly India where the market is growing as rate of 15 per cent.

Conclusion

Needing attention is the fact that even the cost and efforts behind a successful drug cannot be undermined, and the innovator companies should have incentive to come up with more drugs from time to time. However the cost of drugs is also an issue especially in developing or least developed countries. Hence, for the betterment of all and respecting international treaties and also the pressing national needs, some midway may be approached for. Even Patent Offices, courts would be flooded with requests and appeals for and against the compulsory licenses if some guidelines are not there. Some feasible practical approaches may be tried by both the Patentee and the Government such as, either the patentee works with some generic to bring out drugs at an affordable price, or pricing of drug mutually decided by both. The Brazilian model may be tried wherein Government studies the disease needing concern and uses Compulsory License as bargaining tool bringing the cost of drugs down by almost 40 per cent in consultation with the Patentee. Whether its generic companies or major pharma players "drug profiteering" at the cost of interest of general public should not be allowed.

The comments above are solely of the authors and not of the institution they belong to.

Acknowledgements

Mr. Sukhdeep Singh, Examiner, Indian Patent Office, Mumbai for his valuable insight into the Compulsory License decision.

References

1. Amir Attaran and Lee Gillespie-White, Do Patents for Antiretroviral Drugs Constrain Access to AIDS Treatment in Africa? 286 No. 15 J. Am. Med. Ass'n 1886, 1888 (Oct. 17, 2001).
2. http://www.cptech.org/ip/health/cl/us-cl.html
3. David Cronin in EU Threatens Taiwan With WTO Case Over Law On Compulsory Licences, http://www.ip-watch.org/2008/01/31/eu-threatens-taiwan-with-wto-case-over-law-on-compulsory-licences/
4. Katherin Hille in Taiwan employs compulsory licensing for Tamiflu http://www.ft.com/cms/s/0/cebeb882-5dcb-11da-be9c-0000779e2340.html
5. http://www.keionline.org/content/view/90/1
6. *Krishnan Vidya, in Indian drug firms lobby against EU's new directive, http://www.livemint.com/Politics/T8k5joEZilAsENSiqgLQYK/Indian-drug-firms-lobby-against-EUs-new-directive.html*
7. Love, 2001, http://www.cptech.org/ip/health/cl/us-cl.html
8. Love, 2007, http://www.keionline.org/misc-docs/recent_cls_8mar07.pdf

9. Mathew Joe C in MNC drug brands show healthy growth trend in India market, http://www.business-standard.com/article/companies/mnc-drug-brands-show-healthy-growth-trend-in-india-market-112042000004_1.html
10. http://www.moneycontrol.com/news/business/cipla-tells-merck-your-anti-aids-drug-too-costlyindia_533783.html
11. Pilla Viswanath in Natco targets drugs ripe for compulsory licensing, http://www.livemint.com/Companies/ZR7YHsT0xTb6e9ppKDIAuN/Natco-targets-drugs-ripe-for-compulsory-licensing.html
12. Singh Khomba, in Natco examining other drugs to identify compulsory license targets
http://articles.economictimes.indiatimes.com/2012-03-15/news/31197031_1_maraviroc-viiv-healthcare-natco-pharma
13. Tan Ee Lyn in China changes patent law in fight for cheaper drugs, http://www.reuters.com/article/2012/06/08/us-china-medicines-patents-idUSBRE8570TY20120608
14. Unnikrishnan C.H., in Compulsory licensing sets off a wave of price cuts in cancer drugs, http://www.livemint.com/Companies/biLIvDFsDo7YVmXzElUBzJ/Compulsory-licensing-sets-off-a-wave-of-price-cuts-in-cancer.html
15. http://www.ustr.gov/sites/default/files/2012 per cent 20Special per cent 20301 per cent 20Report.pdf
16. USTR Special 301 Report 1999, http://www.keionline.org/ustr/1999special301
17. World Trade organization, Declaration, 2001 http://www.worldtradelaw.net/doha/tripshealth.pdf
18. WTO, 2003 World Trade Organisation. (2003). *Fact Sheet: TRIPS and pharmaceutical.* WTO. http://www.wto.org/english/tratop_e/trips_e/tripsfactsheet_pharma_e.pdf>
19. http://www.worldcrunch.com/business-finance/drug-companies-battle-against-indian-pharmaceutical-pirates-/c2s4890/

Chapter 24

Valorisation of Intellectual Property in Knowledge Based Economy

Dubey Rounak[1]* *and Dubey Rupal*[2]

[1]*Executive-IPR,*
Intellectual Property Facilitation Centre, Confederation of Indian Industry
[2]*Department of Pharmaceutical Sciences,*
Dr. Hari Singh Gour Central University, Sagar, M.P., India

ABSTRACT

Intellectual Property (IP) valorisation is a tool of generating wealth through Intellectual Property. IP valorisation is considered as one of the most important management strategic issues. IP is considered to be valorised when it yields its value. Value when referring to IP is a measure of the benefits received from utilizing the assets. There are numerous individual reasons or motivations for conducting an intellectual property valuation or economic appraisal analysis. IP is to be valued correctly before it is actually valorised. There is no standard for IP valorisation as value of Intellectual Property varies from case to case and is affected by current market environment as well. So it is really required to perform critical assessment of IP while valuing it for specific business purpose. This paper explores numerous individual reasons or motivations for conducting intellectual property valuation for an effective valorisation.

***Keywords**: Intellectual property, Patents, Valorisation, Valuation, Technology Transfer.*

---

* E-mail: rounakdubey03@gmail.com

1. Introduction

The term Intellectual Property (IP) refers to creation of the mind. As the progress and well-being of humanity rest on its capacity to create and invent new works in the areas of technology and culture; legal protection over such creation of mind encourage society to innovate, which further translates into economic growth and hence better quality of life. Intellectual property rights reward creativity and human endeavour, which fuel the progress of humankind. Patents; Trademarks; Geographical Indications; Industrial Designs; Layout-Designs (Topographies) of Integrated Circuits; Plant Variety Protection and Copyright are various forms of reward to protect ones intellectual property. Intellectual property rights are considered as intangible assets as their value is to be realised on the basis of the contribution they made in financial benefits to the business. Intangible assets are defined as identifiable non-monetary assets that cannot be seen, touched or physically measured, which are created through time and/or effort and that are identifiable as a separate asset. Intellectual Property law offers certain exclusive rights to the owner for variety of intangible assets. Exclusive rights granted to the owner of intellectual property allow him to benefit from the property he has created, providing a financial incentive for his intellectual creation and investment. IP is the foundation of knowledge-based economy. It pervades all sectors of economy and is increasingly becoming important for ensuring competitiveness of the enterprises. Intellectual Property often represents one of the most valuable assets of a company whether it is know-how, patents, licenses, brand names or any other form of intangible assets. Ultimate goal of any business is to make financial benefits out of its activities. IP must be regarded as a capital asset rather than just being the short term result of a recent expenditure.

2. Importance of IP Valorisation

Often there is a commercial need to assess intellectual property in a transaction involving intangible assets. IP valorisation is a tool of generating wealth through Intellectual Property. The valorisation of capital is a theoretical concept created by Karl Marx in his critique of political economy. The meaning of valorisation is a use or application of something (an object, process or activity) so that it makes money, or generates value, with the connotation that the thing validates itself and proves its worth when it results in earnings, a yield. Thus, something is "valorised" if it has yielded its value. We use related terms like 'exploitation', 'commercialisation', and 'value extraction'. IP valorisation can therefore be understood as the process of making use of Intellectual Property.

When an inventor creates Intellectual property, he initially uses the same for its commercial exploitation to gain financial benefits out of it. But once its value has been established or created, he begins to valorise IP, *i.e.* increase its value through licensing, technology transfer etc. Some companies use IP to block competition while other uses it to earn royalties. Hence the key question is What IP is worth for me in my business? IP valourisation is seen as the transfer of IP from one party to another, a transfer that needs to result in financial benefit.

Intellectual Property Valuation

Proper valuation of assets whether tangible or intangible, is necessary for effective valorisation. Valuations are necessary in many contexts. These may include investment analysis, capital budgeting, merger and acquisition, financial reporting and taxable events, as well as bankruptcy and litigation proceedings. Correct IP valuation provides necessary support for the strategic decision making processes utilized by investors, management and counsel during these important events. It is true that pre-sale valuations of IP are necessary but difficult to make and, clearly, the value of an IP asset will be seen differently by the seller and the buyer. Therefore, in order to carry out IP valuation it is important to define the following: What is the IP to be valued? (Patents, Copyrights, Design, Trade Secrets and know-how, Trademarks, Brand-names) For whom is the valuation done? What is the purpose of the valuation? The valuation method is appropriate for the circumstances? It is difficult to understand the market value of intangible assets because this depends strongly on the sector and they differ significantly from each other. Furthermore, high tech SMEs do often have a very high percentage of intangible assets and this value does not appear on the balance sheet and is not available for its valuation. There is no such generalised method of IP valuation as Intellectual Property is context specific and value of IP differs from case to case. Intellectual Property valuation in particular, is a specialized process derived from financial and economic valuation concepts. To determine the value of a specific instance of Intellectual Property (such as a trademark, patent or copyright), appropriate methodologies in accordance with recognized Intellectual Property valuation principles need to be applied. To estimate the Market value of a particular land, we do consider factors such as utility, scarcity and desirability and is reflected as price per square foot, but there is no such parameter in IP to estimate the cost. Venture capitalists assess the value of a patent portfolio always in relation to the business model, management, market and product opportunities. Hence a company is valuated, not a patent portfolio. Furthermore, breakthrough patents which bring an entirely new concept that serve as the basis for development of new technology worth more than patents based on incremental improvement over already existing technology. Thus we can say that valuation of IP is a very uncertain process. The real value of IP depends strongly on the context, which makes it difficult to value on some fixed parameters.

4. IP Valuation Methodologies

4.1. Income Approach of Valuing IP

Anticipated future income that is attributable to the Intellectual Property (in the form of Trademark, Patent, Copyright etc) is a key component of the income approach to value IP. This income is discounted to present the IP value as a single amount. Royalty rates are frequently used to drive the income approach to valuing IP. This calculates the amount IP owner would need to pay in royalty income if someone else owned the IP.

4.2. Market Approach of Valuing IP

As a part of market approach to value IP, comparable royalty rate is sourced to fuel the income approach. Royalty rates are sourced from intangible business proprietary database as well as from external sources. Comparable IP transactions are also analysed and benchmarked to support IP valuation.

4.3. Cost Approach of Valuing IP

The cost of creating IP and the associated risks of re-creating a similar IP are key considerations while valuing the asset. These valuations are used primarily to support other IP valuation methodologies.

The Market based method does not work because IP is unique and there are few comparable transactions which makes it difficult to set a price. The cost based approach value IP based on historical or replacement cost. This gives however no indicator of future value. The Income approach is based on the future cash flow and economic profit. Future cash flow are however difficult to predict and therefore IP valuation remains risky. Value is in the eye of beholder. Any valuation method therefore needs to take into account this subjective nature by deliberately choosing the appropriate 'standard of value' (value to whom?) and 'premise of value' (value under what circumstances?). So we can say that standard and sophisticated tool or methodology is still to be developed that can help in IP valuation.

5. IP Valorisation in Industries

The success of any company depends on its innovation capacity and realisation of the value of intangible assets they possess. Successful companies understand the role that patents, trademarks, designs play in maintaining their competitiveness and recognise the worth of intangible assets to their business. Industrial sectors are the real player where technologies develop and commercialised for making capital gains. Industrial research is purely result oriented and demands good amount of profit out of research activities. Serendipitous inventions are very rare at Industrial R&D contrasting their vulnerability at academic research institutions. Several reasons behind this fact could be strategic planning, prior art search, analysis of technology growth (current as well as future) etc. are involved before investing into development of product or a technology at the industries. Successful companies invariably have well managed intellectual property portfolios designed to control access to their inventive advantage and to maximize revenues through licenses, royalties and robust business alliances. Sony, Pfizer, Xerox, Proctor and Gamble, Ranbaxy, Tata, IBM, Ford, Mercedes, Coca cola etc earns greater part of money from their intangible assets. In fact, a 2002 survey of the Fortune 500 companies estimated that anywhere from 45 per cent to 75 per cent of the wealth of individual companies comes from their Intellectual Property Rights. SMEs prefer to protect their IP assets by way of trade secret rather than going for patents due to high cost factor involved in it. One major question SMEs generally face is to assess whether licensing of technology is worth or creating a start-up firm to commercialise IP is beneficial. Answer lies in the proper valuation of IP assets. If IP is giving fair return on investment to the business, SMEs (can commercialise IP on their own). Or else, they may license the IP to larger firms having available infrastructure and capacity to further develop or to commercialise.

6. IP Valorisation in Academic R&D

Although business sector plays a major role for research and development on activities with a commercial objective, many of the fundamental technologies having great implications for everyday life came from publicly funded research that was not intended for immediate commercial use. The importance of ensuring a greater collaboration between the private sector and the public research sector has been recognized in the recent past, and the need for universities and public research institutions to develop intellectual property policies has been emphasized in many countries in order to properly manage the intellectual property rights relating to their research results.

Academic research institutions are the key innovators. These Institutions are equipped with state-of-art infrastructure and technologies required for R& D activities and are well capable of producing successful results. Universities have become innovation ecosystems of major importance. The shift towards knowledge-based development, the increasing importance of science and technology in sustaining innovation and competitiveness, the limitless growth that knowledge can generate, make universities more sensitive to the valorisation of their intellectual capital derived from their research activity. Even though University labs and research institutions produces good results, their innovations do not get proper implementation platform as it does not find the way to market or a strategy to leverage. There are many reasons of not getting market *i.e.* internalities of research effort; weak knowledge transfer mechanisms; communication barriers between academia and industry; failure to meet a critical mass of R&D results due to isolation and lack of cooperation. But scenario has been changed in recent times. Universities are more inclined towards innovation oriented research after the implementation of Bayh-Dole act of 1980. Bayh-Dole act allows transfer of exclusive control over many government funded inventions to universities and businesses operating with federal contracts for the purpose of further development and commercialization. The contracting universities and businesses are then permitted to exclusively license the inventions to other parties. Academic institutes need to work for knowledge transfer by identifying potentially marketable R&D and provide valorisation plans to prospective Industry partners having capacity to commercialise innovations coming from academic R&D. The following are some of the mechanisms of valorisation by research institutions:

- Extending further research by way of contractual agreement.
- Providing consultations during product development phase.
- Licensing out the technology developed as an outcome of research for commercial purpose.
- Creating spinoffs for equity.

7. Technology Transfer: An Effective Way of Valorisation

According to the World Intellectual Property Organization (WIPO), technology is defined as "the systematic knowledge for product manufacture and service provision in industry, farming and commercial fields," and knowledge is reflected in inventions, utility models, designs, and in data forms. Whether from basic research to applied technology or from one firm to another, the transfer of technology is fundamentally a matter of the flow of human knowledge from one human being to another. The use of patents and licensing is a relatively new and increasingly important means of technology transfer. Technology transfer must be recognised as a broad and complex process if it is to avoid creating and maintaining the dependency of the recipient, and if it is to contribute to sustained and equitable development. The end result for the recipient must be the ability to use, replicate, improve and, possibly, re-sell the technology. Transfer of technology is more than just the moving of high-tech equipment from the developed to the developing world, or within the developing world. Moreover, it encompasses far more than equipment and other so-called "hard" technologies, for it also includes total systems and their component parts, including know-how, goods and services, equipment, and organizational and managerial procedures.

Transfer of Technology is one of the important tools of deriving financial benefits from Intellectual property. As patent owner enjoys monopoly over his invention, licensing is a way of granting permission to other to use his patented invention on agreed terms and conditions, while patent owner continues to retain ownership of the patent. Licensing not only paves the way for earnings but it also catalyses further development of technology under defined legal framework of technology transfer.

With the advent of World Trade Organisation (WTO), trade boundaries and barriers are often diminished and free flow of knowledge transfer have been noticed. In such a situation, technology licensing and technology transfer plays an important role in strategic alliances and International joint ventures to maintain competitive edge in a market economy. Following are the benefits of licensing or technology transfer agreements:

- ☆ It provides environment for agreements within legal framework.
- ☆ It provides appropriate climate for investment and economic development.
- ☆ It encourages further development of Technology.

Whether it is an acquisition of technology from particular company or a diffusion of technology from an inventor; technology transfer results in productivity growth. Sometimes sell of patented technology is better than to actually commercialise it. Following example will make it clearer. During early 2011 Mosaid Technologies Inc. sold five patent families at a price of US$11-million to an undisclosed technology company. Patents were related to semiconductors, data compression, encoding and encryption. Mosaid decided to sell the patents as they were not generating any revenues and their sale exemplified a new source of income for Mosaid. In another case, Mosaid obtained more than 1,200 highly lucrative patents related to advance wireless technologies from Nokia Corp. Mosaid paid nothing for the Nokia portfolio, agreeing instead to relinquish two thirds of all gross revenues generated by licensing the acquired patent portfolio. Despite only getting to keep 33 cents of every dollar it makes by enforcing Nokia's patents, the company was able to double the profit by just controlling the new portfolio. Mosaid made $25 million in net income during its

2011 fiscal year. So we can say that technology transfer, technology acquisition, licensing agreement all turn to generate revenues by leveraging Intellectual property.

8. Ways and Means of Technology Transfer

8.1. Foreign Direct Investment (FDI)

FDI or foreign investment refers to the net inflows of investment to acquire a lasting management interest (10 percent or more of voting stock) in an enterprise operating in an economy other than that of the investor. It is the sum of equity capital, reinvestment of earnings, other long-term capital, and short-term capital as shown in the balance of payments. It usually involves participation in management, joint-venture, transfer of technology and expertise. FDI may provide developing countries with more efficient foreign technologies and result in technological spillovers and greater competition. FDI is a more liberal approach of borderless trade in a globalised world. It is believed that foreign direct investment indeed contributes to local firms exports and growth through technology transfer. While technology has been gaining importance aș a vital factor of competitiveness in the world economy, intrafirm technology transfer through foreign direct investment (FDI) has become the predominant channel of international technology transfer (ITT). Factors accounting for enormous growth of FDI include ongoing global trend of FDI liberalisation, large-scale abolition of international trade barriers, increased globalisation of economic activities, and the growing need for technological competitiveness in order to survive and grow economically.

8.2. Technology Licensing of Knowledge

Return on investment by licensing is the most common way technology owner adopts. Since every patented technology is unique, every license agreement reflects the particular needs and expectations of the licensor and licensee. However, certain issues are fundamental to the success of a licensing agreement. For example, in order to conclude a license, the value of the patented technology has to be determined. Valuation of IP assets before entering into licensing agreement would result in 'win-win' deal in financial terms for both the companies. A good IP valuation helps a prospective licensee to compare the financial terms of a proposed licensing deal offered by a particular technology supplier with those of alternative suppliers. Companies believe in licensing their IP assets most often. An example about Hewlett Packard (HP) licensing strategy would explain the concept behind. HP is a technology solutions provider to consumers, businesses and institutions globally. Worldwide, HP added approximately 4,000 patents to its portfolio in 2004. Its total patent portfolio now stands at about 25,000, one of the largest in the world. HP is consistently recognized as one of the world's most innovative companies. Its multi-billion dollar annual investment in research and development has led to thousands of patent grants. HP offers its cutting-edge intellectual property to work for other companies as well. HP assesses technology needs, works within HP to find the patents, technology, trademarks, and other IP that will help achieving objectives of the business of other companies. Though licensing of technology contributes less than 1 per cent of HP's revenue,that too reflects a million dollar figure. HP is hoping that new efforts will eventually contribute hundreds of millions of dollars to its bottom line through licensing. HP is already licensing some technology to other companies, including its spin-off, Agilent Technologies. IBM, again a big software giant, generates roughly $1 billion a year from licensing its technology.

8.3. Joint Venture or Strategic Alliance

Another key external growth strategy which should be considered by both established and emerging companies is the development of partnering relationships whereby two or more companies work together to achieve a specific purpose or towards the attainment of common business objectives. The valuation of IP assets enables parties entering into these types of arrangements to know and to appreciate the value of the other party. In every joint venture or strategic alliance, there arise few questions like; In what manner would each party to the relationship grant or licence its existing intellectual property rights and know-how to other party for the purposes of the relationship? Would each party be able to retain full rights to its existing know-how or inventions? In what manner would the rights to inventions or other intellectual property generated as a result of the relationship in question be dealt with?

Now-a-days, companies are into million dollar business by involving themselves in licensing or technology transfer business. An effective example is Microsoft's patent deal with HTC for Android operating system that is used in cell phones. One of Microsoft's first major successes in implanting their patent licensing strategy was the licensing agreement reached with HTC in April of 2010 which has served as the blueprint for most of Microsoft's smartphone licensing deals. HTC is a Taiwanese company known for its manufacturing of mobile devices. HTC was one of the earliest android partners and was the first company to release an Android phone, the G1 in 2008. HTC was also one of the first companies to produce devices running Microsoft's Windows Phone and Microsoft has acknowledged a long history of collaboration with the Taiwanese company. This relationship is likely why Microsoft chose not to initiate legal proceedings and instead decided to first attempt independent negotiation.

These efforts were ultimately successful and Microsoft was able to negotiate a $5.00 royalty for every Android phone sold by HTC in the US. Financial analysts have calculated that Microsoft licenses its Windows Phone software for $15.00 per license. With Microsoft reporting sales of two million Windows Phone licenses, Microsoft's revenues for their own software is probably around $30 million to date. HTC, however, reported sales of 12 million Android devices in the second quarter of 2011 alone. At a royalty of $5.00 per phone, Microsoft made $60 million off of HTC in the second quarter; a figure that eclipses their Windows Phone revenues by 100 per cent. The deal has thus proven hugely profitable for Microsoft, and has provided a template for later deals with Android partners. Analysts have pegged the profit margins of Android devices to be quite slim, in the neighbourhood of 10-15 per cent or $50.00 per device, so why would HTC agree to a deal that cannibalizes its most profitable line of products without first attempting to contest it in court? Microsoft's legal team was quick to announce that the purpose of the deal was to square away any infringement claims Microsoft might have against HTC, but HTC likely had more than their relationship with Microsoft in mind when they agreed to ink the deal.

Conclusion

In the present globalised world, Intellectual property (IP) plays an effective role in business growth. IP often represents one of the most valuable assets of a company whether it is know-how, patents, licenses, brand names or any other form of intangible assets. Often there is a commercial need to assess IP in a transaction involving intellectual property. Intellectual property must be regarded as a capital asset rather than just being the short term result of a recent expenditure. When undertaking an IPR valuation, the context is all-important, and the valuer needs to take it into consideration to assign a realistic value to an asset. There are quite a few techniques available for IP valuation, each having its strengths and weaknesses, but as is true with enterprise valuation, there is no definitive right or wrong valuation approach. However, it is wise to use several of these methods when valuing a specific IP asset. Finally, we can say that Intellectual Property valorisation has become very important for business houses to exploit their intellectual property through licensing and other means of trading to increase asset value, to obtain financing and to take informed investment and other business decisions.

References

1. http://en.wikipedia.org/wiki/Intangible_asset
2. http://en.wikipedia.org/wiki/Valorisation
3. Valuation of Intellectual Property Assets; valuation techniques: Parameters, methodologies and limitations; WIPO Asian regional forum on the Intellectual Property Strategy for the promotion of Innovative and Inventive activities; Taejon, Republic of Korea, November 22 to 24, 2000.
4. http://www.openinnovation.eu/download/ValueValuationand Valorisation.pdf
5. http://www.wipo.int/sme/en/documents/valuing_patents.htm
6. http://www.wipo.int/patent-law/en/developments/licensing.html
7. http://acta.fih.upt.ro/pdf/2010-2/ACTA-2010-2-Event-01.pdf
8. http://www.cptech.org/ip/health/bd/
9. http://www.technology4sme.net/images/pdf per cent 20floder/ ttps_chapter_3.pdf
10. http://www.gdrc.org/techtran/7-cs.html
11. http://business.financialpost.com/2011/09/14/mosaid-sells-us11m-worth-of-non-strategic-patents/
12. http://data.worldbank.org/indicator/BX.KLT.DINV.CD.WD

13. http://www.oecd.org/daf/internationalinvestment/investmentstatisticsand analysis/2422334.pdf
14. http://www.hp.com/hpinfo/globalcitizenship/environment/commitment/ accenture study. pdf
15. http://eupat.ffii.org/gasnu/ibm/index.en.html
16. A Treaty of Versailles: How Microsoft Wants to, and How They Could, End the Smartphone Patent War by Andrew Pierz

Chapter 25

Patenting Nanobiotechnological Innovations: The Indian Perspective

E. Kalita*

Assistant Professor,
Department of Molecular Biology and Biotechnology,
Tezpur University, Assam, India

ABSTRACT

The term 'Nano' refers to dimensions in the order of 10^{-9} metre. The technology associated with the synthesis, fabrication, assembly/self-assembly of materials and products at nano-dimensions is what we have come to know as –Nanotechnology in recent times. The concept of nano is not novel, as evidence exists across different civilizations throughout time regarding the use of nano-sized products. However, the science behind the understanding of the mechanisms and processes associated with it has been exploding with information in the past few decades. This has been enriched with the convolution of different disciplines like material science, photonics, synthetic chemistry, biotechnology, medicine, tissue engineering etc. to give rise to a slew of new disciplines like nanomaterials, nanophotonics and nanobiotechnology. Nanobiotechnology, which arises out of the confluence of nanotechnology and biotechnology, provides wide scope to researchers to produce solutions for management and control of diseases, detection and diagnosis of disease conditions, agricultural monitors, environmental sensors, nanobio-products, nanomedicines etc. As such, one can easily understand the limitless possibilities they provide and the intellectual wealth this fast growing discipline generates. India being a rich source of qualified human resource generates a great amount of intellectual property in the field of nanobiotechnology. The Indian Patent regime is now over a century old and has been ratified suitably, at different

* E-mail: ekalita@tezu.ernet.in

times, to be in synergy with the global policy on intellectual property policies and reforms (Paris convention, PCT and TRIPS). The advent of nanobiotechnology in India has put forth new challenges and questions pertaining to the protection of the intellectual property generated in India. The Indian patent regime and scope it provides for the protection and commercialization of nanobiotechnological products, in the current scenario, has been discussed within the scope of this paper.

Keywords: *Patents, IPR, Nanobiotechnology, Therapeutics, Nanodevices, Drug delivery.*

1. Introduction

Nanotechnology has had a revolutionary effect on every branch of technology by investigating processes that occur at the nano dimensions. The intersection of different disciplines has given rise to several areas of new-age science like nanoengineering, nanorobotics, nanofluidics, nanocomputing etc. The products of nanotechnology are very diverse, ranging from extensions of conventional physics to completely new approach based self-assemblies, from the development of new materials with unique properties to investigating the science behind such new materials and phenomena. This idea entails the application of fields of science as diverse as organic chemistry, surface science, molecular biology, semiconductors, microsynthesis, patterned organization etc. Nanobiotechnology has emerged with confluence of nanotechnology with the field of biotechnology. Nanobiotechnology primarily serves to manipulate processes at the atomic level, involving biological organisms or processes for the benefit of mankind. Conventionally, nanotechnology entails the development of materials, devices, or other structures having least one dimension sized from 1 to 100 nanometers. Biotechnology, on the other hand deals with metabolic and other physiological processes of biological subjects including microorganisms.

A multitude of applications of nanobiotechnology in diverse fields like disease diagnosis, medicines, targeted drug delivery systems, molecular imaging etc. are being fervently researched at present. Some of the products developed as a consequence of such efforts are also undergoing clinical trials. These advances have the potential of changing the conventions of application of biology for the benefit of mankind, in the future. Realizing such potential, there has been a heavy investment from the different government and private enterprises to develop such futuristic products and devices, in the past decade. The products of such innovation however must be protected to secure the financial investments of the rightful owners, by strong intellectual property laws. Patents being the most powerful territorial protection right, is an important tool for the protection of the rights of the researchers and the products that's have emerged out of their intellect and investments. Patents provide the inventors with the right of exclusive monopoly to practice, license, and transfer (in part/full) the rights and claims relating to their invention. The qualities the innovative products should possess for being patentable are outlined as: novelty, non-obviousness and industrial applicability.

2. Nanotechnology Research in India

The increasing global attention on the nanotechnology has inspired various nations to take proactive measure for promoting funding for research on the subject through different initiatives. The United States had set the pace for nanotechnology innovation worldwide with the National Nanotechnology Initiative (NNI), in 2001. Launched initially with eight agencies, the NNI today consists of the individual and cooperative nanotechnology-related activities of 26 agencies with a range of research and regulatory roles and responsibilities. The NNI budget for the year 2013-14 is estimated to be 1.8 billion US dollars, which is a 4 per cent increase over the 2012-13 budget, with a cumulative investment of $18 billion US dollars since its inception in 2001. Similar public investment initiatives were started in the European Union, China and South Korea with a funding to the order of $650 million, $100 million and $200 million respectively. Taking cue form such global developments, India stated it first initiative under its Department of Science and Technology (DST), Ministry of Science and Technology, Government of India. The Nano Science and Technology Initiative (NSTI) that operated during 2001-2006 under the aegis of the DST, was one of the largest initiatives on nanotechnology in terms of funding and implementation. It was launched with an initial budget of Rs.100 crores (approximately US$ 15-20 million). In addition to funding research in large parts, budget for the NSTI appears to have been spent on developing the various centres of excellence (CoEs) and establishing laboratory infrastructure, throughout the national institutes and universities. The Government of India, in 2006-07 approved the launch of the Nanoscience and Technology Mission (NSTM) with a budget of Rs.1000 crore (approximately US$ 254 million) for a 5-year duration (2007-12). During this time copious amounts are being invested for the development human resource for nanotechnology research.

In addition to the DST, several other agencies with diverse mandates are also actively engaged in supporting nanotechnology research in India. This is an outcome of the discipline's ability to configure itself to several other disciplines and serve multiple sectors. The Department of Biotechnology (DBT), which is primarily involved in developing and supporting biotechnology in India, is keenly supporting research at the junctures of nanotechnology and the life-sciences. The DBT plans to invest around Rs. 1000 crores for promoting nanobiotechnological research in India, though its special programs on nanobiotechnological research. Research ventures with the application of nanotechnological interventions for the other thrust areas of DBT are also encouraged, through the regular research programs. The Council of Scientific and Industrial Research (CSIR), a network of 38 laboratories has also commissioned research in nanotechnology, and is impacting several areas of nanobiotechnology. The Indian Council of Medical Research (ICMR), under the Ministry of Family Health and Welfare and Defence Research and Development Organisation (DRDO), under the Ministry of Defense also has mandates for promoting nanotechnology research for the improvement healthcare and biomedical research as well as development of specific products, strategies and devices for the armed forces. The DRDO is already said to have invested around Rs 200 crore into nanotechnology research in the country . The Department of Atomic Energy (DAE) which is placed directly under the Government of India are also contributing to the expansion of nanotechnology in diverse areas including biotechnology, using its various nation wide facilities, as well as funding research initiatives with nanobiotechnological objectives. This has led to the engagement of a diverse set of players, each with their own agenda and role. Together they shape the trajectory of nanotechnology research activities in their specialized domains. The research and development, except a few cases, is largely being pursued at publically funded universities as well as research institutes. Therefore policy agencies and research organizations are the key players in the national context of India.

3. Patenting Nanotechnological Innovations: Key Challenges

Keeping in tune with the global focus on products emerging out of nanobiotechnology, there has been a steady increase in the number of patents filed for nano-based innovations. In 2011, the USPTO alone granted 792 patents, out of the thousands of applications received. This number is a significant improvement from the 780 patents in 2010, and only 532 patents granted in 2009. The number accounts for 10 per cent of the total patents granted in the USA in 2011. In India, the patent applications for nanotechnological innovations published by the Indian patent office stands at 87 for the year 2011, as compared to 114 international patent applications, as shown in Figure 25.1. The trend of applications from 2005-2010 shows increasing interest among Indian research for patenting their fruits of scientific labour. However, India still has a long way to go to meet the global standards.

The patenting of nanotechnological and nanobiotechnological has been an active arena for debate among IP enthusiasts and legal practitioners. The trends of discussions have concluded on the various practicalities of the legal framework and the provisions available for this highly dynamic and progressive branch of technology.

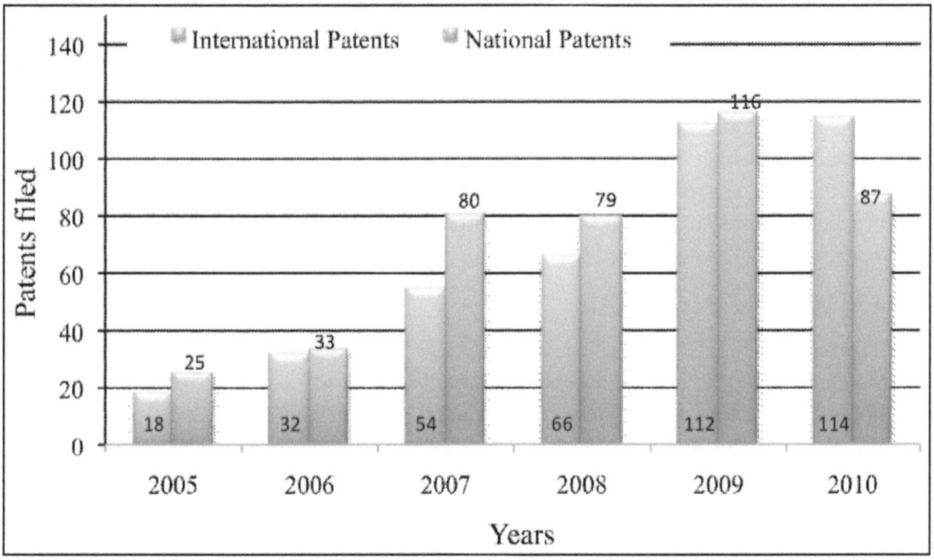

Figure 25.1: Histogram Showing the Trend of Filing International and National Patents Based on Nanotechnology, among Indian Researchers.

As most of the legal frameworks are yet to define specific protective measures for the emerging and nucleating disciplines of science and technology, the protective measures are by means of the currently available models. The challenges faced in providing protection to such dynamic frontiers are far many to be discussed in entirety, however a select few, in context of the Indian Patent framework are as follows:

3.1. Novelty and Existence of Prior Art

The pre-requisite for any invention to be patentable is the novelty of the innovation. The concept of novelty may relative, absolute or territorial under different patent regimes. The Indian patent regime, follows a absolute concept of novelty for patentability of the innovations. As such, patent applications are screened for any form of prior art, publication, communication, display, public working anywhere in the world. The section 2(j) of the Indian Patent Act, lays down the criteria of novelty that pose a challenge to emerging technologies like nanobiotechnology. Such innovations may be ruled out by the fact that process is a mere reduction of size of existing products to nano-dimensions. Further, the effects of the reduction of size may be ambiguous to relate as prior art may overlap with specified size ranges but fail to reveal the "new" property of the patent. Hence, prior art may not necessarily be sufficient to anticipate a nanoscale invention. The concept of novelty and prior art tend to complicate matters further for disciplines like nanobiotechnology. As nanobiotechnology is a product of two pre-existing technologies - nanotechnology and biotechnology, innovations in this area are bound to find some prior art, making the inventions obvious and non-novel. Newer applications of known products are not patentable under the Indian patent regime. This severely restricts the patentability of nanobiotechnological innovations. The debatable issue regarding nanotechnological innovations is process of reducing the size to nano dimensions. It is easily assumed under the current regime that a mere reduction of size does not account for patentability. However, a nano-based innovation may still be novel to a person skilled in the art, if the process of developing the nanomaterials is not obvious to the person, without knowledge of the claimed invention or engaging in inventive activity. In such cases, the process of reduction of size may preserve the novelty of the invention. Although the current patent regime challenges the patentability of nanotechnological innovations, it does provide inroads for rendering novelty for most of the nanotechnological innovations. This is mainly derived from the artful application of well-known patent guidelines to protect the innovations.

3.2. Of What is Patentable

The section 3(d) of the Indian Patent Act 2005, defines non-patentable inventions as *"the mere discovery of a new form of a known substance which does not result in the enhancement of the known efficacy of that substance or the mere discovery of any new property or new use for a known substance or of the mere use of a known process, machine or apparatus unless such known process results in a new product or employs at least one new reactant"*. Multidisciplinary technologies like nanobiotechnology, strongly harps on the functional integration of landmark innovations in different fields, at nanodimensions, for effective benefits to mankind. As such, the *"new property"* of products of nanobiotechnology, wherein the integration of biomolecules and other nanomaterials bring about new applications, may be difficult to patent. This fact is also impacted by the provisions of Section 3(i) wherein any process *"for the medicinal, surgical, curative, prophylactic, diagnostic, therapeutic or other treatment of human beings or any process for a similar treatment of animals to render them free of disease or to increase their economic value or that of their products"* are held non-patentable [14]. Under such circumstances most nanobiotechnological innovations directed towards the development of therapeutic and diagnostic purposes are likely to fall under the "non-patentable" entities. This feature also threatens to impact the nano-based patents for increasing the productivity and health/state of agricultural products. However, the skilled intellectual property practitioner may circumvent the aforementioned provisions by sufficiently highlighting the "inventive process" involved in such cases, to secure effective protection for the products. Such cases can be strongly justified by emphasizing on the development of new products or intermittent reactants, as outlined in the amended Section 3(d). To address the problem, amendments to Section 3(i) modeled on the European and American regimes, having similar modifications, may be executed to broaden the scope of patentability for nanobiotechnological innovations.

3.3. Industrial Potential

One of the salient features of a patentable invention as outlined by the Indian patent regime is industrial applicability. The feature of industrial applicability is difficult to justify for nanobiotechnological innovations as the industry is still in its infancy. It would be a while before the infrastructural capabilities achieve the dimensions of industrial potential. Besides, the nature of nanobiotechnological innovations, make it difficult to predict uniform behavior for a defined innovation. For example, targeted drug delivery systems, developed along the lines of personalized medicine are meant to cater to individual needs, rather than people in general. Also, it may be difficult to ascertain the risks involved in upscaling the production such innovation from a lab to industrial scale. Under such conditions, the industrial potential of the system is difficult to assess, while their innovative strength cannot be undermined. Besides, nanotechnological innovations, designed for therapeutics, imaging, diagnosis etc. are more likely to find niche applications rather than large-scale industrial application. This is keeping in mind the access to technology as well as high production and infrastructural costs in countries like India, where the scientific and industrial potential are not fully explored.

3.4. Technical Know-how

The handling of nanobiotechnological and nanotechnological innovations is another major challenge for the Indian patent regime. As outlined previously, the NSTI in 2001 and NSTM in 2007 were the first initiatives in India to for capacity building and establishment of infrastructure for nanotechnological research. Although scientists have been able to secure a foothold in the global race to develop nano-based products, the country still lacks trained human resource to fully understand and analyze the nanotechnological innovations. Knowledge driven economies like the USA, EU, China and Japan are empowering their respective patent regimes to various capacities, to provide effective protection to "nano" patents, but still have major goals to achieve. In comparison, India is still in its infancy, and has to make significant contributions to be able to compete with the technological advances in this field. By 2010 India, had a total of 80 patent examiners from different technical backgrounds, 26 from biotechnology and allied sciences, 3 from physics, 20 from chemistry, but none from nanotechnology. This problem can be circumvented by the generation of effective human resource and manpower in this discipline.

Major economies like the USA and EU have placed a definite protection regime for all nanotechnological innovations, which is continuously updated to keep track of the technical advancements. The United States Patent and Trademark Office's (USPTO) has a definitive classification for nanotechnology-based innovations under class 977 under 35 USC §8, "Classification of Patents". The European Patent Office (EPO) initiated the classification of nanotechnological patents by tagging it with the Y01N tag. The Y01N2 tag was used to specifically denote nanobiotechnology-based innovations. In a recent development, all patent offices worldwide started to classify nanotechnology uniformly under the International Patent Classification (IPC) system. To facilitate this approach, a new symbol, B82Y was introduced into the IPC on 1 January 2011, building on the basis of the Y01N system that the EPO had been using. The new B82Y symbol makes it convenient to retrieve relevant patent documents, as it is a part of both the IPC and the ECLA (European classification) schemes [18]. Unlike these classifications and nomenclature systems developed in US and EU patent regime, the absence of any nanobiotechnology/nanotechnology patent classification in India makes patent landscaping in effective. Under such circumstances, applicants may be forced to apply for patents without divulging the invention area as "nanobiotechnology".

Conclusion

Nanobiotechnology has been able to excite the mind of researchers and achieve remarkable success in innovation and product base. The legislation and regulations ensure risk assessment and compliance of safety measures, regulating the outcomes of such research. Nanobiotechnology research is still at its infancy in India but holds a promise to widespread application. The present patent regime in India brings to light several contentious issues that pose major challenges to the effective protection of these innovations in India. The absence of consonant patent law provisions in Indian Patent Act, will continue to challenge the products of nanobiotechnology with respect to the criteria of novelty, being capable of industrial application and eligibility of subject matter. For such reasons the Patent Act may be suitably amended, specifically for restrictive sections like 3(i), to broaden the scope of patentability. The Act may include specific provisions for nanotechnological innovations, as available in some of the patent regimes of the advanced countries. Capacity building in terms of having trained manpower for examination of patents, will contribute significantly to the effective examination and grant of patents for nanotechnology.

Acknowledgements

The author acknowledges Hon'ble Vice Chancellor, Tezpur University and Chairman Tezpur University IPR Cell (TUIPR) for constant support and encouragement.

References

1. Goodsell, S.D., 2004. Bionanotechnology: lessons from nature. Wiley-Liss, Inc., New Jersey, pp.1-6.
2. Shaffer C., 2005 Nanomedicine transforms drug delivery. Drug Discov Today, vol.10, pp.1581–82.
3. Moghimi, S.M., Hunter, A.C., Murray, J.C., 2005, Nanomedicine: current status and future prospects. FASEB J, vol. 19, pp. 311–30.
4. Bowman, D.M., Hodge, G.A., 2007. A Small Matter of Regulation: An International Review of Nanotechnology Regulation' 8 Columbia Science and Technology Law Review pp.1-32.
5. NNI website: http://www.nano.gov/(accessed 1 Sep. 2012)
6. DST nano mission website: http://nanomission.gov.in/(accessed 31 Aug. 2012)
7. Annual Report, 2006-07 and 2010-11, Department of Biotechnology http://dbtindia.nic.in/uniquepage.asp?id_pk=50 (accessed 1 Sep. 2012)
8. Annual Report, 2006-2007, Centre for Scientific and Industrial Research http://www.csir.res.in/External/Heads/aboutcsir/Annual_report/annualreport.html (accessed 1 Sep. 2012)
9. Indian Council of Medical Research, Extramural Research Project Division Wise (20102011) http://www.icmr.nic.in/budget2010-11.pdf (accessed 1 Sep. 2012)
10. Department of Atomic Energy website: www.dae.gov.in/(accessed 1 Sep. 2012)
11. FE BUREAU, 2012, DRDO plans to set up Rs 500-cr nanotech foundry http://www. financialexpress.com/news/drdo-plans-to-set-up-rs-500cr-nanotech-foundry/722734/(accessed 1 Sep. 2012)
12. Steven, J.R., Nanotech Patent Counting in 2011: Record Numbers, Slight Growth Good Management. http://www.nanocleantechblog.com/(accessed 1 Sep. 2012)
13. Ramaraju, G.V. 2012. Assessing the economic impact of nanotechnology India Perspective International Symposium on Assessing the Economic Impact of Nanotechnology, Washington DC.
14. Indian Patent Act, 2005 http://ipindia.nic.in/ipr/patent/patent_2005.pdf (accessed 1 Sep. 2012)
15. Annual Report of the Office of the Controller General of Patents, Designs, Trademarks, Geographical Indications Intellectual Training Institute and Patent Information System, India (2009-2010). http://ipindia.gov.in/cgpdtm/AnnualReport_English_2009_2010.pdf (accessed 1 Sep. 2012)
16. Class 977 Nanotechnology, 2012. http://www.uspto.gov/web/patents/classification/uspc977/sched977.htm (accessed 2 Sep. 2012)
17. IPC, 2012, http://www.wipo.int/ipc/itos4ipc/ITSupport_and_download_area/20110101/pdf/scheme/full_ipc/en/b82.pdf (accessed 2 Sep. 2012)
18. Nanotechnology, 2012. http://www.epo.org/news-issues/issues/classification/nanotechnology.html (accessed 2 Sep. 2012)

Chapter 26

Intellectual Property Rights in India with a Perspective on Design, Engineering and Manufacturing

*Rohan Dev Talwar**

Project Assistant,
Centre for Science and Technology of the Non-Aligned and Other Developing Countries (NAM S&T Centre),
New Delhi, India

ABSTRACT

In a field such as engineering, where innovation is brought to the table on a day-by-day basis, it becomes all the more imperative to maintain the credibility of the innovation with the innovator, seeing that technologies in this field thrive by exchanging hands via application in the manufacturing sector through sale and purchase agreements with regards to the machinery/production technique employing the said technology/innovation. Hence it is inevitable that all engineering applications will fall under the domain of Intellectual Property (IP) at some points in their lives. The Indian scenario opens up thriving commercial options for innovations and new design techniques in various fields.

A field in which inventors are constantly striving to make technologies available to meet targets while maintaining a corporation's profit policy, one is constantly at the risk of IP infringement. Once the technology is readily available in the market, it automatically faces an incontrovertible threat from copying hawks, market infringers and rival organizations in the competitive arena.

* E-mail: rohandtal@gmail.com

Engineering designs on a mere sheet of paper or in-house production techniques may fall under the scope of patents/copyright/trademark. It is imperative that during patent filing, not only legal minds, but engineering think tanks are also involved since patents require specifying technical parameters, accurate measurements, invention principles, scientific laws applied/generated etc.

It is highly possible that in today's diversified times, identifying infringement of one's own patent by a player in the market, may become a daunting task and hence it is all the more needed that the engineering industry especially understands, applies, and strives to improve the knowledge of codices, interpretation and covenants of IP and the prerogatives of its acquisition in a corporation's domain, thereby making the knowledge of IP particularly in the field of Design, Engineering and innovation of paramount importance. Moreover the ever expanding Indian industry scenario poses a challenge to technology giants, which face an increased encroachment on their Intellectual Property by the unorganized sector and the cluster of small scale industries which have established a customer base of their own. By default, after technology development and execution of application phase in the market, it becomes the responsibility and duty of the organization to maintain and enforce IP codices in order to curb infringement by existing competitors or new players in the market.

Keywords: *Design, Engineering, Patent, Intellectual property, Copyright, Trademark.*

1. Introduction

Intellectual property in its most basic form is a term used to encompass the outcomes of one's thought process. It is a non-physical property culminating into physical manifestations of the thought process, and the laws falling under the domain of IPR in essence, surround the physicality, rights to produce and control of possible tweaks to the idea in question.

The experience of many countries, corporations, individuals proves the fact that any idea which undergoes widespread application is not free from the threat of infringement, copying and plagiarism especially in the field of engineering, innovation and applied sciences. The concept of IPR was realised centuries ago by ancient philosophers, scientists, innovators etc. and hence IPR has constantly been subject to diversification and modification as civilisation progressed, always adjusting to the ever evolving nature of the global industry. The ever increasing aspiration of industry innovators has constantly maintained the need for an IPR framework both domestic and beyond borders. In order to facilitate governance of IP protection and upholding patent protocols, various organisations on various levels have been formed to regulate the industry functioning in this regard.

For an all round progress of the engineering sector globally, it is necessary to adopt a *quid pro quo* method in order to promote innovation and improvisation in design and manufacturing techniques, which necessitates the need to regulate and counter infringement, if any, by an involved party in the said process. Engineers today work towards maximisation of industrial output through development of improvised and efficient designs and generation of new production techniques hence giving them a lead over existing market players. Industry R&D personnel are always striving towards improving the machinery skill set and to improve and maintain the corporations' income generating ventures, and improving design processes such as development of new softwares, new tool designs, improved aerodynamics in case of applied dynamics in transportation systems etc. All these activities in turn require concerted effort to generate utilization of the developed technologies.

In a planned process after 1947, India embarked on a journey of modernisation of its agriculture and rapid industrial progression under the watchful eyes of its polity. Priority was divided between the rural population and industry so as to attain a comprehensive and robust growth path for the country aimed at self sufficiency, higher employment rates and establishing technological powerhouses aimed at achieving technological advancement in the fields of engineering, innovation, medical sciences etc. making India a frontrunner in innovation. The widespread encouragement by the government and the planning commission to the micro and small enterprises both in the rural as well as urban domain resulted in a wide-spread outburst of technologies being invented in the country.

With the aim of providing due credit, avoiding malpractices, and under its obligations under the TRIPS agreement, the government of India has incorporated a number of legislations which safeguard the interests of this large pool of innovators. The first Indian Copyright Act came into force in January 1958. The Act was a modification of the British Copyright act of 1911. Subsequently, a number of amendments have been made to this law and various other provisions have been incorporated in the government framework with regard to Intellectual Property all of which duly conform to international protocols, conventions and covenants.

The government of India has established several offices for the enforcement and application of these provisions.

Patents, Designs, Trademarks, Industrial Designs and geographical indications fall under the scope of the Controller General of Patents Designs and trademarks. Protection of plant varieties is administered by the Department of Agriculture and Cooperation, Layout designs of integrated circuits is monitored by the Semiconductor Integrated Circuits Layout-Design Registry (SICLDR) which works under the Department of Electronics and Information Technology, a subdivision under the Ministry of Communications and Information Technology of the Government of India.

This paper presents a panoptic view on the existing policy frameworks, existing laws institutional infrastructure and throws light on the status quo.

2. Key Concepts and Notions

With the establishment of some landmark acts and laws and subsequently the comprehensive amendments to them, the Indian lawmakers and polity long realised the importance of Intellectual Property. India had been a member of General Agreement on Tariffs and Trade (GATT) since 1948, which subsequently took shape of the existing WTO in January 1995.

This agreement, inter alia contains an agreement which has been one of the most formidable bone of contention, yet a much needed element among member states since its inception. The agreement on Trade Related Aspects of Intellectual Property rights (TRIPS) lays down the threshold modicums to be maintained in member countries, with respect to the protection and timely enforcement of Intellectual Property Rights (IPR). It obligates the member states to encourage efficient and required protection of IPR in order to counter mutilation of and deterrence to International Trade Policy. This agreement in turn is sought after by government bodies globally in order to align the existing domestic law with the obligations that TRIPS poses to Member States.

3. IPR Sectors Covered by Indian Legislations

3.1. Patents

A Patent is the foremost mechanism in the field of IP protection. It is the most basic and the most matured form of IPR tool that is extensively sought after. Under Indian patent law, as in most patent laws, a patent is a statutory right for an invention granted for a limited period of time to the patentee by the Government, in exchange of full disclosure of his invention for excluding others, from making, using, selling, importing the patented product or process for producing that product for those purposes without his consent.

3.2. Designs

The difficulty arising in solely conferring the proprietorship to an individual or a corporation is inevitable. It is tedious to demarcate a design, on a company to company basis in the engineering manufacturing sector, since the situational utility of a certain component for example a shaft, may change the specifications and body measurements, which will reflect in the drawing

3.3. Trademarks

The law of trademark has gained critical nature in the IPR ambit. A trademark is a sign, graphical indication or a logo with a specified design which is used to differentiate one product entity from another. It becomes a virtual representation for that particular good. Under the Indian policy framework a "trademark" means a mark capable of being represented graphically and which is capable of distinguishing the goods or services of one person from those of others and may include shape of goods, their packaging and combination of colours.

4. Copyright and Related Rights

Copyright is another form of intellectual property that gives the creator of an original work exclusive rights to it, usually for a limited time to get financially compensated for his intellectual creation such as the rights to a photographer or an author for their work. It not only gives the holder "the right to copy" but also to be credited for the work, to determine who may adapt the work to other forms, who may perform the work, who may financially benefit from it, and other related rights.

Essentially, in the Indian framework copyright is a right given by the law to creators of literary, dramatic, musical and artistic works and producers of cinematograph films and sound recordings. In fact, it is a bundle of rights including, *inter alia,* rights of reproduction, communication to the public, adaptation and translation of the work. Variations crop up in the composition of the rights depending on the work.

4.1. Geographical Indications

A geographical indication is a name or a signage used which is used to identify a product to a particular geographical location or origin. Usually they appear due to traditional practices related to the good or to particularly differentiate a good having a single source production location with its produce availability limited to that region. The goods however, are then sold or made available to the customer as the ones belonging to that particular geographical region, comprising of the properties of that particular good from the region. The name attached automatically guarantees the distinct quality and standard which is attributed to that locality, town, city, state or country. It finds wide application in the Indian small scale industry sector, the fruit and vegetable sector and the Indian unorganized sector. The Government of India (GOI) has also encouraged such ventures, with certain quality products renowned around the world.

4.2. Plant Varieties

The Indian economy is basically agrarian in nature, with the government taking up robust initiatives to promote development in this sector. The GOI has tried to leave no stone unturned by enacting legislation that have been helping the countries agriculture sector tremendously. With the immense diversification in this sector, the Government of India has set up facilities to foster technologies which enhance output in this field. With an immensely large pool of scientists and bio-chemical engineers working in this sector, a regularization and credibility accountability mechanism is essential. Under the obligations under TRIPS, India enacted the Protection of Plant varieties and Farmers rights Act in the year 2001, wherein it uses the UPOV convention protocols for protection of new varieties of plants, to acknowledge the accomplishments of new plant variety breeders and make available to them exclusive rights of exploitation if their varieties are distinct, homogeneous and stable.

5. Layout Designs of Integrated Circuits

The electronic revolution that the global civilization witnessed in the second half of the 20th century instigated the need to enact provisions in order to maintain the credibility of the rightful owner of the technology, vis-a-vis semi-conductor integrated circuits layout designs.

This protection is a relatively young one and its need was felt due to the fast paced improvisation in semi-conductor technology that has miraculously reduced the size of components performing high end electronic functions.

With a myriad of electronic giants, striving continuously to gain global dominance in the field of consumer products, defence equipments, telecom hardware etc., a substantial amount of financial resources are diverted in charting details, planned and improved layouts of integrated circuits which have today become the backbone of the electronics industry. Verily, the need to prevent unauthorised reproduction is justified.

5.1. Protection of Undisclosed Information

Contrary to other elements of Intellectual Property, "trade secret" is probably the most specialized IP tool which is diametrically different, in the manner it is employed relative to a patent. With trade secrets the innovative techniques resting with a particular industry/company/individual are not protected under existing IPR legislations. As a result, the responsibility of their protection remain with the owner of the trade secrets.

6. The Indian Scenario: Policy Initiatives by the Government of India

Credited to its enormous size and sheer vastness of Indian industries, the task of employing the IPR regime has not been an easy one in India. Its enforcement therefore always has been under intense scepticism. In tandem with the patterns observed globally, the IPR regime in India too has constantly evolved since the inception of its first patent law in 1856. In recent times, IP is viewed as a distinct entity touching a plethora of socioeconomic, technological, political and societal concerns. The need to incorporate IPR and intensify its influence, effectiveness and viability is something that has seen increased focus in the past years.

7. Approach Towards the Patent Act (Amended-2005)

The patent law of 1856 was replaced by The Indian Patents and Designs Act in 1911. However the need for a comprehensive law was soon felt after Independence so as to counter the detrimental effects of the patent laws to the consumer and industry. The efforts of the concerned stakeholders finally culminated into Patent Act of 1970 which was considered as a timely landmark achievement, since India was on a path garlanded with technological advancement and path breaking innovations in the fields of automobiles, medical sciences etc. In hindsight, this act skipped a very important feature pertaining to the pharmaceutical, food processing and agro-industry. Patents were only granted with regards to the process employed in manufacturing a certain entity. Hence, process engineering was an asset in disguise for industry innovators. For that matter an upscale pharma sector which we are witnessing today, is courtesy this asset. This allowed us to exploit the process improvisation arena, thereby reducing institution, scientific and R&D sectors' dependence on algorithms and formulations devised by institutions and personnel overseas. With changing times, the need also changes, and it is this need that precipitated in the amendments to the act in the year 2005.

The patent office is overseen by the Controller General of Patent Designs and Trademarks, under the Dept. of Industrial Policy and Promotion which is a subdivision of the Ministry of Commerce and Industry. The Controller General has patent reviewers who merely act as reviewers and give recommendations to the Controller General, with whom the authority to grant patents, rests.

The act guarantees that patents are in no ways tools to be used by an individual or a corporation to monopolize while indulging in import activities. It is in essence promoting inventions and ensuing their feasibility for the purpose of commercialisation. The Act mandates that any invention which is in contradiction to universally accepted and established natural laws shall be deemed unfit to be termed as an invention. The act also goes on to define inventions from the morality prospective, and tries to offer a clear distinction between an invention and a discovery.

A general problem which is faced in this regard is especially in the manufacturing sector, wherein a new technology, in process and usage, devised from components under universal use in the sector, are subject to questioning whether it shall be given the status of an invention or not. With the trend of Hybrid technology gaining pace, companies such as Toyota and Antonov found each other at the altars of court rooms regarding patent infringements by Toyota, alleged by Antonov.

8. Copyright Act

The Copyright Act 1957, as amended by Copyright Act 1999 is the sole instrument governing copyright activities in India. With a country as diverse as India, with talent, art, music and work related activities thriving in every nook and corner, the need for a right exclusive to the owner of these particular entities is essential, seeing the traditional as well as economic value they hold. Creativity is one of the most essential driving factors behind progress and socioeconomic advancement of a society. Though critics of the law have pointed out the duality of the law, which they say may hamper cultural and scientific progress if applied rigidly. Generically, the act is a conglomerate of rights including, inter alia, rights of imitation, access to public, interpretation and semantics of the works. Since it is impossible to limit the features of entities as mentioned above, the rights are often tweaked in order to adjust to situation at hand. The act mandates a copyright to be applicable in other countries as well (the condition being the work is first published in India) by virtue of India being a member of Berne Convention. Thus, obtaining copyrights in India will establish copyrights across several countries. Another facet is the extension of copyright protection to works published outside India upon India's signing of the International Copyright Order-1999.

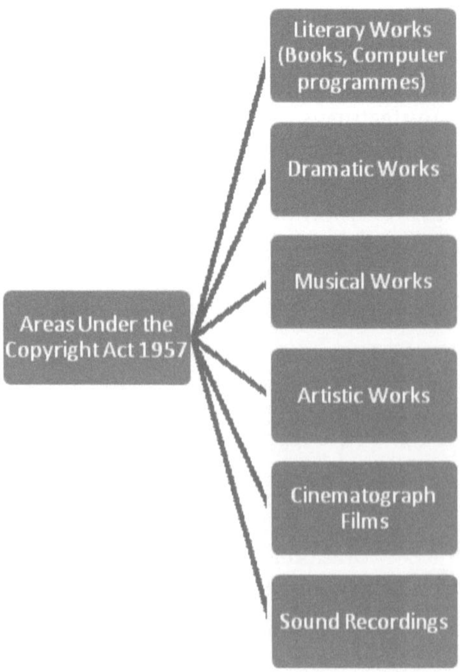

9. Designs

Designs form an integral part of any entity being made commercially available by a corporation be it a mechanical component, be it a consumer durable or the packaging in which the product is sold in the market

Under the India's Design Act, 2000, "design" is defined to mean only *the features of shape, configuration, pattern, ornament, or composition of lines or colours applied to any article, whether in two or three dimensional, or in both forms, by any industrial process or means, whether manual or mechanical or chemical, separate or combined, which in the finished article appeal to and are judged solely by the eye; but does not include any mode or principle of construction*. The holder of an industrial design will have the exclusive rights to make, import or sell any objects to which the design is applied. The essential purpose of design law is to promote and protect the design element of industrial production. It is also intended to promote innovative activity in the field of industries.

In India, the duration of the registration of a design is initially ten years from the date of registration, but in cases where claim to priority has been allowed the duration is ten years from the priority date.

This act also comes under the office of the Controller General of Patents, Designs and Trade Marks, and he is the sole authority to grant a certificate of registration to the proprietor. The Indian Design offices are currently located in Kolkata, New Delhi, Chennai and Mumbai which come under the administrative control of the Department of Industrial policy and promotions, Ministry of Commerce and Industry.

An example of the relevance of this act was seen in the Escorts construction Equipment Ltd. vs. Action construction Equipment Pvt. Ltd., 1999, wherein the court rejected the plaintiffs complaints that the there was infringement on the part of the defendant with regards to certain mechanical components employed in hydraulic cranes which are imperative to its functioning and are generic requirements for any such equipment and hence do not fall under the ambit of being classified as a specialised design to be registered under the Design Act, 2000.

Another such ruling was in the case of M/s B Chawla and Sons Vs M/s Bright Auto Industries wherein the court established that a mere tweaking or addition of a feature to an already well recognized shape which is well recognized in the market and of common use cannot be deemed fit to be accorded as new or original in design.

10. Trademark

The trademark law is one of the cardinal features of the IPR regime in India. The Trademarks Act of 1999 amended the Trademarks Act of 1958 making it TRIPS compliant.

In the post '91 reforms era, it was felt that the 1958 Trademarks law was little more than short to accommodate the changing needs of the trading sectors, the boom in manufacturing and commercial sectors, the robust injection of new technology and FDI&FII in the country.

The 1999 Act makes provision for "Well known Trademarks". *A "well known trade mark", in relation to any goods or services, means a mark which has become so to the substantial segment of the public which uses such goods or receives such services that the use of such mark in relation to other goods or services would be likely to be taken as indicating a connection in the course of trade or rendering of services between those goods or services and a person using the mark in relation to the first- mentioned goods or services."*

A remarkable judgement pertaining to the Trademarks Act was in the case Satyam Infoway Ltd. vs. Sifynet Solutions Pvt. Ltd. wherein the court recognised the ramification of the said law in case of domain usage and the internet activity. The court recognised the changed role of Internet as a contributor to commercial interests and how one domain name could be used to exploit an existing domain's reputation in order to give way to one's commercial interests. Since time immemorial, trademark has helped customers identify a certain product belonging to the respective corporation, and has become a tool of ensured quality and reliability. With the massive Industrial sector, that India is witnessing today, corporations and giants are facing a threat from this covert market. The industry has seen an influx of substandard pirated and copied products under names or logos which have been slightly tweaked from their original counterparts. The worst affected is the electronic sector and mainly the cellular phone domain. With an increased market and requirement for cheaper technology yet keeping the design and logo intact, the mobile phone market is flooded with phones similar in designs and parameters to that of major giants. It has been hard to track down such defaulters as these are mostly small sized units large in numbers working independently on a region-by-region basis. Similar is the case in the Computer Hardware sector. The logos of some major giants have found rampant usage on products assembled in small factories and sometimes shops in the Indian market. In a similar case, TATA, on 9th June 2013 filed a trademark lawsuit against unknown persons, involved in infringement of the company's trademark. FICCI (Federation of Indian Chambers of Commerce and Industry) estimated that the loss to counterfeiting and piracy could be up to 100,000 crore to the Indian Industry. A shocker/damper of almost any car/bike make is readily available at any road side tyre shop in the country, with the part carrying all logos and identification marks justifying its genuine nature, the reality is obviously different. Albeit the industry is aware of such practices, it has found it difficult to curb it due to lack of proper enforcement infrastructure and the ready acceptance of substandard equipment by the money conscious Indian customer. Hence, the industry feels best to keep at bay, though remains actively seized of the matter by trying to make products difficult to replicate and tough to manufacture.

11. Layout Designs of Integrated Circuits

This IP protection is a relatively new tool in the international scene and its need was felt due to the sudden onset of advancement in the field of semi-conductor technology. It was felt that corporations tend to invest vast amount of its human and financial resource pool in order to develop layout designs of integrated circuits and it was relatively easier for it being copied by simple reverse engineering processes. This gave reason for introduction of legislations in this field. Similarly, as has been the case, due to the function specific nature of IC's, their protection viability is complex. The Semiconductor Integrated Circuits layout Design Act, 2000 is the sole mechanism in the country available for protection of IC layout and electronic circuitry.

The owner of the layout designs and circuitry may issue licenses for production of the same layout and chips by another manufacturer.

The electronic industry has in recent years, faced increased threat with ease of availability of technology to develop and manufacture cheap counterfeit products, which are now giving stiff competition in the low range Indian electronic market, which has a massive customer base. Major giants are now looking towards reducing costs of products and entering the low cost market in order to attract customers and retain its customer base. An excellent example of the outcome of such competition was the launch of Asha series mobile phones in the low cost segment, which the company took up robustly after its depleting market share in this segment. In recent news, Micromax, the largest domestic mobile phone manufacturer in India, has been sued by Ericsson, which despite exiting the mobile phone market, hold majority of patents in the sector. Though it does not target its IC layout per se, it has challenged usage of its GSM, EDGE and 3G technology which is more or less likely to trickle to concern it internal IC layout.

12. Protection of Undisclosed Information

India, under its obligation, will have to protect undisclosed information. There is no provision or legislation at the moment available which to counter violations in this regard. However, as in a general case, issues in this domain are currently dealt with general by breach of contract mechanisms and secondly under tort for breach of confidentiality.

This IP facet literally concerns a scenario wherein an owner does not wish to divulge details regarding a certain entity, product, part, process, recipe employed by the company towards manufacturing its products.

13. Plant Varieties

TRIPS agreement gives leverage to member nations to make it optional, protection of plant varieties through the traditional patent protection establishing the correct criterion or by enactment of a new specific regime solely dealing with the protection of Plant varieties. In India, the Protection of Plant Varieties and Farmers Rights Act 2001. The act aims to give a boost to the R&D in this sector and to help ensure investment returns to rightful owners.

14. Geographical Indications

A country's natural resource is one of the most important factors towards its commercial and industrial development. These resources are sometimes characterized by the region of its availability, consisting of certain characteristics which add to its economic as well as aesthetic value. When the name of a place to which the resource or product belongs to, is attached to it for marketing, it acts as a geographical indication. The name itself denotes the place of origin of the product, the quality assurance, the method used-traditional or modern etc.

The need for geographical indication was realized long after the world woke up to its needs. The reason being the massive product range in India attached to states, regions, villages etc. admired world over. The mango variety, the range of rice varieties or the handicraft work from Bihar, Orissa, Andhra Pradesh etc. have all established a strong market in India as well as overseas. Darjeeling tea was the first product to be instated with a geographical indication in 2004-05 and since then 172 Geographical Indications have been awarded in various sectors.

In January 2013, a manufacturing tool for the first time was given a Geographical Indication protection, from MSME (Micro and Small Medium Enterprise in India) "Meerut Scissor Manufacturers". The tool awarded the GI is the Mirror scissor which is applied to home use and by garment factories. It is the only scissor cluster in India, and is made from metal scrap.

Another GI in the manufacturing sector is that of Coimbatore Wet grinders, Tamil Nadu. This geographical indication has been awarded due to the difference in the manufacturing of wet grinders, using stones which are available in and around the Erode and Coimbatore districts only, hence emphasizing the uniqueness of the product. Wet grinders are used for manufacturing of tools required in cutting of hard materials, as well as churning of batter in Indian cuisines, using lubrication or appropriate cooling liquid. This geographical indication, makes it impossible for other wet grinders manufacturers to sell substandard quality under the same name.

15. Institutional Support in India to Boost IP Protection

After gaining its independence, the Indian polity chose to adopt a mixed economy approach to IP with the public sector dominating. The core and development sectors were majorly under the control of the government, with the private sector having little role to play. The reason behind this was the lack of capital and experience in the private sector. The responsibility for the country's complete R&D activity was conferred upon government institutions. The Indian patent laws made an effort to align with the changing industry needs, but the act of 1970 missed out on the pharmaceutical industry, and hence a lot of small scale private ventures were able to manufacture drugs patented overseas. As the country progressed, situations arose which sprouted the needs of amendments to the act in front of the Indian polity. Controversies and industrial lawsuits culminated into the amendments of the act in 1999.

The post 1991 era saw the manufacturing sector open up, for a sufficiently developed private sector which welcomed the move. The concerns due to Foreign Direct Investment and increased liberalization were particularly felt in the fields of computer hardware, machinery, Pharmaceuticals, software development and sale of music. Since then, the government has concentrated it effort in a robust manner towards establishing an efficient IP regime in the country.

Various support institutions have been established in the country in this regard.

16. NASSCOM (The National Association of Software and Services Companies)

NASSCOM was founded by Dewang Mehta and Nandan Nilekani, a non-governmental organization. The main aim of NASSCOM at the time of its inception was to facilitate global trade in terms of software development seeing the boom that Indian industry experienced with the onset of the computer age. NASSCOM took up the issue of software infringement aggressively, seeking protection under the Copyright Act thus it succeeded in amending the Copyright Act to reflect their concerns in 1994. Their sole aim was to prevent privacy in the software market, which was gaining momentum and was the cause of major losses to firms in India and abroad.

The association itself is an enforcement agency, with a mandate to raid and check on piracy practices. Hence, suggestions were made to the effect that industry itself should take steps to manage the IPR regime in the country.

16.1. Institute of Intellectual Property in India (FICCI)

FICCI (Federation of Indian Chambers of Commerce and Industry) is an apex body, which identified the role of IP protection in the Indian industrial sphere. Keeping this in mind, it established IIPD (Institute of Intellectual Property in India) in New Delhi, which acts as an awareness creating body amongst the industrial conglomerates in the country. FICCI observed that there was little effort by the corporate houses in generating awareness regarding IPR amongst their managers, engineers, technical staff etc. The institute has been fairly active in its effort of making the industry personnel cognizant of the existing regime and has been appreciated by industry.

16.2. Confederation of Indian Industries (CII)

The Confederation of Indian Industries (CII) has taken the lead in spreading and garnering support for the idea of Utility Patent Legislation. The legislation aims to make only those inventions patentable whose utility cannot be challenged. In other words, an invention based on hypothetical terms, such as a perpetual motion machine cannot be deemed fit to be recognized as an invention capable of being granted a patent, due to its lack of utility in reality.

16.3. Federation of Associations of Small Scale Industries of India (FASSII) and the Federation of Indian Small and Medium Enterprises (FISME)

These two associations have provided a platform for the small scale producers or manufactures to display their products amidst global competition. Craftsmanship, manufacturing techniques, weaving etc. have been existent in India for centuries and today have culminated into clusters of small and medium scale industries. These two institutions have concentrated their efforts towards making such clusters cognizant of their rights and means to access IP rights. The most recent development in this sector has been the conferring of Geographical Indication to Meerut scissor manufacturers with the help of FISME, which is currently working on getting Three (3) more GI in the MSME sphere.

16.4. United Nations Industrial Development Organization (UNIDO)

UNIDO has been giving policy advisory service in various countries under its mandate. Based on the needs and priorities of the country, UNIDO has identified the pattern of working of small scale units in clusters. It has been observed that there are certain products which are specific to a particular cluster hence, UNIDO has been lobbying to establish collective trademarks for these products.

16.5. National Program for the Development of the Toy Industry-Ministry of Micro, Small and Medium Enterprises

The Ministry in its effort to promote production and industrial contribution by small scale industrial clusters, initiated the National Program for the Development of the Toy Industry in 2000, which aims to put the Indian toy industry on the world map. Also, it aims to specify certain toy designs as ones belonging only to India. Under this programme, an institute for Toy Design and Development has been established, which is directing its efforts towards toy manufacturing technology development, facilities for providing certification and testing with regards to non hazardousness of the toys, and training programmes.

16.6. National Research Development Corporation (NRDC)

The corporation aims to bridge the gap between the R&D powerhouses of the country and the market. It acts as a marketer for the research work and the technology developed by R&D setups across the country, providing services through programmes and helping innovators to transform the innovations into profitable technology. NRDC has tried to boost the rural sector through services and runs a technology development and utilisation programme, including, initiating "The Invention Promotion Programme" to support inventors. This programme, awards prizes to meritorious inventers for their inventions while providing assistance for patenting inventions of R&D organisations and universities both in India and abroad, as wells as providing assistance to commercialise their patented inventions.

16.7. National Innovation Foundation (NIF)

NIF is an autonomous organization under the Department of Science and Technology, GOI and is involved with scouting and supporting innovations and making them achieve self sufficiency. The Society for Research and Initiatives for Sustainable Technologies and Institutions (SRISTI) is a Honeybee Network which have been working in identifying innovations particularly in the rural sector while Gujarat Grassroots Innovations Augmentation Network (GIAN) that improves innovations are its network partners. The foundation has been able to identify over 100,000 innovations and traditional practices have been identified. It has a database of patents filed in India, USA and has a tracking system for Design Registration application, Trade Mark Applications and Application under PPV&FRA (Protection of plant varieties and Farmer's Rights Authority) on its website.

16.8. Technology Information Forecasting and Assessment Council (TIFAC), Department of Science and Technology

This council is an autonomous body which provides assistance to innovators in developing technologies that are of vital national importance. The Agriculture sector has taken the forefront of its efforts, and its efforts have yielded positive results in the past. It covers almost all industrial sectors ranging from Agriculture, Agro-Food Processing, Health, Bioprocess and Bio products, Automobile, Education, Judiciary, Advanced Composites, SME. The council also maintains a database of patent licenses granted overseas and in India.

16.9. Patent Information System (PIS) under the Ministry of Commerce and Industry

The Patent information system aims to provide information regarding the patents already filed, under consideration, those up for technology transfer and subject to opposition. It has information regarding the R&D institutions in India Businesses indulging in innovations, corporations and government schemes and organizations.

16.10. Small Industries Development Organization of India (SIDO)

SIDO has been established to assist the central government in policies regarding the development of the small scale industries in the country. It has played a very constructive role and has been one of the major pillars of policy formulations. It has collaborated with World Intellectual Property Organization (WIPO) in order to spread information regarding IP regime and its management and has conducted numerous workshops on IPR sensitization.

Observations and Conclusions

India today is going through a transitional phase in its IPR regimes, with certain decisions by its judiciary proving to be landmark judgements, establishing the credibility of the IPR regime in the country. The private sector which was first averse to the idea of liberalization and entering of foreign investors is now reaping the benefits of the reform undertaken by the polity in 1991. Technology sharing and collaborative research mechanisms have been established which has increased the country's value of output and increased employment and expertise. The private sector has itself taken initiative to establish IP management systems and is now taking the shape of a consumer centric entity. Their support institutions and initiatives have ironically proven to be a role model for certain government ventures. The government is constantly pushing up its effort in order to fill its experience pool in the international sphere with respect to IP management and has collaborated with international organizations such as WIPO to strengthen its policies and setups. Its support to the small and medium enterprises has resulted in creation of a large pool of exclusive techniques, technology, creativity and practice prevalent in the industry to be indexed, and tabled with a global perspective.

References

1. World Trade Organization, Website: http://www.wto.org/english/thewto_e/whatis_e/tif_e/org6_e.htm.
2. IGNOU, Indira Gandhi National Open University, Website: http://webserver.ignou.ac.in/schools/sos/ipr_web2/IPR_Awareness/Web per cent 20pages/UNIT per cent 204.pdf.
3. CGPDTM, Controller General of Patents, Design and Trademarks, Website: http://ipindia.nic.in/ipr/design/design_act.PDF.
4. Trademarks Act-1999, Website: http://ipindia.nic.in/tmr_new/tmr_act_rules/TMRAct_New.pdf.
5. Handbook of Copyright Law, Website: http://copyright.gov.in/Documents/handbook.html.
6. FAO Corporate Document Repository, Website: http://www.fao.org/docrep/003/x7355e/x7355e05.htm.

7. Mauritius Research Council, 2003, Basics of Intellectual Property Rights, Mauritius Research Council, September 2003.

8. Shriram Institute of Industrial Research, 2005, New IPR Regime-Converting a Challenge Into an Opportunity, Shriram institute for Industrial Research, 2005).

9. Copyright Act, GOI, Website: http://copyright.gov.in/Documents/handbook.html, http://copyright.gov.in/Documents/CopyrightRules1957.pdf.

10. Indian Designs Act 2000, GOI, Website:http://ipindia.nic.in/manuals/Manual_DesignsPractice_and_Procedure_31March2011.pdf.

11. Indian Trademark Act, Website: http://ipindia.nic.in/tmr_new/TMR_Manual/DraftManual_TMR_23January2009.pdf, http://ipindia.nic.in/tmr_new/tmr_act_rules/TMRAct_New.pdf.

12. Sanjay Pandey, 2002,Legal Regime of Undisclosed Information: Indian Perspective, Journal of Intellectual property Rights, Vol. 7, November 2002, Website: http://nopr.niscair.res.in/bitstream/123456789/4940/1/JIPR per cent 207(6) per cent 20526-529.pdf.

13. Geographical Indication registered, March 2012, Website: http://ipindia.nic.in/girindia/treasures_protected/registered_GI_29March2012.pdf.

14. Amita Bhatnagar, Need Assessment Study Amita Bhatnagar Meerut scissors industry design consultant, Delhi, march 2012, NID/MSME Design Clinic Scheme, Website:http://fisme.org.in/document/SCISSORS_MEERUT_DESIGN_CLINIC_ per cent 20WORKSHOP_Full_Report.pdf.

15. UNIDO, India, Website: http://www.unido.org/where-we-work/offices/regional-offices/officeindia/projects/india.html?ucg_no64=1 per cent 2Fdata per cent 2Fproject per cent 2Fdata per cent 2Ffileadmin per cent 2Fmedia per cent 2Fdocuments per cent 2Fpdf per cent 2FEmployment per cent 2FInternship per cent 2Fdata per cent 2Fdata per cent 2Fdata per cent 2Findex.php.

16. National Program for the Development of the Toy Industry-Ministry of Micro, Small and Medium Enterprises, Website: http://dcmsme.gov.in/emerge/npdti.htm.

17. NRDC, National research Development Cooperation, Website: http://www.nrdcindia.com/support.htm.

18. NIF, National Innovation Foundation, Website: http://www.nif.org.in/

19. TIFAC, Technology Information Forecasting and assessment council, Ministry of S&T, Website: http://www.tifac.org.in/

20. S.K. Tuteja, 2002, Role of SME support institutions in promoting effective industrial property management; acquiring protection, commercializing inventions, marketing brands, WIPO Asian regional workshop on the use of information technology and management of industrial property rights by small and medium-sized enterprises, 2002,Website: http://www.wipo.int/edocs/mdocs/sme/en/wipo_ip_bkk_02/wipo_ip_bkk_02_7.pdf.

21. Improved internal combustion engine working on four stroke principle WO 2005042954 A1, Website: http://www.google.com/patents/WO2005042954A1?cl=en.

22. Delhi High Court, B. Chawla and Sons vs. Bright Auto Industries on 21 November, 1980, Author: O Vohra, Bench: R Sachar, O Vohra, Website: http://www.indiankanoon.org/doc/819445/

23. Delhi High Court Escorts Const. Equipment Ltd. and vs. Action Const. Equipment P. Ltd. 16 October, 1998 Author: M Siddiqui, Bench: M, Website: http://www.indiankanoon.org/doc/1315312/

24. Bajaj Patent, Website: http://www.google.com/patents/WO2005042954 A1?cl=en.

www.ingramcontent.com/pod-product-compliance
Ingram Content Group UK Ltd.
Pitfield, Milton Keynes, MK11 3LW, UK
UKHW041643031026
15587UKWH00001B/461

9 789351 302681